DRAPING

FOR FASHION DESIGN

D-S
CF
BUST
CF

DRAPING

FOR FASHION DESIGN

Theresa Parker

THE CROWOOD PRESS

First published in 2021 by
The Crowood Press Ltd
Ramsbury, Marlborough
Wiltshire SN8 2HR

enquiries@crowood.com

www.crowood.com

British Library Cataloguing-in-Publication Data
A catalogue record for this book is available from the British Library.

ISBN 978 1 78500 953 2

Cover design: Sergey Tsvetkov

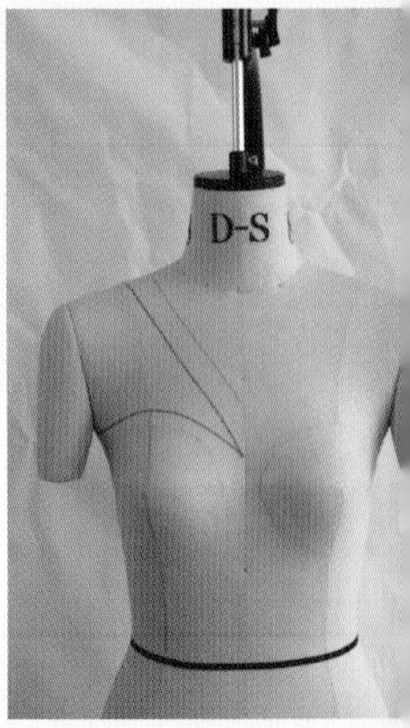

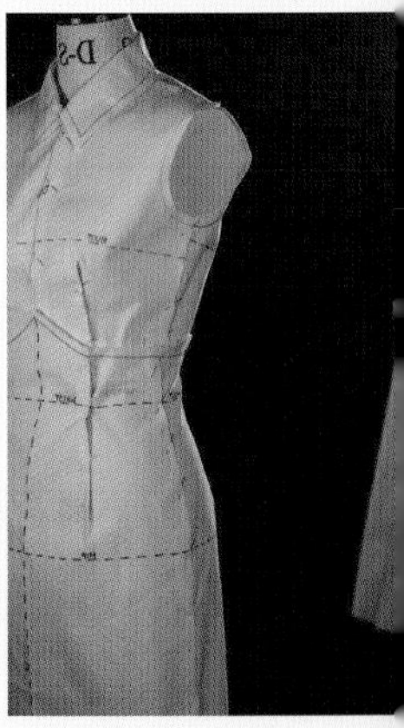

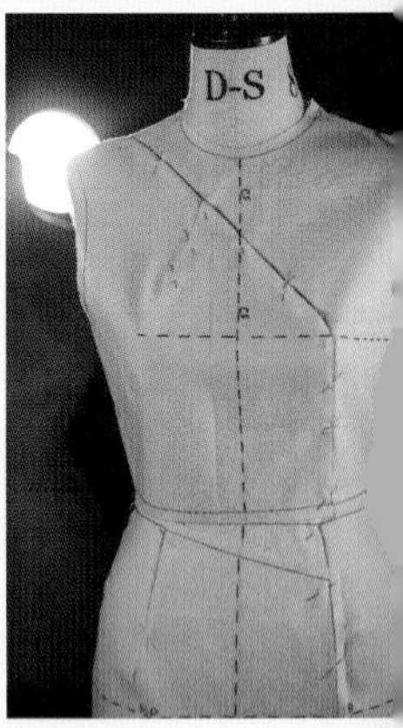

Typeset by Sharon Dainton Design.
Printed and bound in India by Parksons Graphics

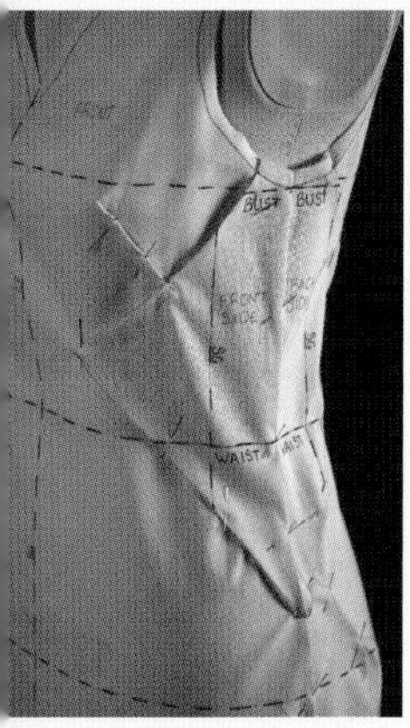

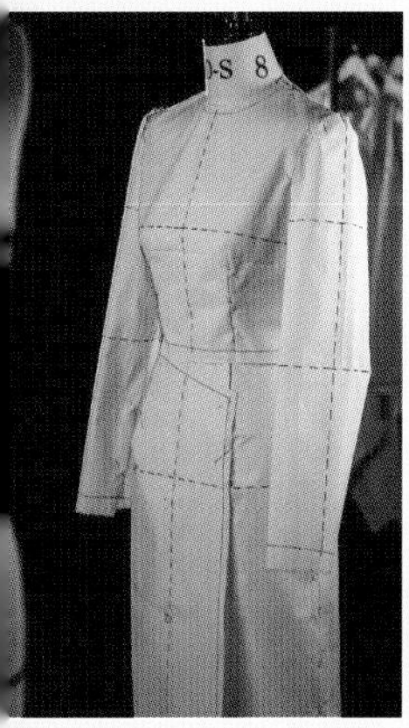

Contents

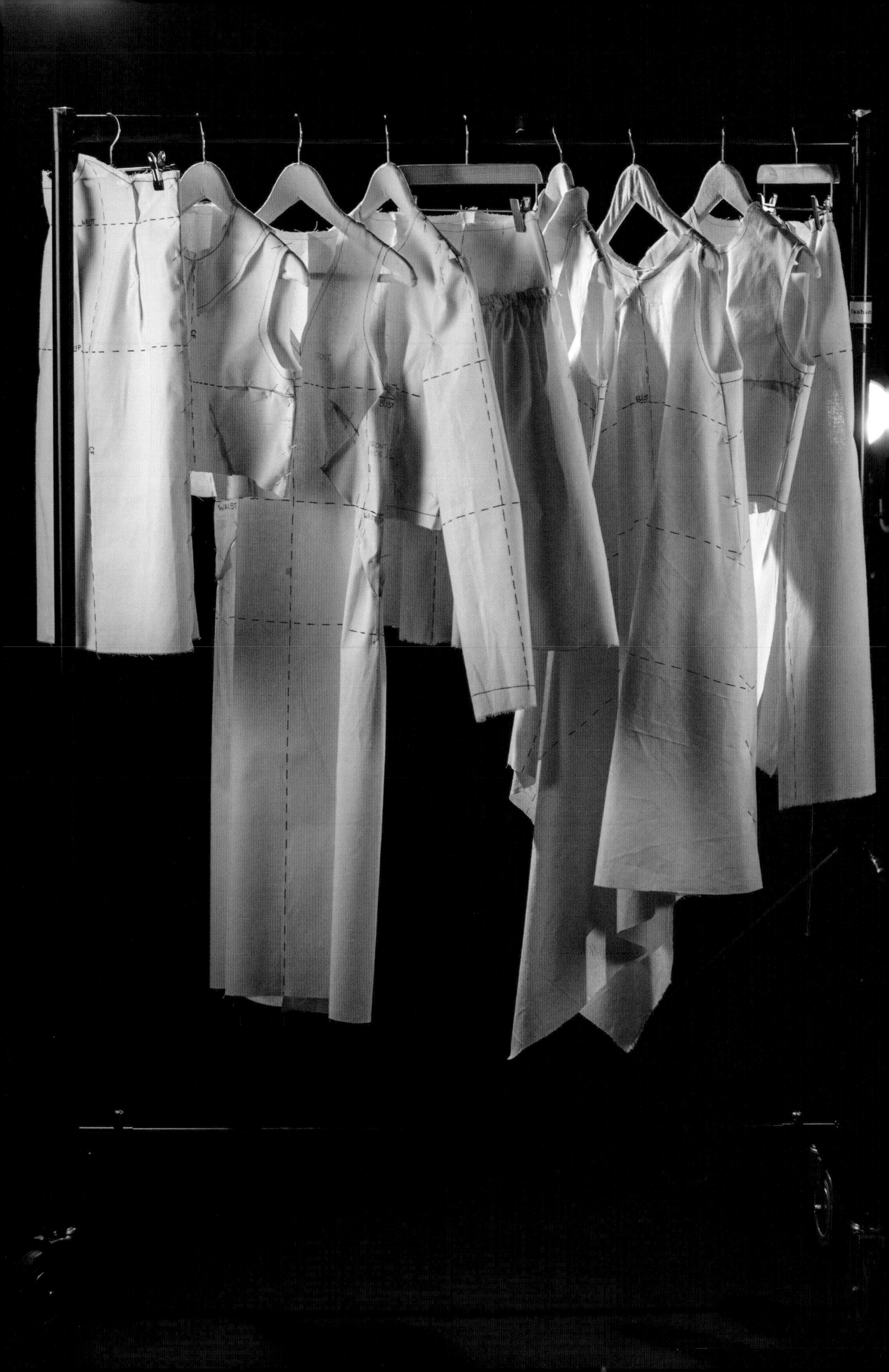
WAIST
BUST

Preface

... the prevailing system of draping, which dates from the first half of the twentieth century, is utterly impervious to modernization. It was good right from the start and cannot be bettered ...
(Duborg et al., 2014).

Fashion designers conceptualize their ideas in two ways: two-dimensional drawings and pattern making or three-dimensional draping. It does not matter whether a designer begins with an idea, a sketch or a fabric; in each case the design process ultimately ends with a three-dimensional prototype or sample. Draping, or *moulage* as it is known in France, generates a considerable amount of freedom from a design perspective as the fabric envelops a mannequin or model. It has to be readable as a garment as well as a pattern when the design is transferred to paper. The technique has been used frequently in couture houses where bespoke mannequins are kept, replicating the bodies of their most important clients and garments commissioned to suit the specifics of both their client's bodies and their lifestyles. Draping is also an important prerequisite for the commercial fashion industry, where it informs the use of computer-based design tools like three-dimensional body mapping, virtual reality apparel design software and augmented reality software. The act of real-life draping reveals not just important information about the design content but also enhances the designer's understanding of the fabric and the garment's fit.

A mastery of the basic principles of pattern drafting is not a prerequisite for learning draping skills, as most of my students will testify, but some flat pattern knowledge definitely helps. There is some very specific pattern cutting terminology consistently being used, which is listed in the glossary at the back of the book. Beginners will find this book a useful introduction to the discipline and experienced students and professionals a means to expand their existing knowledge and skills base, particularly if they are more used to drafting than draping. The book is written as a series of chapters with step-by-step instructions and tips. Each new chapter introduces a new design element and/or garment type with a little social history to put it in context. It then builds on the techniques learnt in the previous chapter. It is not necessarily about creating a final garment that I have already designed and made for you to see; it is more about looking at the sum of a garment's parts and learning the techniques for developing a bodice or a sleeve so that you can do your own design work with a clearer idea of how to set about achieving it. If you were to start from the beginning and work your way through the whole book systematically you would be able to design and cut a rich and varied collection of dresses, skirts, shirts and blouses. Please note I have not included jackets and trousers in the book as they are more technically advanced, but what is included in this sculptural process will allow you plenty of opportunities to develop and identify your own individual style aesthetic and preferences for cut and fit. You will get visual feedback from what is happening with the calico on the mannequin almost immediately and can adjust and amend as you please for the silhouette you want.

Garment visualization is a key skill for a fashion designer and draping is a great way not only to learn it but to become more confident with your own creative visions. The book also includes how to take a drape into a master pattern, then into a paper production pattern for toile and review. It also includes advice and top tips to help avoid some common pitfalls; for example, the importance of using the correct grain lines for balance and stability in your garments. There is also a section on working at half scale: this is a separate skill on its own and probably really useful as more fashion education delivery moves online, and it is not something I have seen much in other draping books. I have also included calico preparation diagrams so you do not have to spend time calculating them.

Draping could be considered a niche skill in today's fashion school training but it can lead to spectacular results and an excellent fit. With practice, pattern cutting can be put at the heart of the design process with the two key elements – design and creative cutting – developing harmoniously in tandem. Fabrics can be tested simultaneously, thereby informing the designer's understanding of its properties and suitability for her/his design idea, making this holistic approach more exploratory and sometimes faster than more conventional techniques. What's not to like about any of that? Enjoy ...

Left: Finished drapes for this book. (Photo: Yousef Al Nasser)

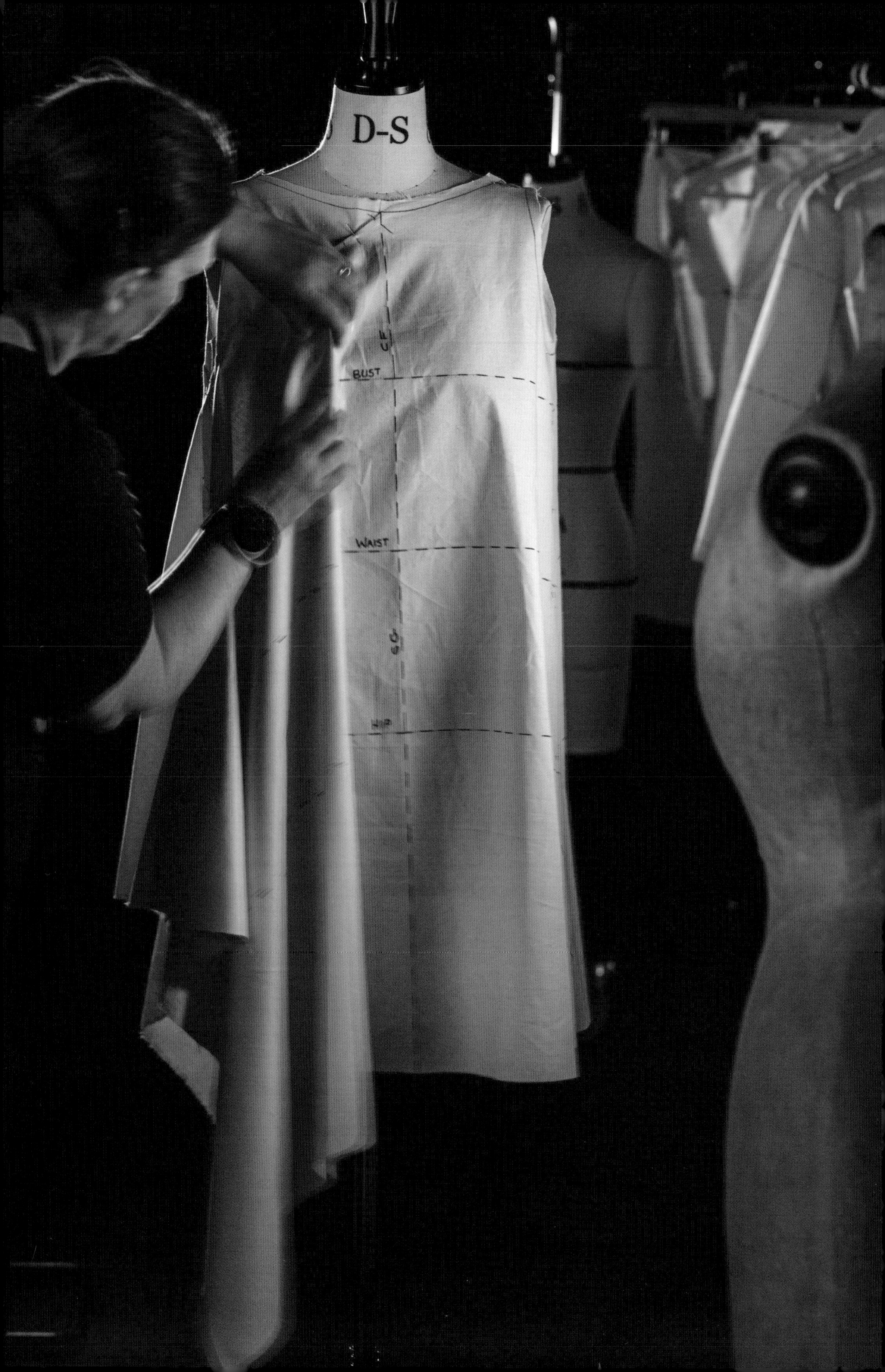
D-S
BUST
WAIST

Introduction

Historically, the evolution of all clothing relies on two principles: cutting cloth and draping cloth. With the former, cloth is cut according to a pattern tailored to specific measurements and the separate pieces are joined together to create a definitive three-dimensional form. In contrast, a draped garment often has no fixed form and relies on one piece of cloth being wrapped around the body and fastened at strategic points. The two approaches are often combined, or at least operated in harmony, to develop the prototype garments that form the basis of modern haute couture and luxury prêt-à-porter brands (Fig. 0.2).

Fig. 0.2 Finished calico toiles draped for the Fashion Atelier 'A Question of Angles and Curves Exhibition', The Zandra Rhodes Gallery, UCA Rochester. (Photo: Grace Elliot)

'Drape' is the term usually used to describe the way a fabric or garment hangs, and *moulage* techniques allow a designer to see their ideas come to life three-dimensionally as they manipulate and pin fabric on the dress form or house model. The designer may start out with a sketched design but during the draping process a new or more interesting garment idea can often take shape unexpectedly that could never have been conceived two-dimensionally on paper. This aspect of working with the unknown is why draping is often considered to be a more creative method of pattern making and design realization. Unlike two-dimensional pattern-making processes where a flat block or 'sloper' is manipulated, draping allows the designer to get a feel for the handle of the fabrics selected and their suitability for particular garment styles. The designer can also make alterations for fit (for example, by repositioning darts, ease and hemlines) before committing to the final idea and transferring the drape to a master pattern in paper.

Paris was the world leader in fashion aesthetics and tastes for several centuries in the Western world so our understanding of pattern-making systems and terminology are often expressed in French (*see* the glossary). For example, the term '*moulage*' comes from the French '*moule*' – a mould or container – and is the name for creating a product with the aid of a mould. When translated into fashion processes it means moulding around the body or dress stand in a three-dimensional way to achieve both the design and pattern simultaneously. This draping process is undertaken by either a designer or a toiliste in couture houses. The cloth, often the actual cloth of the final garment, which can sometimes be pre-cut into small pieces for resolving specific details or dimensions, is placed or arranged on the body. Alterations and corrections become immediately clear and are usually dictated by what the cloth itself wants to do. The cloth used for draping is called the 'toile', the French word for fabric (Fig. 0.3).

The toile is made of different weights of unbleached cotton, such as calico.

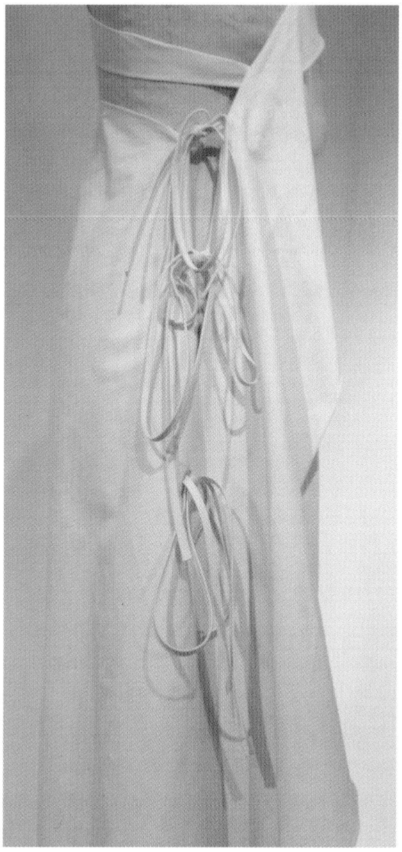

Fig. 0.3 Calico toile draped from one continuous piece of cloth by Fashion Atelier student Georgia Stevens. (Photo: Grace Elliot)

Left: Fig. 0.1 The author pinning a drape. (Photo: Yousef Al

Depending on the weight or type of the garment different thickness can be used. The cloth is a plain or neutral colour so that the fit and silhouette are not disrupted by pattern or motif at this stage. As soon as the toile is completed it is taken apart, with the separate pieces making the pattern for the final garment. The expected final result is already known before the garment is re-toiled and presented for approval. This is the process being used consistently throughout this book to realize a series of garment types and key design features. For all toiling, I have worked with mediumweight calico unless otherwise stated.

The craft of draping is considered a niche skill in today's fast fashion industry and in fashion training and education. Draping can be time-consuming and, sometimes, a resource-heavy technique with significant fabric wastage as an idea evolves. Drape-based modules and assignments are included in most fashion education curricula but it is not an approach that underpins the whole ethos of the majority of fashion courses and, as such, it can be difficult to find many good technical manuals on the technique. Draping is also an intuitive process open to personal interpretation (such as what constitutes a beautiful fit or aesthetic); consequently this is often difficult to capture in a series of instructions, especially where the skills have been passed down by word of mouth from master to apprentice or learned 'on the job' in a particular way unique to a specific atelier environment. There are only a limited number of people who are still able to teach the art of draping. Many of them are now in their seventies and although most of them still work in the fashion industry in some capacity they do not always have the opportunity to share or pass on their knowledge. I feel privileged to have met some of them in the course of my working life and, in 'old-school style', to have seen them demonstrate techniques that they have been using successfully for some fifty years to create beautiful clothes for high-profile clients or the luxury fashion market.

Contents for a book such as this never come from one source alone and in addition to working alongside other practitioners I have also waded through, and in some instances attempted to transcribe, collections of manuscripts from the libraries and archives at UCA, the V&A and Worthing Museum and Art Gallery to identify a clear set of instructions for draping. On occasion I have been looking closely at actual garments where the pattern and construction is so unusual or exceptional that collection curators have concluded that it could only have been arrived at through draping directly onto the body of a house model to evolve. This method is called object analysis and involves close examination of a garment's technicality (in pattern, construction and fabrication) to identify further areas for research. In these examples it has been to establish a designer's draping methodology. This part is a very fluid, trial-and-error process of working backwards from the finished garment. I often have to rethink the sequence of processes or test some of them out in calico to establish a definitive tried-and-tested methodology, particularly where, in the case of the Madame Grès dresses, the original couturiers are not here to ask. It is obviously not fail-safe but as a practitioner a lot can be learned through the re-creation of historical garments.

Brief History of Creative Cutting and Draping

Greeks, Romans and Antiquity

Moulage is a relatively new Westernized fashion process but its origins could arguably be traced back to Graeco-Roman times when dress was based on a simple system of different-sized rectangles of fabric that varied depending on its use and the size of the wearer, with little to differentiate between men's and women's wear. For

Fig. 0.4 Ancient Graeco-Roman statue of a headless woman in a chiton. (Photo: Mohammed Zarovski, Pexels)

example, the chiton was a single rectangle of wool or linen strategically pinned or sewn at the shoulders, along the arms or down one side, worn plain or with an over-fold kept in place with one or more belts (more common to women). The length was usually longer than the wearer was tall to allow for the folding when the excess was pulled above the belts to create a blouse-like effect (Fig. 0.4). The chiton was often worn with a heavier himation draped diagonally over it which acted like a cloak. A surprising variety of looks were achieved with a limited number of basic forms and is reflected best in Roman and Greek statues seen in museums today where they are characteristically the same but achieve very varied results. The practicality of this dress system probably accounts for such remarkable longevity (about BCE 600–100 Greece and BCE 275–330 CE Rome). Interestingly, there were ways in which these pieces were expressed differently and that we could loosely term as trends. For example, the early archaic periods were often defined by coarse heavily decorated wools and the later classic period by finer lighter linens. The hang of the drapery and the

Fig. 0.5. Ancient Roman statues in a variety of himations and togas. (Photo: Engin Akyurt, YUA Unsplash)

positions of the folds in the Late Hellenistic period were wider than previously seen and held in place with lead weights at the bottom to enhance the fall of the drapery.

Originally the Roman toga, a Roman version of the himation, was a simple and egalitarian form of dress and not draped diagonally across the body as we have come to think of it. Instead, it enclosed the body in a straightforward manner. It evolved into something less democratic over time as it became more gaudy and embellished for nobles during the Roman Empire. As it became synonymous with wealth and status it also became longer and more voluminous, with the cloth being folded double before being wrapped in more elaborate and sophisticated ways (Fig. 0.5). This way of dressing was comfortable and elegant and gave the body a certain degree of movement. Conceptually, the ideals of democracy and personal freedom much cherished in ancient Rome and Greece were epitomized in this simple style of dress; this period with its classic egalitarian ideology was later to become a rich source of inspiration for Parisian couturiers like Fortuny, Madame Vionnet and Madame Grès in the late nineteenth and twentieth centuries.

Court Fashions in Europe before 1850

Historically speaking, this will seem like a mammoth jump in time but the truth is that whilst there is a lot of visual information and even excellent examples of textiles, colour texture, components and silhouettes, there is very little identified documentation for pattern making and construction processes for clothing from Roman times until mid-sixteenth-century Spain. The control of volume in European garments from the fifteenth to nineteenth centuries suggests that draping directly onto a body must have occurred as it is unlikely that such designs could have been arrived at in other ways, but the lack of consistent information on historical draping suggests that no specific system had been formalized. We must surmise that tailors more or less invented their own systems based on what the client asked for. Tailors were generally of low social status and consequently have not been named or remembered kindly throughout history, which is probably the key reason why there is a shortage of information about technical detail or process. The earliest recorded example of a published book on dressmaking techniques was written by a Basque tailor called Juan de Alcega. What remains of the book can now be viewed online in the World Digital Library. It is unlikely that paper patterns or tape measures existed – a good tailor was expected to work directly from measurements on strips of paper or knots in string indicating their own handspans, transferring these onto fabric. The fabric could be a variety of different widths, so many chapters were devoted to resolving problems caused by not having a universal system either for measuring a client or for a woven cloth width.

The book, entitled *Libre Ede Geometria: Practica y Traca*, was extremely mathematical, depicting complex pattern lays that demonstrated how clothing for men, women, clergy and commanders of military orders could be arranged and cut out to minimize or eliminate waste on up to fifteen different widths of cloth. The information was then consolidated into tables cross-referencing pattern yardage for combinations of three possible lengths and fourteen possible widths. The book was a considerable undertaking because of the contradictory nature of the 'fashion industry' at that time and in the preface the author tells the reader how he nearly quit on numerous occasions.

Marie-Jeanne Rose Bertin, milliner, couturier and fashion adviser to Marie Antoinette throughout her entire reign, is credited as being the first celebrated French fashion designer with a significant and extravagant body of work that is well documented and archived. It is through her far-reaching influence that France emerged as the fashion capital of the world from the 1770s onwards.

Haute Couture and the Influence of Paris

Charles Frederick Worth

The British dressmaker Charles Frederick Worth (1825–95) opened a salon in Paris in 1858. He took what is now viewed historically as a revolutionary approach to fashion business. Rather than letting the customer decide how their clothes should look, he designed a collection himself and presented it on live models. The customer could select

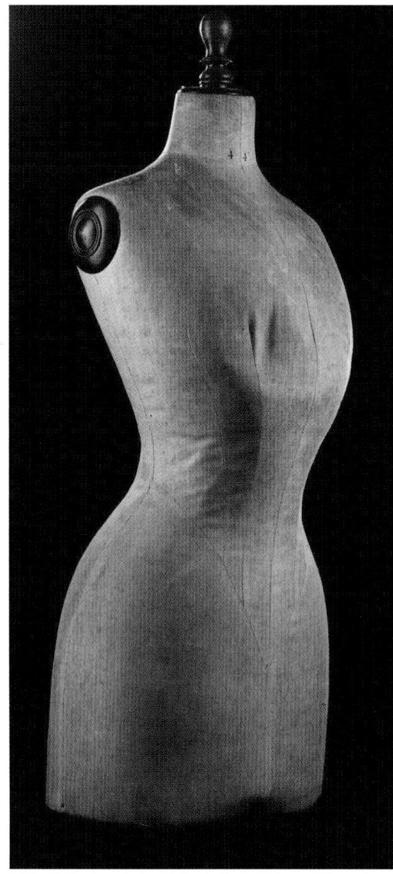

Fig. 0.6 Antique mannequin used to 'build' an S-bend silhouette. (Photo: Yousef Al Nasser)

what they wanted from the collection and have it re-toiled and made to fit them. This heralded a new era in terms of raising the profile of tailors and dressmakers, with the fashion designer being celebrated for the first time as an artist. The quality of workmanship coming from the Paris houses was undeniable; their far-reaching influence has been well documented, which has allowed us to see the diversity of working practices and philosophies so clearly abundant in one small microcosm of Europe at that time. For centuries women's dresses had been constructed around the corset and petticoat and this aesthetic did not really shift until dress reforms emerged in the late nineteenth century. The prevailing silhouette for women since Renaissance times had been to divide the body into two masses above and below a waistline that shifted depending on the length of the corset. In 1881 the Rational Dress Society began to spearhead a movement away from the corset on the grounds that it was detrimental to women's health and by championing looser-fitting clothing. By 1900 the S-curve silhouette, with large forward-projecting bosom and an equally large backward-protruding bottom was all the rage and a look championed by the influential House of Worth. Fig. 0.6 shows a Parisian mannequin from that era with its distinctive bustline. The fashionable lady's derrière would have been further enhanced with hoops, bustles and paniers. It was not really until 1906 that significant sartorial and political changes began to emerge and then they were not necessarily driven by health concerns for women but by a new theatrical aesthetic.

Paul Poiret

In the early 1900s the couturier Paul Poiret took up the cause, with his fluid, comfortable corset-free designs which were deemed so shocking at the time that people were said to have fainted at the sight of a woman wearing them in the street. Poiret had learnt his craft by working at the House of Worth so it is interesting to see that having trained in such a revered traditional fashion environment he then set out to subvert or break the established conventions of dressmaking with such vigour. He is now most famous for his exoticized aesthetic and love of orientalism which was often expressed through his choice of vivid colour coordinations, pattern and embellishment on harem pants, kimonos and 'lampshade' tunics. The silhouette he created was a far cry from the tight-fitting bodices and full skirts of the previous decades and his collaborations with artists and high-profile theatre companies ensured that his work was consistently in the public eye. From a creative cut perspective Poiret's work was a radical departure from the couture traditions of the nineteenth century which were based on men's tailoring techniques and relied on flat pattern pieces to utilize suppression to get the correct fit. Poiret looked at alternative garment systems, such as the Greek chiton, the Japanese kimono and the kaftans of North Africa and the Middle East, for inspiration in evolving a system using rectangles and straight lines and allowing the fabric to fall and drape more naturally. He introduced simple shapes that hung from the shoulders, offering the wearer a multiplicity of options for styling rather than the restriction of the bodice.

Madame Vionnet

Madame Madeleine Vionnet (1876–1975), a contemporary of Poiret, also embraced an alternative approach to the conventions of the couturier craft, setting out to disrupt the basic construction of European fashion but in a slightly different way. As a woman her career opportunities were somewhat restricted by comparison to Poiret's, although she did of course have first-hand experience of the restrictions of wearing corsetry! Vionnet was one of the most influential couturiers in the 1920s and 1930s and, like Poiret, her love for classicism and antiquity is believed to be the source of inspiration for many of her designs which also used basic geometric forms or 'quadrants' that adjusted themselves to the body (Fig. 0.7). Her often complex cutting or construction was not fully revealed until the garment was off the body or taken apart. Unlike Poiret she relied less on embellishment and surface pattern for her designs and more on the handle and drape of the cloth. Another source of inspiration is also likely to have been her love of mathematics which, as a girl, she was not encouraged (read 'allowed') to study. Instead she apprenticed herself to a dressmaker. Her knowledge and understanding of three-dimensional realization was greatly elevated when she went to work as head of the workroom for the highly respected couture house Callot Soeurs. The sisters relied solely on her to transform their ideas into fully working toiles and ultimately into garments highlighting the ways in which fabric could be manipulated and design content developed and progressed through draping on the stand.

She is most well known for her draping applications and particularly for working on the bias (Fig. 0.8). The fluidity in her designs was achieved by cutting the cloth at a 45-degree angle to the selvedge edge rather than along the warp or weft of the cloth. The bias cut allowed her to create sculptural gowns that would closely hug the figure as the fabric draped around the contours of the female body. She

Fig. 0.7 Sketchbook page for a Vionnet quadrant dress. Courtesy of the Stuart Aitken Archive

Fig. 0.8 Sketchbook page for a geometric Vionnet dress with knot. Courtesy of the Stuart Aitken Archive.

refined a method to stabilize the cloth by using the straight grain in diagonal seams to create body-skimming tubes of cloth that slipped over the head and clung to the curves of the body. She had a preference for silks, satins and crêpe de Chines that helped to create her elegant, modern silhouettes. She ordered these fabrics to be woven 1.8 metres wider than normal (so up to 3 metres) to give her more freedom to manipulate the cloth and create drapery. Her initial designs were often worked out on a half-scale mannequin – rather like a three-dimensional sketch – before being fully resolved at full scale: this minimized the costs of the toiling process. After WW1 Vionnet was one of the most successful couture houses of the era, employing 1,200 people and influencing the working practices of many. Vionnet's expertise, innovation and craftsmanship ensured that draping was used as a technique in all the great ateliers in Paris up to and including the 'Golden Age of Couture' in the 1950s where urban myths abound about different couturiers' working practices. For example, Nina Ricci only worked directly onto a live model and Jacques Fath often draped on himself whilst a few trusted assistants observed and made quick sketches of his discoveries.

Madame Grès

Perhaps the other best-known proponent of drape is Madame Alix Grès – born Germaine Krebs (1903–93). Originally a sculptor, she cared little for the current fashions of the day but instead shared Vionnet's passion for classism and was also inspired by Greek drapery (Figs 0.9 and 0.10). She preferred to realize her draped designs in silk jersey, crêpeline or muslin, with a single gown using 21 metres of cloth or more as a direct result of her trademark pleating and folding. Her garments also often included perfectly positioned cut-outs to reveal the skin of the wearer's back or shoulder – something that could only be determined by working directly onto the stand with the fall and handle of the cloth dictating the silhouette of the design. Her design house was known as Alix from 1934 to 1942 and was dubbed by the *New York Times* as 'the most intellectual place in Europe to buy clothes'. She had an extraordinarily long career, working up until the 1980s and refusing to be swayed in her design aesthetic. Her working practices were not dissimilar to those of Vionnet, with the use of three-dimensional sketches on scaled-down mannequins and an intuitive understanding of how her cloth would behave. The marriage of this creativity, coupled with her technical knowledge, seems perfectly aligned when you see her clothes first-hand and the methodology, knowledge

Fig. 0.9 Madame Grès-inspired bias-draped toile in final cloth by Fashion Atelier student Isobel Tustin.

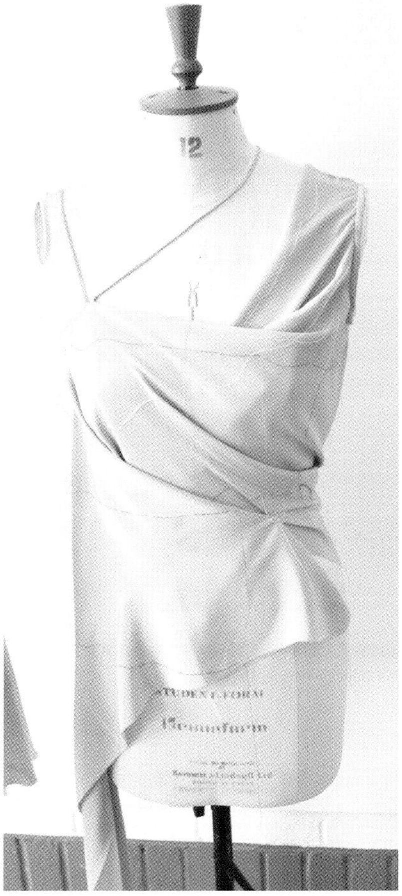
Fig. 0.10 Madame Grès-inspired bias-draped toile in final cloth by Fashion Atelier student Cliona Gissane.

and skill become somewhat clearer. In reality, for example, the weight of an evening dress would mean the need for an invisible support which would need to be considered and designed simultaneously with the dress shell. The support, most likely a corset, would then have to be made first and placed on the mannequin before the dress could be draped from a single large piece of jersey. The smaller three-dimensional version would have highlighted in advance any issues with regard to excess cloth and functionality but it would still have been necessary to investigate how to connect the shell to the support.

Madame Grès was not alone in her approach but in fact part of a group of influential Parisian designers that included other masters of creative cut – Jeanne Lanvin, Pauline Trigère, Richard Tyler and, the most well-known, Cristóbal Balenciaga. What these couturiers had in common was their 'hands-on' approach and a shared belief that design evolved by working on a living body or mannequin rather than starting with a sketch. Balenciaga was particularly influential at the time and apprenticeships in his house highly sought-after by emergent designers. André Courrèges, Oscar de la Renta, Emanuel Ungaro and Hubert de Givenchy were amongst those who trained under him and then went on to launch their own influential fashion houses or work for other often ailing houses to reinvigorate them. Another famous contemporary was, of course, Christian Dior and his house's characteristic play on female proportion was epitomized in his 1947 New Look. Although significantly more tailored and corseted than Balenciaga's, the look was hugely influential and ultimately became the defining look of that decade in spite of its opponents who rejected the notion of putting women back into what was effectively a pseudo-Victorian corset and skirts. This era of Paris couture really demonstrated the diversity of the designers' visions, with an emergent plurality to fashion that had not really been witnessed before.

John Galliano

It's a never-ending learning process with the bias, because each fabric reacts differently ... a dialogue develops and you have to be attentive because it's alive, ... It teaches you, you can't read about it from a book ... you are not forcing it to do anything, it tells you what to do

(John Galliano, *The Guardian*, 2018).

Galliano is a British visionary who emerged fresh-faced from the London fashion school of Central Saint Martin's in the 1980s. His work is highly influenced by the bias cutting of Vionnet and the sculptural techniques of Madame Grès but with his own modern-day spin. His collections could not be produced in any other way than draping; they remain consistently edgy and extravagant, with what looks at first glance to be purely sumptuous embellishment but which is actually combined with creative cutting and is integral to the garment pattern. Unfortunately, Galliano is possibly now most well-known for his public sacking as Creative Director at the House of Dior after a drunken anti-semitic outburst in a café just before Paris Fashion Week 2011. However, his atonement for the incident is also much publicized and has enabled him to sustain his creative and strategic roles in couture where he headed Givenchy and Dior before joining Maison Margiela as Creative Director in 2014. Famous for his trail-blazing approach, his work at Margiela has included the controversial launch of his first couture menswear range for Spring/Summer 2019. Speaking in a *Guardian* newspaper podcast to the fashion journalist Scarlett Conlon about his work, Galliano described the designs as 'artisanal' rather than 'couture' because they bring together the separate elements of a traditional womenswear couture collection by combining bias cutting, soft sewing and tailoring but for menswear. He explained: 'We are trying to define what artisanal means for us ... It's rooted in craftsmanship and is the highest form of dressmaking, but for men. Its backbone is in tailoring, but we are trying to further explore the bias cut.'

Charles James

Before Galliano's time but clearly an inspiration to him, Charles James is another designer who showed his collections in Paris after WW2, albeit for a short period. I first discovered his work whilst working on a costume exhibition for Brighton Museum and Art Gallery entitled 'Fashion and Fancy Dress'. It was an exploration of the Messel Family Dress Collection, largely womenswear, most of which was collected and worn by Anne, Countess of Rosse and her mother Maude Messel. Part of the British aristocracy and social elite, the family were all able

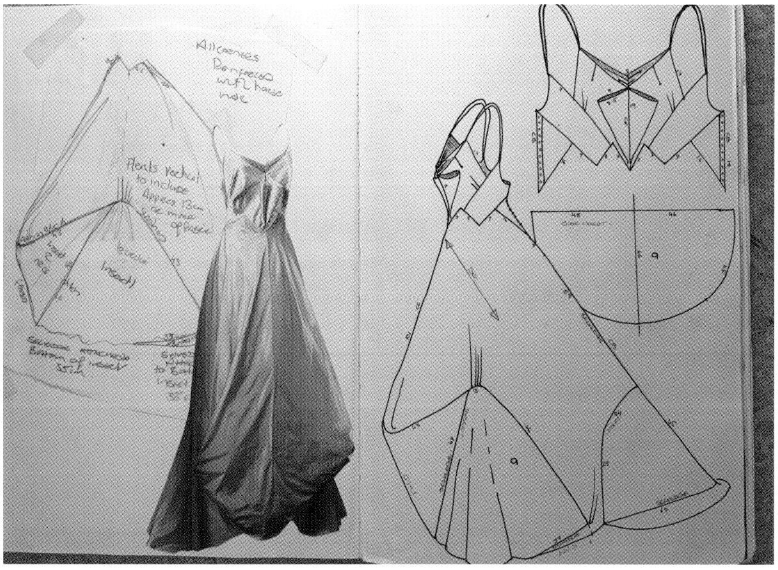

Fig. 0.11 Charles James pattern analysis sketches. (Author's own)

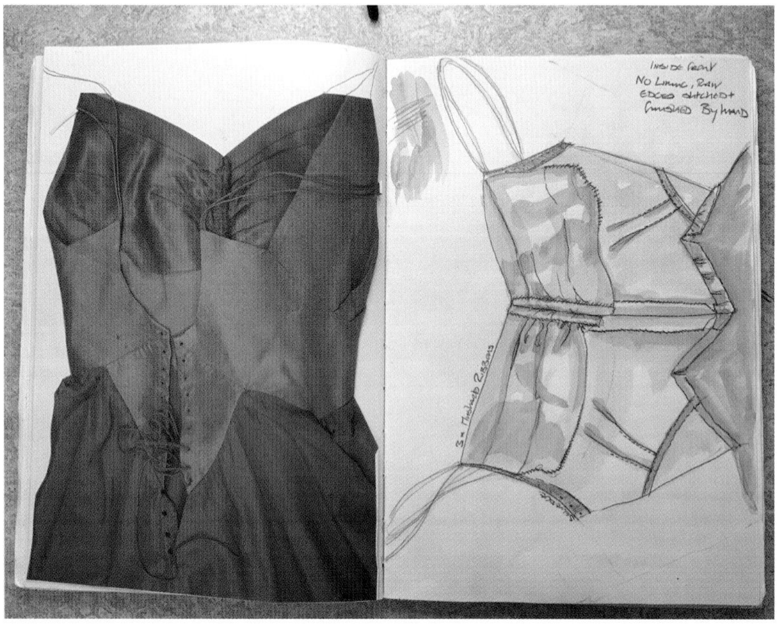

Fig. 0.12 Charles James pattern analysis sketches. (Author's own)

to commission and wear couture indulgently and in amongst the 500 pieces or so that they owned was the debutante dress designed by Charles James (Figs 0.11.and 0.12). James was, in fact, an Anglo-American milliner turned fashion designer living in the US whose practice was more akin that of an architect or engineer than a dressmaker. He predominantly worked and sold one-off pieces from his atelier in New York and, unlike his peers from this period, was never apprenticed in Paris. He is the least well known outside of the fashion industry but to fashion insiders he is considered to have been a staggering visionary talent with far-reaching influence who had a major impact on the draping methodologies of designers in Europe and America for decades.

It would be inappropriate not to mention him here when talking about draping techniques although his designs were often not about the softness and fluidity we associate with draping techniques. James took a very sculptural approach towards investigating the relationship between the female body and the surrounding space and frequently created/engineered enormous stiff-boned gowns with incredible silhouettes. Whilst his work was about the manipulation and drape of the fabric around the female form it was also about the sculptural development of the form itself: one major example would be his 'Clover Leaf' ballgown with a skirt hem shaped like a huge four-leaf clover in 1953 which was worn by Austine Hearst at the Eisenhower inaugural ball. The dress, which can be seen as part of the online collection at the Metropolitan Museum in New York, weighed nearly 7kg (over 15lb) and held its unique shape because the designer had first created a four-leaf clover dress stand from plaster-covered papier mâché, wood and metal and then draped fabric over it. This allowed him and his team of '*petits mains*' to see how his cloth of choice – silk taffeta and velvet – performed and to create a bespoke boning and horsehair support structure unique to that design that allowed the gown to hold its shape without collapsing or being filled up with petticoats. Most ateliers would have a version of padding out a conventional dress form to match a client's measurements and aid in the fitting of garments but James's concept took this to an entirely different level by constructing his own customized mannequins in unconventional proportions in much the same way he would have used a moulded head form to block a hat. He pushed the boundaries for how the dress form could be used to create new gravity-defying garments in a process he was referring to by the 1960s as 'metamorphology'. James's rich patrons allowed him to embrace often controversial approaches, such as the development of new dress forms in clay in a sculptor's studio to ensure that what he made for them was an individual walking work of art and a true couture piece.

Draping and Zero Waste

The zero waste movement of the twenty-first century is the practice of encouraging a sustainable lifecycle for fashion products, particularly as a pre-consumer intervention, by reducing wastage that ends up in landfill. Research by zero waste designers like Holly McQuillan and Timo Rissanen have demonstrated that up to 15 per cent of cloth ends up on the cutting room floor when using traditional pattern-cutting systems. Zero waste cutting works by knowing the dimensions of the amount of cloth to be used before beginning to design. The pattern can be developed in a variety of ways depending on the aesthetic to be achieved; for example, by draping on the stand to create garments with minimal seams or by embedding a fixed point like a neckhole and shoulder somewhere on the fabric and then developing the rest of the pattern as interlocking pieces like a jigsaw. Yeohlee Teng is a Malaysian-born American designer who has been spearheading the zero waste movement since the 1980s and is known for her minimal, functional clothing. She uses geometric shapes to create carefully considered designs that are carefully draped and analysed to achieve the perfect fit and fabric efficiency. This concept is being more frequently adopted by emergent designers and fashion students, as demonstrated in the toiling and pattern diagrams in Fig. 0.13.

Thoughts from an Emergent Practitioner

Draping very much continues behind the scenes of the contemporary fashion world, depending on the quality and exclusivity of the end product. I recently spoke with Hannah Ralph who works as the Atelier Coordinator for the ready-to-wear brand Hussein Chalayan. Her role involves production management for the UK atelier but it also involves making toiles at a very high level. A graduate of the Fashion Atelier BA Honours degree, she is clear that the prevailing system of draping traditionally used by couturiers is impervious to modernization and she marries this tradition with modernity comfortably in her practice. For example, she can create exclusive prototype products by draping at half-scale for designs being patterned for serial production in the company's Japanese studio. Her work requires a lot of draping and each drape serves as a technical aid in realizing a design sketch and as an indispensable part of the design process itself (Figs 0.14 and 0.15). She describes her approach like this:

When approaching a design, I like to explore words associated with my inspiration through 3D experimental play, with a range of media. I then like to contextualize the conceptual ideas

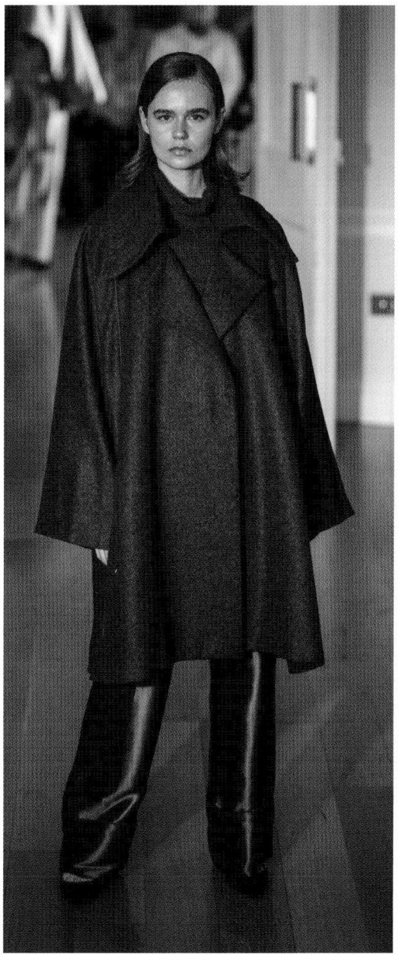

Fig. 0.14 Hannah Ralph, Graduate Collection, Asia House. (Photo: Yousef Al Nasser)

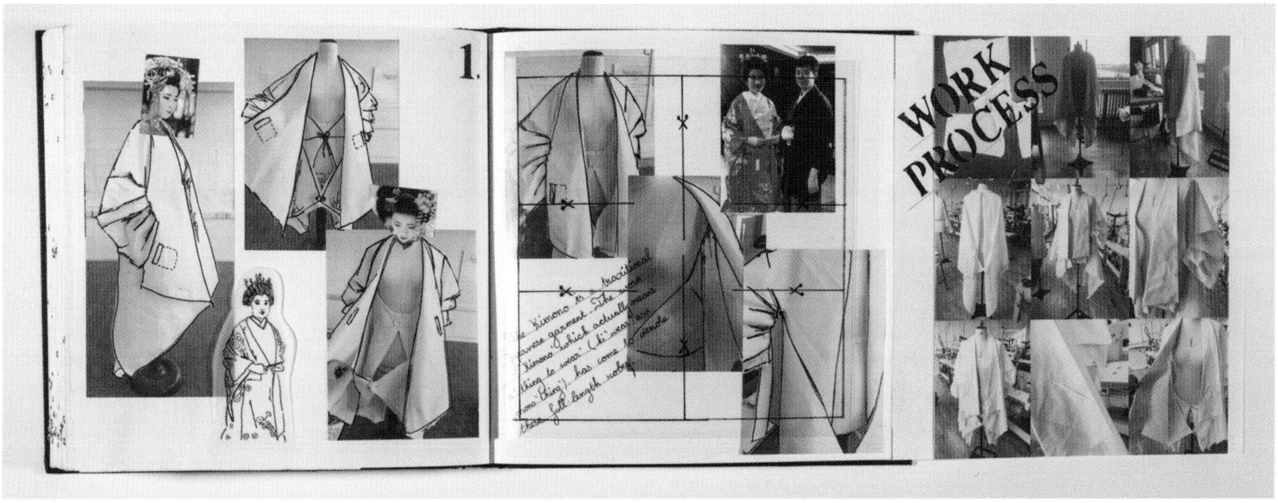

Fig. 0.13 Zero waste garment and pattern diagram based on a square from Fashion Atelier student Rosalie Key.

Fig. 0.15 Hannah Ralph, Graduate Collection, Asia House. (Photo: Yousef Al Nasser)

that come from this, by working them into the dimensions of the body ... Because my ideas start in 3D, draping is the natural next step. My first drapes will always start with the grainline on the centre front, but then a lot of fabric, way more than the panel will end up as. This ensures I have no constraints to the shapes and volume I am creating, but I can always transfer to paper pattern knowing the grainline. I want my designs to be organic and natural, and designing whilst draping allows this. I can see how the shapes work and see how panels and seam lines should naturally form through the drape of the fabric. And I work out the correct proportions and the type of fit I want from the beginning. I am creative when I drape but by also following traditional draping techniques, I know whatever I am designing is always possible as a working garment.

My first drapes will be toiled and may become a final design. But often I will further develop the design from the toile. I may cut and drape into it, or remove sections, or drape layers on top. I also like to put the drape on the mannequin at new angles or on different parts of the body. Or if there is a shape I like in one toile, I extract it and use it as a starting point for a new drape. So I am constantly re-draping to exhaust my designs.

Object-Based Research and Costume History

Designers are consistently inspired by what already exists and their new designs are often in response to their analysis of something they have seen and taken inspiration from. Extra research is key here: say, for example, if you have seen an image of a dress but only from the front and want to know more. It is often difficult to work out a garment's true cut and construction from photographs online or in books alone and there really is no substitute for going to see it first-hand. A good way to explore couturier working practices is therefore to look at their garments first-hand, either in a store if they are a contemporary practitioner, or at auctions or vintage stores or in private collections and museums if they are historical. If you want to really expand your research content and knowledge nothing can beat a hands-on approach to exploring historical artefacts in museum archives with the help of a curator. I have used quite a few sketchbooks so far in this introduction and that is because observational drawing and analysis really helps to cement an understanding of the working practices of practitioners who create the garments you find inspirational. This process is called object-based research.

The Dress Detective by Ingrid Mida and Alexandra Kim is a practical guide to object-based research in fashion; this requires you to book an appointment to go behind the scenes and see something specific in a museum archive with the support of the curator. It is a great starting point for providing a framework for a deductive approach to analysing fashion objects and ephemera. It sets out criteria and a ticklist of what to look for to ensure you find out what you need to know through close analysis of well-chosen fashion objects. It can, for example, greatly enhance and enrich our knowledge of cut, construction, use of materials and techniques and social context in which the object has been worn. Evidence and inference gained from the object can then be used to corroborate existing ideas you may have or generate new ones. In the past, information that might have been missed or passed on informally has begun to gain substance. Object analysis is now seen as a legitimate route of academic research for museums, curators, fashion designers and collectors alike and I have used this process to influence some of the decisions made for the development of ideas in this book. This process never disappoints for me and always offers up a wealth of new knowledge for cutting and finishing and amazing insight into the working methods of other practitioners. However, be aware that with regards to museum collections, the drawback is often that, for conservation purposes, you cannot touch the garments yourself. It is therefore necessary to be clear about what you want to find out before booking an appointment. By working collaboratively with curators and by asking the right questions you can find out what you need to know. I work on the bias a lot with students and in the first example described below I wanted to identify seam positions in the pleated Grecian drapery of Madame Grès to see if the dresses were draped from a single piece of cloth or if there were concealed panels. I wanted to know if they were cut on the bias or not and also how the fluid pleating was being controlled so that the dress looked exactly the same each time it was taken on and off. I also work with quite a lot of fabric manipulation techniques at work and wanted to know, in the second example, whether or not the aesthetic of the Galliano dress and coat was created through embellishment or creative cutting. I was also interested to look at the finishing techniques used for such complex garments in such delicate fabrics to see if I could use them in my own or my students' practice.

Object Analysis for Madam Grès

For this book, and also for my own teaching practice, I looked at two Madame Grès dresses from the V&A's costume archive that had been draped and not cut on the flat. (They can be seen in the catalogue on the 'gres-madame' pages of the 'collections.vam' website listed at the end of the book.) Both dresses would be considered typical examples of her work and craftsmanship and they support what I had previously surmised about her working practices. They are faithful replicas of Paris originals designed in 1955 and re-made in the Grès atelier before being donated to the V&A by the designer. They make up a small part of the Cecil Beaton Collection – an extensive collection of pieces brought together by the society photographer of that name, who contacted the well-dressed elite of Europe and North America to ask for donations to create a monument to contemporary couture. The whole collection was exhibited in 1971 although a lot of it is now in storage and only available to see on request.

Both dresses have a Grecian aesthetic. They look minimal, being unadorned, and appear at first glance to be made from one cylinder of cloth (Figs 0.16 and 0.17). Yet they are also complex in appearance, with tiny micro pleats constructed to create a flattering fit through the bust and waist but volume and movement through the floor-length skirts. The cut and construction methods for both garments are similar as they are part of the same collection. They are constructed with a mix of hand and machine stitching. They also both have an invisible waist-length corset foundation that provides a base for the pleating to be mounted whilst supporting the weight of the dress (Fig. 0.18). The internal corsets are both fully boned, with silk ribbons to make the casings. The bra cups have underwires and are also boned over the bustline through the princess seams. The underwire casings and bridge are made of bias silk velvet sewn by hand and the cups and natural bra line are reinforced by a silk half-cup that has been strengthened with a grid of machine stitching across it. The edges have been finished by hand and sewn in by hand. The necklines of both dresses have been faced with silk and stitched closed by hand (Fig. 0.19).

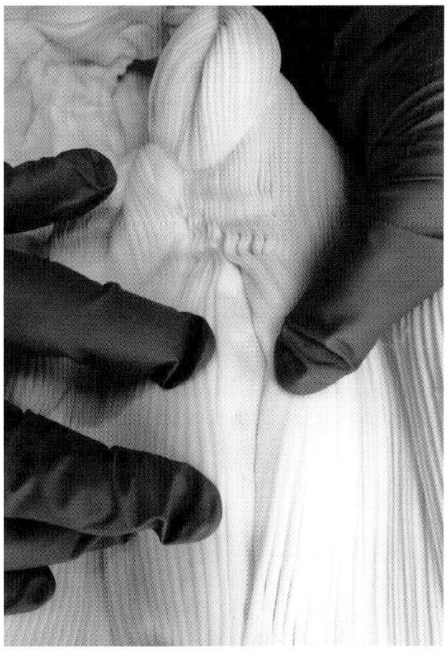

Fig. 0.16 Examining the pleats of a Madame Grès dress, The Clothworkers' Centre, V&A Museum.

Fig. 0.17 Madam Grès dress laid out for object analysis, The Clothworkers' Centre, V&A Museum.

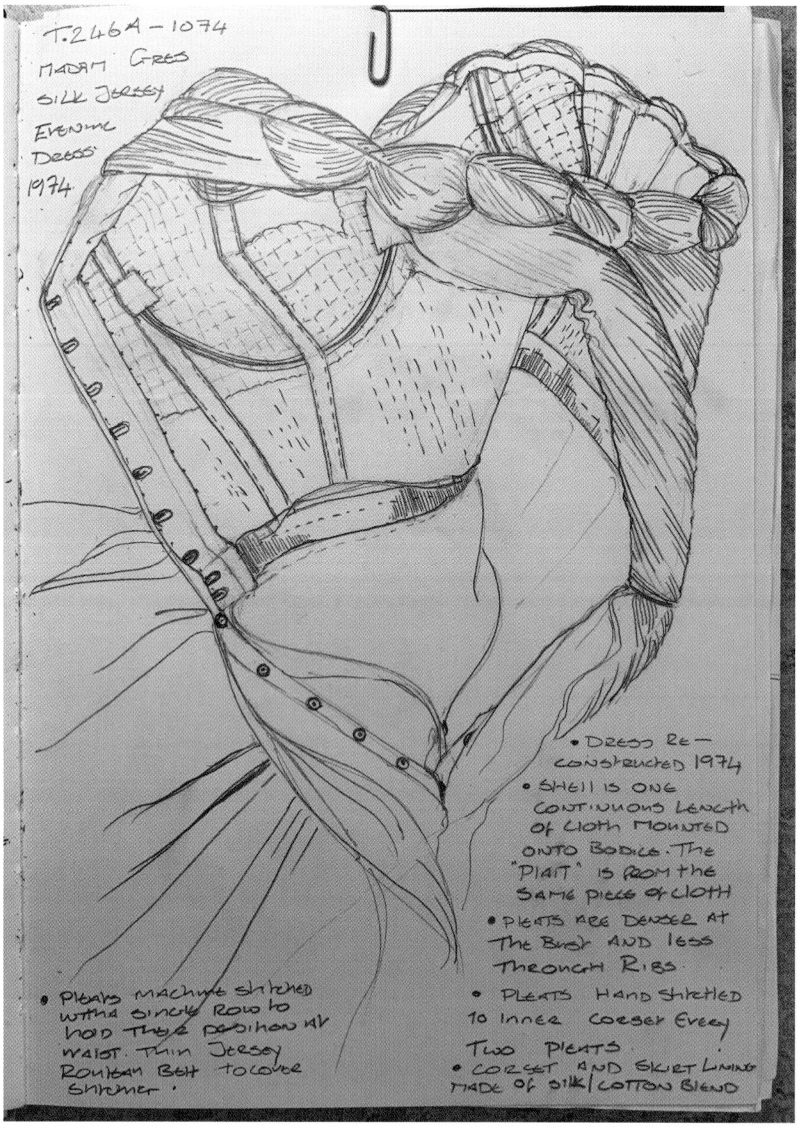

Fig. 0.18 Author's object analysis sketches, showing construction analysis.

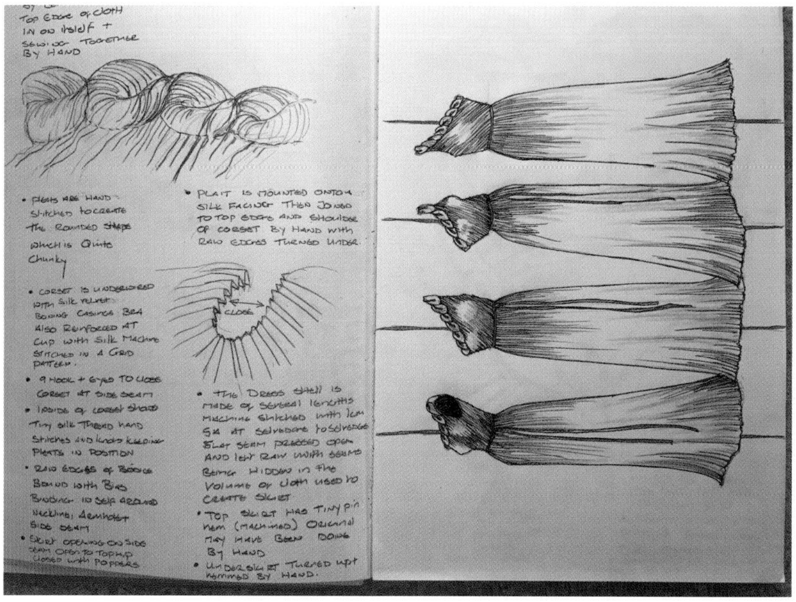

Fig. 0.19 Author's object analysis sketches, showing construction analysis for neckline detail.

Both designs have one armhole, with the drapery continuing over the shoulder. The armholes have also been faced in silk and closed by hand but where the shape of the armhole is squared off at the underarms, the corner edge has an additional small triangular reinforcement to match the facing and is also stitched in by hand. What is most notable about the inside of both corsets are the rows of tiny, fine hand stitches anchoring the pleats in place on the dress shell. At first glance the pleating appears to be held in place by a simple, thin rouleau belt. On closer inspection it is apparent that it is actually a row of machine stitching to securely anchor the pleats densely into position around the bottom of the internal corset and that they are not free-flowing at all. This is concealed on the inside with a piece of silk petersham ribbon in both corsets and in one of the dresses only it also serves to conceal the seaming of the lining to the corset at the waist.

The pleats themselves are a real demonstration of the level of skill and craftsmanship that has gone into each piece (Fig. 0.20). The pleats have been put in by hand by experimenting with draping them across the mannequin's torso and getting them in the most flattering position. They are almost completely even in a depth of about 3mm (⅛in) each. They are anchored into place every two to three pleats with a tiny invisible hand stitch with more around the bust or where the pleating changes direction. The pleating is left to drop open at the hemline, exploiting the sheer volume of fabric to create movement and fluidity. The pleating is finished by hand with a tiny delicate pin/rolled hem about 2mm (bare ⅛in) in depth. There are panels in both skirts along the princess seams where it is evident the fabric has been stitched on the straight of grain, selvedge to selvedge, and left raw as the fabric does not fray. I have included some pages from my own object analysis sketchbook that show the garments and notes on the construction. What is evident is that this design could not have evolved without working directly

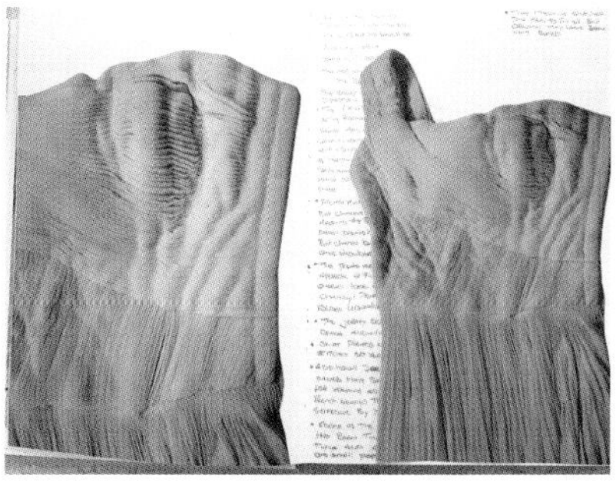

Fig. 0.20 Author's object analysis of pleating technique for silk jersey dress.

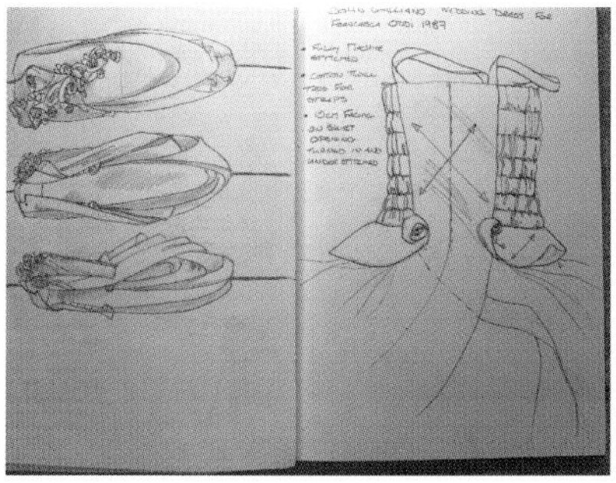

Fig. 0.21 Author's object analysis for seamed embellishment on John Galliano wedding coat.

on the body to organically synchronize the flow of cloth with the curvature of the torso. This is particularly borne out by the positioning of the pleats over the integral corset at the bustline.

Object Analysis for John Galliano

This dress is also part of the V&A archive and can be viewed online (look at the 'galliano' page of the 'collections.vam' website as listed at the end of this book). Galliano's silk, satin, chiffon and organza cream wedding ensemble is an excellent example of his technical skill in creative cut (Figs 0.21 and 0.22). Mainstream bridal wear in the 1980s was dominated by extravagant interpretations of the traditional white wedding dress, and frequently copied or referenced the David Emanuel design for Princess Diana's dress for her marriage to Prince Charles in 1981. Galliano's design, made for Francesca Oddi in 1987, was both experimental and groundbreaking in regard to cut

Fig. 0.22 Author's object analysis, quick sketches of the John Galliano wedding coat and of the pattern and construction of the John Galliano wedding dress.

and construction and his imaginative handling of the surface embellishment. The wedding outfit comprises a dress, blouse, veil and coat. Roses gathered from folds of ivory silk cluster and trail over the shoulder and back of the wedding coat. More roses are placed amongst the complex folds of material. The dress is strapless with shirred decoration and has more roses at the hips. It is worn over an organza blouse with long sleeves. The highly decorative soft-tailored coat is collarless, with an edge-to-edge closure at the centre front. Typical of his complex cutting techniques, the left rever is a separate piece that is twisted to create a rose. The two-piece sleeve has been extended to create extra fabric at the sleeve head that is also rolled to create a rose before being machine stitched into the shoulder seam. The rose-covered surface of the coat back is created by extending the fabric at the centre back seam and suppression points to create excess fabric and allow the designer to make the roses integral to the cut of the seams themselves. This method creates a characteristic asymmetric fold of cloth synonymous with Galliano's early cutting practices. Additional roses embellish the rest of the surface; they are made by hand in chiffon to match the veil, with the leaves that are self machine stitched and bagged out for sharpness. The coat is closed with one button and a rouleau loop at the centre front waist. The skirt of the coat hangs from the waist seam with a twisted drape at the side bottom hem and is asymmetric – something that could not be achieved without a certain degree of experimentation with the cloth on a mannequin or model first.

The coat is designed to be worn over a strapless dress with shirring and more integral roses at the hip. The dress bodice is fitted through the body using six panels that eliminate the side seam. Seven casings for wide elastic gather in the volume in the side panels. The asymmetric tulip-shaped drape of the skirt is created by adding volume over the side hips in a series of four box pleats with a double box pleat at the side point where it intersects the top hip and the bottom of the side casing panel. The pleats are anchored into position with a pocket jet and then bagged out into functioning side pockets and concealed with a large pocket flap. The front edge of the pocket flap is extended to create an integral rose on each front hip. A rouleau and button keep the pocket under the flap closed. The skirt has a wrap-over at the centre front but the skirt is cut in one piece from centre front round to the centre back.

It is most likely that this design was cut using a combination of draping on the stand and flat pattern cutting. To establish the behaviour of the fabrics they would have been draped first and the manipulation tested in three dimensions to allow the design to evolve and be resolved more realistically. The best way to embed fabric manipulation is to test it on a large piece of cloth first to see how it adapts around the contours of the body. The design process then becomes a more harmonious balance between the two-dimensional and the three-dimensional, with the designer moving between the two approaches towards the final outcome.

Tools of the Trade

1

*Draping is like any other artisanal craft and has its own 'tools of the trade', which I have listed in this chapter. The most important are the **dress stand** or **mannequin** and the **calico/muslin** or other cloth you are using for draping and toiling. I have therefore unashamedly talked about these in significantly more detail than everything else.*

The Mannequin

The mannequin or dress form is the primary piece of equipment you will need to drape and it takes up the lion's share of this chapter. Without a body you have nothing to drape on or around. It is used in the fashion industry for design development and fitting garments, allowing the designer to see their designs take shape, either in calico or the intended final fabric choice. Pattern cutters and designers use mannequins to fit and drape garments, check proportions and check the balance or hang of a garment. Choosing one depends on your needs and finances but get the best you can afford, regardless of its age or the state of its cover. It should be sturdy with a metal base. Do not choose one with an adjustable centre front and centre back as these are the most important points to drape from so there needs to be something solid to pin calico to. This is even more apparent if you are only working on a half toile (which is customary when the garment you are draping is symmetrical) and working on one half of the stand only. It is better to pad up a stand for different client requirements than use an expanding stand if you want to perfect your draping skills and use the technique as your preferred method for garment development (Fig. 1.2).

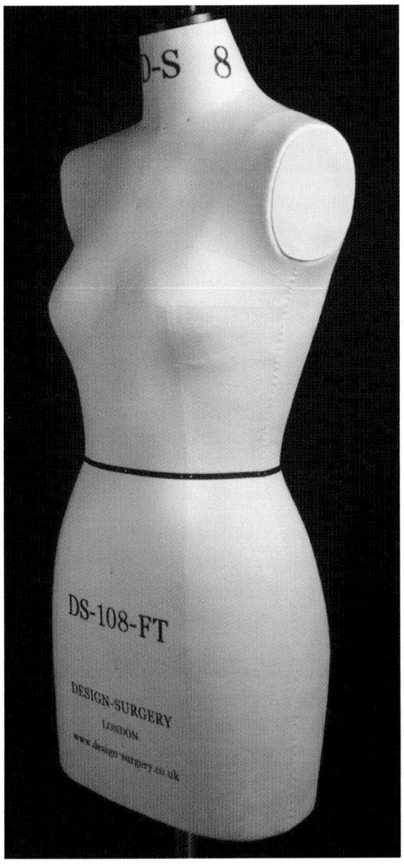

Fig. 1.2 Design-Surgery® 'Florence' female mannequin used in the book.

History of the Mannequin

Historically speaking, the very first shop window mannequins appeared in about 1780 and were woven in wicker like a basket to make male and female forms. As the needs of the fashion industry dictated, a flourishing dress stand industry emerged in Paris in the mid-nineteenth-century replicating the fashionable silhouettes of the day. A dress stand that could actually be worked on seems not to have been available until around 1850. Although it was still made of wicker, it was now covered with a layer of horsehair or waste cotton and upholstered with linen. By 1880 practitioners had begun to use a more solid version made of papier mâché with a linen cover, although still a far cry from the fibreglass, batting and canvas stands we are used to seeing in workrooms today (Figs 1.3 and 1.4). Mannequins reflected the desired body aesthetic for the men and women of a particular era; for example, a mannequin from the early 1900s will have the characteristic S-bend silhouette with a high round bust and rounder bottom with a significantly smaller waist than we would expect to see today.

In its costume archive, the Worthing Museum and Art Gallery has a Home Dress Making Course designed for the Woman's Institute of Domestic Arts and Sciences Ltd. Initiated in the US, this was an offshoot of the otherwise voluntary and non-profitmaking Women's Institute (WI) movement. The WI was only established in the UK in 1915 so this was one of their relatively early initiatives in teaching its members new skills. The course comes as a box set with its original receipt and application for membership (Figs 1.5 and 1.6). The original owner was a thirty-year-old housewife called Mrs E. Horlock, who in 1925 paid the princely sum of £10 10s. for her annual membership and the complete course entitled 'Dressmaking and Designing'. The course comprises a box set of sixteen illustrated booklets which, according to the receipt, would have been dispatched one at a time, setting work tasks that would have had to be completed and sent in to the local WI for correcting before Mrs Horlock received the next manual. The first manual (Figs 1.7 and 1.8) also came with a solid or non-adjustable form made of papier mâché to be padded up to replicate her own figure and a manual for it entitled *The Dress Form*

Left: Fig. 1.1 Antique mannequin, toiles and pattern blocks. (Photo: Yousef al Nasser)

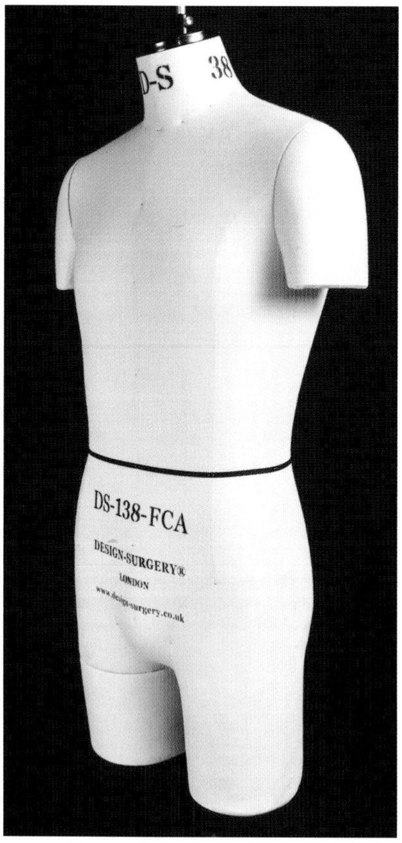

Fig. 1.3 Design-Surgery® 'Thomas' male mannequin, with crotch and thigh used for the design of menswear and men's intimate apparel. (Photo: Design Surgery, London)

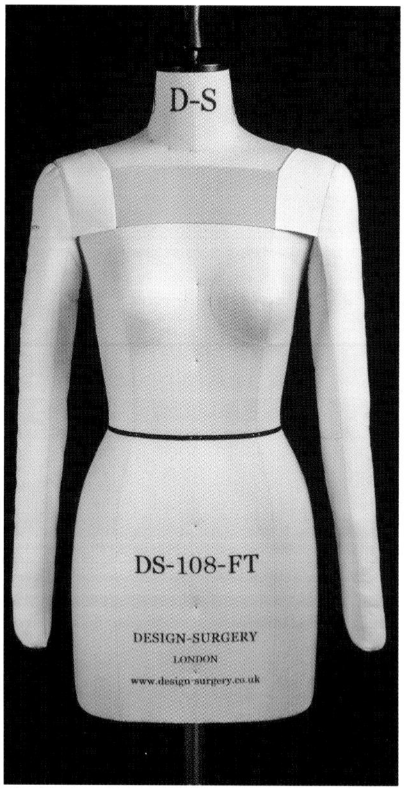

Fig. 1.4 Design-Surgery® mannequin with detachable arms. (Photo: Design Surgery, London)

and Its Use. The WI advocated and also sold adjustable forms although they were expensive. Cheaper options included a 'Pneumatic Dress Form' made of rubber that could be inflated like a tyre. The cheapest option was a 'Paper Shell Form' that ladies made themselves using strips of gummed paper pasted onto a gauze shirt worn by the woman the mannequin was for (Fig. 1.9). She was then cut out of it through the centre back and the form was allowed to dry solid before either being placed over an existing smaller stand or used on its own. It was assumed that the form ordered by Mrs Horlock would need altering to fit. She would have had to make or have fitted a cotton lining that was an exact fit to her own body or, if she supplied her vital statistics, the WI would cut the pattern and do it for her. The lining would then have been placed over the papier-mâché form to check the fit and make note of further adjustments. Sometimes these processes were incredibly 'hands on' as these images for making adjustments reveal in Figs 1.10 and 1.11. It does, however, reinforce the importance of having the right-sized mannequin to work on from the outset.

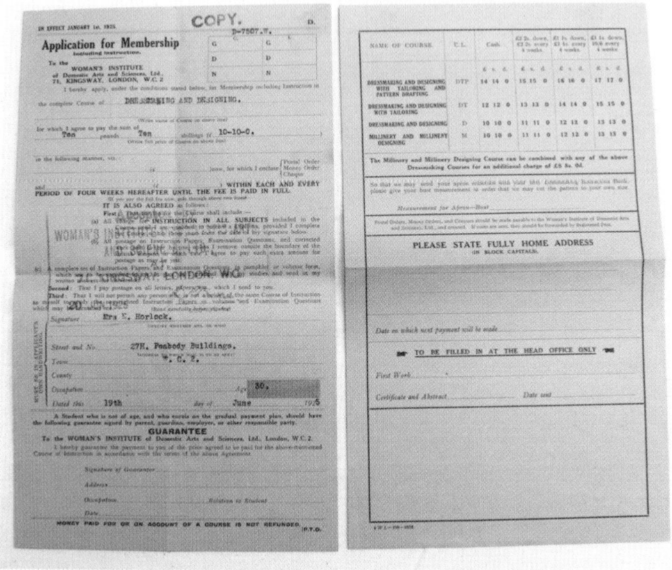
IN EFFECT JANUARY 1st, 1925.

COPY.

D-7507.W.

Application for Membership
Including Instruction

To the
WOMAN'S INSTITUTE
of Domestic Arts and Sciences, Ltd.
71, KINGSWAY, LONDON, W.C.2

the complete Course of DRESSMAKING AND DESIGNING.

for which I agree to pay the sum of Ten pounds Ten shillings (£ 10-10-0.

WITHIN EACH AND EVERY PERIOD OF FOUR WEEKS HEREAFTER UNTIL THE FEE IS PAID IN FULL

IT IS ALSO AGREED as follows:

INSTRUCTION IN ALL SUBJECTS

Signature Mrs E. Horlock.

Street and No. 27H. Peabody Buildings.

W.C.2.

Age 30.

Dated this 19th day of June 1925

GUARANTEE

To the WOMAN'S INSTITUTE of Domestic Arts and Sciences, Ltd., London, W.C.2

MONEY PAID FOR OR ON ACCOUNT OF A COURSE IS NOT REFUNDED.

PLEASE STATE FULLY HOME ADDRESS
(IN BLOCK CAPITALS)

TO BE FILLED IN AT THE HEAD OFFICE ONLY

Fig. 1.5 Application for WI membership and enrolment onto a dressmaking course. (Photo: Worthing Museum and Art Gallery)

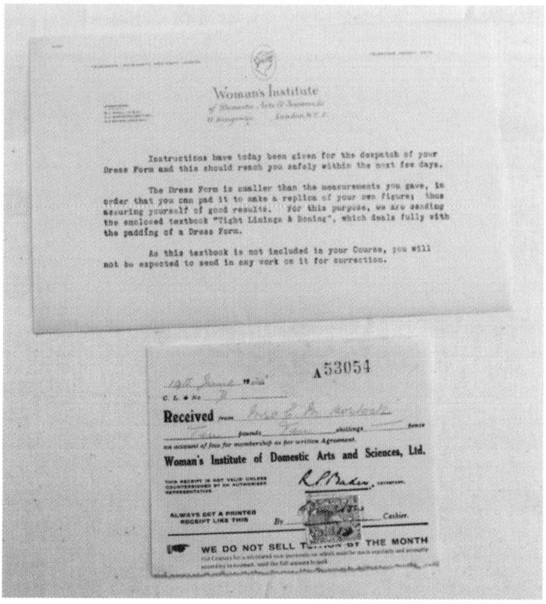
Woman's Institute
of Domestic Arts & Sciences Ltd.
London, W.C.2

Instructions have today been given for the despatch of your Dress Form and this should reach you safely within the next few days.

The Dress Form is smaller than the measurements you gave, in order that you can pad it to make a replica of your own figure; thus assuring yourself of good results. For this purpose, we are sending the enclosed textbook "Tight Linings & Boning", which deals fully with the padding of a Dress Form.

As this textbook is not included in your Course, you will not be expected to send in any work on it for correction.

A53054

Received from

pounds shillings pence

on account of fees for membership as per written Agreement.

Woman's Institute of Domestic Arts and Sciences, Ltd.

ALWAYS GET A PRINTED RECEIPT LIKE THIS

Cashier.

WE DO NOT SELL ... THE MONTH

Fig. 1.6 Despatch note and receipt for the WI dress form. (Photo: Worthing Museum and Art Gallery)

The Mini Mannequin

(Fig. 1.12). If designing in three dimensions is your preference then this small but expensive piece of kit is invaluable. The half-scale mannequin is proportionally scaled down by 50 per cent of a full-sized dummy, meaning that all the suppression points and seams are in the same position. Working at this scale forces you to be more precise but also saves on material costs when you are trying to develop a garment idea from scratch and it is easier to manipulate for pinning on fabrics or work on fine details.

The miniature mannequin originated in the fifteenth century where it was first used to demonstrate fashions for customers. It is thought that they were more akin to the miniature jointed artist's mannequins we are familiar with today and that it was really the refinements of the Parisian fashion industry in the nineteenth century that revived the notion and made it into the perfectly scaled version of a tailor's dummy that we will be using in this book. The format was one used by Monsieur Dior for trunk shows after WW2 to showcase the savoir-faire of French haute couture at a time when the sector had to reinvent itself and find new ways of reaching new and existing clients. *'Le Théâtre de la Mode'* was originally conceived as an itinerant show travelling between Paris, London and the US. The 'trunk shows' were initiated by the Chambre Syndicale de la Couture Parisienne for the French market in 1945 and went global in

Fig. 1.7 Front cover of *The Dress Form and Its Use*, published by the WI. (Worthing Museum and Art Gallery)

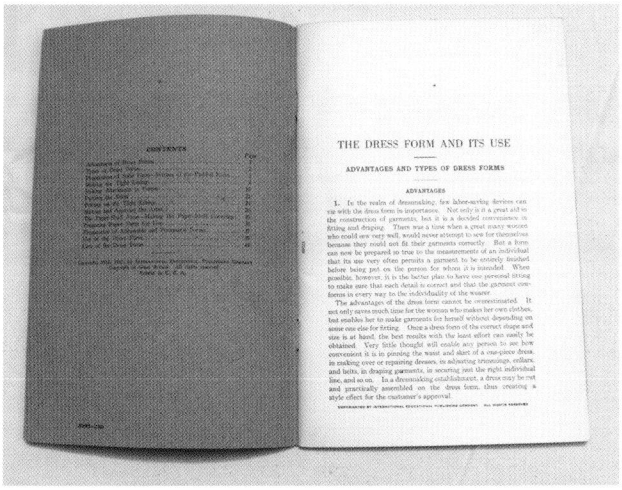

Fig. 1.8 Inside the front cover of *The Dress Form and its Use*, published by the WI. (Worthing Museum and Art Gallery)

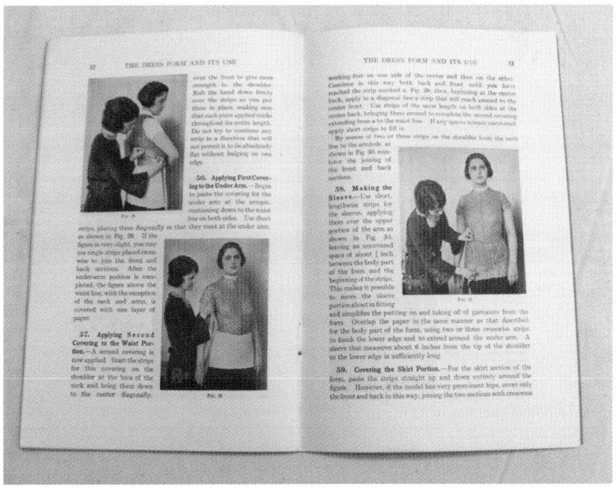

Fig. 1.9 Instructions from *The Dress Form and Its Use* for making a 'Paper Shell' dress form from sticky paper tape. (Worthing Museum and Art Gallery)

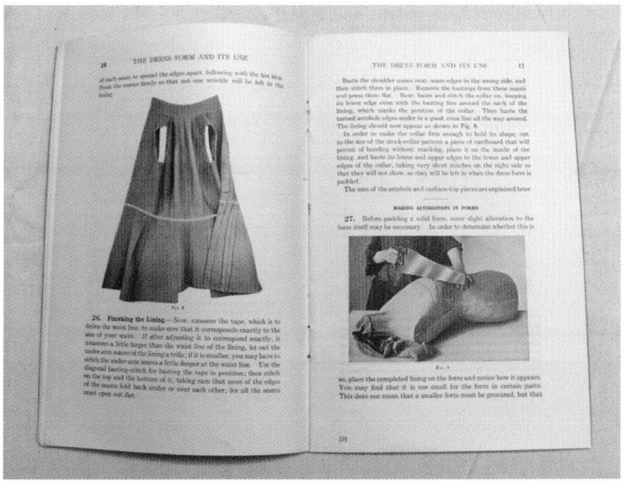

Fig. 1.10 Delightfully brutal instructions for adjusting the WI mannequin with a saw. (Worthing Museum and Art Gallery)

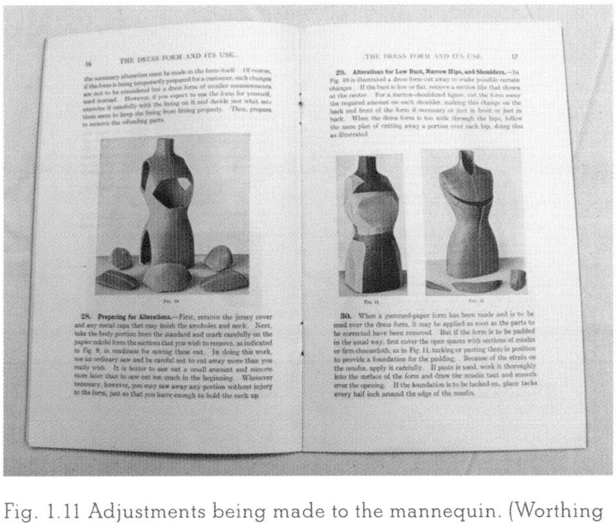

Fig. 1.11 Adjustments being made to the mannequin. (Worthing Museum and Art Gallery)

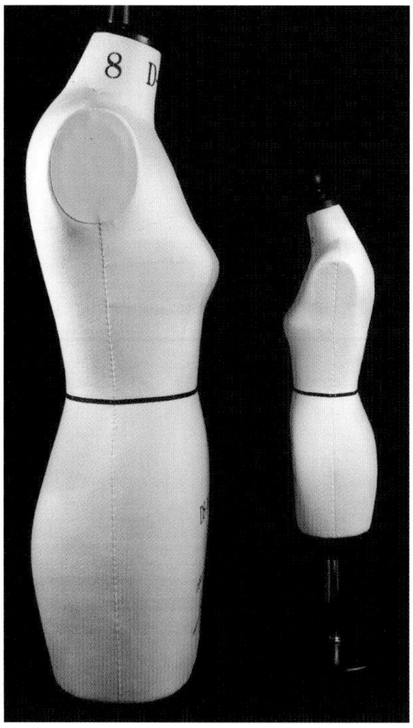

Fig. 1.12 Design-Surgery® 'Violet' female mannequin at full scale and half scale. (Photo: Design-Surgery®, London)

1946. The first was a tableau of miniature mannequins in custom-made dresses accessorized with hats, gloves, shoes and jewellery, all perfectly scaled down. Dior collaborated with artists and friends, including Christian Bérard and Jean Cocteau, to create the tableaux, with music by the composer Henri Sauguet. The first performance was in Paris at the Pavillon Marsan, now the Musée des Arts Decoratif.

It looks as though the concept of the miniature is undergoing a revival as a result of the Dior Autumn/Winter 20/21 haute couture collection by Maria Grazia Chiuri. The whole collection evolved through a process that saw each piece created twice – once in miniature and once full-size. The mini mannequins used are a third the size of a real mannequin, standing only 55cm (22in) tall with a 40cm (16in) torso, but each one is perfectly proportioned in its scaling down. Ateliers draped directly onto them in the real fabrics, with intricate beading and trims being meticulously re-created for the tiny new proportions. All the garments have the same processes as their full-scale counterparts with combinations of draping and pleating and embellishment, down to the linings and miniature fastenings and zips. For example, the stands are taped up exactly the same as the full-scale version and the metreage of cloth is multiplied by three for the later scaling up. Some of the gowns require micro spaghetti rouleaux details and fine pleating and the *petits mains* openly admit the need for 'fairy fingers' to successfully and faithfully create the designs at a one-third scale. In a Covid 19 era it is somehow timely for Maria Grazia Chiuri to revisit the idea with its beacon of hope with her tableau set in a beautifully crafted trunk that replicates Dior's store on Avenue Montaigne and aptly named 'Kingdom of Dreams'. Look at Dior's website to see the miniatures.

Buying a Mannequin

Standard modern mannequins usually follow the measurement specifications of commercial sizing but vary physically dependent on their use. For example, a mannequin developed to design women's cocktail dresses on may have a smaller waist and more bust and hip definition than one designed for outerwear and coats. One used for lingerie and contour wear will have a bustline with each bosom clearly sculpted and defined by a series of tiny darts and with far more suppression; it will also most likely have a crotch and two separate thighs. Mannequins also vary dependent on target market, gender and age groups, so it can be confusing when you are shopping for one.

There are obviously some shortfalls to working with mannequins but you learn to accommodate them. For example, it is sometimes better to work with a mannequin that has collapsible shoulders so that you can get tight-fitting and tailored garments on and off more easily. You can then use the shoulders to which you can firmly pin pads for sleeves. Most mannequins do not come with arms (although the Design-Surgery® model I have used in this book does) so you have to make them if you want to test the fit of a sleeve. The body rise or thigh girth is often too small or too big; the bustline is not like a natural bust that separates so you may need to add a bra and pad it; there are no buttocks, and so on.

All of this makes the sound of buying a mannequin for your personal use a bit of a minefield. It is possible to find old dress stands on eBay or in flea markets and whilst they are beautifully formed they are not much use for draping because they are so physically dated. The modern human body has undergone some major changes as a result of change in our diet and lifestyles, with people today being significantly taller and heavier than our ancestors. Women no longer wear corsetry so the waistline is considerably thicker and research shows that our busts are all much larger, rounder and fuller than those of our predecessors, even from thirty years ago. Older stands can, of course, be adapted and I have included instructions for adapting a stand to a personal set of measurements in another chapter. When purchasing a stand, which is after all a significant financial investment, consider the following: are the proportions modern? Is the covering suitable for sticking pins into? Do the bust, waist and hip deviate much from the measurements you need? It is always better to get a stand that is slightly small that can be padded up; if it is too big there is nothing to be done to change the size. Fortunately, with practice you learn to work with whatever quirks and peculiarities your own mannequin has and after a while you begin to make little adjustments to compensate for it to achieve the fit or silhouette you need.

A relatively new company called Design-Surgery® launched a contemporary range of mannequins in 2015 which have been widely adopted in UK universities' fashion degrees as well as in the industry (Figs 1.13, 1.14 and 1.15). The company owners both work in the fashion industry and are

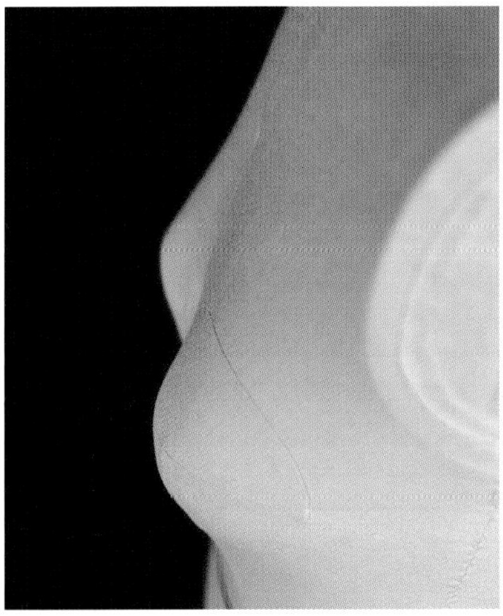

Fig. 1.13 Design-Surgery® mannequin bustline with additional seaming to create a more realistic body shape.

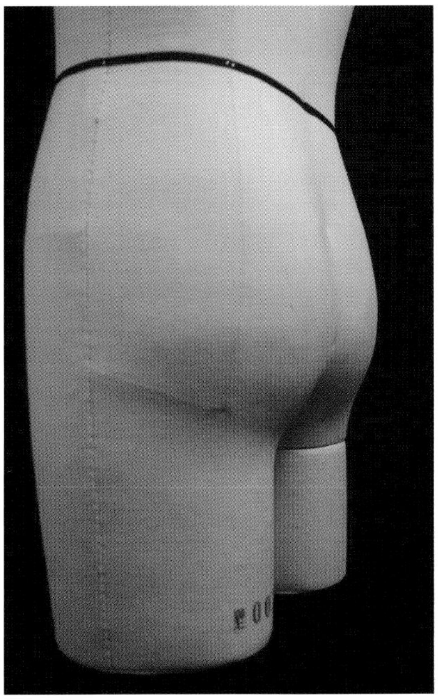

Fig. 1.14 Design-Surgery® mannequin bottom and thigh, unusually sculpted to have a proper buttock.

familiar with the shortcomings of existing mannequins and the difficulties faced by designers and pattern cutters. They have evolved a new type of dress stand that more closely reflects the anatomy of men and women today by creating a more natural body shape; for example they are the only mannequins I have seen that have separate breasts and actual buttocks. They also have a collarbone. The other thing that is great about

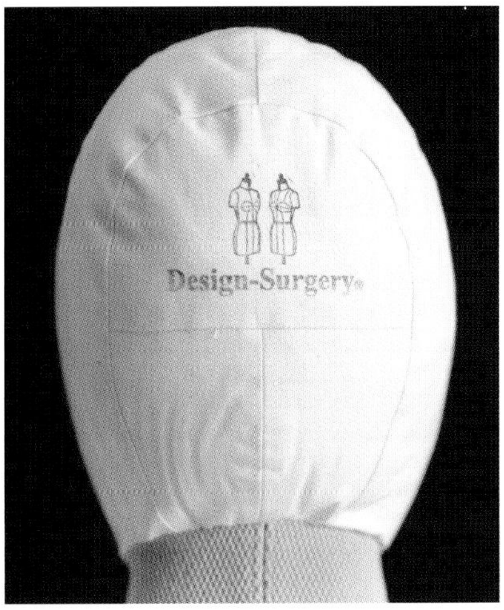

Fig. 1.15 The Design-Surgery® detachable head!

them is that they can be bought with a range of additional body parts like arms, legs and heads. For years I have been working on Kennett & Lindsell stands which are much flatter and have no buttocks or separate breasts at the bustline, so it has been really interesting to work on a different type of body. Think about what you are looking for – it should be indicative of your needs and your working processes. You must definitely shop around for it – don't impulse buy.

Calico (Fig. 1.16)

Calico is a plain-woven textile made from unbleached semi-processed cotton which may contain small unseparated husk parts in the cloth once it is woven. It originated in India where it served as a base cloth to be dyed and printed on and was adopted in the UK in the late eighteenth century when it was imported for furnishings and fashion. It is traditionally used in the garment industry to make toiles or fitting prototypes. It drapes differently from the final fabrics you are likely to use to realize your designs so you have to learn to make allowances for that when you work with it. For designers and creative cutters, as they experience the qualities of other fabrics more in their work, they are able to make an educated guess as to how the final fabric will behave compared with the calico and thus make allowances at the toiling stage for it.

Although calico is often stiffer and drapes differently from other fabrics, it does have other qualities that are beneficial to the draping process. It is light, supple and easy to fold or crease with your fingers. It is fairly inexpensive and not too precious, allowing for the development of a mindset that permits the designer or cutter to rip it, tear it, mark it and experiment with it without becoming too attached to it. If an idea isn't working it is OK to start another toile. Its neutral colour allows the designer to see the fit and silhouette of an idea that is emerging from a sketch and better visualize how it could be improved without the initial distractions of surface pattern, colour or texture. From a practical perspective its most important quality is that it has a stable grain line that can be seen easily.

I will mainly be using a mediumweight calico throughout the book (Fig. 1.17). It is crisp and works well for most garments. It is easy to manipulate but holds its shape well for a variety of bodices, skirts, sleeves and so on. I will also use muslin or lightweight calico which is a looser

Fig. 1.16 Mediumweight calico with grain line indicated by blue stitch line.

weave than the mediumweight and is semi-transparent. It is good to drape with where you are working with thinner lighter fabrics that have enough body to hold a shape or where multiple layers of cloth might be used. I occasionally use a heavyweight calico for outerwear or where I am intending to use heavyweight wools, leathers or performance fabrics for clothing. If I am working on the bias I will most likely use a cheap crêpe de Chine or georgette (Fig. 1.18) as the fall of the drape is softer, bouncier and more fluid. However, it is also very unstable and more difficult to sew. Jersey knits can also be draped and have a soft fluid handle but the stretch in them can make them hard to work with (Fig. 1.19). As a general rule of thumb, it is always best to toile in the real fabrics if you can but this is generally prohibitive in terms of cost for most projects so, where possible, use a calico or alternative that closely resembles the weight and handle of your actual cloth and therefore drapes in a similar way. I have included some images of the different toiling fabrics being draped across the torso of a mannequin so that the difference in which the fabric falls is apparent (Figs 1.20, 1.21 and 1.22). The grain line is indicated by a row of blue stitching after we pulled a thread from each cloth; this is more fully explained in Chapter 4.

Other Tools (Fig. 1.23)

In addition to the mannequin and calico you will need to keep some other items in your toolbox. You will need a **tape measure** and a variety of **rulers** for drawing lines on your master patterns. Of the latter I would recommend as essential a short clear plastic one of 46cm (18in) and a metal 1-metre rule. A **set square** is essential, particularly for drawing curves even though that sound counter-intuitive. Other practitioners will probably advise a French curve or a Pattern Master® so I have included them although I never use them anymore: my preference is to draw my curves freehand or use the set square and pencil. Dedicated **fabric shears** are absolutely essential; these should have at least a 23cm (9in) blade, longer if you can hold the weight properly. Get the best you can afford and look after them, then they will last you a lifetime. Never cut paper with your fabric scissors as it will blunt and ruin the blades, so buy a cheaper separate pair of **paper scissors** for cutting your paper patterns out. A pair of small **snips** are also handy for trimming threads. You will also need **style tape** for marking style lines onto the dress form. There are adhesive and non-adhesive

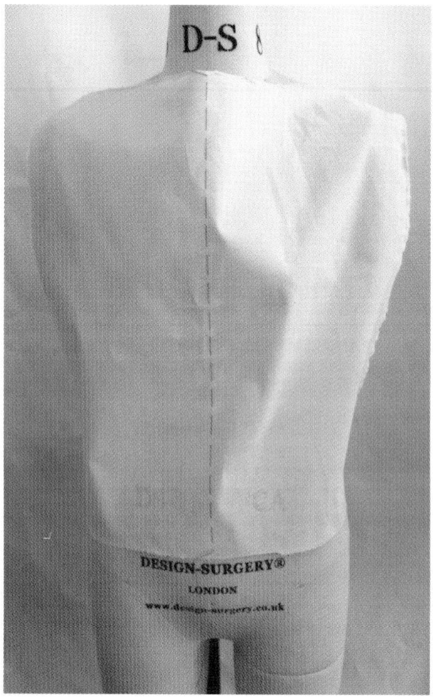

Fig. 1.17 Mediumweight calico pinned on mannequin to see the hang; grain line is marked with blue stitch line.

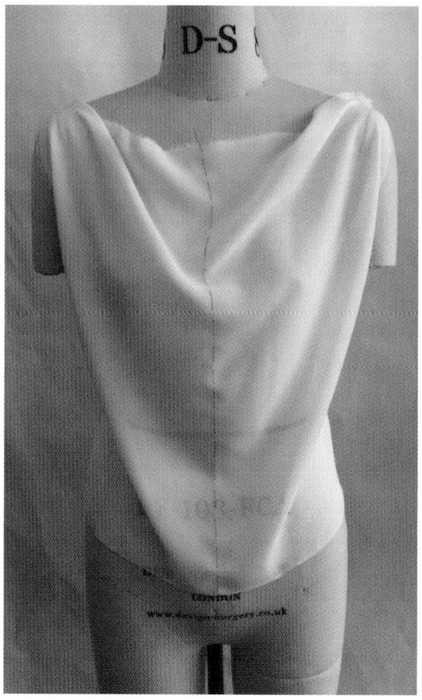

Fig. 1.18 Georgette polyester pinned on mannequin for hang; grain line is marked with blue stitch line.

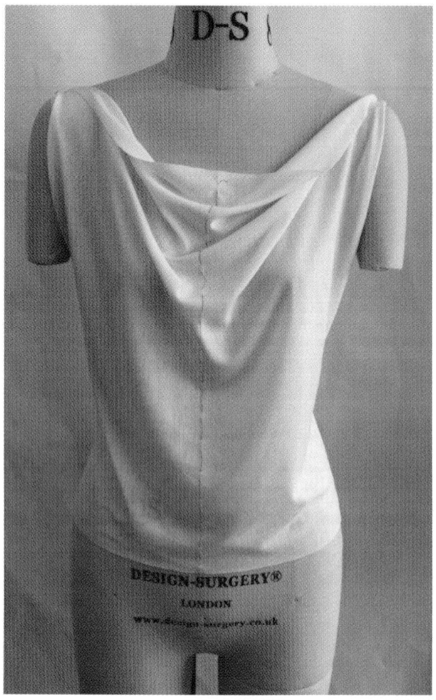

Fig. 1.19 Cotton jersey pinned on mannequin for hang; grain line is marked with blue stitch line.

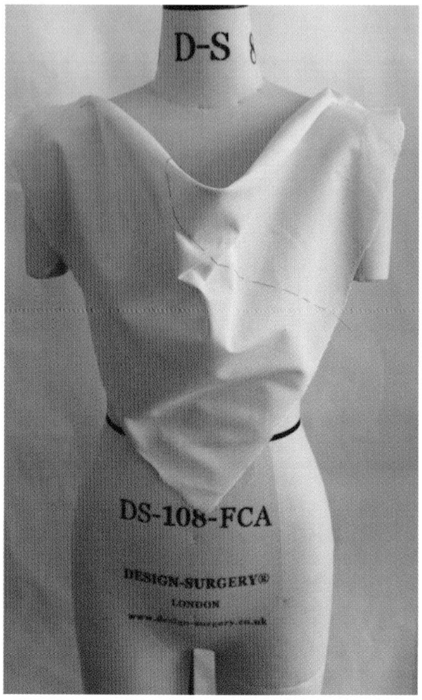

Fig. 1.20 Mediumweight calico on the bias.

versions available, both with their own merits. I prefer to use a 5mm (¼in) non-adhesive version and pin it into place. I have used the adhesive tapes to indicate some style lines in the book in contrast to the black twill stay tape but it can be quite fiddly to work with. You will need pins to pin the calico in place

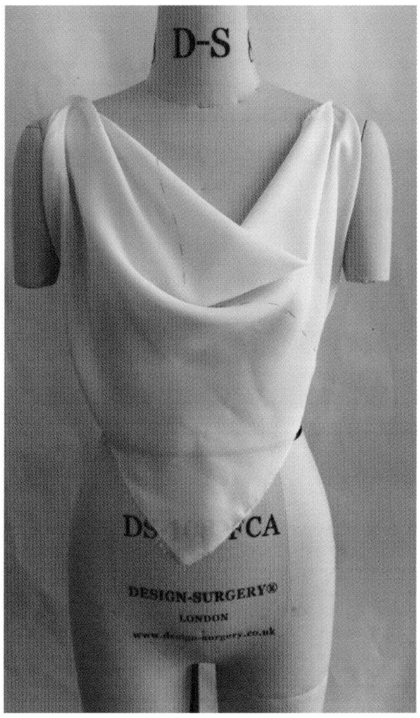

Fig. 1.21 Georgette polyester on the bias.

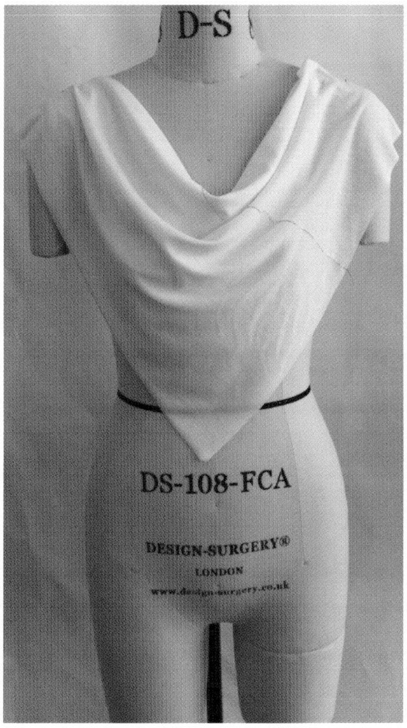

Fig. 1.22 Cotton jersey on the bias.

(17mm/⅝in to 27mm/1⅛in are good sizes for draping) and a **wrist pincushion**, which is much more efficient than keeping pins in a box where they seem to gather fluff. **Push pins** or drawing pins will also be required for pattern drafting. You will also need a **tracing wheel** for transferring the patterns from calico to paper and refining the pattern on paper to paper.

I use a **mechanical pencil** in varying widths of lead as it gives a sharper accurate line and I don't waste time sharpening every five minutes. I recommend 0.5 and 0.7 leads as I am quite heavy-handed but a colleague of mine with a feather-light touch swears by a 0.3 lead for delicately marking out her calico. Also have different **coloured pencils** (I'm using blue and orange here) for marking off corrections, although a **biro** is just as good for this. In addition, make sure to have hand **sewing needles and thread** as well as a **sewing machine** with a **general purpose presser foot, bobbin and screwdriver.** For pressing you will need a **steam iron, ironing board, sleeve board** and ideally a **ham**.

It is also important to mention the **workspace** here as there needs to be room for the dress stand and space for you to move comfortably around it. The **pattern cutting table** should be adjusted to a height that is comfortable to stand at and as large as the room will allow. There also needs to be room for the iron and ironing board, the storage of toiling materials and **pattern paper** which comes pre-cut on a roll, and ideally a rail to keep finished toiles or garments on in **plastic dress bags**.

The **pattern cutting table** should be as large as the room will allow. The height and the length you need are dependent on two things: the type of work you are likely to be doing (for example, you often need to roll out large lengths of calico to drape or cut out fabrics for final garments) and how tall you are. Ideally you would have a table at least 2 metres long or more; in reality just get the biggest one you can for the space you have. It is essential that it is adjustable to the height that is comfortable to work at: you do not want to bend over too much as it will put a strain on your back. The average cutting table height is between 90cm (39in) and 102cm (40in) so is significantly higher than the average dining table! The width is less important but as a minimum it needs to be around 80cm (31½in) wide. The widest cloth woven for the fashion industry is 152cm (60in) so you would need to be able to fold this in half on your table. You will also need the top of the table to have a soft top like a cutting mat so that your tracing wheel can make track marks successfully. Amazon sells **self-healing cutting mats** or, if you are making a bespoke table, use a flat lino to cover the top instead. This should be separate from your **sewing table**, which is set much lower with appropriate seating.

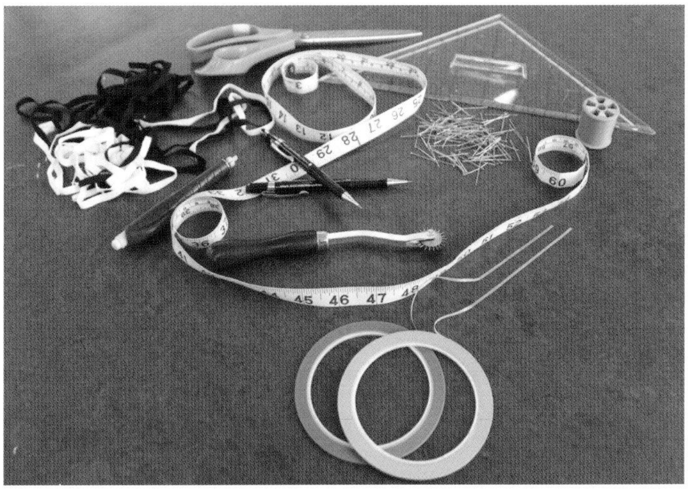

Fig. 1.23 Assortment of other draping and pattern drafting tools and tapes.

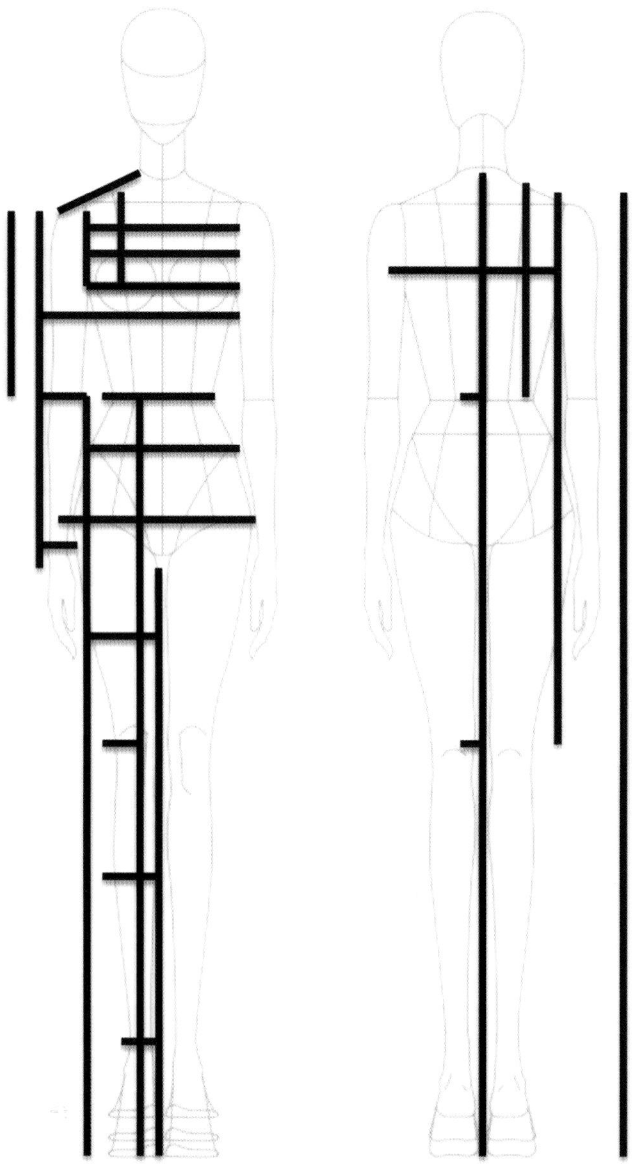

BODY MEASUREMENT CHART
Hold tape measure close but not skintight to the body. Use the *croquis* as a guide and mark up your measurements in sets (e.g. horizontal, vertical). Memorize the set sequence.

CLIENT NAME	
DRESS SIZE	
HEIGHT	

BUST:

WAIST:

HIP:

OVERBUST:

UNDERBUST:

CHEST:

CROSS BACK:

TOP HIP:

SHOULDER:

SCYE DEPTH:

SHOULDER TO BUST:

SHOULDER TO UNDERBUST:

SHOULDER TO KNEE:

SHOULDER TO WAIST:

SHOULDER TO FLOOR:

SHOULDER TO ELBOW:

SHOULDER TO WRIST:

BICEP:

ELBOW:

FOREARM:

WRIST:

NAPE TO WAIST:

NAPE TO INSIDE KNEE:

NAPE TO FLOOR:

WAIST TO KNEE:

WAIST TO FLOOR:

OUTSIDE LEG:

INSIDE LEG:

THIGH:

CALF:

Fig. 2.1 Measurement chart.

Measuring the Body

2

A good fit is the quality that sets bespoke garments apart from their high-street counterparts. Very few of us are lucky to have an off-the-peg body or have a mannequin that exactly replicates our own body's quirks and characteristics so it is important to take measurements accurately for any adjustments; this is explored in Chapter 3. If it is your own measurements you are taking, get someone else to measure you and fill out the chart. Failing that, stand in front of a mirror so you can see what you are doing. Measure with the tape held closely but not tightly round the body; I was actually taught to keep two fingers between the tape measure and the body when I did fittings for clients. The personal measurement chart is written in the order in which you need to take the measurements. As a general guide, start with your height, then continue with the horizontal measurements, then the others. The term 'croquis' is the word for an outline or sketch.

MEASURING REMINDERS

Stand in front of a mirror so you can see what you are measuring and ensure that the tape measure is level all the way round. Hold the tape closely to the body but not skintight. I was taught to keep two fingers between the tape measure and the body to ensure that the clothes being made do not end up too small: it is easier to take excess fabric out of garments than to try and add it in later on! Check that you are wearing the shoes that you are likely to wear with the garment. Measurements in this book are given in both metric and imperial. Work with one or the other as suits you; do not mix them as they do not always convert exactly.

Height: Stand erect without shoes and with your back against the wall. Place a ruler or small piece of board flat on the top of your head and lightly mark the point where it touches the wall. **Measure from the mark to the floor:** this gives a common reference point. Now add the shoes that you are likely to wear with the garment you are working on; their heel height will affect the finished length measurement.
Bust: Measure around the fullest part of the bust. An additional measurement you might want to include is horizontal bust point to bust point or nipple to nipple. If you have a fuller bust or are draping lingerie you may also want to include a vertical measurement of bust point to underbust. Also remember that different bras affect the position and shape of your bustline so think about the silhouette you are trying to achieve before you begin draping and make sure the mannequin is padded up to reflect it.
Waist: Tie a cord around your natural waist. It should be the thinnest part of your midriff and not necessarily where the waistbands on your clothes sit. Keep it tied on whilst you take the other measurements. The cord stretches a bit with your body heat and this is what happens to your clothes provided the waist is not too tight to begin with. Take it off and measure it at the end of the process.
Hip: Horizontal measurement around the fullest part of the hip.
Overbust: Measure around the body above the bust and under the arm.
Underbust: Measure horizontally around the rib cage.
Chest: Horizontal measurement from armpit top to armpit top.
Cross back: Horizontal measurement from armpit top to armpit top.
Top hip: Measure horizontally at the abdomen or top of the hip bone.
Shoulder: From neck point to the end of the shoulder.
Scye depth: Vertical measurement from the shoulder to the armpit.
Shoulder to bust: Vertical measurement from the shoulder to the bust point.
Shoulder to underbust: Vertical measurement from the shoulder to the underbust.
Shoulder to waist: Vertically measure down the back from the shoulder to the natural waist.
Shoulder to knee: Vertically measure down the back from the shoulder to the knee.
Shoulder to floor: Vertically measure down the back from the shoulder to the floor. Note that if you are making a garment for a specific occasion, take the measurement with the right shoes on: their heel height will impact on the finished length measurement.
Shoulder to elbow: Lift the arm, bend it slightly and measure from the shoulder bone to the elbow joint.
Shoulder to wrist: Lift the arm, bend it slightly and measure from the shoulder bone to the wrist joint.
Bicep: Horizontal measurement at the top of the arm.
Elbow: Horizontal measurement around the elbow joint.
Forearm: Horizontal measurement halfway between the elbow and wrist.
Wrist: Horizontal measurement around the wrist joint.
Nape to waist: Top of the spine to the natural waist.
Nape to inside knee: Top of the spine to the back of the knee.
Nape to floor: Vertically measure down the back from the top of the spine to the floor.
Waist to knee: At the front, measure vertically from the natural waist to the kneecap.
Waist to floor: Vertically measure down from the natural waist to the floor, ensuring you have the right shoes on if you are making a garment for a specific occasion.
Outside leg: Measure the outside of the leg from the natural waist to the ankle.
Inside leg: Measure vertically from the top of the thigh at the crotch to the ankle.
Thigh: Measure horizontally at the widest part of the top of the leg.
Knee: Measure horizontally around the knee joint.
Calf: Measure horizontally around the widest part of the lower leg.

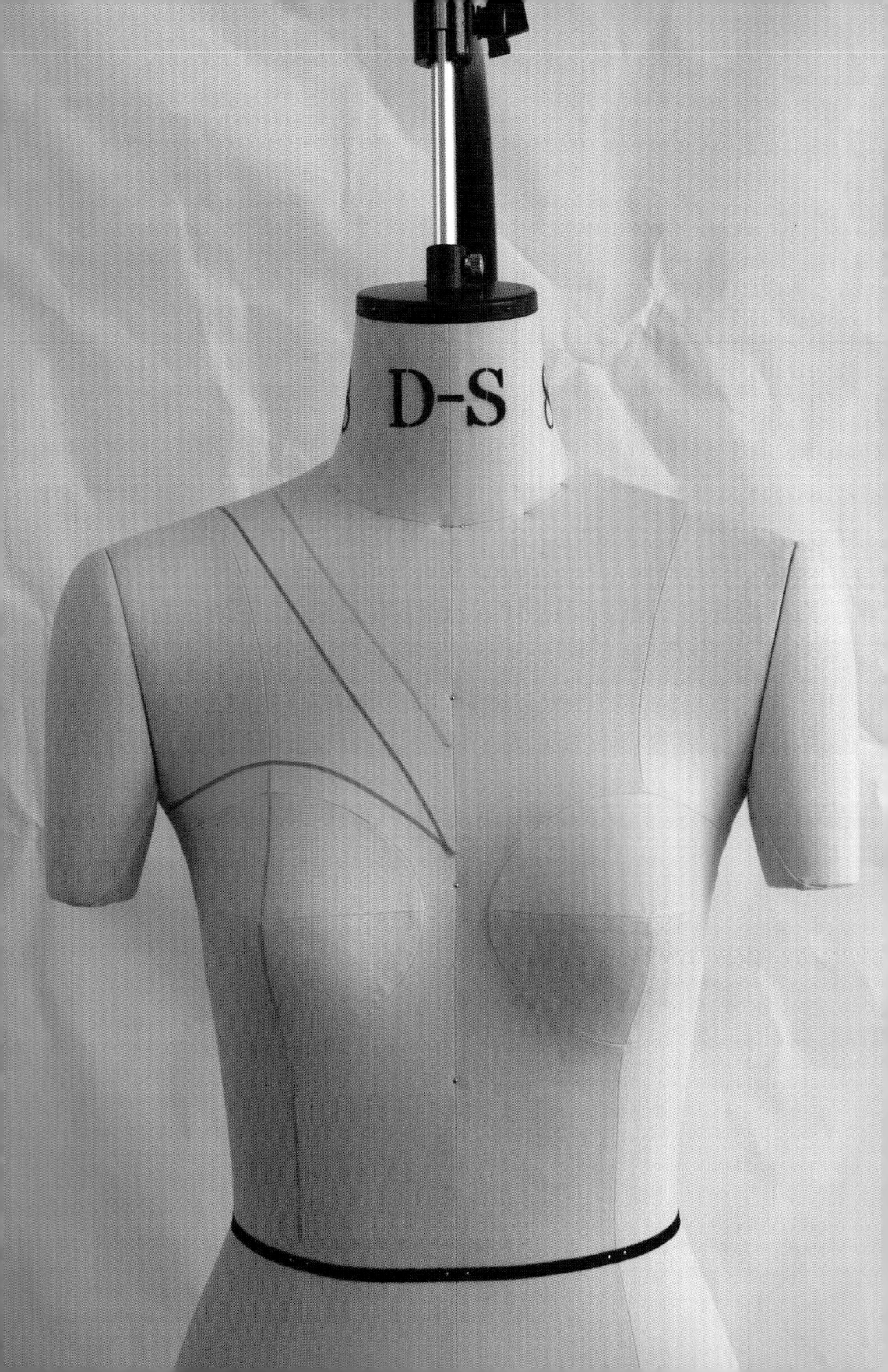
D-S

Preparing the Stand

3

Permanent Demarcation and Balance Marking

Whenever practitioners drape they mark out the mannequin first. There are fixed points on the dress stand which are used consistently as reference points for the draping process and need to be marked off before starting. The vertical permanent demarcations usually already exist in the construction of the mannequin's canvas cover unless you are using a shop display one with a jersey cover. They are the centre front (CF) (Fig. 3.2), the princess seams (PSs) at the side front (SF) and side back (SB) (Figs 3.3 and 3.4), the side seams (SSs) and the centre back (CB) (Fig. 3.5). (Note that we will be using these abbreviations throughout the rest of the book.) Some practitioners put a tape that contrasts with the mannequin cover on top of these seams to form an obvious series of vertical panels but this is not really necessary so long as you can feel the position of the seams underneath your calico with

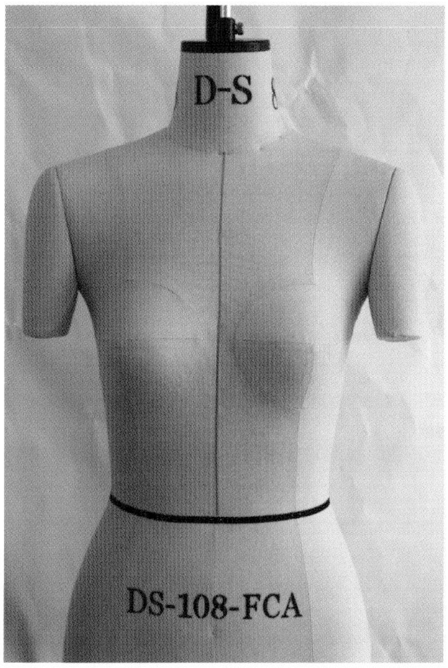

Fig. 3.2 CF position marked in blue.

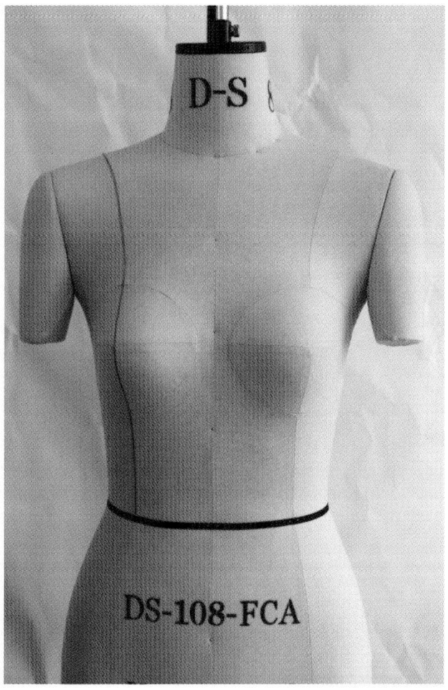

Fig. 3.3 Front PS position marked in blue.

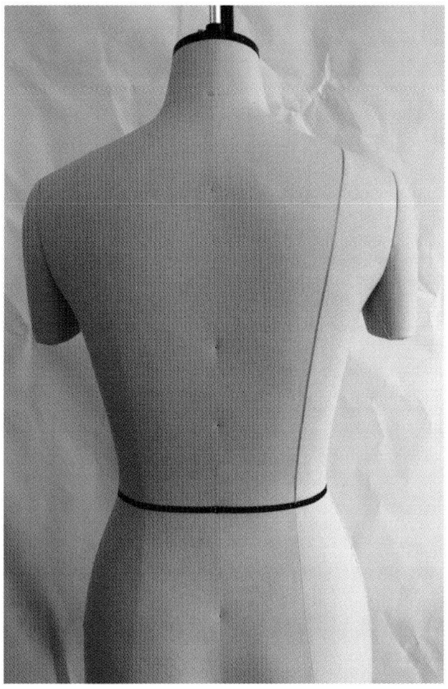
Fig. 3.4 Back PS position marked in blue.

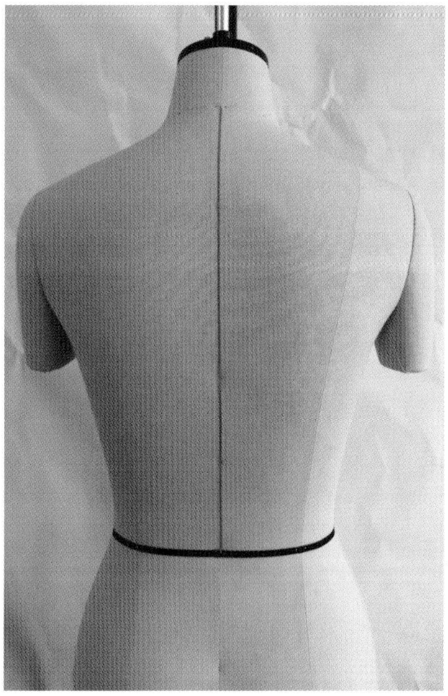
Fig. 3.5 CB position marked in blue.

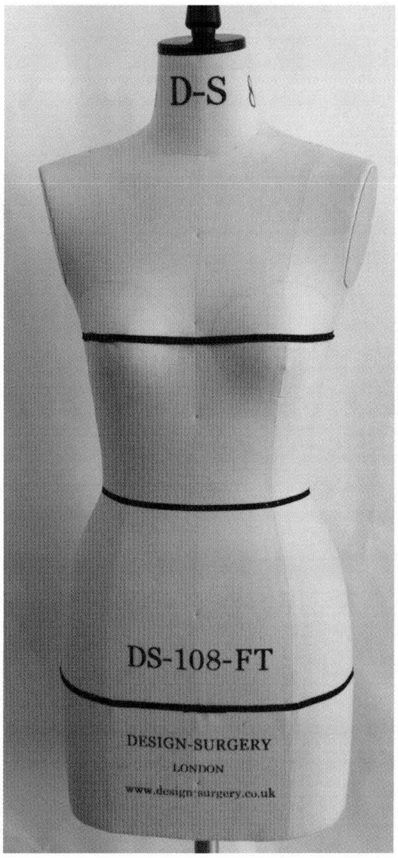

Fig. 3.6 Mannequin with bust-, waist- and hiplines intersecting CF, CB and SS.

Left: Fig. 3.1 Style lines taped on Design-Surgery® mannequin.

your fingers whilst you drape. (Incidentally, this is also why it is so important to work on a solid stand rather than an adjustable dressmaker's stand.) It is customary to also create horizontal demarcations to indicate the bust, waist and hip. This effectively creates a grid system around the body where the horizontal and vertical lines consistently intersect one another, creating a series of fixed reference points in three dimensions. Their purpose is to correspond with the position of the same lines marked on your calico to allow you to keep track of what you are doing. Using this grid makes it significantly easier to take a developmental drape on and off the stand and re-position it in exactly the right place each time. The taped mannequin will look like the one in Fig. 3.6.

Note that when we refer to 'right' and 'left' with regard to the mannequin, it is right or left on the mannequin itself, which is standing in for the wearer of the garment, rather than the observer's right or left. However, when we refer to, say, drawing a line on the right-hand side of a piece of calico it is the conventional 'right' as you look at it.

Taping the Bustline

There are different ways to do this although the outcomes are effectively the same so this is down to personal preference. For example, in *Draping Techniques for Beginners* by Francesca Sterlacci (*see* the Suggested Reading list at the end of the book) places a stay tape from bust point to bust point (BP) only and uses this as her guide line, saving both time and tape. Any further demarcations are made directly onto the calico before it is placed at the intersection of the CF and bustline to begin the draping process. My preferred method is to use a stay tape pinned firmly to the mannequin all the way around the torso regardless of whether I am doing a full or half drape. My issue with only having the tape at the CF is that if, for example, I want to drape a design that has no SS I cannot see how the front and back align

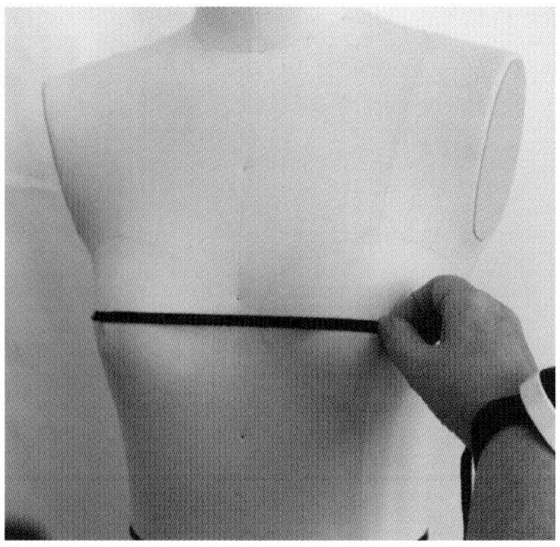

Fig. 3.7 Taping BP to BP.

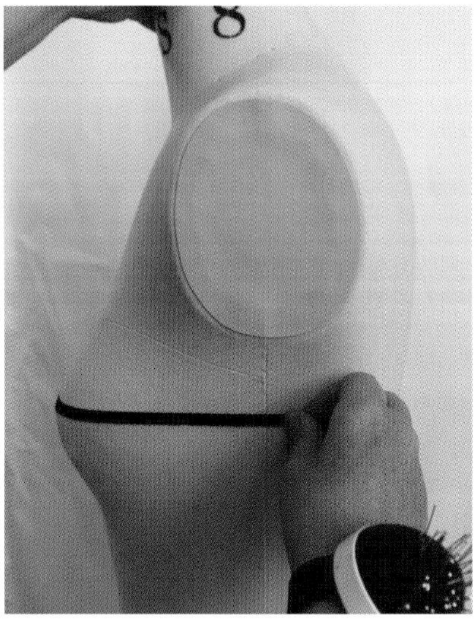

Fig. 3.8 Taping bustline round side of body and under arm plate.

together as easily without the bustline reference running cross back.

Here is my preferred method (Figs 3.7, 3.8, 3.9 and 3.10). Pin the tape to the right BP, then keep the tape level in one hand whilst turning the mannequin round, slowly running the tape all the way round it. Pin at the left BP and continue to pin firmly every 4cm (1½in) or so, making sure the tape line is parallel to the floor. On a flatter mannequin you can run the tape from BP to BP without pinning at CF or distorting the line. On the Design-Surgery® mannequins there is a lot more shaping at the bust so in this instance I have had to pin it down. Remember that if your tape is wobbly your pattern will be too.

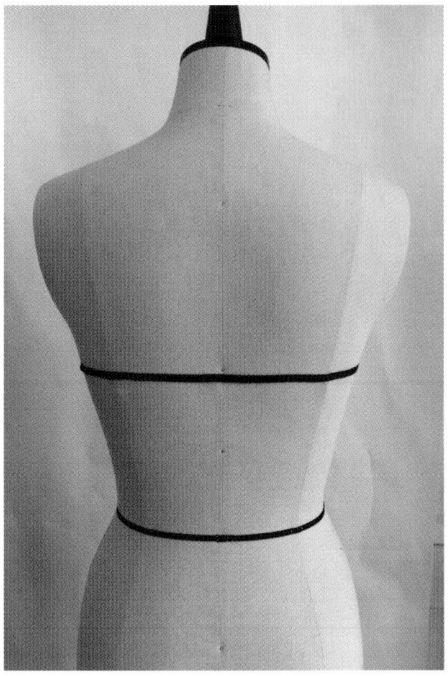

Fig. 3.9 Taped bustline running round back of mannequin parallel to floor.

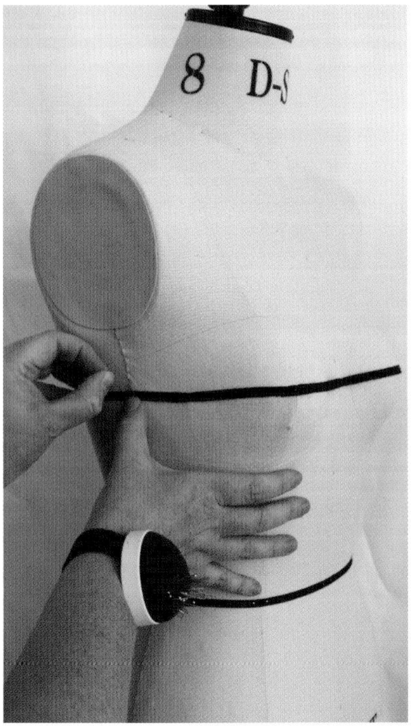

Fig. 3.10 Straightening the bustline.

Taping the Hipline

Pin the tape at the CF at the widest part of the torso (Fig. 3.11). Hold the tape level and turn the mannequin round, running the tape all the way round the body and then pinning firmly. Make sure the hipline is parallel to the floor. The hipline is usually 18cm (7in) below the waistline for a UK size 8 but check

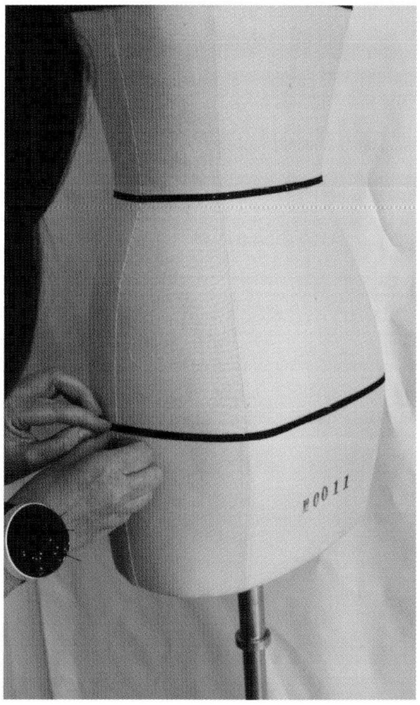

Fig. 3.11 Taping the hipline; waistline position is already pre-indicated on the Design-Surgery® stand.

against either the measurements of your client or the measurement chart in Chapter 2. The logo on most modern mannequins is usually positioned over the hipline so that works as a good visual clue for its positioning. Stand back from the mannequin and check the tape line is level with the floor and make minor adjustments where needed.

Taping the Waist

The Design-Surgery® mannequin used here comes with the natural waist already taped as in Fig. 3.11 but most mannequins do not. I usually put the waist in last, depending on the garment type, because not all garments are draped using the natural waist. As a general guide for beginners though, pin the tape to the CF at the narrowest part of the torso. Hold the tape level and turn the mannequin round, running the tape all the way round the body, and pin firmly to the mannequin. In terms of the position this can vary depending on the garment type you are draping but usually dips slightly lower by a couple of centimetres at the CB.

Style Lines and Temporary Demarcation and Balance Marking

These vary from garment to garment and style to style depending on the design. A style line is a seam or feature in a garment made primarily for its visual effect rather than for the purpose of shaping or structuring the garment. It is really drawing the design again but full scale in three dimensions instead of two-dimensionally in a sketchbook (Fig. 3.12) and happens before you start to drape. I use the black stay tape for this too although other practitioners may use a black and white or coloured adhesive style tape to draw on key details like necklines and panels. Marking these on top of the grid of permanent reference points already mentioned allows you to see the proportion and complexity of your design quickly without having yet drafted a pattern or toiled anything. Style lines are temporary and can be repositioned, unpinned and adjusted before starting to drape the actual garment to give the best aesthetic. For most of the projects in the book they will go onto the mannequin before draping. However, this is dependent on the garment type and sometimes if there is a lot of volume of calico it is better to drape a basic shape first and pin the style lines to the fabric

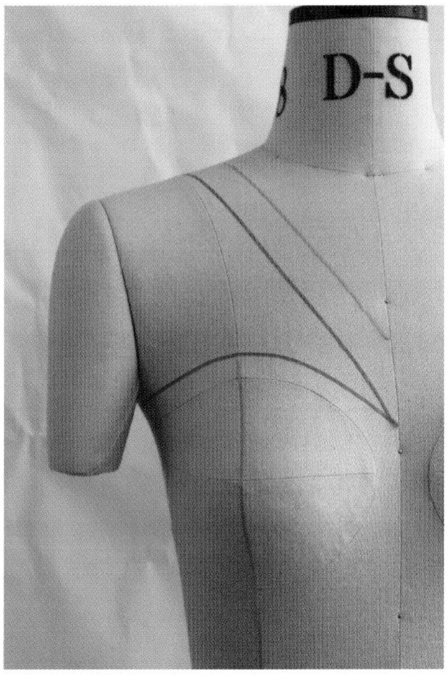

Fig. 3.12 Style lines using coloured adhesive tapes.

STYLE TAPE ACCURACY

Decide which side of the style tape you are marking off from and stick to it consistently. If you inadvertently change sides your drape will be inaccurate by the width of the tape.

afterwards. Trial and error is the best way to understand when to do what; be open to the fact that you may have to adapt your approach sometimes.

Altering a Standard Dress Stand for a Specific Body Shape

Obviously the stand can't be made smaller although the difference in measurements can be taken into account when making the toile. The stand can, however, be adjusted to take a number of other factors into account.

Height

All mannequins come with a mechanism for adjusting the height (Fig. 3.13). Make sure that it is set at a height where you can comfortably see

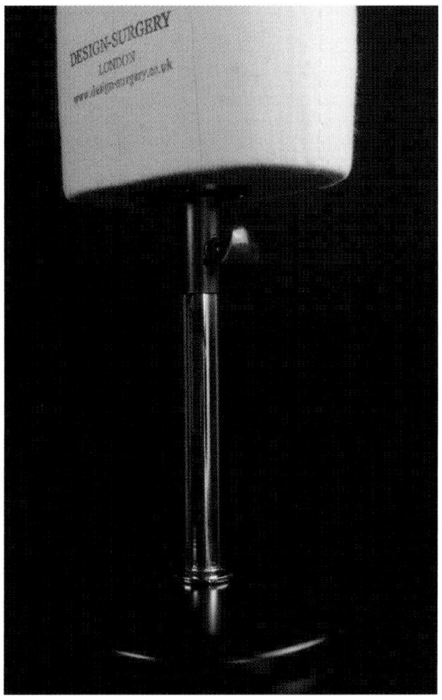

Fig. 3.13 Mannequin height adjuster.

the seam on the shoulder. If you imagine the mannequin has a head you would effectively be looking straight into its eyes! Draping becomes inaccurate really quickly if the stand is too high or too low to work on properly. Drape standing up; don't sit down to do it unless you really have no choice. To get a true sense of the garment's proportions and silhouette, adjust the mannequin to your client's height or to a model height of 1.78m (5ft 10in) and take a look before making any adjustments.

Hip Girth or Tummy

The extra has to be added on before marking off the bust-, waist- and hiplines. Determine where the extra padding needs to go, then pin or sew some wadding or fibrefill onto these places in an approximation of the extra girth or body shape you want to achieve (Figs 3.14 and 3.15). Fibrefill is a synthetic manmade fibre similar in appearance to candy floss. It is soft and expands and contracts according to how densely you pack it and it is often used for stuffing toys and pillows. It comes flat on a roll and will create a smooth contour when it is built up layer by layer – a bit like contours on a map. If the wadding is fuzzy then smooth it down with a piece of gauze or batting over the top and pin or stitch down to the mannequin cover. The hipline can then be taped as per the instructions above. It is also worth using tape to mark any of the vertical seams (such as princess, CF or CB seams) now covered by the wadding. The example in the photo is intended to mimic a real client so the measurements needed to be checked to make sure they corresponded with her measurement chart. Some designs may also require expanded or sculpted hips, so the same technique can be employed but, in this instance, you would effectively be sculpting the silhouette first with wadding to create a foundation or structure over which to drape the rest of the garment.

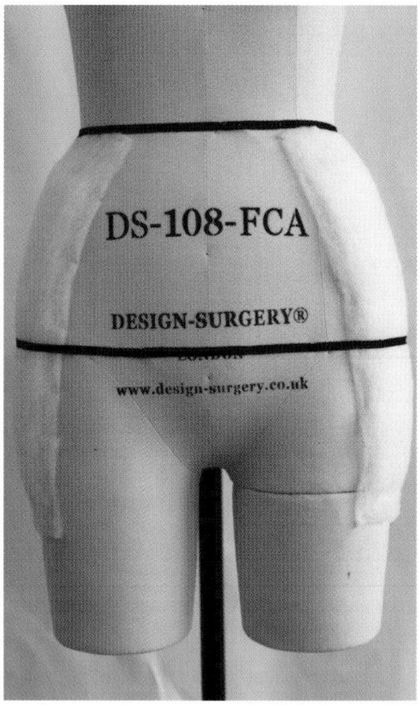

Fig. 3.14 Padded hip taped, front view.

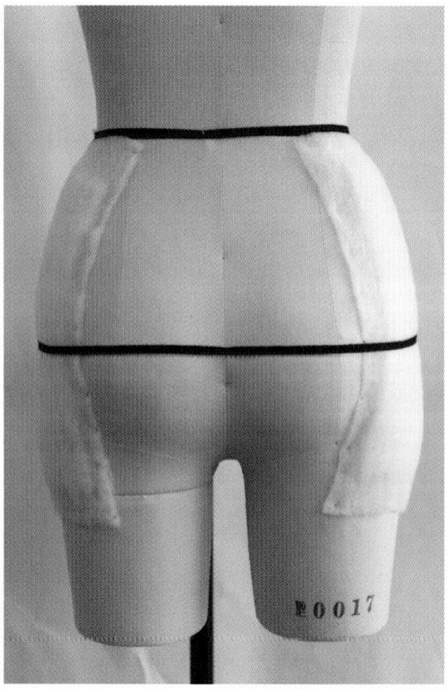

Fig. 3.15 Padded hip taped, back view.

Bust

If the bust has to be increased then put a soft bra with the right-sized cup and lift on the stand and pad it out with fibrefill (Figs 3.16 and 3.17). Pin the fibrefill into place. You have the option of either keeping the bra on whilst you drape or removing it and creating a fitted cover to keep the wadding in position. Tape the bustline as per the previous instructions and re-mark any vertical seams on the mannequin that are now covered.

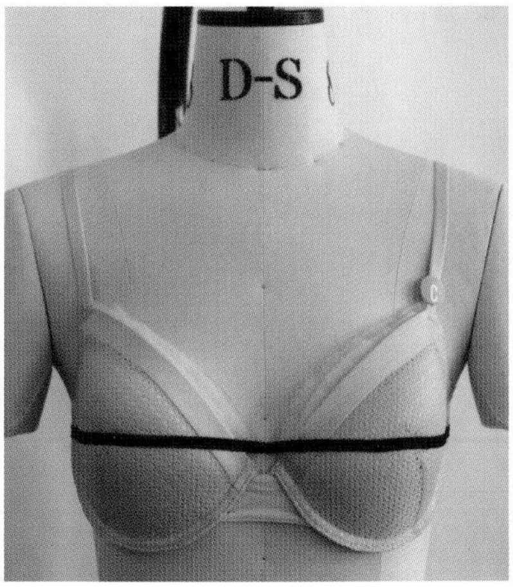

Fig. 3.16 Padded bust with bustline taped, front view.

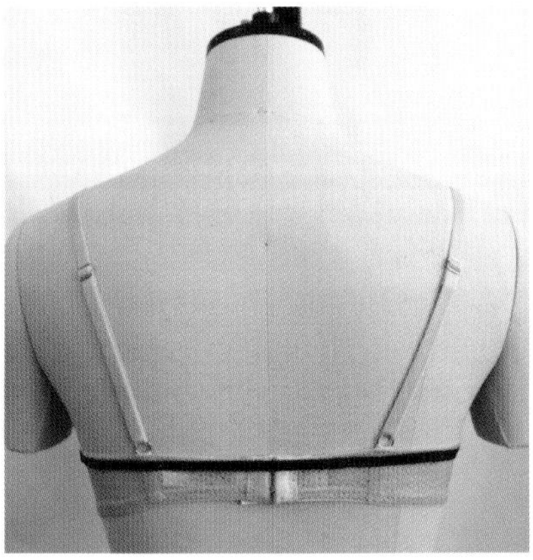

Fig. 3.17 Padded bust with bustline taped, back view.

Shoulder Pads

If the garment being draped has a padded shoulder then the correct pad needs to be pinned firmly to the mannequin first (Figs 3.18 and 3.19). I like to pin tape across the top of the shoulder pad to indicate the shoulder line beneath it. This is particularly useful if the intended garment's seam is going to be further forward or backward of the actual shoulder line. Some practitioners like to tape around

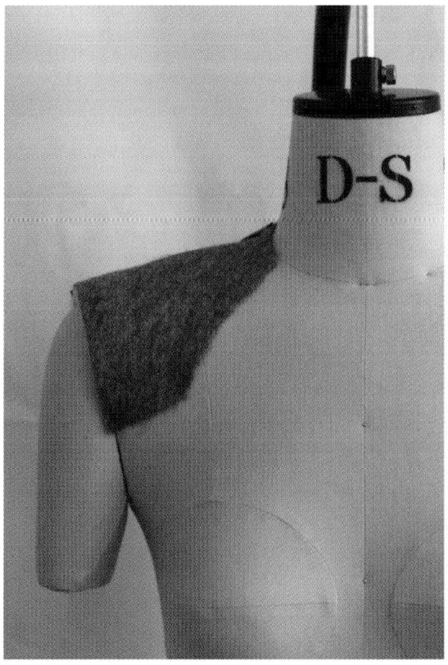

Fig. 3.18 Shoulder pad positioned on stand.

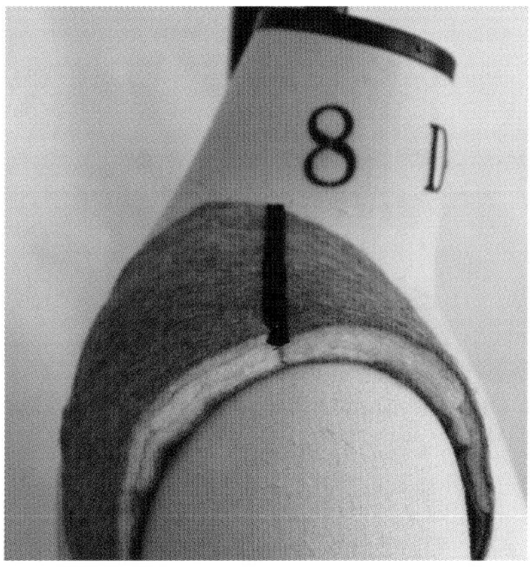

Fig. 3.19 Shoulder line taped onto pad.

the armhole but I don't think that is necessary and use a method to finish the armhole when the calico has been removed from the stand.

Arms and Other Body Parts

One of the great things about the Design-Surgery® mannequin is the number of accessories you can buy cheaply for it; for example, you can buy an additional pair of pre-made arms held in place with surgical elastic (Fig. 3.20). However, if this is not an option then you can always make an arm. There is a detailed method for drafting and constructing a calico and fibrefill arm in Duborg et al.'s *Draping: Art and Craftsmanship in Fashion Design* which works very well. It is unlikely that you will always be able to avoid draping anything with sleeves so it is worth bothering to make at least the right arm if not a pair. As a last resort and a temporary fix, twist a large piece of pattern paper to the approximate dimensions of an arm and pin it to the mannequin's shoulder; this works but obviously is not accurate or durable.

GETTING IT RIGHT

When taping the bustline and hipline, take your time and step back several times – at least by a couple of metres – so you can see if the lines are running parallel to the floor all the way round the torso. If you don't have much room, walk away and then come back: you will see at a glance if the lines are parallel. If either is incorrect, don't use it or all of your draping will be wrong from the start.

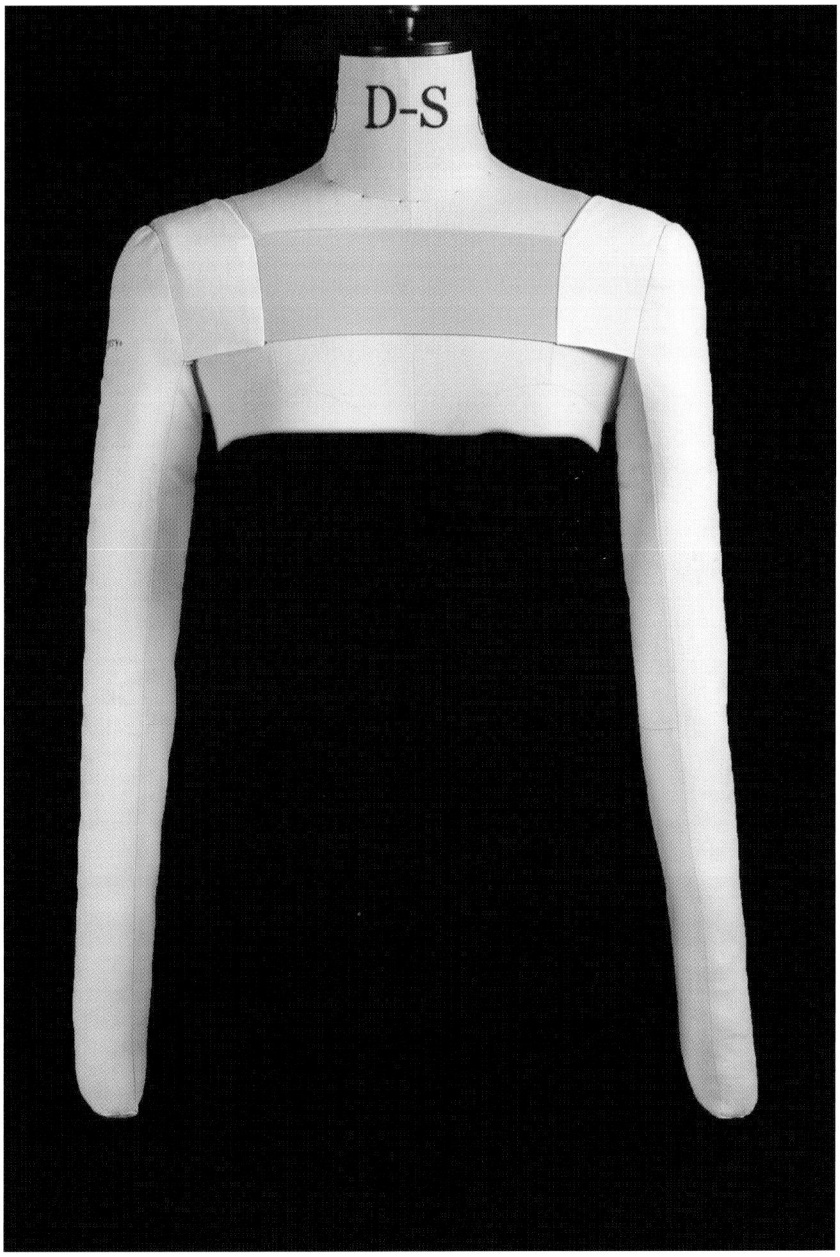

Fig. 3.20 Design-Surgery® detachable arms on surgical elastic.

BUST
WAIST
HIP

Preparing the Fabric

4

Designs can be draped in their actual end-use fabric or in a reasonable representation of it. The latter is usually called muslin although fabric suppliers will call it by their own product names. Usually it is a light-, medium- or heavyweight calico. It is an inexpensive cotton that is unbleached and unsized, which means it has no coatings or finishings on it and is therefore easier to work with. Calico is neutral in appearance and its absence of colour helps one to stay focused on the silhouette being created or to create a blank canvas on which to design. It has a relatively loose weave but stable construction, making it easy to see the lengthwise and crosswise grains in the fabric. The lightest weight has the most open weave and is useful for draping soft silhouettes, cowls and drapery. The heaviest is the most densely woven and primarily used for coats, jackets and tailored pieces; it is the most difficult to handle because of its thickness. For most of the drapes in this book I have used a mediumweight calico because it is easy to work with but has a bit of structure. Getting to grips with how different fabrics drape is best remedied by pinning sample pieces roughly the same size onto a mannequin in exactly the same way to see how they fall as outlined in Chapter 1. It can be a bit of a mental leap to visualize your design in its real fabric when you have toiled it in calico so it takes practice. It is also worth knowing the properties of your fine fabrics first so that you can make mental comparisons between how you think it might perform and what the calico is actually doing.

Grain Lines

The ability to identify and utilize a fabric's grain lines correctly is key to draping accurately. Any garment draped off grain or on the wrong grain will not hang properly and may not give a good fit or wear as well as it should. That would be a waste of resources, so it is important to get this right.

The grain refers to the direction that threads run in a fabric. A plain weave like calico is made by interlacing two sets of yarns. The warp runs vertically down the full length of the cloth and is normally the stronger of the threads because it provides the supportive framework for the cloth, taking most of the strain during the weaving process. It is always parallel to the selvedge edge and is known as the true grain or the straight of grain – SG. The weft or cross grain runs across from selvedge to selvedge. The fabric is at its most stretchy and unstable on the bias, which is at a 45-degree angle to the SG.

The true grain or SG can be found by pulling a thread (Fig. 4.2). My own preferred method is a technique called the 'drop pencil' where the lead of a mechanical pencil is put in between two warp threads and dragged firmly along the cloth. You do need a steady hand but with practice this will be straight and accurate without any wobbles (Fig. 4.3). If necessary, to prepare for this, a push pin or map pin can be positioned between the warp threads and dragged down to create a slightly wider groove in which to put your pencil and draw along. Don't ever use anything like a marker or Sharpie for this: it needs to be fine and accurate. Don't use a ruler: this is just drawing on top of the warp threads and ignoring the fact that they might not be straight to begin with; the result will be a buckling garment that doesn't sit flat to the body.

Fig. 4.2 Pulled thread to show SG.

Fig. 4.3 Drop pencil technique.

MARKING

When drawing lines on calico a fine mechanical pencil or a 2HB is best (so long as it is sharp). The H denotes the hardness and the B the blackness of the lead. Keep the line hard and sharp, not fuzzy and soft.

The Selvedge

The outside edge of any cloth is called the selvedge and is woven more densely than the body of the cloth to stop the sides unravelling or fraying during the weaving process. We tend not to include it when draping because it can distort the grain and make the calico pucker. This is remedied by simply removing it, using a process known as blocking. To remove the

Left: Fig. 4.1 Calico drape for top and skirt. (Photo: Yousef Al Nasser)

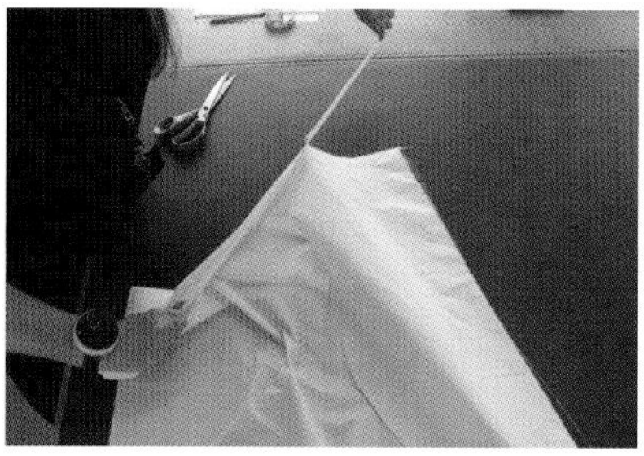

Fig. 4.4 Removing selvedge of calico where weave is denser.

selvedge, snip with scissors just inside it at the point where the weave density visibly changes, then tear it off by hand. Don't use a ruler and pen to mark anything out as a cutting line; just rip and your calico will split along the grain line with the selvedge coming away as a long thin strip (Fig. 4.4).

Determining Dimensions

Dimensions are included for blocking throughout the book. However, should you feel the need to calculate your own at some stage then you need the widest and the longest measurement on the torso for the panel you are draping, then add a generous 5cm (2in) or so around the outside edges to allow for adjustment. Each pattern piece of a garment has to be individually draped and will need to be pre-torn to size

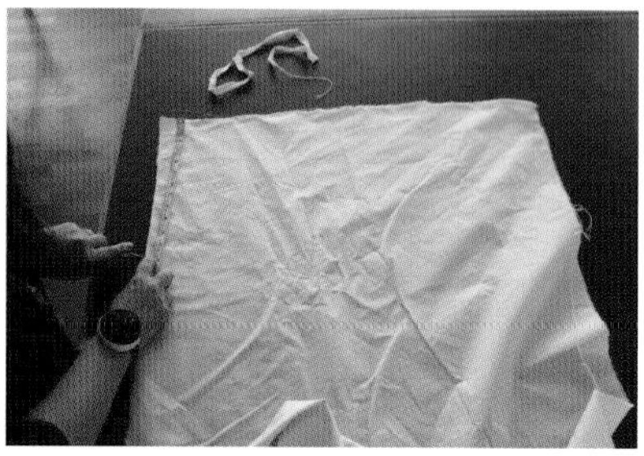

Fig. 4.5 Measuring the dimensions of the block.

Fig. 4.6 Ripping calico to size.

(Figs 4.5 and 4.6). To establish the size of each piece of calico required, measure the dimensions against the dress stand and add extra all the way round. Measure the calico to the desired length, snip with scissors and rip. Then turn the calico round, measure to the desired width, snip and rip again. Never just draw out the dimensions with a ruler, then cut out with scissors, as the result is likely to be off grain. By ripping you are actually tearing directly down the warp and weft of the cloth and although it doesn't look it, it is actually the most accurate way. You can also tell if you are on grain by pulling a strand of thread from the edge – if you are on grain a single thread should come out in one long strand from end to end.

The Blocking Process

The warp and weft need to be at right angles to each other before draping. Often they are not and they need to be manipulated back into position through the process called blocking. Line the corner of the calico up against the table corner (as it is a right angle) or use an L square or set square (Fig. 4.7). If the edges of the fabric do not align then they need to be blocked. Begin by pulling the corner to the position where it should be. The fabric can also be pushed on the diagonal with the palm of your hand but this needs to be done firmly to work properly (Figs 4.8 and 4.9). Intermittently check against the table corner or square to see if the calico has aligned and repeat as necessary (Fig. 4.10).

An alternative way to check is to fold the calico in half on the cross grain and see if the corners match up. Then turn the fabric the other way and check again (Fig. 4.11). Then proceed as above if necessary.

Once the calico is blocked, press without steam to get rid of the wrinkles and flatten down the edges (Fig. 4.12). Press in the direction of the grain or it will stretch and have to be re-blocked. The calico is now ready to be marked off with guide lines for draping.

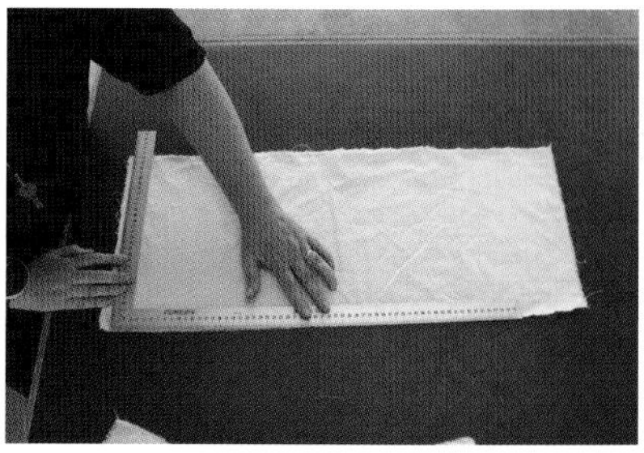

Fig. 4.7 Lining calico up with an L square.

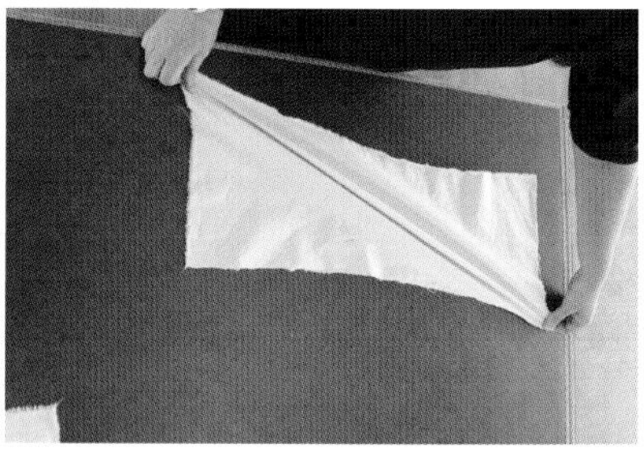

Fig. 4.8 Stretching calico into shape on the diagonal by pulling the corners.

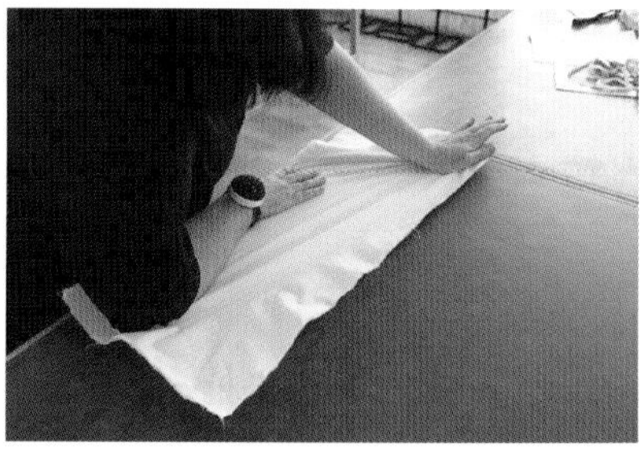

Fig. 4.9 Pushing calico grain lines back into position with the heel of the hand.

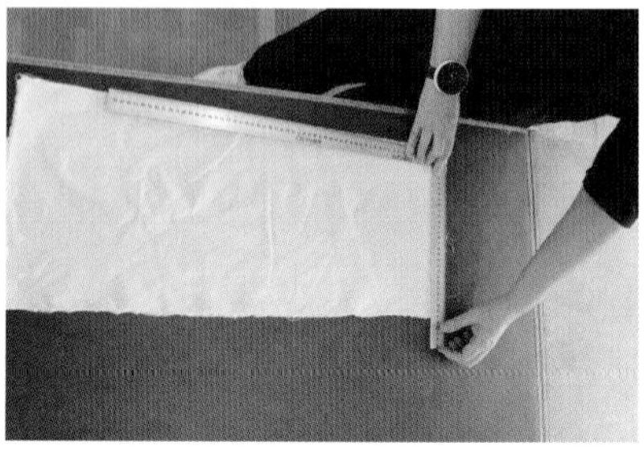

Fig. 4.10 Re-checking alignment of outside edges with L square.

Fig. 4.11 Folding calico to check corners line up.

Fig. 4.12 Pressing calico without steam.

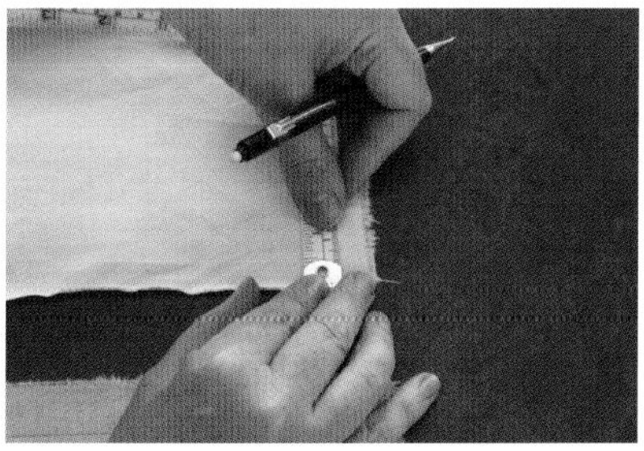

Fig. 4.13 Marking 2cm in from edge of calico.

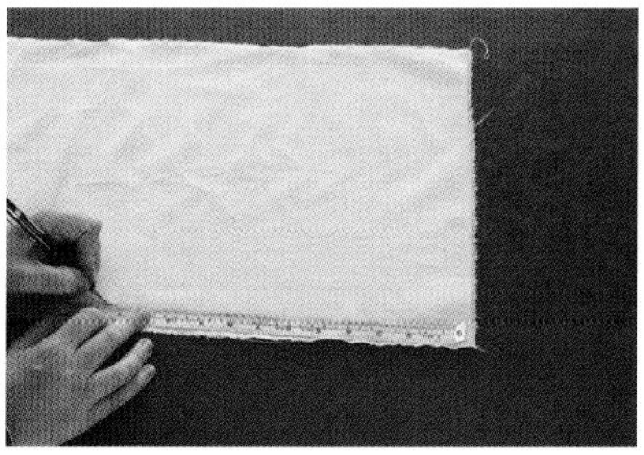

Fig. 4.17 Marking corresponding measurement on CF or CB.

Marking Out

Starting with the front piece, the SG gets marked onto the calico first. Generally, the SG is also the CF or CB and can be marked in 2cm (¾in) from the edge of the calico (Figs 4.13 and 4.14). If you are draping on the right then the CF will be on the right-hand edge and the CB on the left-hand edge of the calico piece. Sometimes, depending on the piece to be draped, we begin by placing the SG on the SS instead and then it is marked in the middle of the cloth. The calico will also always include a cross grain to align with either the bustline for a bodice or dress or hipline for a skirt rather than the waistline (Figs 4.15, 4.16, 4.17 and 4.18). For example, to work out its position for a bodice on the calico, measure the position of the bustline on the mannequin from the shoulder line and the hip from the waistline, then add on the extra to get the total length. Measure down from the top edge of your calico, turn it round and use the drop pencil technique to mark in the bust- or hipline along the cross grain for both pieces so that you have a pair. Again, start with the front and include the BP (Figs 4.19 and 4.20).

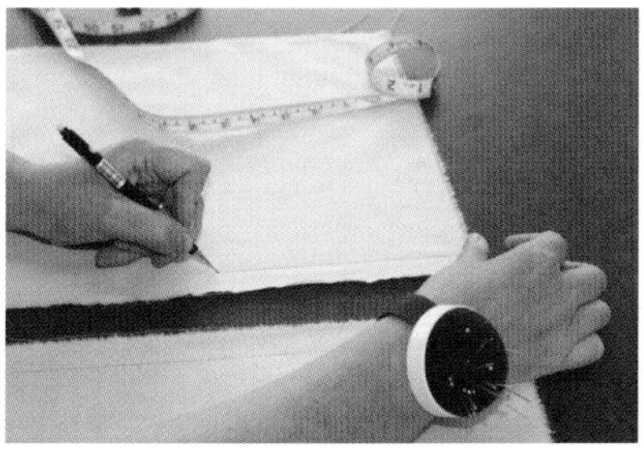

Fig. 4.14 Using drop pencil technique to draw CF and CB; note CF is on right and CB on left for a right-sided drape.

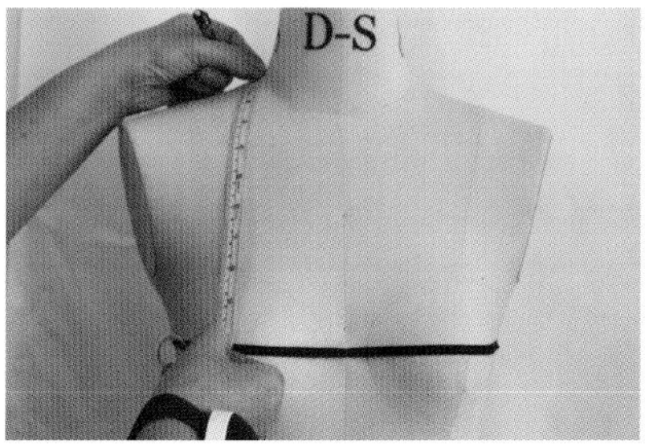

Fig. 4.15 Measuring from neck point to BP on mannequin front.

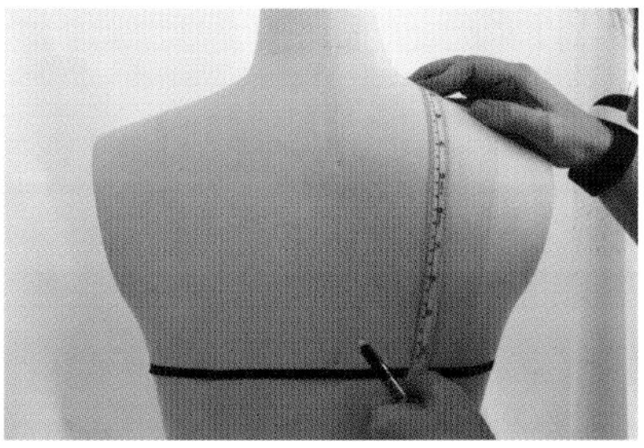

Fig. 4.16 Measuring from neck point to bustline on mannequin back.

Fig. 4.18 Using drop pencil technique to square across on calico.

Fig. 4.19 Marking off the BP.

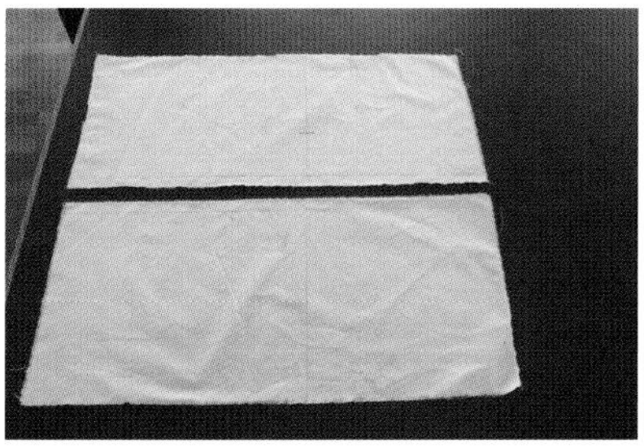

Fig. 4.20 Prepared front and back pieces of calico for a bodice block.

8
CB
BUST
BUST
HIP
HIP
CB

The Draping Process

5

Understanding the Sequence of Work

For a symmetrical womenswear garment it is usual to drape a half toile only from CF to CB on the mannequin's right side. Always allow a 2cm (¾in) seam allowance on the CF and CB to ensure there is something with which to pin the calico onto the stand securely. If a whole toile is needed later on (for example, for fitting a client), then there is also sufficient seam allowance (SA) to join the two halves down the CF or CB. If your design is asymmetric then the whole garment will need to be draped. Each part of the pattern will need to be draped separately and systematically, working round the body a section at a time. The seam lines and piece edges will all need to be marked out as a series of dots in pencil. It is important to mark out each pattern piece as accurately as possible and include as much information as possible, particularly for more complicated toiles (Fig. 5.2). Each piece can be taken off the mannequin and the dots 'trued' or joined up to create smooth seam lines (Fig. 5.3). When blending curves or straight seam lines sometimes a dot is out of alignment; in this instance exercise common sense and just use the tools to create a nice smooth line. When all the pieces have been draped they are pinned together in sequence on the stand – not flat on the table – to accommodate the curves of the female form more precisely (Fig. 5.4). Adjustments can then be made to each panel and marked onto the calico in a differently coloured pen or biro to ensure that all seams match up, the darts are in the right places and the fit is right and so on before taking it off the stand and truing up again (Figs 5.5 and 5.6). Notches or balance marks indicate where the pattern pieces join at strategic points along the seam lines and are added once the drape is right. The whole toile can then be removed from the mannequin and taken apart again ready to be traced onto paper to create the master pattern.

USING NOTCHES

Notches are used to match parts of a garment during pinning and sewing, so make sure they are marked onto the drape from the outset. Put them on the SS and shoulder seam where the front joins the back but also include for the CF and CB and in the middle of any other panels and style lines. Use one line for front notches and two for the back.

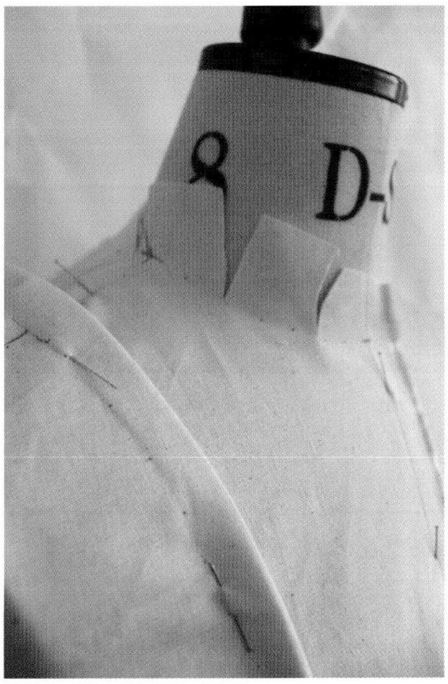

Fig. 5.2 Marking out neck and shoulder on a drape.

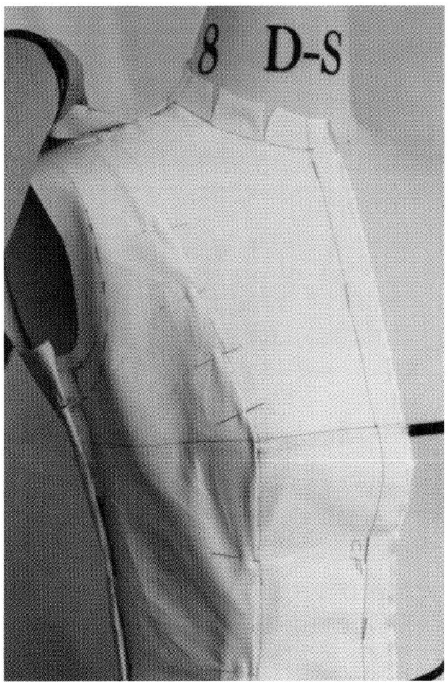

Fig. 5.4 Pinning from the top.

Fig. 5.3 Truing up a drape on the flat.

Fig. 5.5 Marking out alterations in contrasting colour.

Left: Fig. 5.1 Draped bodice and skirt. (Photo: Yousef Al

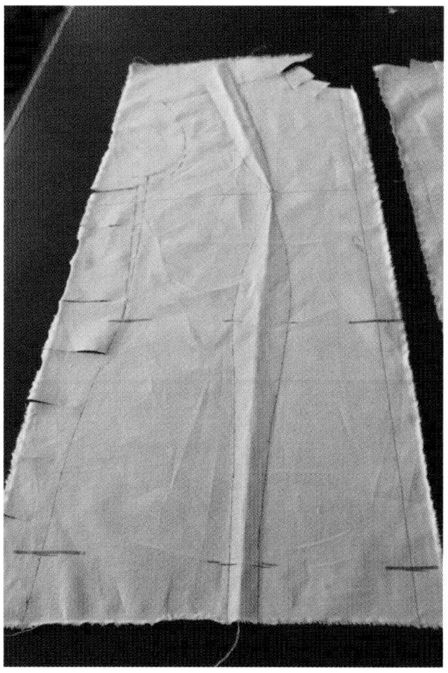

Fig. 5.6 Notches or balance marks added, denoted here as short single blue horizontal lines.

Marking Terms

- A **dash** indicates the direction of marking; for example, round the neck or arm plate.
- A **dot** indicates the outside edge of the pattern piece.
- A **cross** indicates a right angle; for example, at the neck point where the neck intersects the shoulder line and where the shoulder line intersects the armhole. A cross also indicates the top of a dart.

It is very important to be consistent with your marking terms so you can navigate your way around your drape when you take it off the stand.

Positioning the Cloth on the Body

The draping process always starts at the CF and the CB. The intersection of the bustline for bodices and hipline for skirts is aligned with the corresponding points taped out on the mannequin, with the fabric being draped up, down and out from the centre towards the side, waist and neck if it is a drape for a bodice or top (Figs 5.7 and 5.8).

Fig. 5.7 Pinning calico at CF and BP for draping front of bodice.

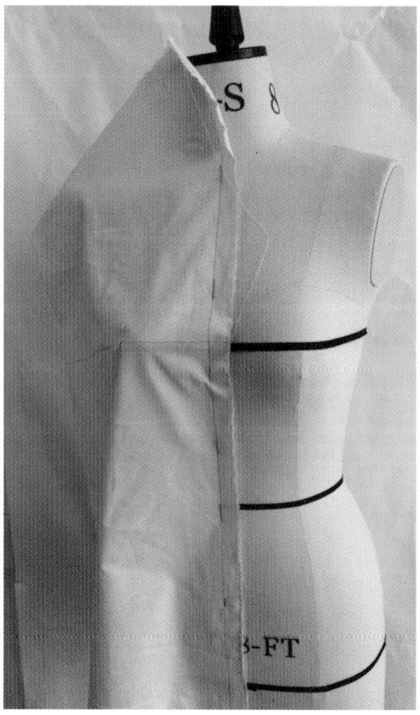

Fig. 5.8 Smoothing calico down the CF; the calico CF and BP are aligned to the corresponding position on the mannequin.

Pinning and Marking Out

Ideally, you will have relatively short pins without glass heads for draping. How you pin will also matter. When first placing the calico, pin vertically downwards with the pin point going into the mannequin cover once. This holding pin position allows for the fabric to be positioned but easily adjusted. As you smooth the calico over the body of the mannequin it will shift a little so this is one way of allowing for natural movement of the calico. Each piece of the drape will need at least 4cm (1½in) SA round it to drape but this can be trimmed down to 2cm (¾in) on the flat when you true it up. For complex patterns with more seams you will be draping to a style or seam line. When you are confirming the fit of each piece you can pin in and out through the calico and mannequin cover, either vertically or horizontally. When putting the toile together, the seams will need to be folded inwards at the seam line (Fig. 5.9), with one piece layered over the other, aligning at the seam line. The pieces can then be pinned together from the top by putting the pins diagonally (or horizontally if you prefer) through the three layers of calico but not the mannequin cover (Figs 5.10 and 5.11). This is a more secure way of pinning but still allows for adjustments to be made easily, which is why we don't ever pin from the underneath/back. The final drape for a longline bodice

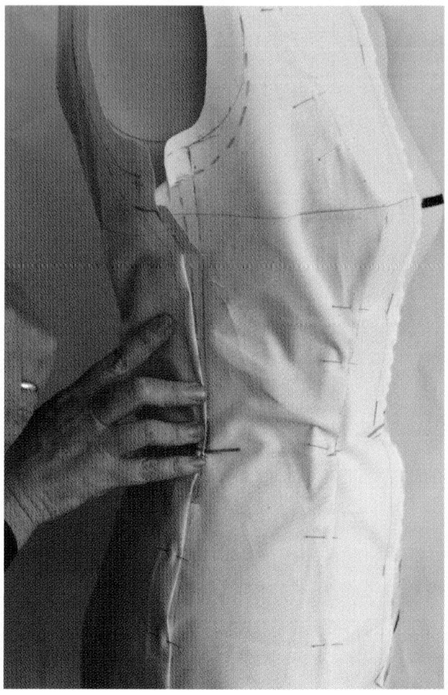

Fig. 5.9 Pinning SS together, with top layer of calico's allowances turned under.

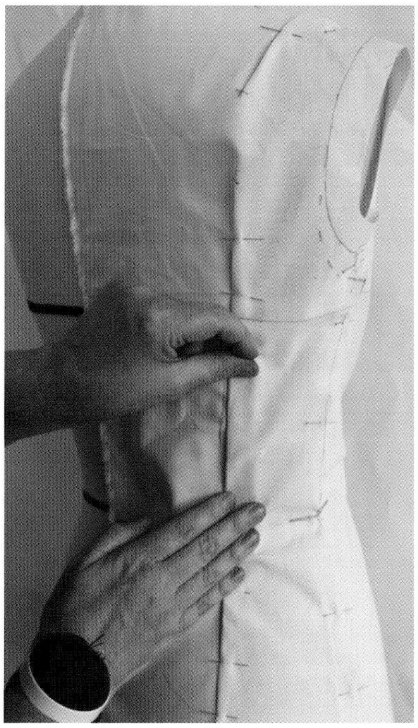

Fig. 5.10 Pinning seams and darts together on longline bodice; the pins go in and out through all the fabric layers and the stand cover.

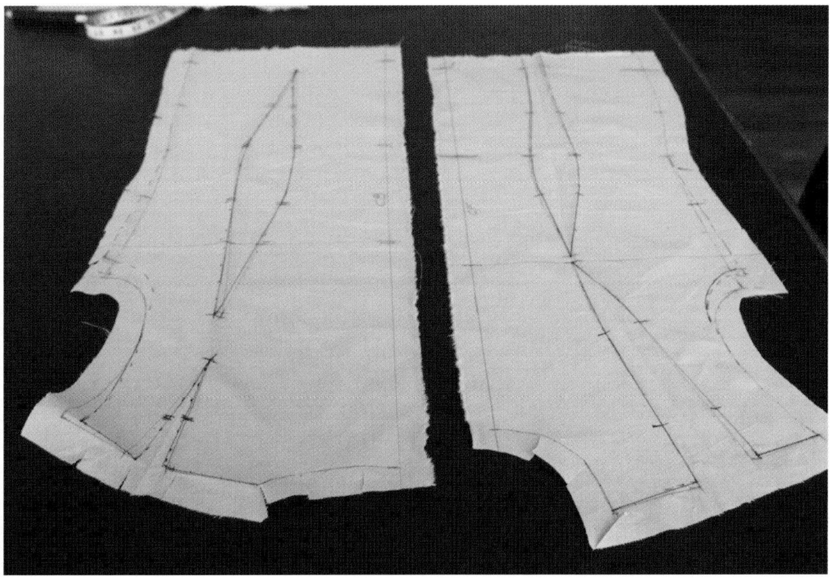

Fig. 5.12 Completed drape for longline bodice on the flat.

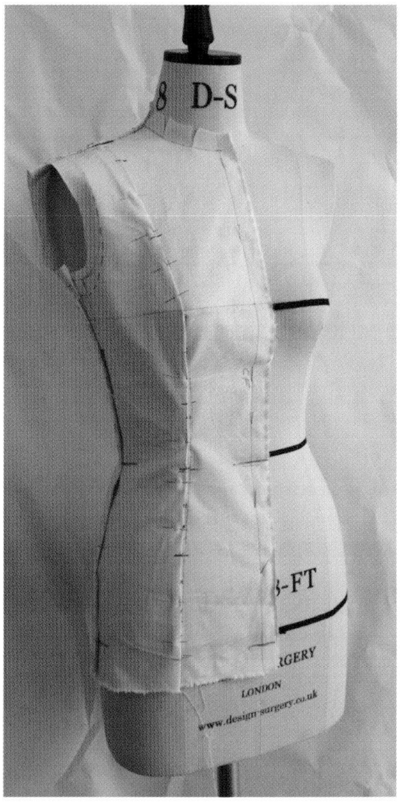

Fig. 5.11 Completed drape for a longline bodice on the mannequin.

ACCURATE PINNING

Pin close to or directly on what will be folded edges for your symmetrical garment; for example, the CF and CB, or on darts or SSs. When learning to drape people often pin too far away from what will eventually be a stitch line: this causes the drawn guide lines to shift or be pinned incorrectly and inaccurately from the outset.

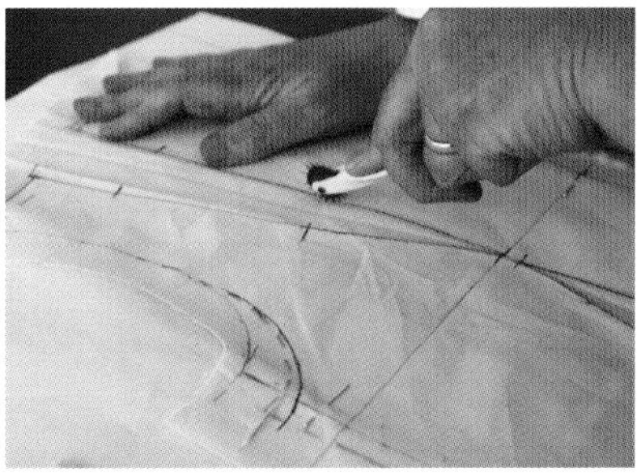

Fig. 5.13 Using tracing wheel to trace off drape onto paper.

after it has been trimmed down with all amendments marked out can be seen in Fig. 5.12.

The Master Pattern

This is where all the information on the calico is traced off onto paper with a tracing wheel, including grain lines and notches (Fig. 5.13). The master is only created after the drape has been altered and trued up. It is the first plan for a design and is 'nett', meaning it does not include any SA. The master serves the same purpose as a block used in traditional two-dimensional pattern drafting and is never cut up or used directly on fabric. Instead, it is used to trace off onto more paper, where it can also be altered (with new style lines, seam and hem allowances, yokes, button wraps and so on) to turn it into a production pattern or working pattern for a variety of new designs. This is what is used on fabric in preparation for cutting out and machining to construct the garment.

Creating the Master Pattern

Fig. 5.14 shows what you are aiming for, in this case a longline darted bodice. The same method is used for this process regardless of the garment type and works by systematically positioning the pieces along a horizontal and vertical axis:

1. On a piece of pattern paper draw a vertical line all the way down the

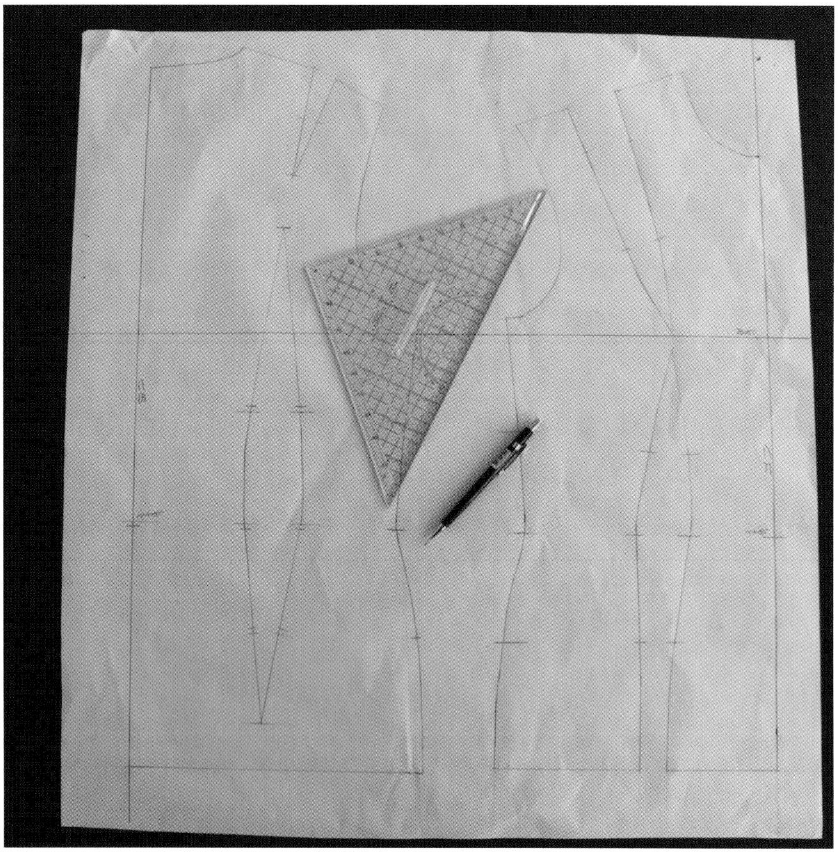

Fig. 5.14 Finished master for longline darted bodice.

right-hand side with a metre rule (Fig. 5.15). This will represent the CF of a garment that has been draped on the right-hand side of a stand. If you were draping menswear and therefore draping on the left-hand side of the stand you would begin on the left-hand side.

2. Draw in the cross-grain line. This will be the bustline for a bodice or dress and the hipline for skirts and trousers. This must be at a right angle intersecting the CF so use a set square and metre rule to do it accurately.
3. On the left-hand side of the paper, draw in another vertical line that intersects the cross grain at a right angle: this will be the CB of the drape. The object of the exercise is to lay the calico drapes sequentially in the order in which they connect together at the seams to eventually make the garment. Sometimes they are odd shapes or they don't have the cross grain marked on the panel as a reference point. When this happens, it is best to position the piece logically above or below the cross-grain line. It is also acceptable for the pieces to overlap on a master pattern so you don't utilize too much paper for complex patterns.
4. Starting with the CF piece, align the calico drape with the CF line and bust- or hipline you have drawn on the paper (Fig. 5.16). When it is positioned accurately, pin or weight it down and use a tracing wheel to trace the drape off.
5. The tracing wheel will leave a series of small holes or track marks provided you pressed down firmly enough; you can now draw in the line with your mechanical pencil.
6. When you have transferred all of the visual information from the first piece, you can unpin the first drape and move onto the next piece and repeat the process, aligning it up to the bust- or hipline. Work your way sequentially through all the pieces finishing at the CB.
7. Double-check that the pattern pieces are clearly labelled with all the notches and grain lines marked off. If you have given your garment a style name or number also include that, plus the garment size and how

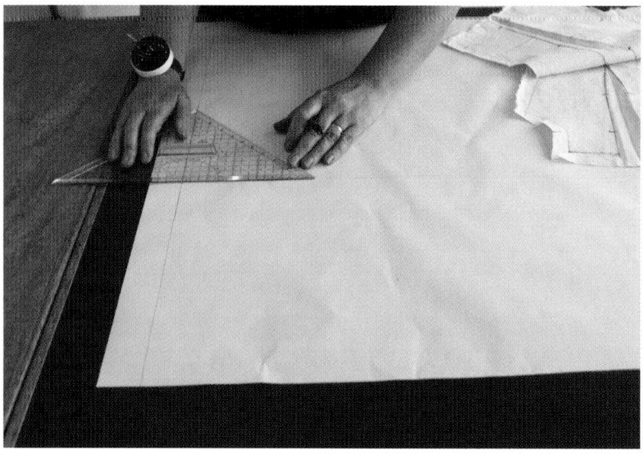

Fig. 5.15 Drawing in CF and bustline on pattern paper with a set square.

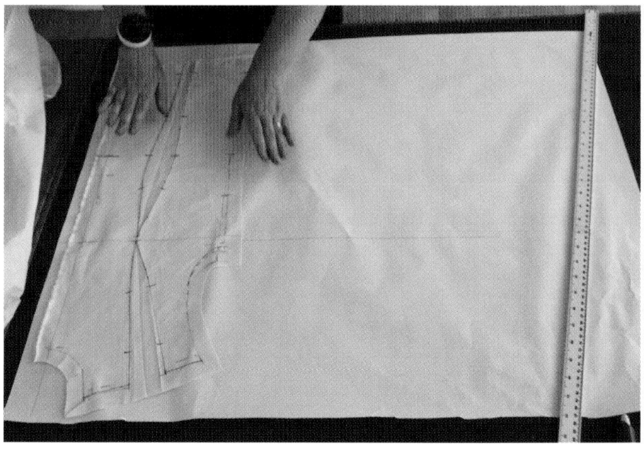

Fig. 5.16 Aligning front bodice to CF and bustline at point where they intersect.

many times each piece needs to be cut out.

8. *Never cut out the master!* Keep it as it is and trace it off onto fresh pattern paper for the production pattern. Any amendments made at the toile stage can be transferred to the production pattern with a note of them; don't waste time endlessly altering the master until the design is fully resolved. If you are making multiples of the design then trace it off onto something more robust like card and have the final version as your style block.

Golden Rules for Draping

- Always prepare the calico/toile by indicating horizontal and vertical grain in pencil.
- Don't be over-economical with the calico – it is cheap and more can be cut.
- Always place the calico on the dress stand with accurate straight of grain or true bias as appropriate.
- Pin the toile onto the cover of the stand and adjust. When it is totally straight, secure by pinning in and out through all the calico layers and the mannequin cover.
- If the toile does not mould around the body in the desired way, snip into it to release the tension (see next chapter).
- For seams and darts always pin one layer of fabric over the other. Pin from the top.
- Accurately mark off the pinned toile with a sharp pencil and include notches.
- Always true the marked-off lines to create the pattern pieces with the calico flat on the table.
- Trim away the excess SA and re-pin the calico pieces back onto the stand (working from the top and pinning diagonally through the calico layers but not the mannequin cover).
- Transfer the calico to the master pattern (no SA).

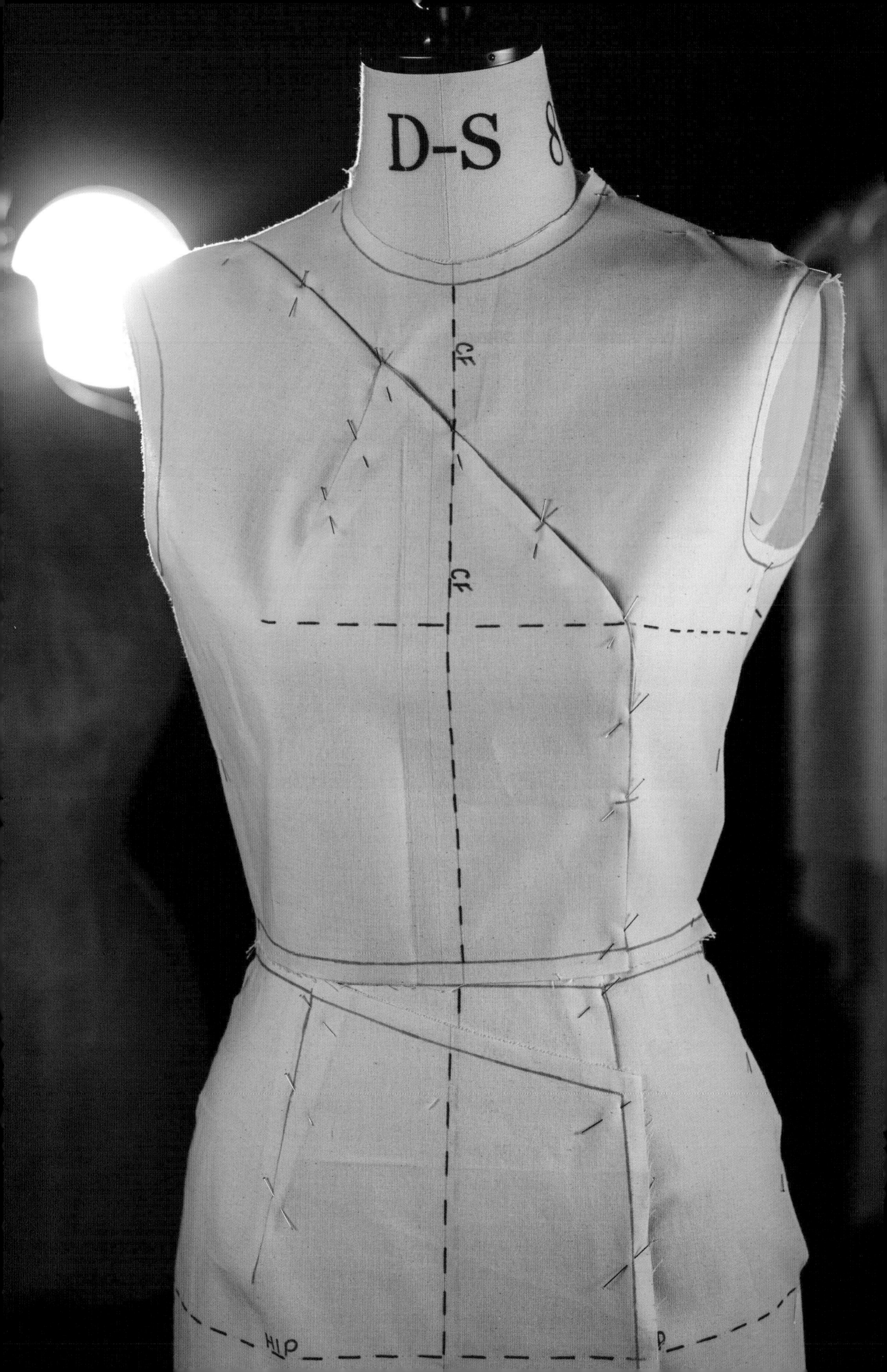
D-S 8
CF
CF
HIP

The Bodice

6

Anatomically speaking, human bodies are divided up into a number of hypothetical planes with a grid of vertical and horizontal placement either perpendicular or parallel to the ground. The planes are used to describe anatomical structure and direction of movement. The body is effectively divided up into left and right, back and front and head and tail portions, all divided at the waist or hip. For womenswear in particular there is so much contouring and shaping required to get the perfect fit that we are often left with an excess of cloth that needs to be controlled by using seams and darts at the points where these planes change direction. These points are known as the key suppression points, of which there are three: the bust, waist and hip. Fig. 6.2 is a design; Fig. 6.3 indicates how the suppression points and style lines are taken into account before the pattern is draped. You have to work with the suppression points if you want to design clothes that fit!

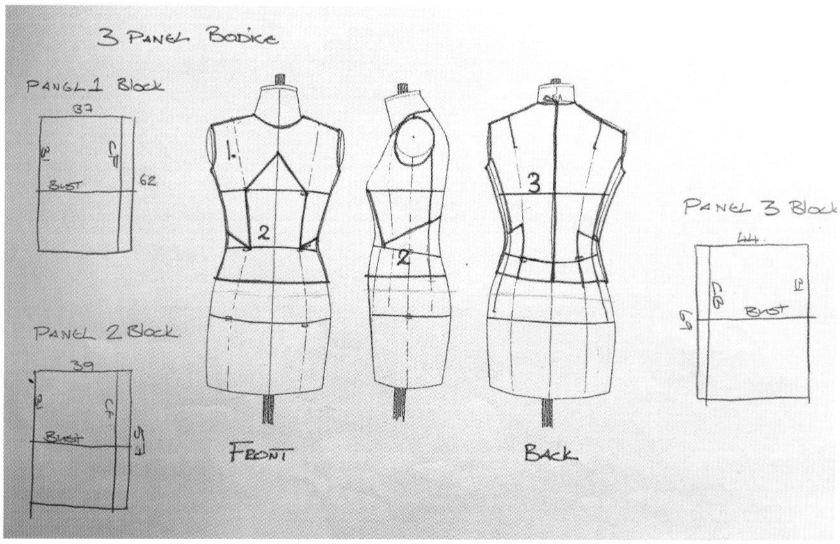

Fig. 6.3 All-round view of a design using the suppression points.

Suppression

If a piece of cloth were to be wrapped around the body it would look like a cylinder with no obvious shaping. It is the designer's job to refit the cloth to reveal the bust-, waist- and hiplines in a creative and flattering way by controlling the volume of cloth at key points on the body. The usual way to add shape to a garment is to use darts although it can also be done with a variety of pleats, gathers, tucks and seams or panels. All of these methods enable us to make a two-dimensional piece of fabric into a three-dimensional garment by suppressing the excess cloth. 'Suppression' is used to create garments that will sit smoothly whilst acknowledging the planes of the body underneath and create a flattering silhouette. Draping directly onto the body really helps to see how suppression or excess fabric can be manipulated in a variety of different ways to suit the design aesthetic or customer requirements.

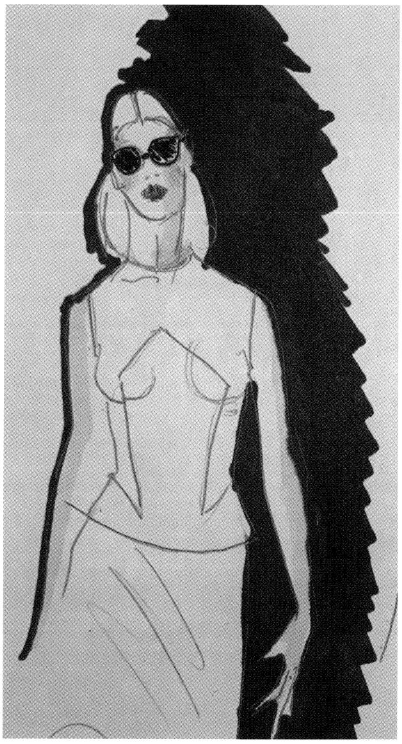

Fig. 6.2 Design for a bodice using suppression points.

Darts and Dart Manipulation

Darts are the most common method of suppression used to shape the curves and hollows of the human figure and enable flat two-dimensional cloth to become a three-dimensional form. The dart is formed as a tapered fold; its widest and smallest points reflect the position of the suppression point over which it is travelling (Fig. 6.4).

Back bodice: This will have darts at the shoulder to shape the top of the shoulder blade (Fig. 6.5) and below the shoulder blade down the back midriff to the waistline.

Front bodice: This will have a longer shoulder dart to shape the bust from

Left: Fig. 6.1 Draped asymmetric bodice. (Photo: Yousef Al Nasser)

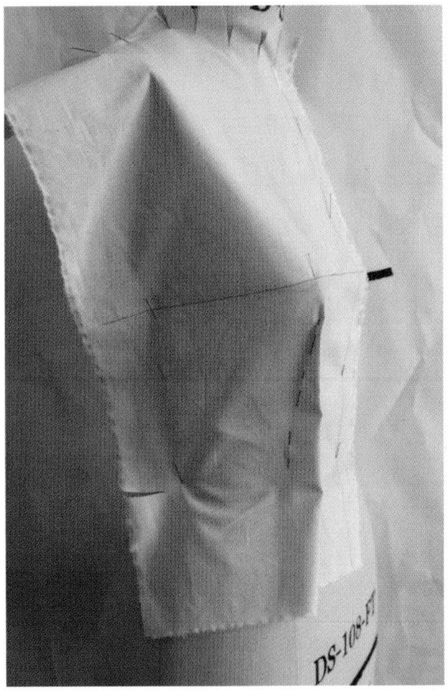

Fig. 6.4 Pinning tapered triangle or dart from BP to waist on the front of a bodice.

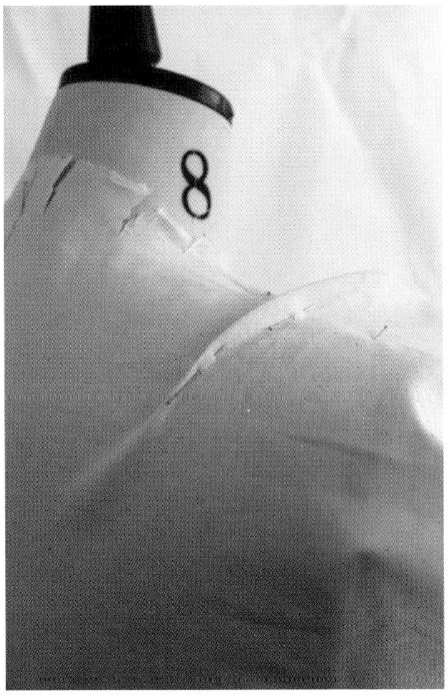

Fig. 6.5 Pinning tapered triangle or dart over the back shoulder.

the top, and a waist dart to shape from under the bust down the front midriff to the waistline (Fig. 6.6). Both darts on the front bodice are drafted to converge at their apex at the bust point (BP). This allows the darts to be moved to different areas around the front bodice whilst still maintaining the same basic fit as in their original position.

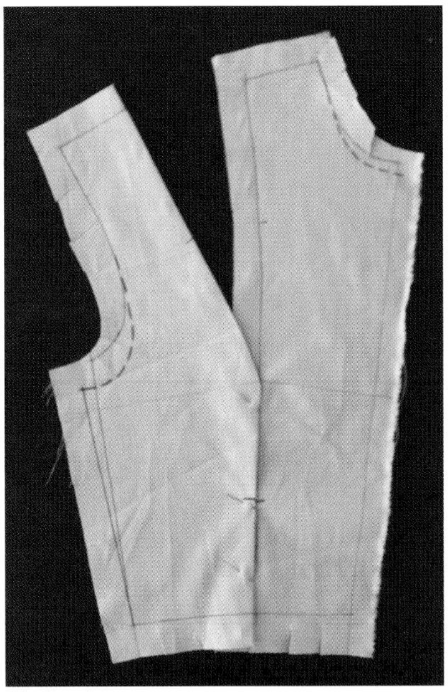

Fig. 6.6 Flat dart drape showing darts running from shoulder to BP and waist to BP.

Types of Darts

Aesthetically, darts can take on a variety of forms to address both form and function; as you can see in Fig. 6.6, the basic front darts are not particularly pretty. The concept is that the fit remains the same whilst stylistically the positions of the darts and seams change.

1. Straight darts: these give a semi-fitted effect.
2. Curved darts: these serve the same purpose as straight darts but are shaped and used as a particular design feature.
3. Contour darts: these follow the curves of the body more closely to create a more fitted effect most obviously achieved by draping rather than flat pattern drafting.
4. Multiple darts: two or more darts are used in conjunction for a tighter fit or as a design feature.
5. Dart tucks: where darts are sewn in place but left to form a type of pleat rather than fully sewn closed.
6. Dart seams: a design feature, when darts converge from different directions to produce, say, a square-shaped panel.
7. Concave darts or double-pointed darts: may be used in a dress to suppress the waistline.

Draping a Basic Bodice with Waist Darts (Fig. 6.7)

This waist-length sleeveless bodice has a waist dart at the front (Fig. 6.8) and a shoulder dart at the back (Fig. 6.9). Its appearance is rather functional but demonstrates the basic suppression points well so it's a good starting point

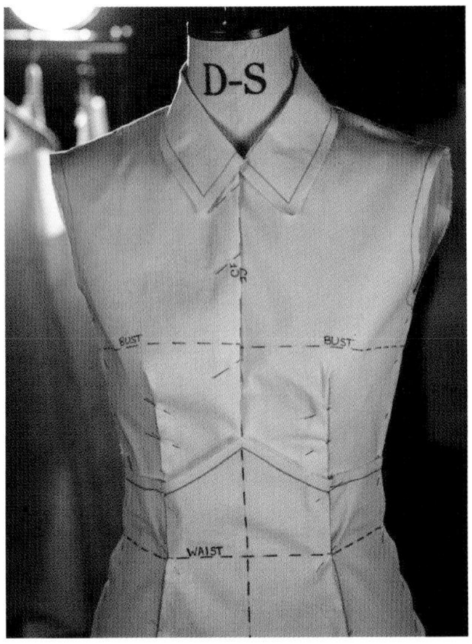

Fig. 6.7 Completed bodice with waist darts.

before moving onto something more creative. This classic type of utilitarian darting is usually seen on dresses and blouses or tops where flare needs to be removed from the front part of the garment and minimal shaping might be required through the back.

1 Prepare and block your calico as per the dimensions in Fig. 6.10.
2. To drape the front, begin on the right front by positioning the calico as shown in Fig. 6.11. Align the bustline on the calico with the bustline tape on the mannequin where it intersects the CF. Pin vertically on the CF above the bustline and at the BP to hold the calico in place. Put another pin under the bustline on the CF.
3. Ease the calico into the neck point

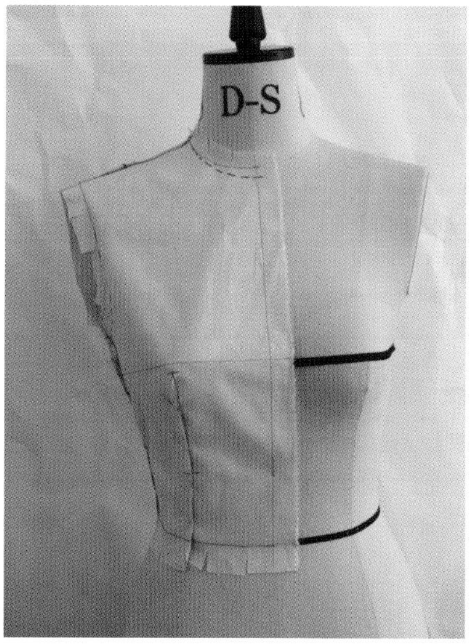

Fig. 6.8 Bodice with waist dart, front view.

and pin. There will be some pulling so release the tension by snipping around the front neck and trim away the excess fabric (Figs 6.12 and 6.13).

4. Smooth the calico along the shoulder seam of the mannequin and pin. The object of the exercise is to get the calico to sit flat, but not skintight, to the mannequin (Fig. 6.14).
5. Pin at the SS just under the arm plate, allowing the volume to swing into the front of the calico through the BP and down to the waist (Fig. 6.15). The arm plate is the plastic plate on your mannequin that denotes where an arm should be.

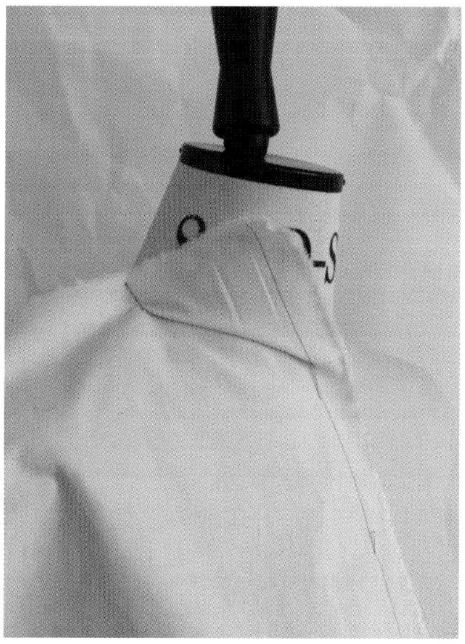

Fig. 6.12 Easing calico into neck point.

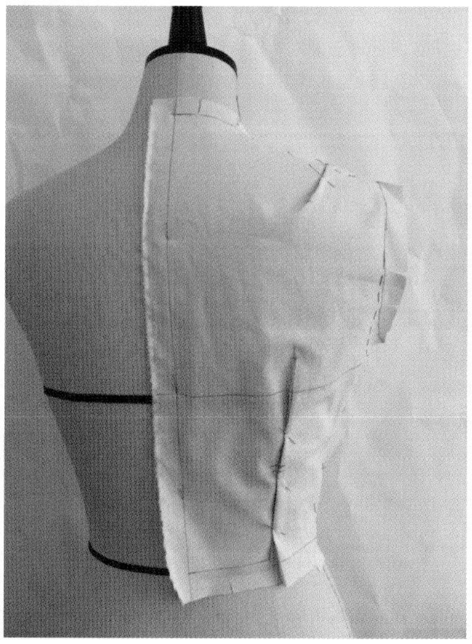

Fig. 6.9 Bodice with waist dart, back view.

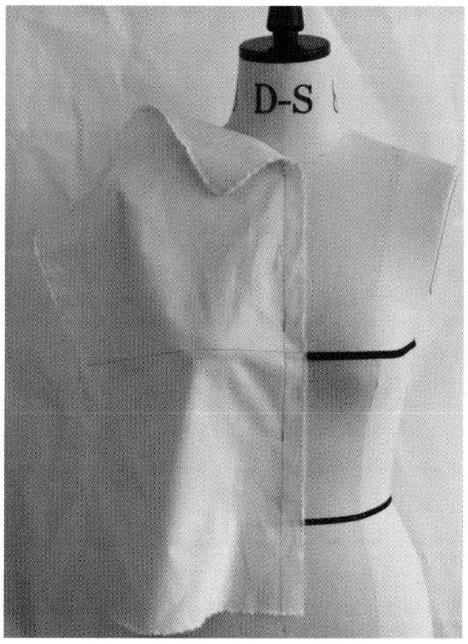

Fig. 6.11 Aligning calico to CF and bustline to drape the front bodice.

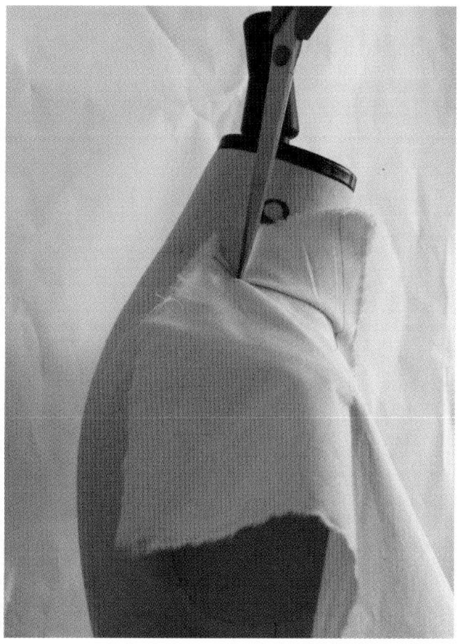

Fig. 6.13 Snipping into neck point to release tension.

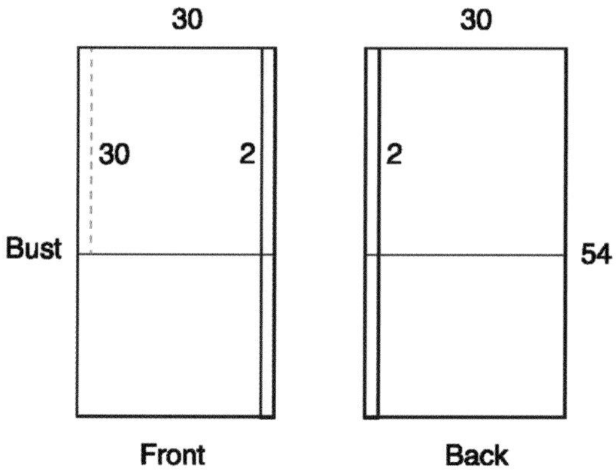

Fig. 6.10 Block dimensions for bodice with waist darts.

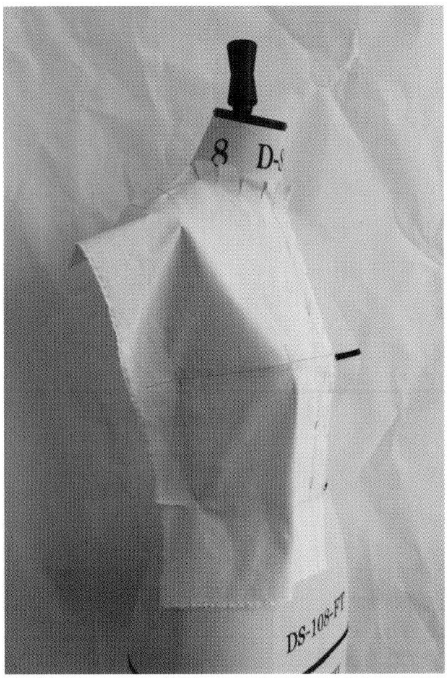

Fig. 6.14 Calico with snipped neck is smoothed along shoulder line and pinned, allowing excess volume through bust to waist to show.

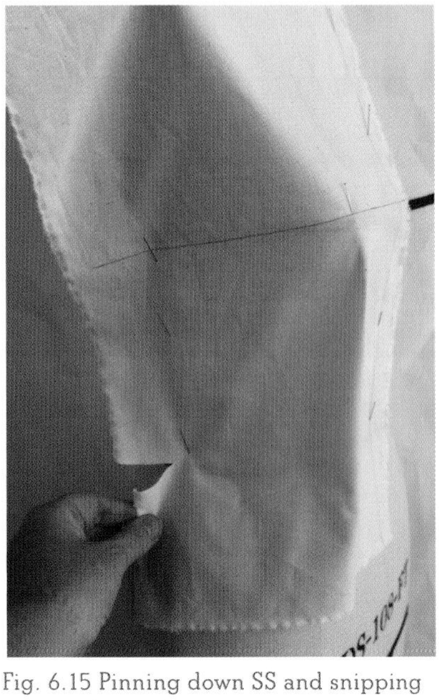

Fig. 6.15 Pinning down SS and snipping in towards waist.

Note that although it is the anatomical equivalent of the armpit position it is too high to use as a guide for a well-fitting armhole on a garment (Fig. 6.16).

6. Form the waist dart from the excess fabric, trying to keep the amount of suppression. Check you are happy with the fit and silhouette being created before pinning the darts into position. Make sure it is not too tight. To pin the darts ensure that your pins travel diagonally in and out through both layers of fabric in the fold; this will anchor them securely. The darts should be straight and run out just before the BP with a clean end and no puckering (Fig. 6.17).
7. Pin down the SS. If there is any tension through the waist or side the fabric will pull, so release it by snipping up to, but not through, the waistline or SS.
8. Using a mechanical pencil, make a series of dots to mark off the neckline, dart, SS and waist. Also mark off the position of the armhole and the position of the bottom of the arm plate where it joins the SS. Use dashes to indicate corners or

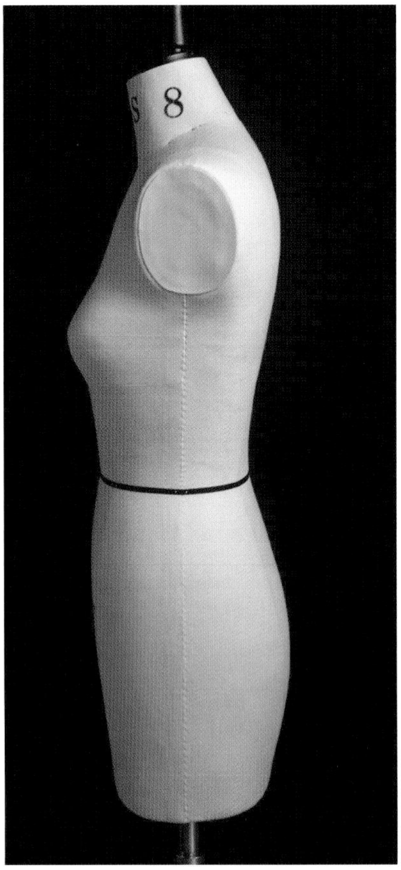

Fig. 6.16 Arm plate on Design-Surgery® mannequin.

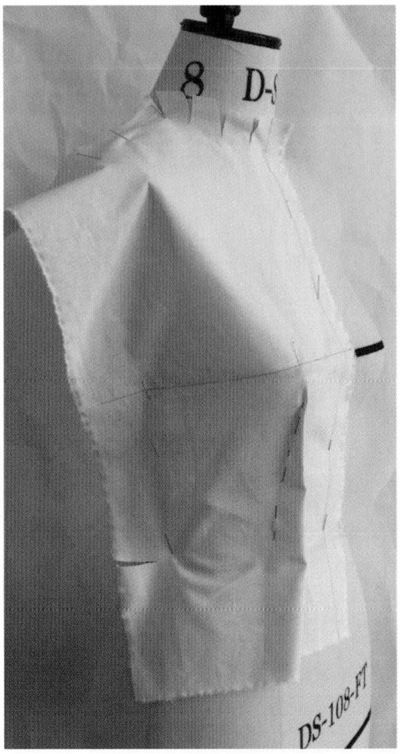

Fig. 6.17 Pinning waist dart in and snipping into waist from side allowance to release tension.

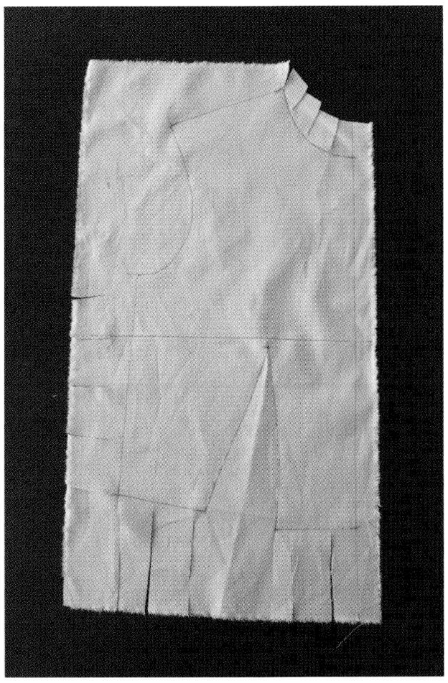

Fig. 6.18 Trued-up bodice front with waist dart on the flat.

Fig. 6.19 Marking off dropped neckline at CF by 1cm.

junctions where seams intersect one another and crosses to denote the fine ends of your darts.

9. Remove the calico from the stand and true up (Fig. 6.18).
10. With the calico drape flat, drop the neckline at CF by 1cm and run it out to the neck point. This will take account of the throat muscles on the neck. Draw the new neckline (Fig. 6.19).
11. The armhole can be draped with tape on the mannequin but the following method gets a good fit every time. On the flat, drop the armhole down from the base of the arm plate by 2cm and out by 1cm (Fig. 6.20) and draw the new SS, running it out to the waist. Draw in the new armhole by joining the original armhole to the adjusted armhole at the SS. You can do this with a variety of pattern-cutting tools (such as PatternMaster®, French curve, set square, etc. or by eye (Fig. 6.21). It is also worth checking the length of the darts and adjusting if necessary. Ideally they need to be 2cm short of the BP to give a nice point and not pucker, so foreshorten and redraw if you need to.
12. Trim off excess calico at armhole, neck, shoulder and SS but leave a 2cm allowance all round the new drape.

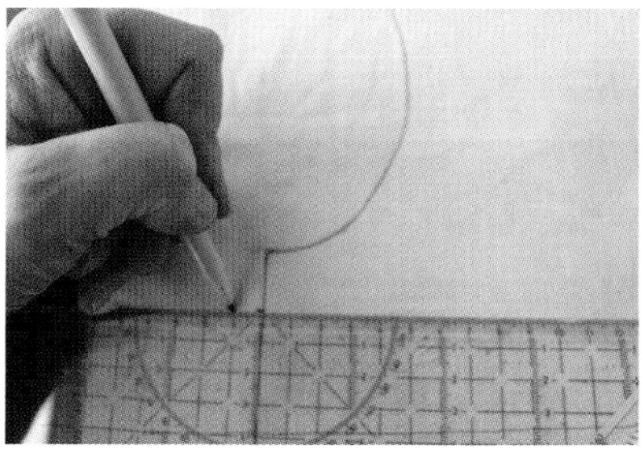

Fig. 6.20 Dropping underarm down and out on the flat for the front bodice.

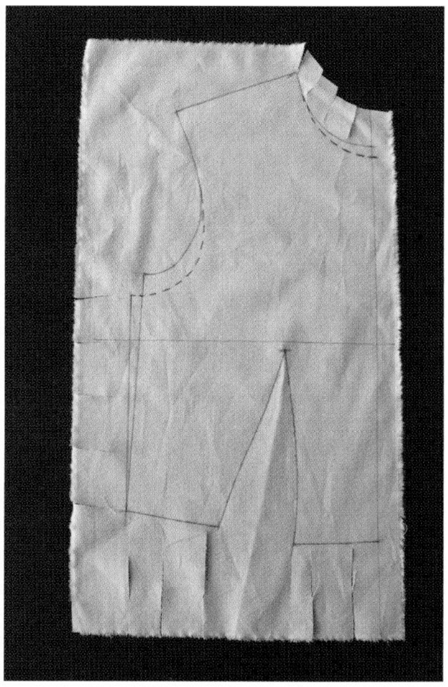

Fig. 6.21 Amended front bodice with new neckline, armhole and foreshortened bust dart.

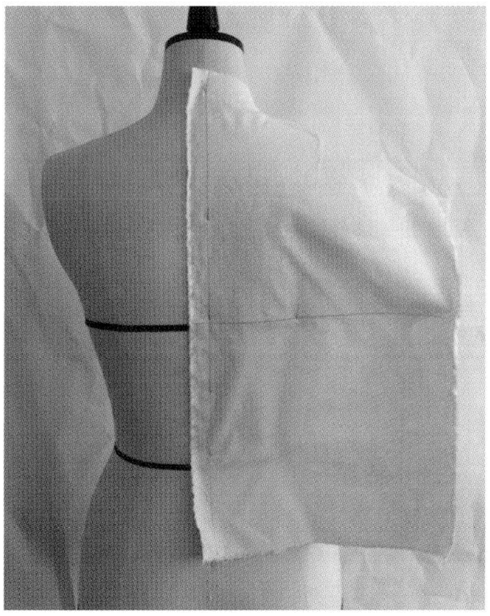

Fig. 6.22 Positioning back bodice calico against CB and bustline.

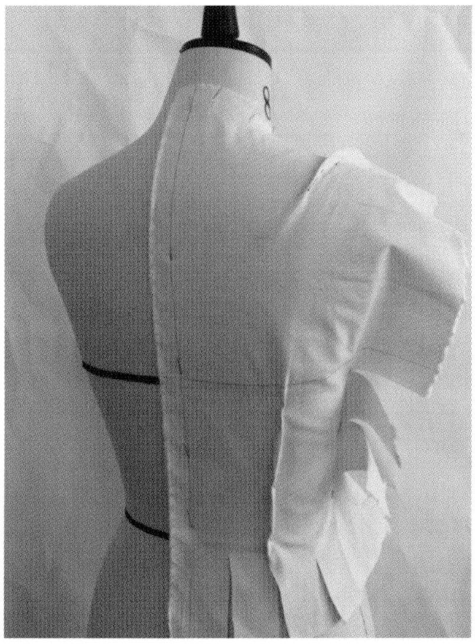

Fig. 6.23 Pinned back shoulder and back waist darts; note where the calico has been snipped along waist and side to release tension in the cloth.

13. To drape the back, the technique is the same as for the front but with less suppression to address: obviously a lady's back is flatter than her front! Begin on the right back by positioning the calico as shown in Fig. 6.22. Align the bustline on the calico with the bustline tape on the mannequin where it intersects the CB. Pin vertically on the CB above and below the bustline to begin with to hold the calico in place.
14. Ease the calico into the neck point and pin. Again there will be some pulling so release the tension by snipping round the front neck and trim away the excess fabric as you did on the front neck.
15. Smooth the calico along the shoulder seam of the mannequin and fold a small dart about 1cm in depth on top of the princess seam (PS) and pin. This shoulder dart allows for ease of movement at the shoulder bone and should taper out just above the middle of the shoulder blade.
16. Pin at the SS just under the arm plate, allowing the volume to swing into the back of the calico, and shape the dart by folding the fabric. Ideally the dart should taper out towards the bustline and must not join up to the shoulder dart (Fig. 6.23).
17. Using a mechanical pencil, make a series of dots to mark off the neckline, darts, SS and waist. Also mark off the position of the armhole and the position of the bottom of the arm plate where it joins the SS. Use dashes to indicate corners or junctions where seams intersect one another and crosses to denote the fine ends of your darts.
18. Remove the calico from the stand and true up as per the front. Repeat the process for dropping and drafting the armhole only. As the back neck is already a good fit, you do not need to adjust it this time. Trim down leaving a 2cm allowance around the adjusted drape.
19. To join the front to the back, reposition and pin the front onto

the mannequin, aligning the bustline and CF. Anchor through the CF. Fold in the bust and waist darts and pin. Then reposition and pin the back onto the mannequin, aligning the bustline and CB. Anchor through the CB. Fold the shoulder dart into position, then fold the allowance on the back shoulder under and along the shoulder seam and align it to the shoulder seam for the front. Pin

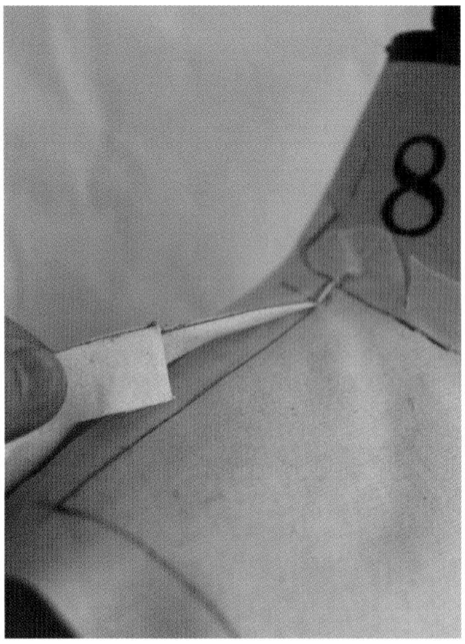

Fig. 6.24 Pinning back bodice piece to front at shoulder; shoulder dart is already folded and pinned.

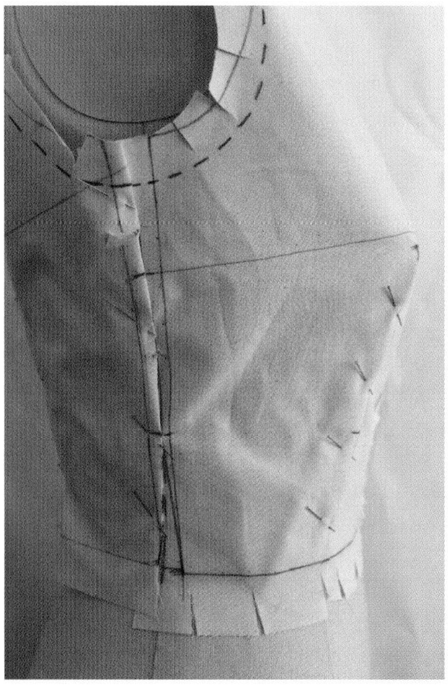

Fig. 6.25 Back bodice piece is pinned to front bodice piece at SS.

diagonally through both layers to hold everything (Fig. 6.24).

20. Fold the back side SA under and align the front and back SSs. Pin diagonally through both layers to hold them (Fig. 6.25).
21. As this is a drape you may need to adjust it once it goes back onto the mannequin. It is better then to pin on the top of the seams to check the fit rather than to pin from the back as you would do for a garment you are about to sew. If you are happy with the fit and silhouette then you can transfer the drape onto a paper master pattern.

If you need to adjust then just unpin and get another coloured pen to mark off the adjustments. Then remove from

FINGER-PRESSING

While draping the basic bodice you may well already be doing a certain amount of finger-pressing without realizing. The term is self-explanatory. It is a useful method for creasing the centre of darts instead of using an iron when folding the darts into position. It is also good when overlaying one piece of calico on another, such as at the SS or shoulder seam, to get a more accurate seam line.

SHOULDER SEAM FIT

When working on any of these bodices you will get a better fit if you true up the front shoulder seam straight but the back shoulder seam about 6mm to 1cm (¼–⅜in) longer; this creates a slight curve which allows for the curvature of the shoulder blade and roundness of the back. The back seam should then be eased onto the front seam, even when pinning, to check the fit and make alterations.

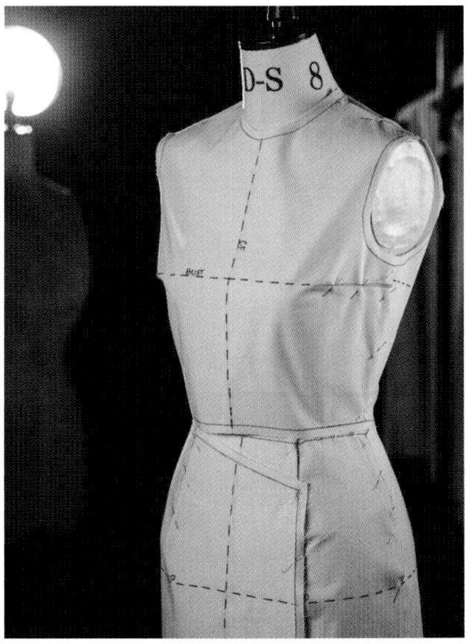

Fig. 6.26 Finished basic bodice with bust darts.

the stand and transfer the adjusted version to your master.

Having examined how to drape the basic bodice you can move on to some variations.

Basic Bodice with Bust Dart (Fig. 6.26)

Figs 6.27 and 6.28 show the positioning of the volume at the bust

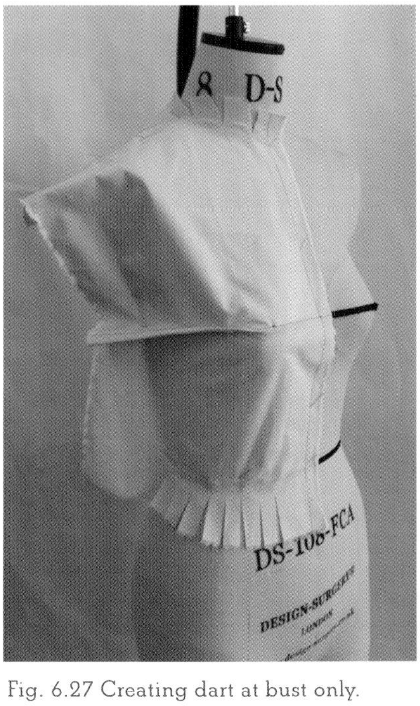

Fig. 6.27 Creating dart at bust only.

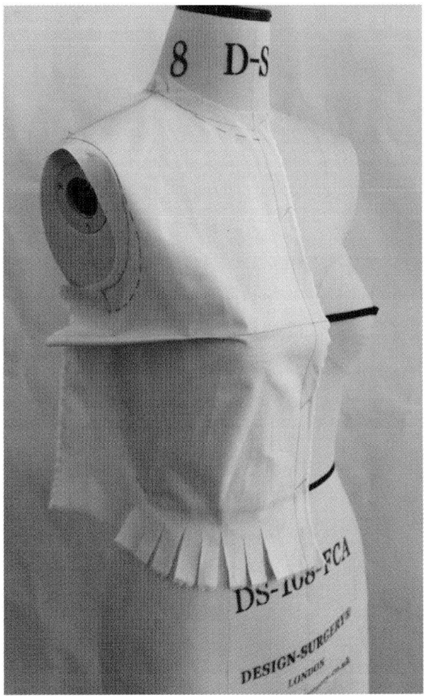

Fig. 6.28 Bust dart with lowered armhole and neckline.

instead of the waist. The process is very similar to the process for the waist dart with a result that is still very functional. A key difference is that with the dart coming from the SS to the BP there will be more volume at the front of the garment from the BP down to the waist. All that has really happened is that the suppression has moved around the body from the waist to the bust whilst the fit remains the same. The dimensions for blocking the calico will be the same as for the basic bodice with waist dart.

Repeat steps 1–5 given for the bodice with waist darts; you will be able to use the same dimensions to block.

6. Form the side bust dart by folding the lower fabric upwards along the bustline. Pin through both layers to hold and check the silhouette.

Repeat steps 7– 21 listed for the bodice with waist darts.

Basic Bodice with French Dart (Fig. 6.29)

This has a side bust dart but it is angled sharply from the side waist to the BP. It effectively combines a bust and waist dart in one. It was used a lot in the 1950s where the underwear worn created significantly more exaggerated curvature to women's bodies. It creates a closer fit to the body, particularly the underbust.

Repeat steps 1–5 listed for the bodice with waist darts.

6. Form the French dart by folding the lower fabric upwards from the waist diagonally to the BP. Pin through both layers to hold, then check the silhouette.

Repeat steps 7–21 listed for the bodice with waist darts. Note that the darts tend to be large with this style, so when transferring to a paper pattern it is better to have SA along the inside of the dart and cut the excess away.

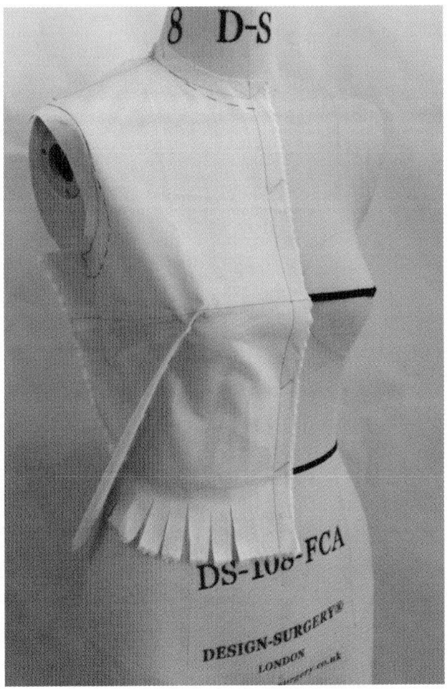

Fig. 6.29 Positioned French dart with dropped neckline and armhole.

Bodice with Princess Seams/Princess Line (Fig. 6.30)

These days we tend to call any bodice with vertical seams a princess line but historically the style was characterized in the 1880s in honour of Alexandra, Princess of Wales. She was the first to adopt a crinoline that had no horizontal waist seam and instead had her skirts and bodices cut in one piece with vertical seams and tucks to closely fit the waist and emphasize the bust and hips. There is no need for darts with this bodice; instead the

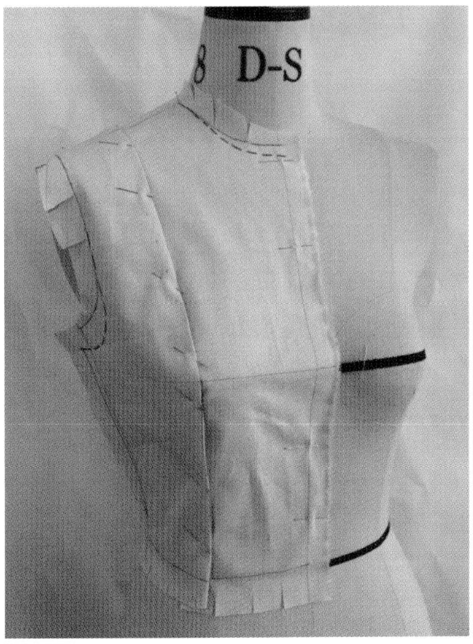

Fig. 6.30 Bodice with PS.

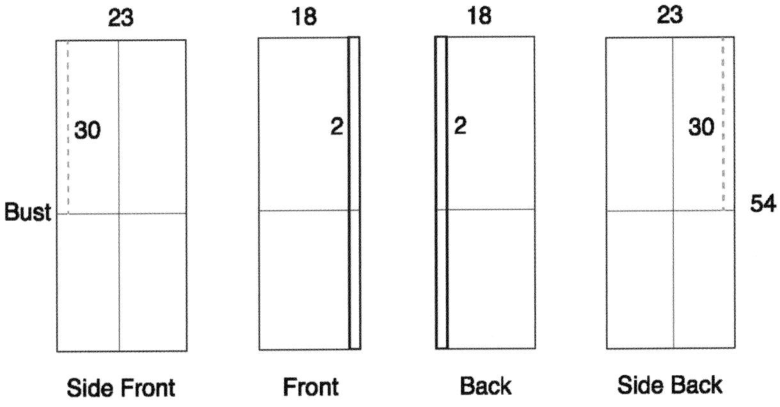

Fig. 6.31 Block dimensions for PS bodice.

suppression is moved out into vertical seams, either with two panels to make a half front or three for the whole front which will now comprise the CF panel and two SF panels. The same goes for the back which is now cut as a CB panel and two SB panels in total. Prepare and block your calico as per the dimensions in Fig. 6.31.

1. Begin at the CF panel and work out towards the SS. Align the bustline and the CF on the calico to the bustline and the CF on the mannequin. Pin vertically to hold along the CF (Fig. 6.32).
2. Ease the calico into the neck point and pin. There will be some pulling so release the tension by snipping around the front neck and trim away the excess fabric.
3. Smooth across the shoulder to the PS and pin to hold.
4. Pin calico down the PS so that it sits flat. Snip up to the waistline if you need to release any tension.
5. Using a mechanical pencil, make a series of dots to mark off the neckline, dashes for junctions and a dash to denote a notch at the BP. A corresponding notch on the other panel piece at the BP will allow you to line up the pieces to check the drape later.
6. Remove from the mannequin and true up (Fig. 6.33).
7. For the front side panel, align the SG to the SS and pin to hold.
8. Pin down the SS. If there is any tension through the waist or side then release it by snipping up to, but not through, the waistline or SS (Fig. 6.34).
9. Smooth upwards around the armhole and chest and along the shoulder. Pin to hold.
10. Smooth along the PS and pin to hold; then, using a mechanical pencil, mark off the PS with a notch at the BP, the shoulder, armhole, arm plate and SS (Fig. 6.35).
11 Remove from the mannequin and

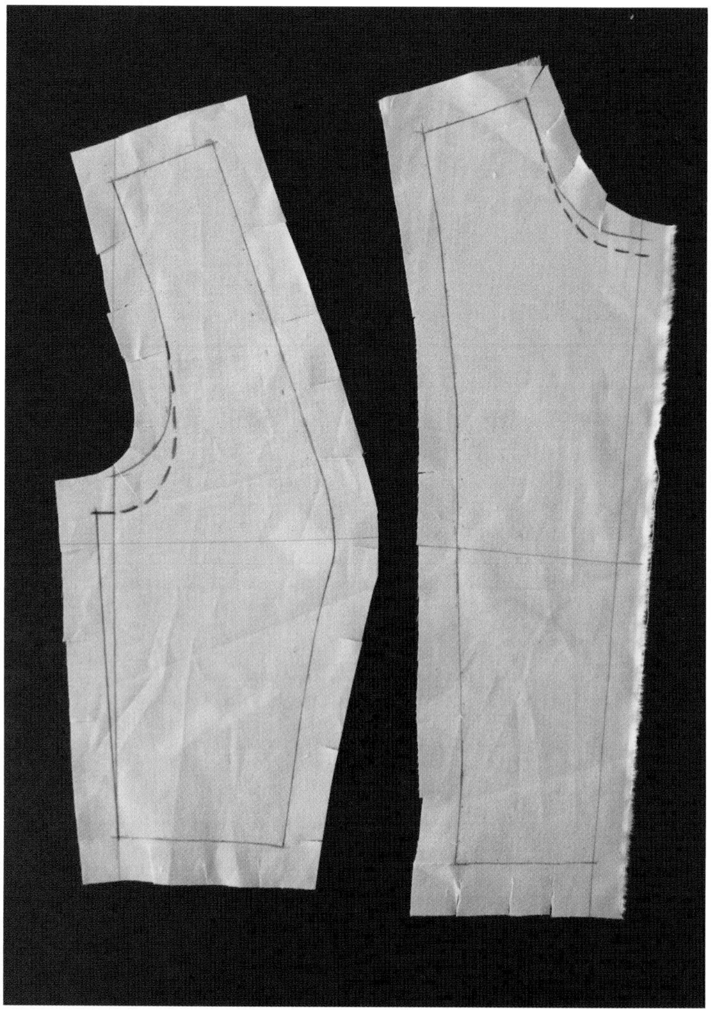

Fig. 6.33 Trued-up front and SF panels on the flat, with dropped neckline and armhole.

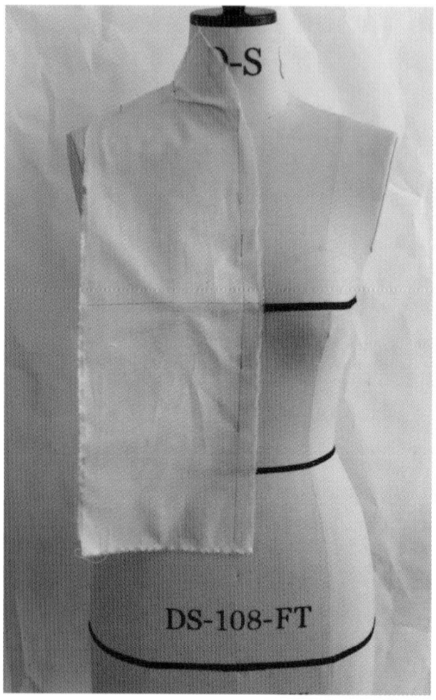

Fig. 6.32 Pinning CF panel to mannequin and aligning to where CF and bustline intersect.

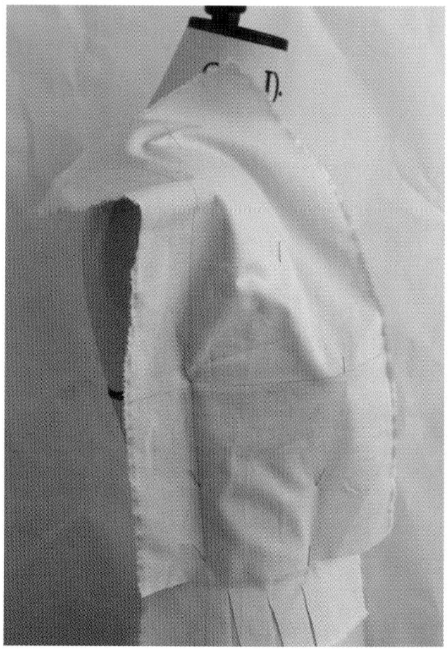

Fig. 6.34 Positioning calico block to drape SF panel; SG is running along SS.

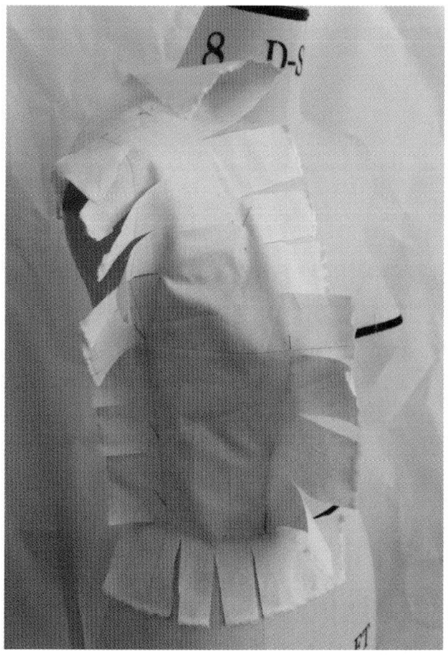

Fig. 6.35 Releasing tension in SF drape by snipping into it.

true up.

12. For the back, repeat the process as per the front, starting from the CB.
13. For the armhole, repeat step 11 for the basic bodice with waist dart by dropping it down and out for the front and back. Trim the excess away from each panel to leave a 2cm allowance.
14. To check the drape, begin by realigning the bustline and CF and pinning back into position. Fold the allowance on the side panel under at the PS and align the edge to the CF front panel at the PS. Make sure the notch at the BP lines up and then pin on top of the seam (Fig. 6.36).
15. Repeat from the back, beginning at the CB.
16. Fold the allowance under on the back SS and align to the front.
17. Adjust if necessary and mark the alterations in a different colour before transferring the adjusted drape to a paper master pattern ready to toile (Fig. 6.37).

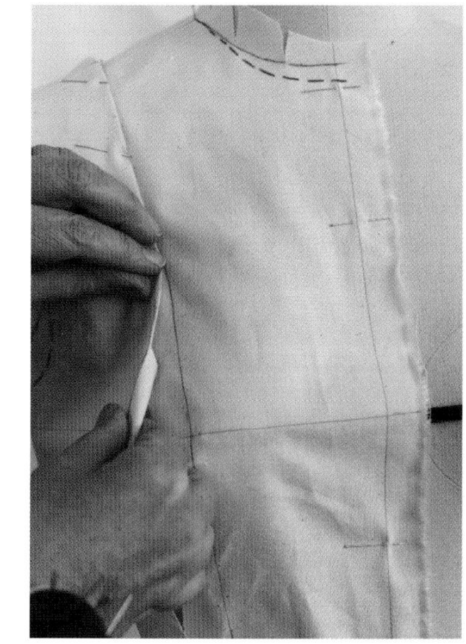

Fig. 6.36 Aligning front panels to check fit.

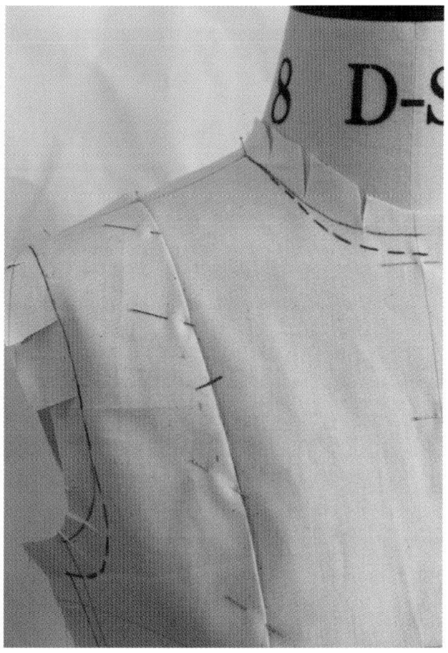

Fig. 6.37 Adjusted PS bodice with notches marked.

Strapless Bodice with Princess Seam

The origin of the strapless dress or bodice as outerwear is thought have been a late 1930s invention named the 'Naked Look'. It was only adopted by one or two of the Hollywood glitterati at the time because of its lack of modesty and although it features in a lot of 1950s couture gowns and swimwear it was not widely adopted until the 1970s when elasticated fabrics became more accessible. Now it predominantly resides in the bridal wear and occasion wear sector. This bodice is a variation on the previous princess-line bodice with PS and has no darts. It is very form-fitting, with the suppression taken out through the PSs as before. It is the premise for a basic corset pattern and to stay up it needs to be tight without tolerance or ease. The neckline can be any shape of your choosing; just don't let it get too low towards the BP or it will be too revealing and not offer the wearer much support.

Prepare the mannequin as before with bust- and waist lines. Pin the waist tape at the thinnest part of the mannequin and it will denote the position of the bottom of the corset.

1. Tape a style line for the neckline. Start by pinning the tape at the CF, then run it all the way round the mannequin and back to the CF. Stand back from the mannequin to see if you are happy with the line as this denotes the position of the top of the corset. Adjust and pin into place.
2. Prepare and block your calico as per the dimensions in Fig. 6.38.
3. Begin with the CF panel and work out to the PS. Align the bustline

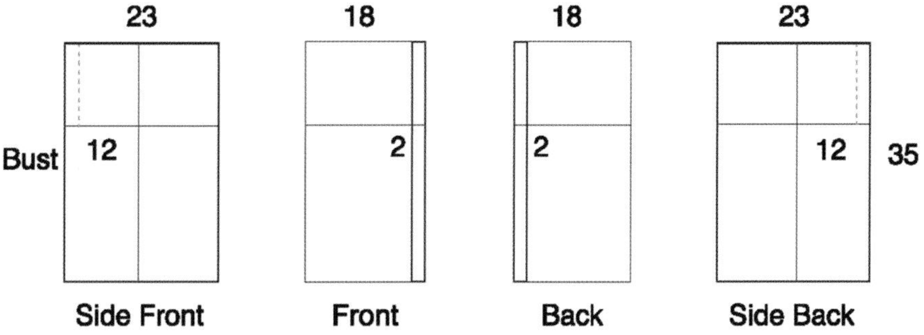

Fig. 6.38 Block dimensions for strapless bodice.

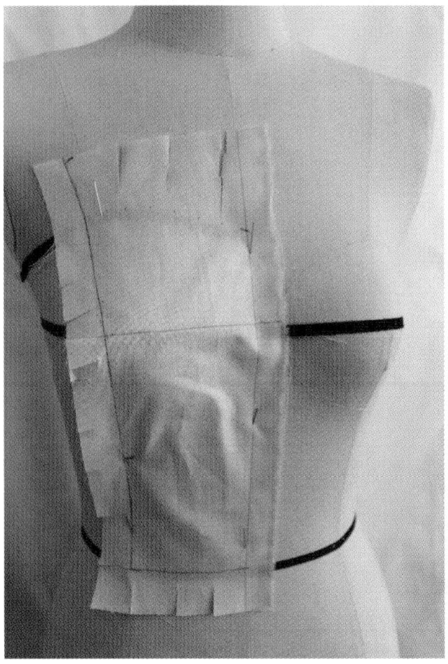

Fig. 6.39 Draping the CF panel of strapless bodice.

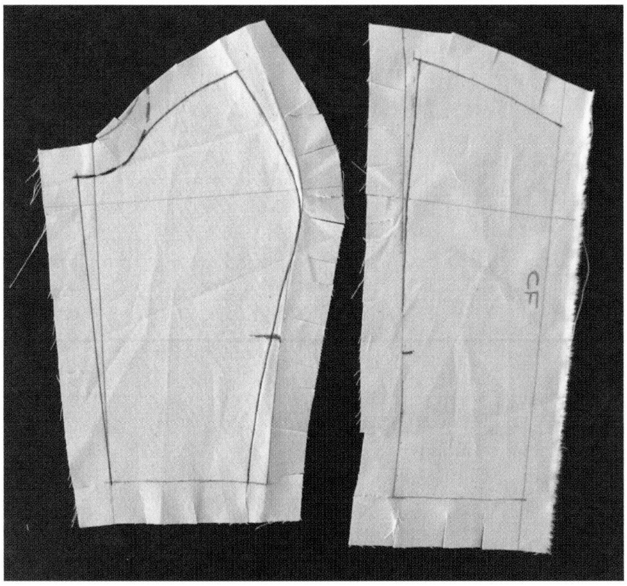

Fig. 6.40 Trued-up and altered front bodice pattern with adjustments under the arm.

and the CF to the bustline and the CF on the mannequin. Pin vertically to hold along the CF. This time you are only draping up to the style line on the overbust and not to the shoulder. (Looking at Fig. 6.39, you can see the neckline tape through the calico and how the excess calico at waist and PS has been trimmed away. The style line has been marked with a series of dots on the calico.)

4. Pin calico down the PS so that it sits flat. Snip up to the waistline if you need to release any tension.
5. Using a mechanical pencil, make a series of dots to mark off the neckline, plus dashes for junctions and a dash to denote a notch at the BP. A corresponding notch on the other panel piece at the BP will allow you to line up the pieces to check the drape later.
6. Remove from the mannequin and true up.
7. For the front side panel, align the SG to the SS and pin to hold, smoothing the fabric towards the PS and the CF.
8. Pin down the SS. If there is any tension through the waist or side, release it by snipping up to, but not through, the waistline or SS. Again, you are only draping to the style line so this negates the need to drape an armhole. Mark off with a mechanical pencil and remove the calico from the stand to true up (Fig 6.40).
9. Move to the back and repeat the process, starting at the CB to the PS, then the SS to the PS.
10. Check the drape using the method as per the bodice with PSs and don't forget to include notches (Fig. 6.41).

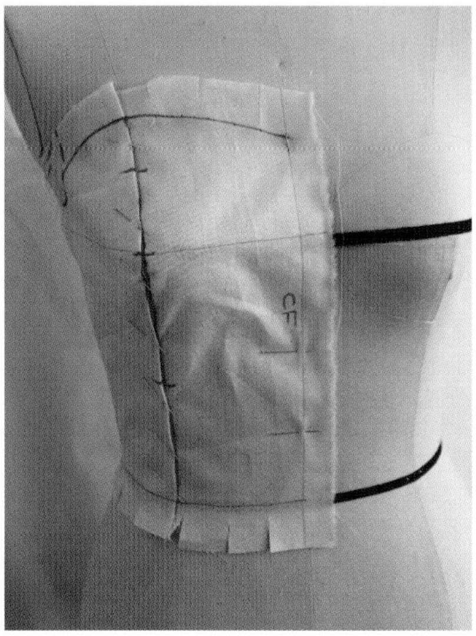

Fig. 6.41 Finished strapless bodice on mannequin.

Asymmetric Bodice (Fig. 6.42)

This bodice has really been created to show how the suppression of some of the previous bodices can be adapted to create less conventional design content but still have the right fit. This particular design has an asymmetric front and a plain fitted back. As the back is the same as the basic bodice with waist and shoulder dart listed earlier in this chapter, I have only draped the front. It has two asymmetric front panels and therefore the whole

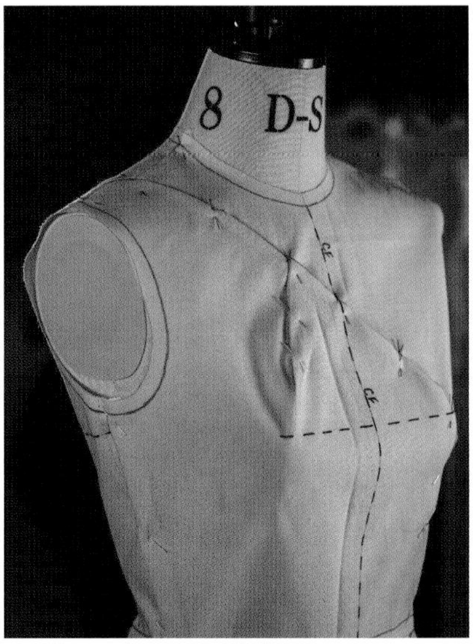

Fig. 6.42 Asymmetric bodice, front. (Photo: Yousef Al Nasser)

front has had to be draped rather than just the right-hand side. The seam runs from the right shoulder diagonally to the left BP, then down the PS to the waist. The suppression on the right-hand side is formed by a dart running from this seam to the right BP. It is the same design as in Fig. 6.1 at the beginning of this chapter.

1. Tape your style lines onto the mannequin, including the position of the bust dart. This way you can see if you like it or not and move it around before starting to drape (Fig. 6.43).
2. Prepare and block your calico as per the dimensions in Fig. 6.44. Note the position of the CF.
3. Position the calico on the CF where the bustline intersects and pin above the bust to hold. You can drape either panel first – the start point is the same – but I am beginning with the top panel with neck and shoulder lines (Fig. 6.45).
4. Smooth the calico across the chest up to the neck points and pin, snipping in to release the tension.
5. Smooth the calico along the left shoulder and pin flat. Smooth the calico along the right shoulder to the style line and pin.
6. Pin down the style line, then smooth the calico out to the SS. Snip into the waist if you need to release the tension at the bottom of the drape. Note that for the calico to sit flat on this half of the body you have to move the suppression out of this panel. If you are doing this correctly you should see the half of the calico you don't need in this panel start to stick out from the body from the BP (Fig. 6.46).
7. Mark off the panel with a dotted line along the shoulders, neck, armhole, SS, style line and waist, making sure to stay on the same side of the tape line each time (Fig. 6.47).
8. Remove from the stand and true up on the flat.

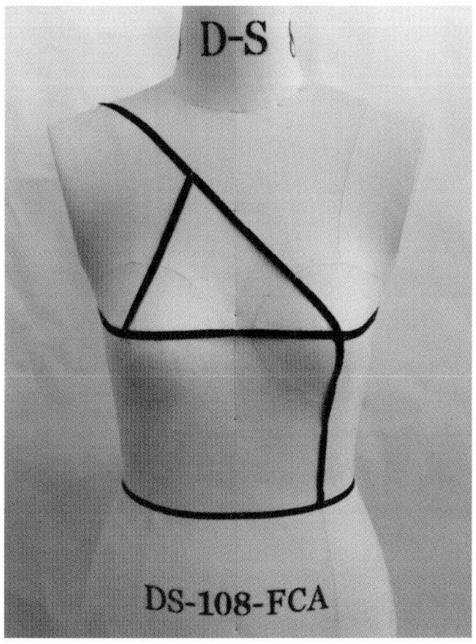

Fig. 6.43 Taping style lines to mannequin before draping.

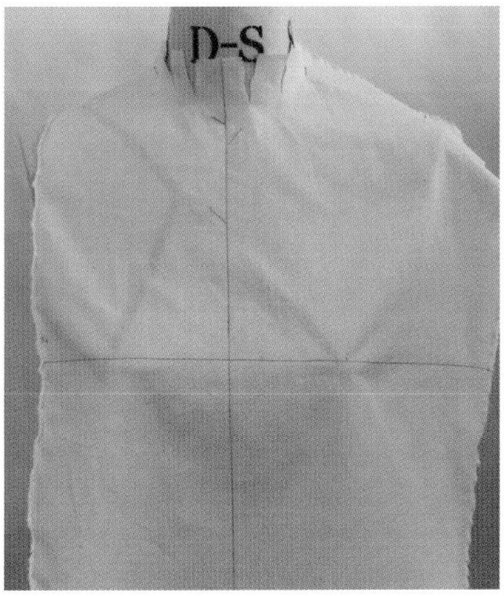

Fig. 6.45 Calico positioned for draping top panel of design that includes neckline and left armhole; neck is snipped to release tension.

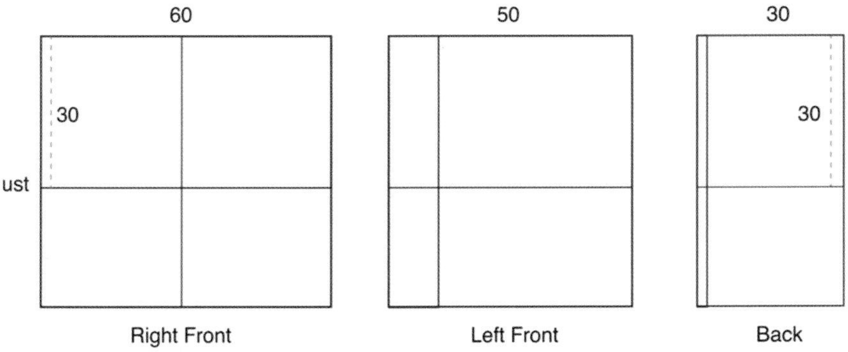

Fig. 6.44 Block dimensions for asymmetric bodice front.

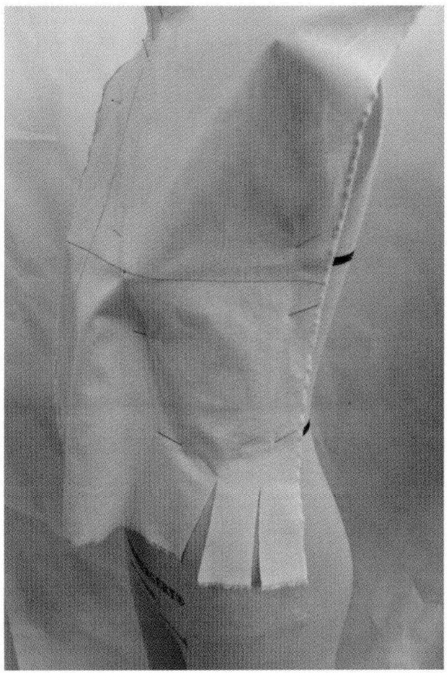

Fig. 6.46 Fitting drape for bodice left side and moving the suppression beyond style line.

Fig. 6.47 Marking style lines in with dotted line.

9. To drape the right side, align the CF and bustline of the next piece of calico and pin to hold on CF and BPs. It will look as though you are about to do the same thing twice but remember this is for the other side (Fig. 6.48).
10. Smooth the calico below the bustline out towards the SS and pin across to the left-hand PS. Snip into the calico up to the waistline to release the tension in the calico and create a snug fit.

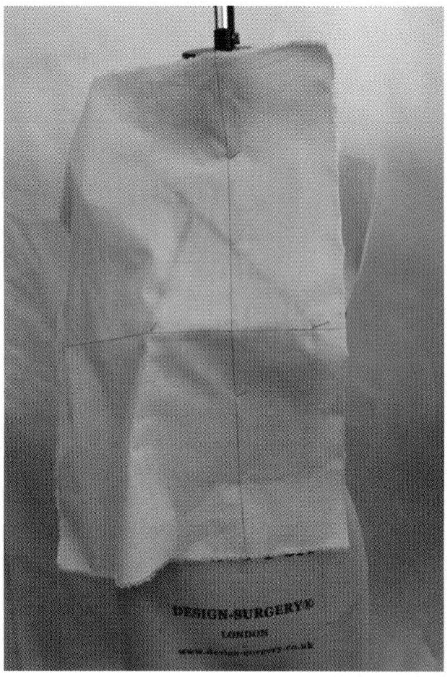

Fig. 6.48 Aligning calico to drape right front panel of asymmetric design with dart.

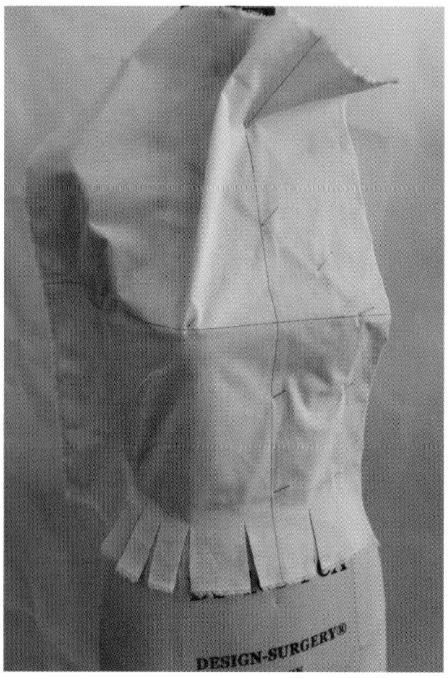

Fig. 6.49 Putting in bust dart.

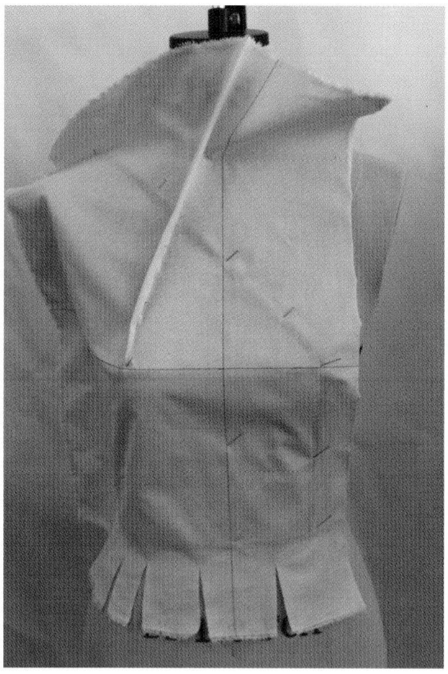

Fig. 6.50 Fit is refined and re-pinned firmly.

11. Smooth the calico up along the style line across the chest and roughly create the dart running from the style line to the BP by folding the calico and running the fold out at the BP (Fig. 6.49).
12. Smooth the calico up to the shoulder line and pin. Adjust the fit and the dart before pinning properly (Fig. 6.50).
13. Mark out the style lines, waist, dart, shoulder, armhole and SS with dotted lines before removing from the stand and truing up.
14. On the flat, drop the armhole down by 2cm and out by 1cm and drop the neckline at the CF by 1cm. Foreshorten the dart by 2cm. Trim away the excess allowance to 2cm

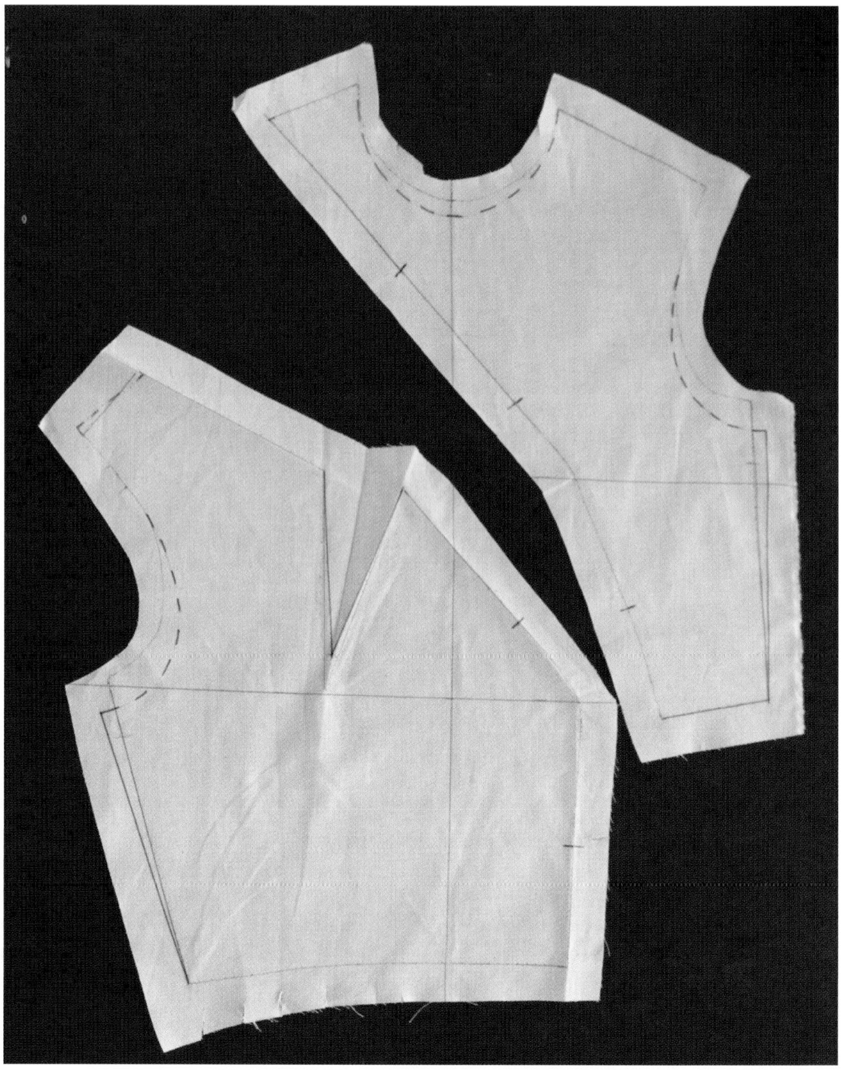

Fig. 6.51 Two panels on the flat with dropped armhole and neck and foreshortened dart.

so that your drape looks like Fig. 6.51.

15. Check the drape by putting the left/top panel back into position first and pinning. Position the right-hand panel at CF and bustline, folding the dart in and pinning it closed. Turn the allowance along the edge of the style line under and align it to the style line on the top panel. Pin the two panels together from the top. Note how few pins are being used but the drape is still nice and flat (Fig. 6.52).
16. Make any adjustments necessary and transfer to the master pattern.

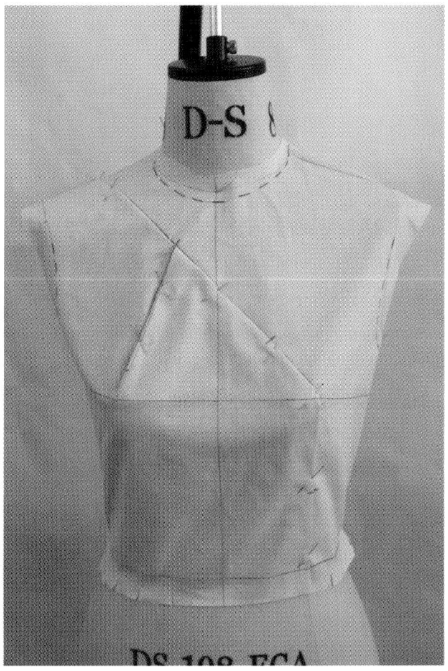

Fig. 6.52 Checking drape of asymmetric front panels.

Other Stylistic Variations

Armhole variations: It is better to use the process described in the previous bodices and get the basic block/sloper right first before modifying your armholes. Your armhole can be whatever shape you want and this can be drawn on the flat after you have adjusted the armhole. If you want to play around with it in three dimensions to see if you like it or not first, use one of the adhesive styling tapes to draw it onto your bodice and have a look (Figs 6.53 and 6.54).

Neckline variations: As with the strapless bodice, your neckline can be styled as you want just by taping it onto the mannequin before you drape. Alternatively, it can be done on the flat or on the stand using the styling tape (Figs 6.55 and 6.56).

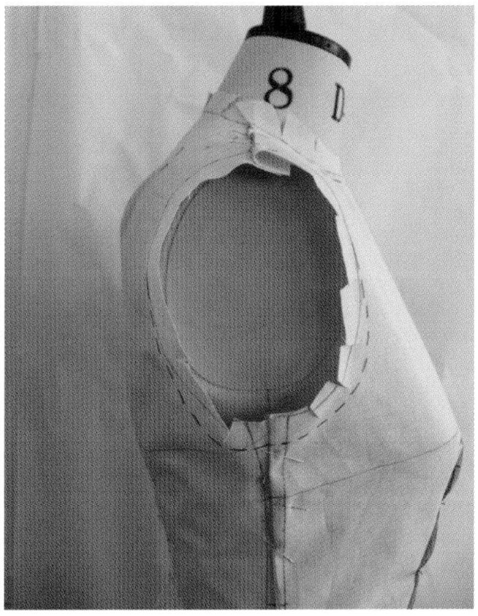

Fig. 6.53 Basic armhole dropped down and out by 2cm from arm plate.

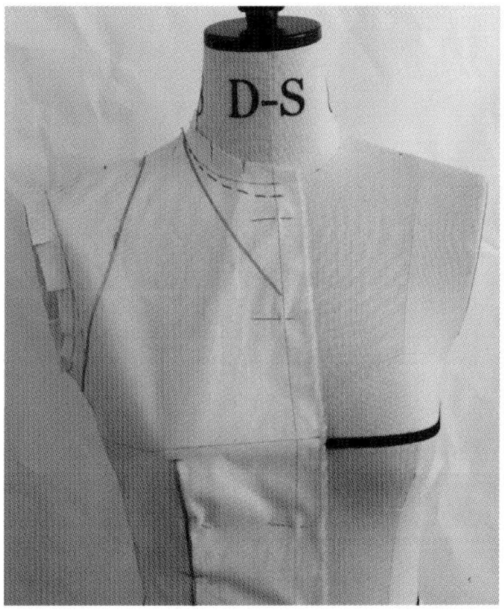

Fig. 6.55 Drawing new armhole and neckline with tape.

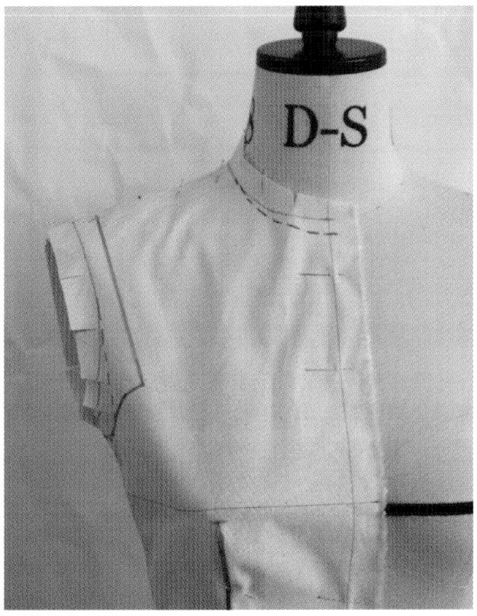

Fig. 6.54 Drawing new armhole with tape.

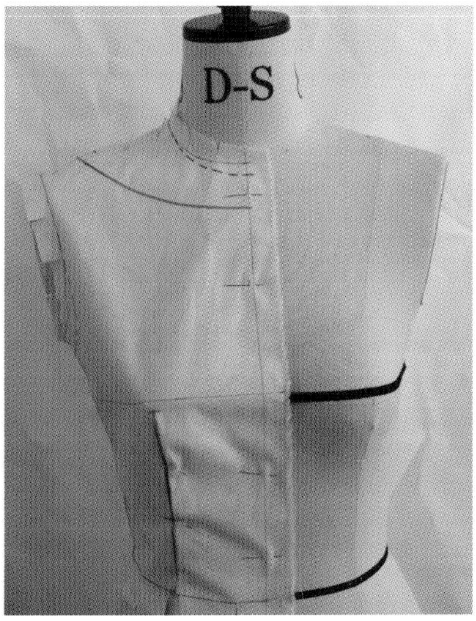

Fig. 6.56 Drawing new neckline with tape.

The Skirt

7

The modern-day Western skirt is both highly gendered and sexualized, with a controversial history remarkably different from its humble beginnings. The skirt is actually the second-oldest garment known to mankind, only pre-dated by the loin cloth. Originally it was a simple, genderless garment as it was effectively a rectangular piece of cloth wrapped around the body for practicality's sake. In Ancient civilizations, men often adopted a knee-length skirt whilst women wore floor- or ankle-length versions; the necessity for wearing something akin to trousers was dictated only by the extremities of the climate you lived in or the need to ride a horse frequently. As the latter in particular seems to have been more of a masculine occupation, it is thought that this practicality may have been a driver in the gendering of trousers and skirts. According to the Victoria and Albert Museum, the big change that definitively brought trousers into the mainstream for men was tailoring. Prior to this, both men and women wore unshaped tunics but as such garments became tighter and shorter in the fifteenth century CE, fashionable men began to wear tight legwear or hose as outerwear. Whilst there was still a propensity for volume in the rest of men's clothing, these revolutionary steps in garment technology and tailoring saw a clearly defined sartorial gender divide being created for the first time in Western society, with the wearing of the bodice and the skirt relegated to women.

This perspective is, of course, a very one-sided one, as in several cultures from India to Japan and South East Asia, robes and skirts have always been and still remain completely acceptable attire for adult men. Occasionally, the male skirt is seen in catwalk shows and promoted by European designers but it is never widely adopted for mainstream wear. Presumably this resistance is due to our Western perception that the skirt is inherently feminine and therefore the wearer must be less of a man to wear one.

It was not until around the sixteenth century that the skirt started to take on social importance and become exclusively synonymous with womenswear. In the seventeenth and eighteenth centuries more volume was added; as the yardage and the weight increased so the necessity for internal supports did too. Skirts became so large that they had to be supported with hoops, petticoats and crinolines which, combined with corsets, created the illusion of the very tiny waist, thus setting the benchmark for perceived ideals of female beauty and modesty. The nineteenth century saw the skirt silhouette become leaner as all of the volume moved around to the back of the body into a bustle over a lady's derriere and for the first time hemlines were raised about 15cm (6in) off the ground to allow more freedom of movement and to demonstrate that the polite society of the Victorian era would not implode with the occasional glimpse of a lady's ankles!

By the 1920s most of the corsetry and hoops had been stripped away, with designers like Chanel designing shorter, wider skirts that finished just below the knee and provided a significantly more practical silhouette that was more in keeping with the lifestyles of its wearers. This is quite likely the turning point in the politics of the modern skirt which was to see a yo-yoing of hemlines over the next few decades defiantly linked with politics, economics and societal divisions over women's roles in the home and workplace. With the Swinging Sixties came the Western world's most controversial skirt yet – the mini. Credited in the UK as being the invention of the designer Mary Quant, in France it is believed to have been the creation of the Parisian couturier André Courrèges. The rising hemline was linked to increased prosperity and sexual liberation. Prior to this, the skirt hadn't revealed much skin; it was always a conservative length, often with uncomfortable cuts and fabrics. The thigh-high miniskirt was considered scandalous by many but also seen as a sign of women's liberation by others in an era of unprecedented social change. What is not in doubt is the absolute totality with which Western women adopted it, regardless of their age, job or body type. Its unabashed links to rebellion have seen it make many a comeback, decade after decade.

NOTE ON DRAPING SKIRTS

If your skirt is symmetrical you need only drape on the right half of the body. With regard to length, you only need drape to the bottom of your stand, then the pattern can be extended to the full desired length on your master pattern. Ensure that you know the length you are working to before you begin: knee, midi, maxi, etc.

Left: Fig. 7.1 Gathered skirt with yoke. (Photo: Yousef Al

Simple Straight Skirt (Fig. 7.2)

The silhouette of the skirt is obviously straight, with a hem parallel to the floor: sometimes it is called the pencil skirt. According to *Vogue*, the origin of the pencil skirt as a fashion icon stems from an incident in 1908 when Mrs Edith Hart O. Berg became the first American woman to fly as a passenger on an aeroplane. Allegedly, on being seated, she tied a length of rope around her ankles to save the fabric of her skirt from billowing in flight, thus inspiring a trend for skirts that tapered sharply around the shins and forced the wearers to move with short rapid steps. The severity of this style ensured it was dubbed the 'hobble skirt' and most women opted for something they could actually walk in. The pencil skirt became a defining garment for 1950s sex appeal with its obvious physical restrictions on gait and its emphasis on particular parts of the female anatomy. My own spin on it as a pattern cutter is far less thrilling: it is, in fact, the skirt equivalent of a basic block from which most other designs are derived and a direct fit to the body. From a creative point of view it is the starting point for realizing more challenging designs.

1. Tape up your mannequin with waist- and hiplines. Make sure the hipline is parallel to the floor by stepping away from the mannequin to check.
2. Prepare and block your calico as per the dimensions in Fig. 7.3.
3. Align the hipline on the calico with the hipline on the mannequin where it intersects the CF. Pin vertically on the CF to the bottom of the stand to hold the calico in place. There should be quite a bit extra above the waistline of the mannequin (Fig. 7.4).
4. Ease the calico across the mannequin along the hipline and towards the SS. Pin to hold on the SS. Allow a little ease or fullness for

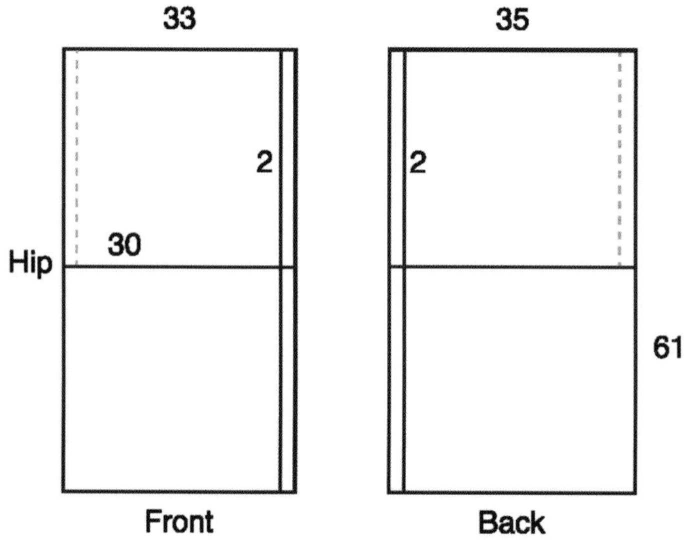

Fig. 7.3 Block dimensions for straight skirt.

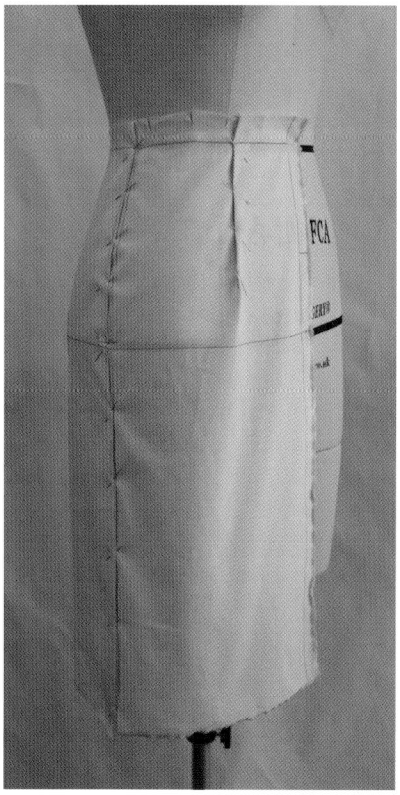
Fig. 7.2 Half drape for simple straight skirt.

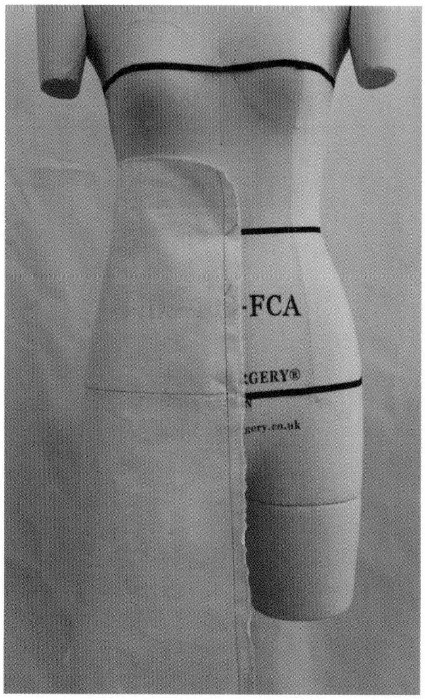

Fig. 7.4 Aligning CF and hipline to begin draping skirt front.

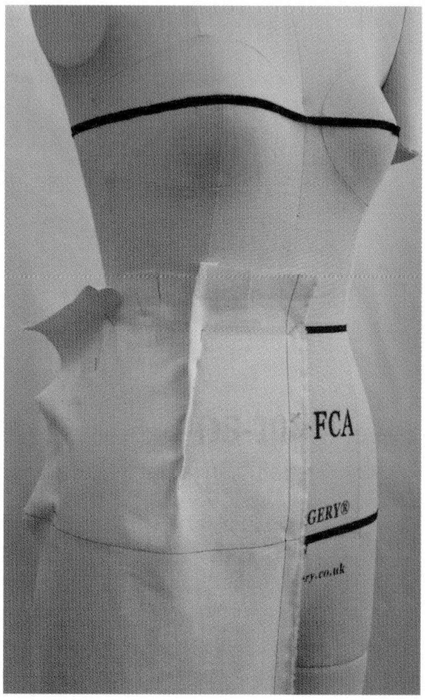

Fig. 7.5 Putting waist dart into skirt.

movement – if the drape is skintight you won't be able to sit down in your skirt!

5. There will be excess fabric at the waist which will need to be suppressed to create a dart over the PS. If there is a lot of excess then consider splitting the volume across more than one dart. Pin the dart position. There may also be some tension at the waist so snip down vertically towards the waist point and snip horizontally through the side to the SS if you need to. As this will relax the waist and SS you may need to adjust a little and re-pin (Fig. 7.5).
6. With a mechanical pencil, mark off the waist SS and dart with a line of dots. Use a bar to denote corners and edges. Remove from the mannequin to true up.
7. Align the hipline on the calico with the hipline on the mannequin where it intersects the CB. Pin vertically on the CB to hold the calico in place.
8. Ease the calico across the mannequin along the hipline and towards the SS. Pin to hold on the SS. Allow a little ease or fullness for movement.
9. There will be excess fabric at the waist which will need to be suppressed to create a dart over the PS. Pin the dart position. There may also be some tension at the waist, so snip down vertically towards the waist point and snip horizontally through the side to the SS if you need to. As this will relax the waist and SS, you may need to adjust a little and re-pin.
10. With a mechanical pencil, mark off the waist SS and dart with a line of dots. Use a bar to denote corners and edges. Remove from the mannequin to true up (Fig. 7.6).
11. Trim off the excess calico leaving a 2cm allowance around the side and waist on the front and back.
12. Check the drape by re-aligning the front and back pieces on the mannequin, then fold the calico back under along the sewing line at the SS before pinning to the SS for the front panel as in Fig. 7.2. The back can be seen in Fig. 7.7. Make any alterations necessary and re-mark in a different colour before taking the assembly off the stand and transferring it to a master.

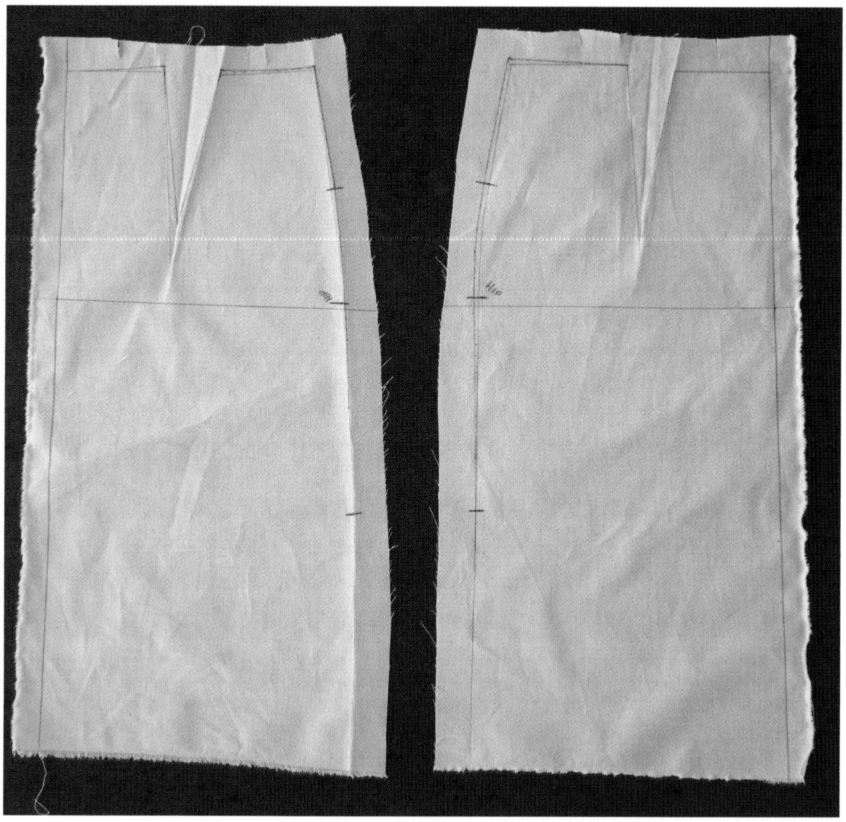

Fig. 7.6 Front and back pieces of straight skirt on the flat.

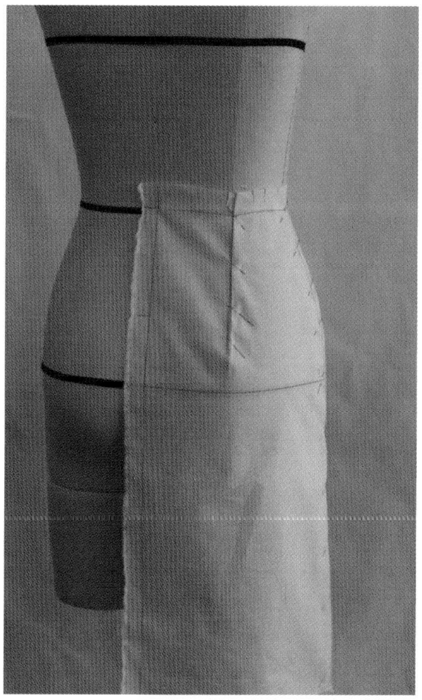

Fig. 7.7 Straight skirt, back view.

EFFECT OF DARTS

The vanishing point of a skirt dart is determined by the fullness of the hip. The fuller the hip the shorter the dart will be. Front skirt darts are usually shorter than back skirt darts and both must end above the hipline for a flat fit.

High-Waisted Straight Skirt (Fig. 7.8)

This variant on the straight skirt extends the top of the waist higher above the natural waist of the mannequin and up the ribcage. Where it finishes is a stylistic decision and a good fit can be achieved through the use of extended darts.

1. Tape up the mannequin with waist- and hiplines. In addition, mark off the style line to denote the top of the skirt (Fig. 7.9).
2. Prepare and block the calico as per the measurements in Fig. 7.10. Note that the allowance above the waistline is more than for the straight skirt to accommodate the higher waist.
3. Repeat steps 3–12 as for the straight skirt. This time there will be significantly more shaping through the darts to reflect the suppression of the body through the waist. Look at Figs 7.11, 7.12 and 7.13.

Fig. 7.8 Finished drape for high-waisted skirt with shaped waistline. (Photo: Yousef Al Nasser)

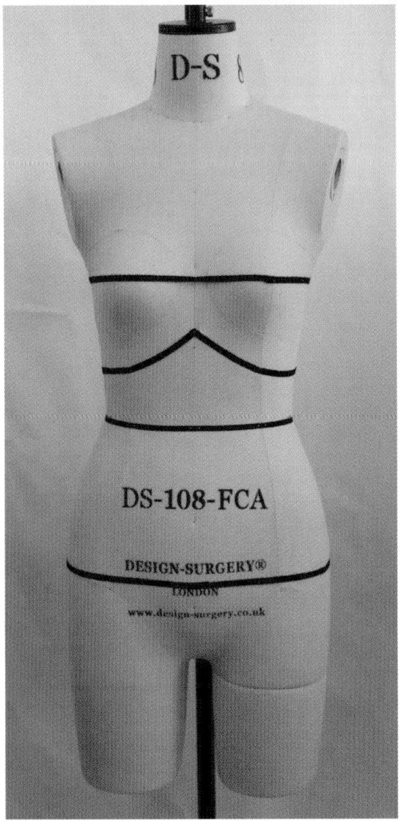

Fig. 7.9 Mannequin taped for high-waisted skirt.

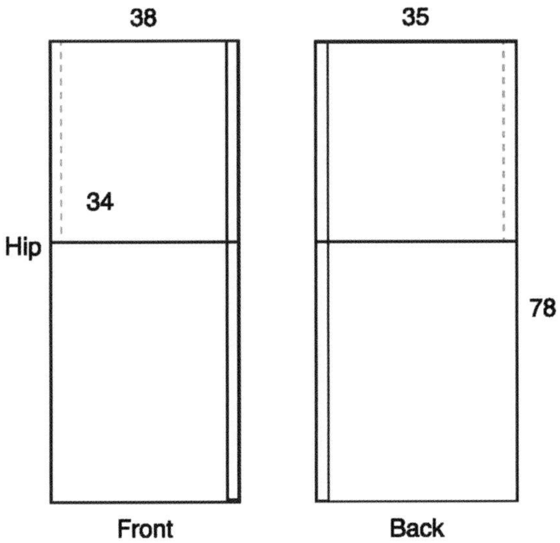

Fig. 7.10 Block diagram for high-waisted skirt.

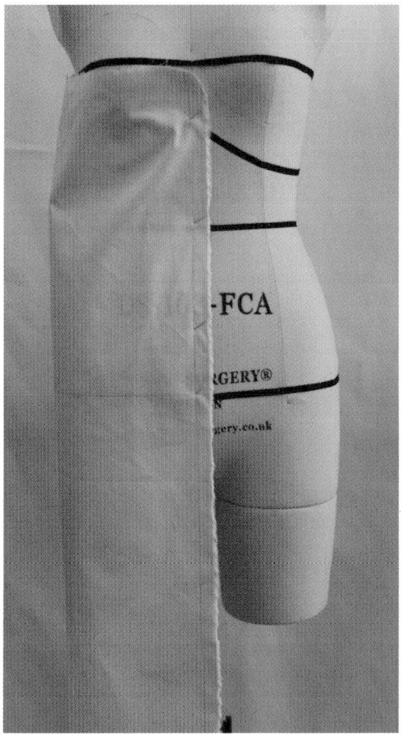

Fig. 7.11 Positioning calico for high-waisted skirt front.

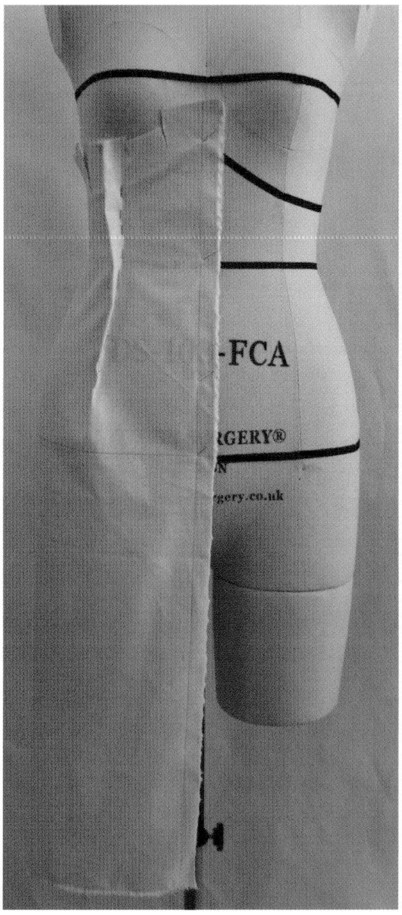

Fig. 7.12 Dart is elongated as it runs from above the waist downwards.

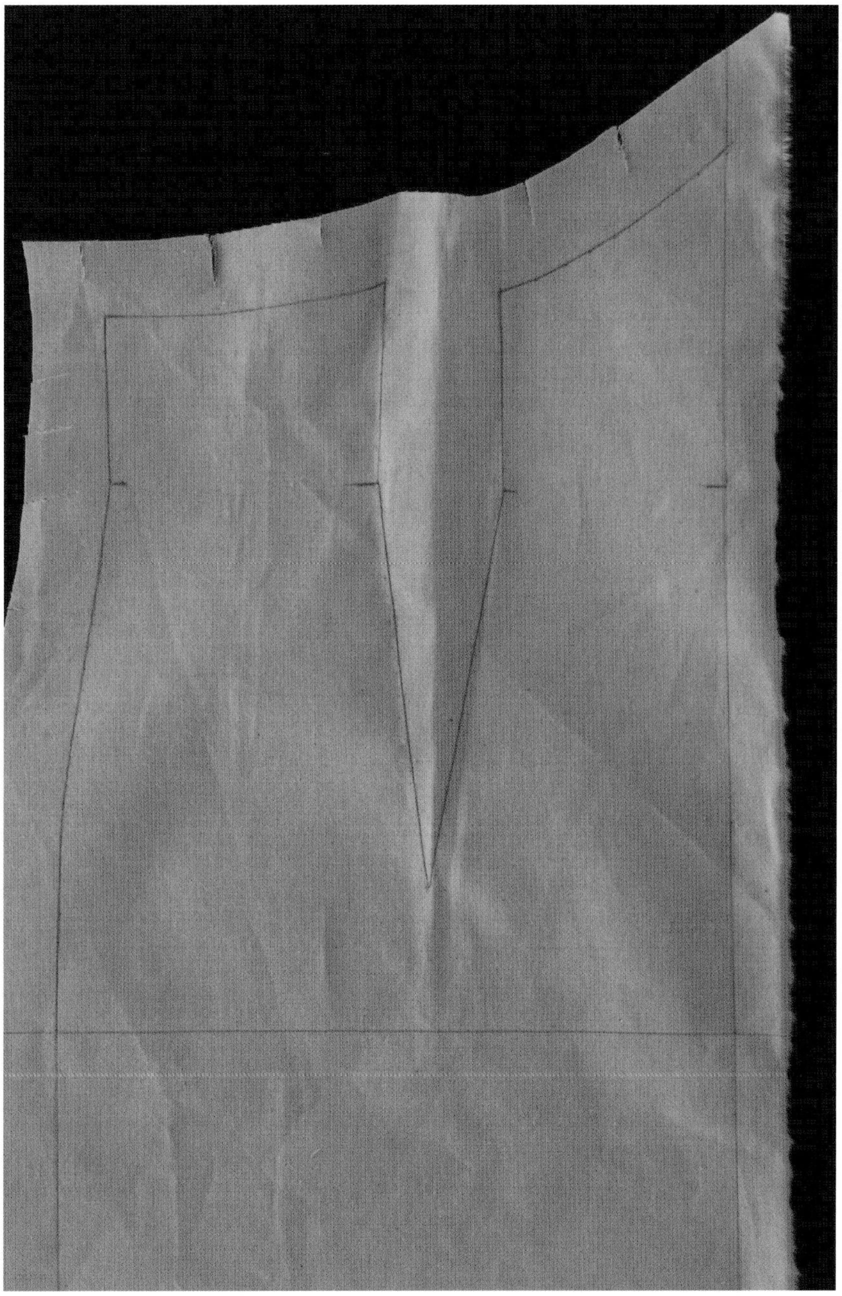

Fig. 7.13 Shape of elongated dart on the flat.

Wrap-Over Skirt (Fig. 7.14)

This drape is for a skirt that effectively has two front pieces that extend one over the other at the CF to fasten at the princess or side seams. You will only need to drape the right side even though the front pattern pieces are slightly different at the waist.

Mark off the right waistline and the left on the same piece of calico. Trace the right side off as is and flip the calico over to trace off the left for the master pattern.

1. Tape up your mannequin with waist- and hiplines. Make sure the hipline is parallel to the floor by stepping away from the mannequin to check.
2. Prepare and block your calico as per the dimensions in Fig. 7.15. You will have two front pieces for your skirt – a left and a right. Make sure that you are marking your drape guidelines on the front of each piece so that you do actually have a left and a right and that the fit is the same both sides.
3. Pin on any style lines – in this instance the PS indicates the outside edge of the skirt wrap and the right half of the wrap is slanted downwards away from the waist slightly. There is no practical reason for this – it is purely stylistic (Fig. 7.16).
4. Align the hipline on the calico with the hipline on the mannequin where it intersects the CF. Pin vertically on the CF to the bottom of the stand to hold the calico in place.
5. Smooth the calico along the hipline from the CF towards the SS and pin to hold (Fig. 7.17).
6. Smooth the calico along to the PS where the wrap ends and pin in place. Don't pin too tightly as there needs to be some ease across the hip. Create the dart and pin through the waist. Follow this in Figs 7.18, 7.19, 7.20 and 7.21.
7. Repeat stages 5–12 as given for the straight skirt but transfer a right front and a left front onto the master pattern.

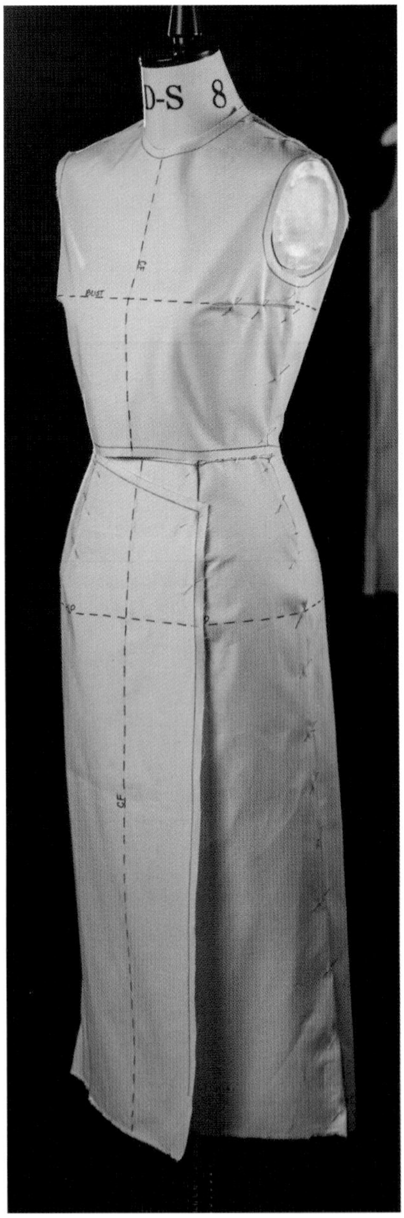

Fig. 7.14 Finished drape for wrap-over skirt. (Photo: Yousef Al Nasser)

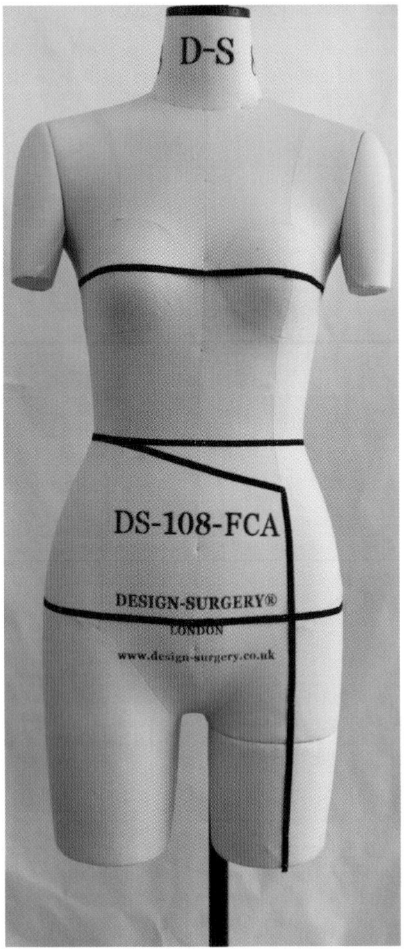

Fig. 7.16 Mannequin taped for wrap-over skirt.

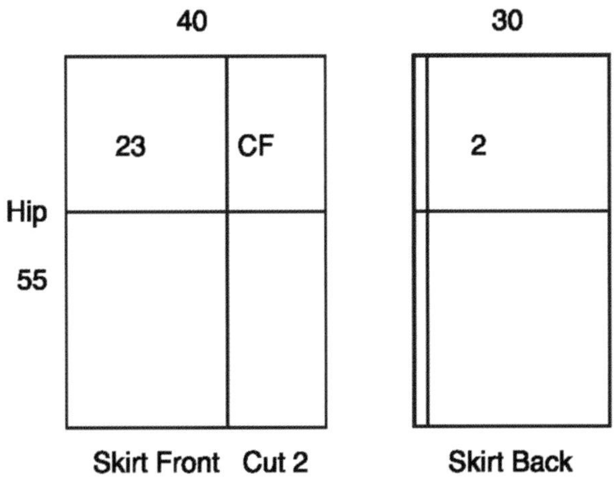

Fig. 7.15 Block dimensions for wrap-over skirt.

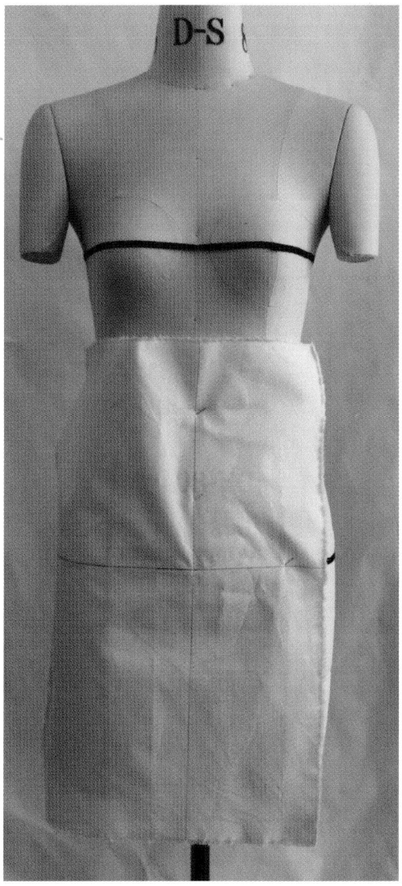

Fig. 7.17 Draping right-hand side of wrap-over skirt; calico is smoothed to SS and pinned down the style line and a dart has been created for fit.

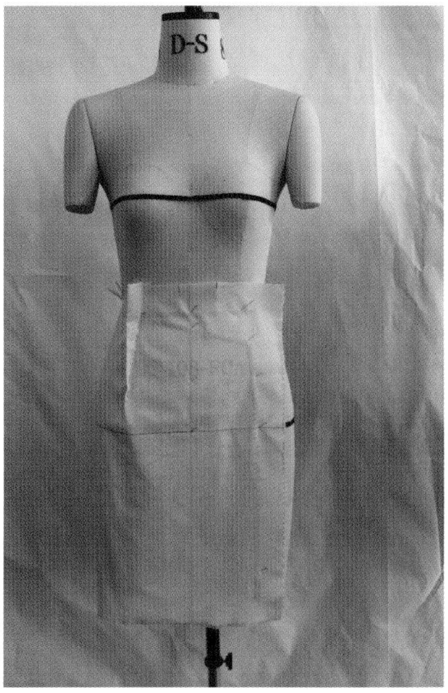

Fig. 7.18 Refined front piece trued up, with excess allowance trimmed away.

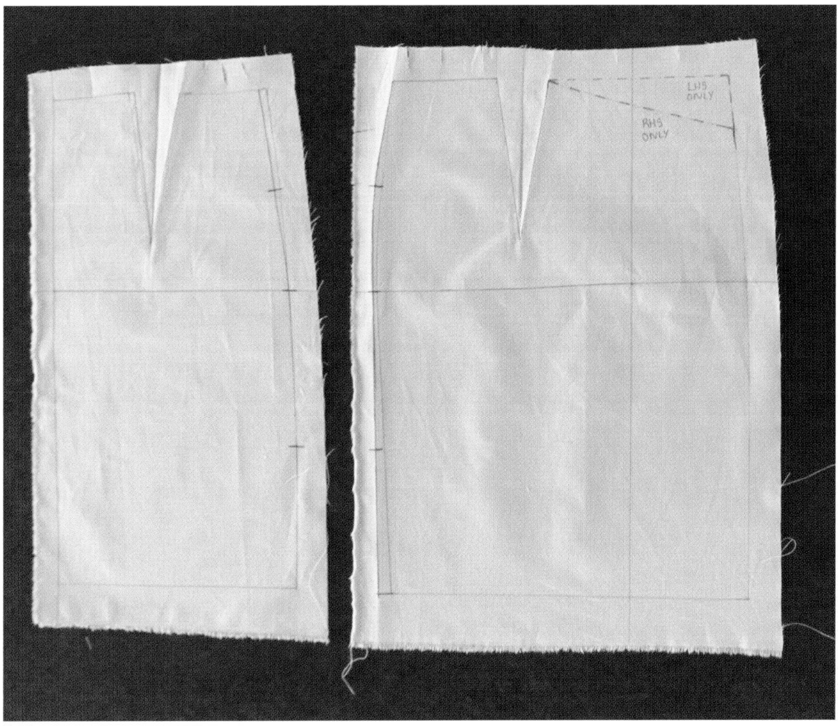

Fig. 7.19 Finished drape for wrap-over skirt on the flat.

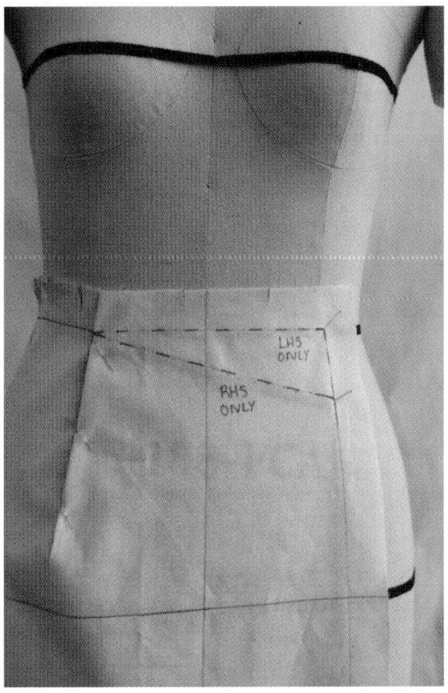

Fig. 7.20 Final drape for wrap-over skirt, front, with right and left side waistlines marked out.

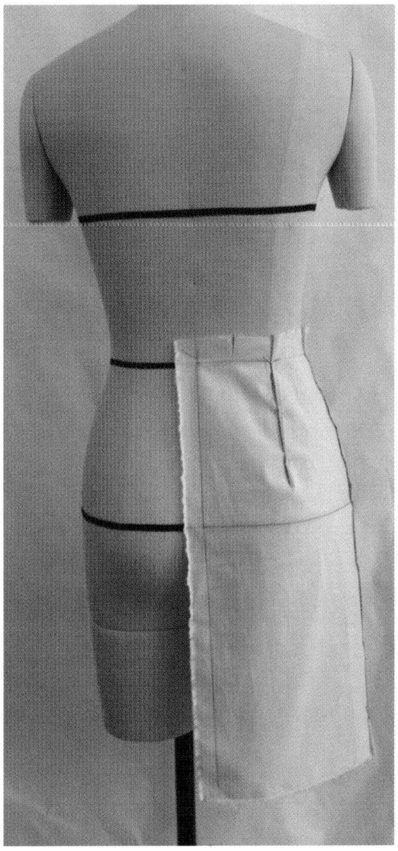

Fig. 7.21 Final drape for wrap-over skirt, back.

A-Line Skirt

This drape removes the dart at the waist, putting the suppression at the bottom of the skirt. This is what gives it its characteristic A-shaped silhouette with a flat front and back from waist to hip (Fig. 7.22).

1. Tape up the mannequin with waist- and hiplines.
2. Prepare and block the calico as per the measurements in Fig. 7.23.
3. Align the hipline on the calico with the hipline on the mannequin where it intersects the CF. Pin vertically on the CF to the bottom of the stand to hold the calico in place.
4. Smooth the calico along the hipline from CF towards the SS. This time the calico needs to be flush to the mannequin to eliminate the dart at the waist. As a result the hipline on the calico will start to tilt downwards from the hipline on the mannequin at the PS, making a triangular silhouette and moving the volume round into the hemline and away from the stand (Fig. 7.24).
5. Snip down towards the waist and horizontally into the SS to alter the fit.
6. Mark off waist and SSs and the new position of the hipline which will now be curved. Remove the calico from the stand.
7. True up (Fig. 7.25).
8. Repeat the process for the skirt back, working outwards from the CB.
9. Put the pieces together to adjust and make final alterations before transferring to paper for the master pattern. Extend the hem on the master pattern for the final skirt length.

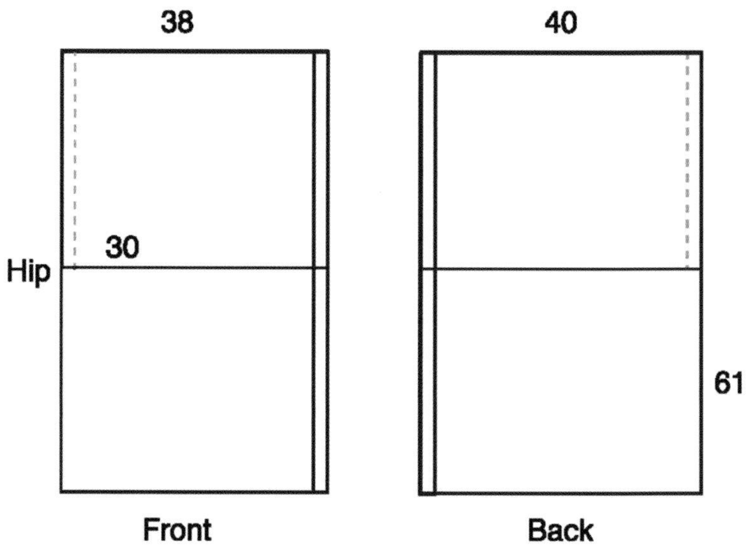

Fig. 7.23 Block dimensions for A-line skirt.

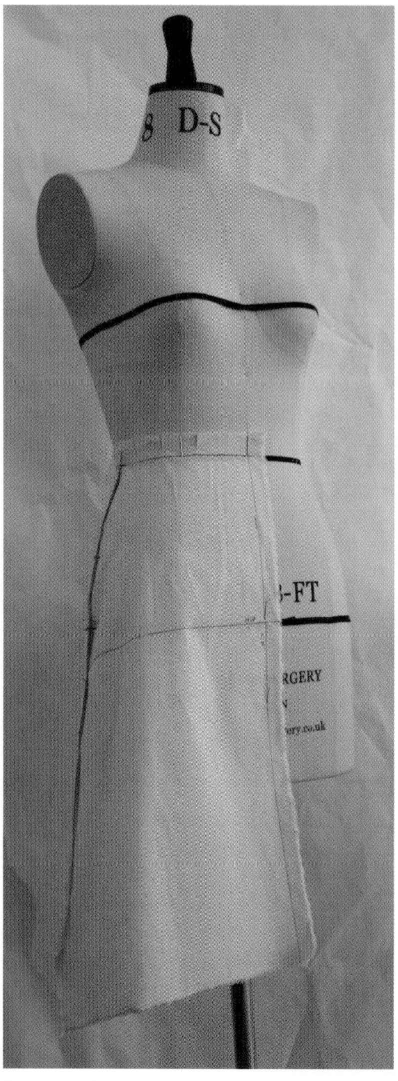

Fig. 7.22 A-line skirt drape.

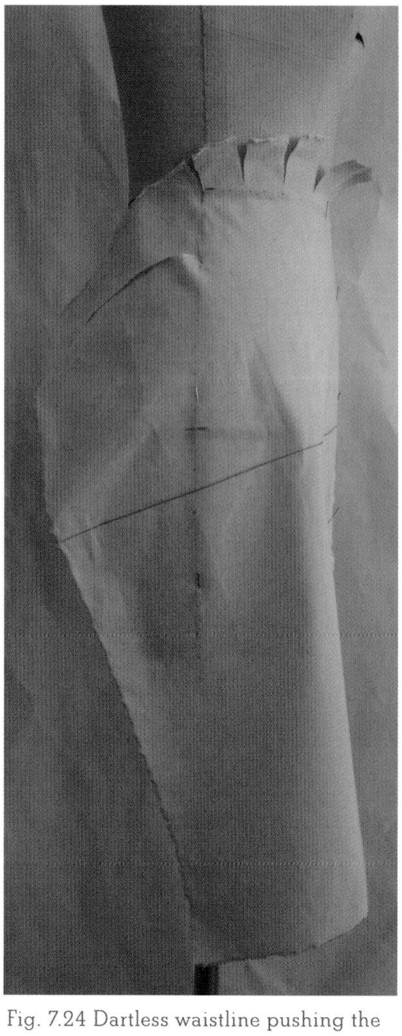

Fig. 7.24 Dartless waistline pushing the suppression into hem to create A-line the hipline moves downwards.

Fig. 7.25 A-line skirt on the flat.

Circular Skirt (Figs 7.26 and 7.27)

This basic circle skirt has no suppression at the waist and minimal seaming. The fabric is smoothed over the waist and hip and allowed to fall freely to create a voluminous flared hemline. The SG is on the CF but will start to shift downwards so that part of the skirt is on the bias. (The bias is at a 45-degree angle to the SG.) The generous volume of fabric at the hemline and its use of the bias creates wonderful movement and is synonymous with clothes from the 1950s. The circular skirt can also be easily flat pattern cut, with the pattern piece looking something like a doughnut, with a small hole in the middle for the waist. However, the benefit of draping, particularly in the real fabric, is that designers can see how their cloth will hang and behave. With practice you will be able to control whether the SG is at the CF or SS.

1. Tape up the mannequin with waist- and hiplines.
2. Prepare and block the calico as per the measurements in Fig. 7.28. in this instance we are blocking a front quarter and a back quarter on the right-hand side. The pieces are quite large so you may break into a

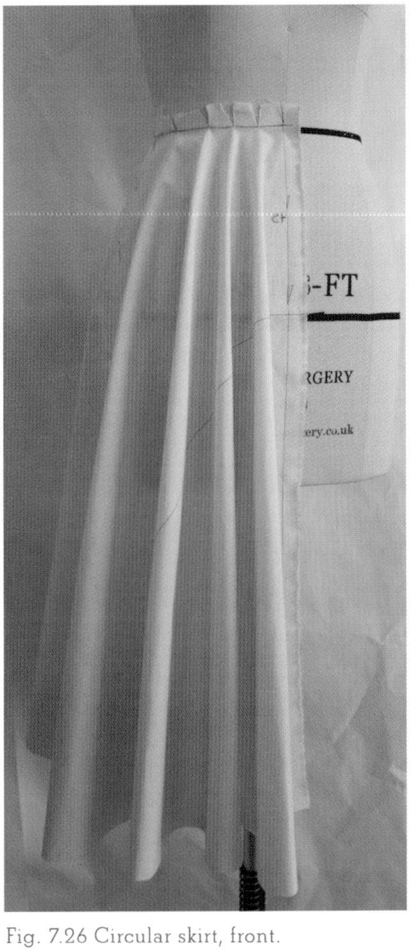

Fig. 7.26 Circular skirt, front.

Fig. 7.27 Circular skirt, back.

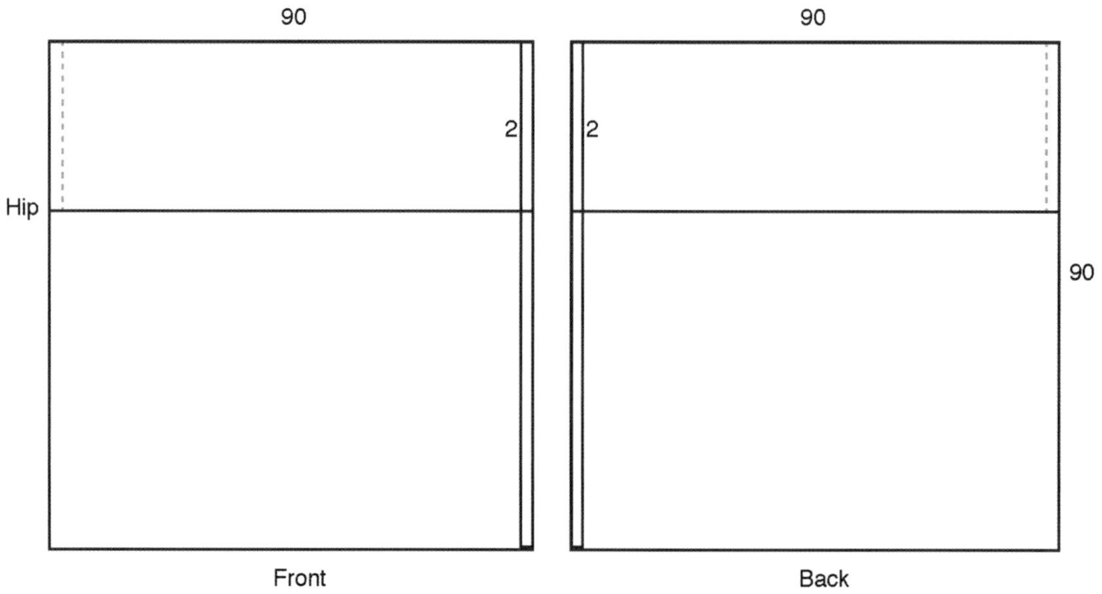

Fig. 7.28 Block dimensions for circular skirt.

sweat if you are blocking correctly!

3. Align the hipline on the calico with the hipline on the mannequin where it intersects the CF. Pin vertically on the CF to the bottom of the stand to hold the calico in place.
4. From the CF, slash 2.5cm horizontally at 2.5cm above the waistline and put in a pin. A triangular fold of cloth will naturally appear at the base of the pin in the skirt as you begin to manoeuvre the volume down and

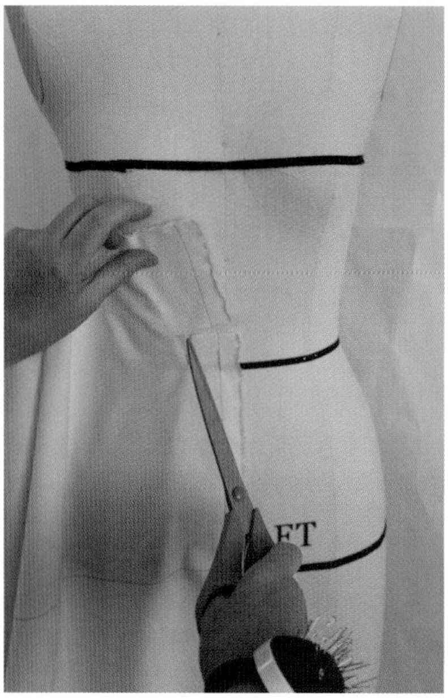

Fig. 7.29 Snipping in from CF on front quarter to start angling the volume of fabric downwards.skirt.

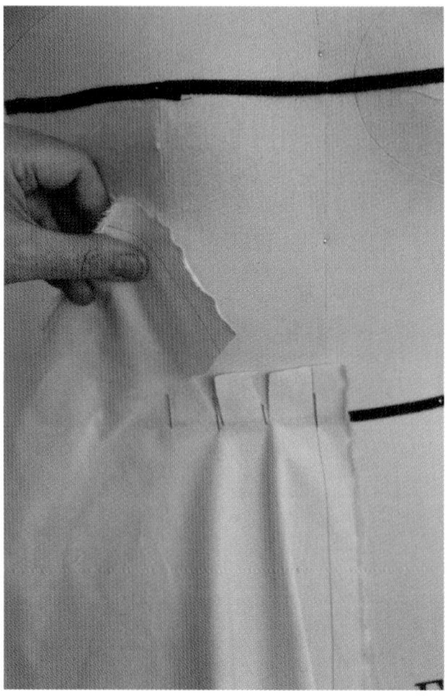

Fig. 7.30 Snipping down to waist, creating volume at base of each snip.

out through the hemline.

5. Move the top edge downwards and snip across 2.5cm horizontally, then vertically, and pin. Continue to the SS (Figs 7.29, 7.30 and 7.31).
6. Mark off the new waistline and SS with dots.
7. Take off the stand and true up (Fig. 7.32).
8. Repeat for the back quarter.
9. Put both halves back onto the mannequin with the back SS overlapping the front SS. Pin together from the top, check the fit,

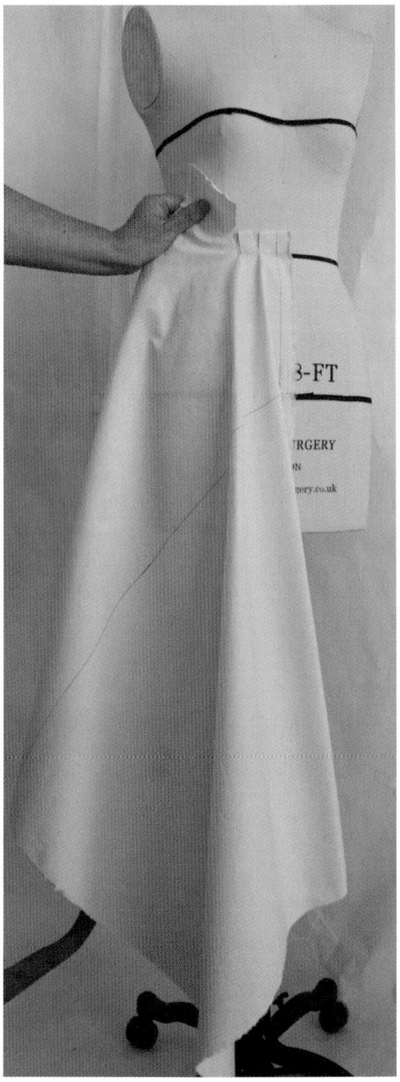

Fig. 7.31 Volume moves into the flare at the hemline with the help of gravity.

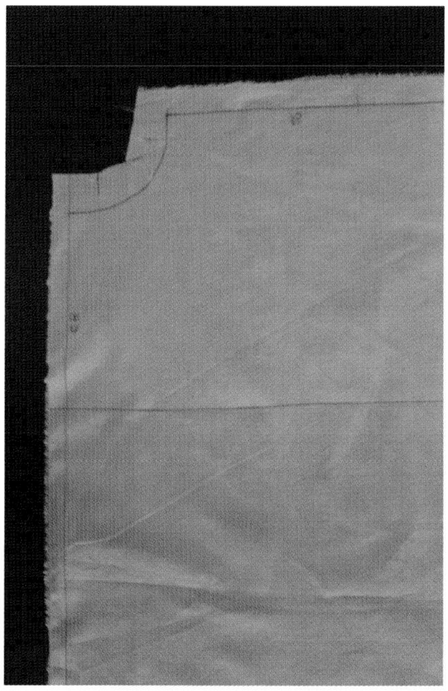

Fig. 7.32 Front quarter with curved waistband on the flat.

adjust and add notches.

10. The final drape will still have its corners creating a handkerchief hem so this could be left or levelled off (*see* Levelling Skirt Hems) depending on your aesthetic (Fig. 7.33).

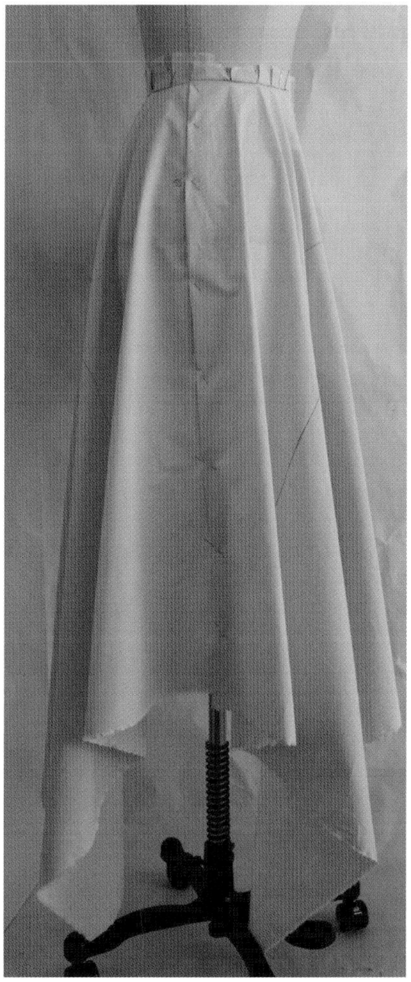

Fig. 7.33 Circular skirt half-drape before hem is levelled.

Double Circular Skirt

This is a variant on the circular skirt but with twice the volume. Instead of draping with quarter-circles you will be draping with a half-circle per quarter waist. The resulting effect is an extremely voluminous and often quite weighty skirt – think Dior's iconic 'New Look' from 1947 with the 'Bar Suit' as a reference. In America in the 1950s and 1960s the style was called the 'Poodle Skirt' and its characteristic volume was exploited to show off pictorial border prints of lifestyle-orientated designs like bowling scenes, music and dancing, etc., on printed cotton. The skirt's true origin is actually the *folklorico* skirt from Mexico: traditionally two full circles of indigenous textiles are sewn together and tied at the waist. These highly decorative pieces were frequently worn by Frida Kahlo as a political statement about her cultural identity and allegiance to Mexico. Beware – it will take a significant length of cloth to create. This particular drape used 1.8 metres to create a quarter!

1. Tape up the mannequin with waist- and hipline.
2. Prepare and block the calico as per the measurements in Fig. 7.34. In this instance we are blocking a front quarter and a back quarter on the right-hand side.
3. Measure the quarter waist, making a note of the PS.
4. From the CF of your calico block use a tape measure to create a small half-circle the length of the waist quarter from CF to SS. Include the PS position and mark off in pencil. Slash through the middle towards the PS to help with positioning on the mannequin.
5. Align the hipline on the calico with the hipline on the mannequin where it intersects the CF. Pin vertically on the CF to the bottom of the stand to hold the calico in place.
6. From the CF, slash 2.5cm horizontally at 2.5cm above the waistline and pin.
7. Continue snipping across and down, manipulating the top edge of the cloth downwards as you go, as per the circular skirt, until you reach the SS.
8. Repeat steps 6–10 as given for the circular skirt (Fig. 7.35).

GENEROSITY WITH FABRIC

The amount of flare you can add to a skirt is dependent on the width of cloth you drape with and how much extra calico you have given yourself above the waistline. The more fabric you have the more you can drop into deeper flares. If even more fullness is required you will need to include additional seams; these can be incorporated into the design or hidden in the folds of the finished skirt.

FABRIC BULK

When positioning larger volumes of calico on the stand you may need to pin some of the excess to the back or the other side to keep it out of the way whilst you continue to pin on the CF and hipline. The weight of the extra volume will distort the CF by pulling it downwards if it is not pinned out of the way.

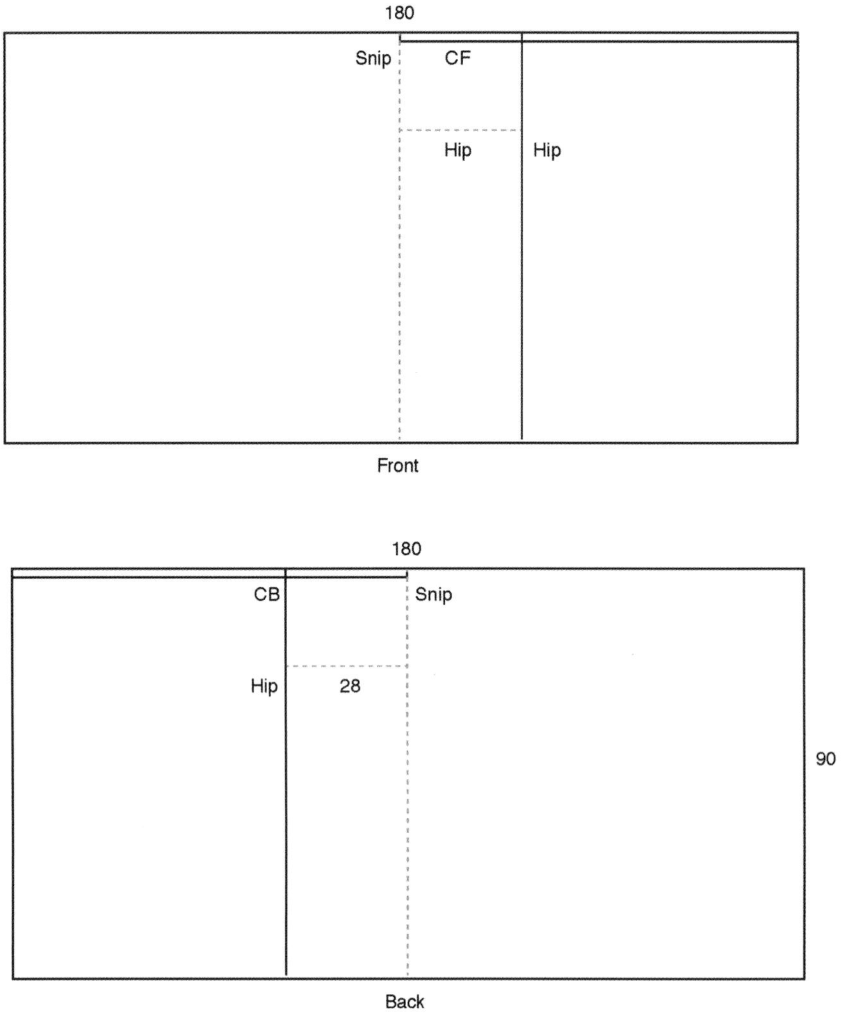

Fig. 7.34 Block dimensions for double circular skirt.

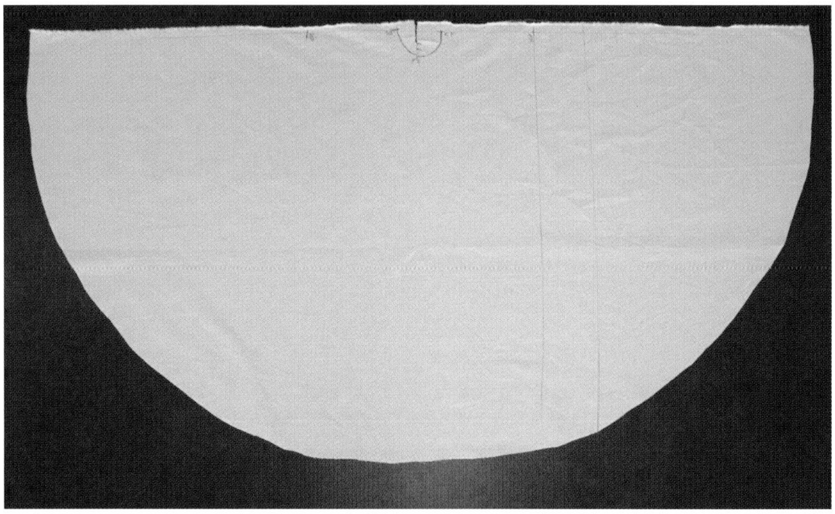

Fig. 7.35 Front quarter of double circular skirt on the flat is actually a half-circle.

Gathered Skirt with Waistband/Dirndl Skirt (Fig. 7.36)

A dirndl is a skirt that accompanies a bodice as part of the traditional two-piece Bavarian folk dress for women and girls. Originally it was workwear but was adopted into high fashion in the 1950s. Characteristically it has a gathered waist mounted onto a waistband. This time, the volume at the hem of the skirt is dictated by the volume in a series of gathers at the waist as the fabric hangs down perpendicular to the floor creating a rectangular pattern piece. The amount of gathering is controlled and varies depending on the weight of the cloth and how bulky it becomes. To create the dirndl's characteristic silhouette, the drapery at the waist has to be higher at the CF, flattening out towards the SS. There are a variety of methods to create the gathers in this skirt; for example, one method is to run a gathering stitch through the hipline before aligning it to the mannequin and draping upwards to the waist. This technique is really well documented in Francesca Sterlacci's *Draping for Beginners*. My preferred method (and the one I have used here) uses a piece of elastic to firmly hold the gathers temporarily whilst I adjust them to create the aesthetic I want.

1. Tape up the mannequin with waist- and hiplines.
2. Prepare and block the calico as per the measurements in Fig. 7.37.
3. Tie a piece of elastic around the mannequin's waist and knot it.
4. Align the hipline on the calico with the hipline on the mannequin where it intersects the CF. Pin vertically on the CF to the bottom of the stand to hold the calico in place.
5. Arrange the calico under the elastic at the waist and adjust the volume to create gathers that are even and aesthetically pleasing (Fig. 7.38).
6. Using a mechanical pencil, mark off the waistline and SS, and add notches halfway from the CF to the PS, at the PS, and from the PS to the

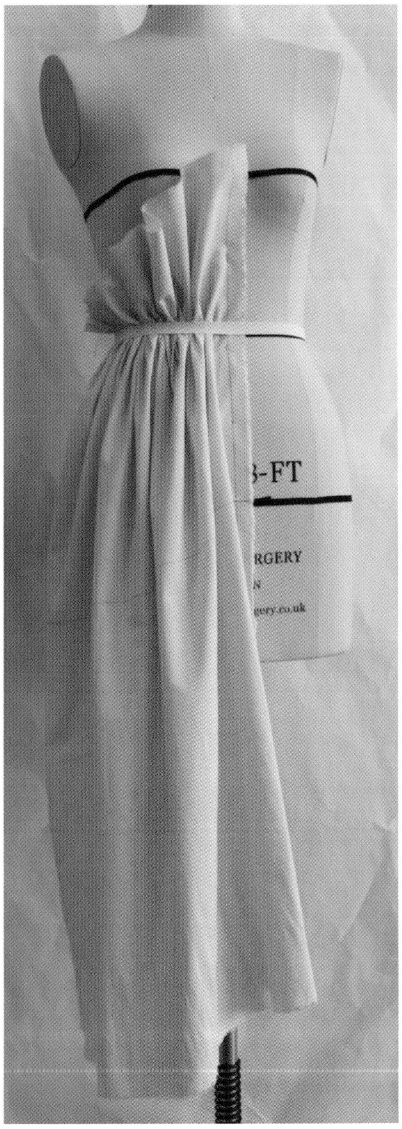

Fig. 7.36 Gathers at waist dictating both silhouette and volume at bottom of dirndl's skirt panel.

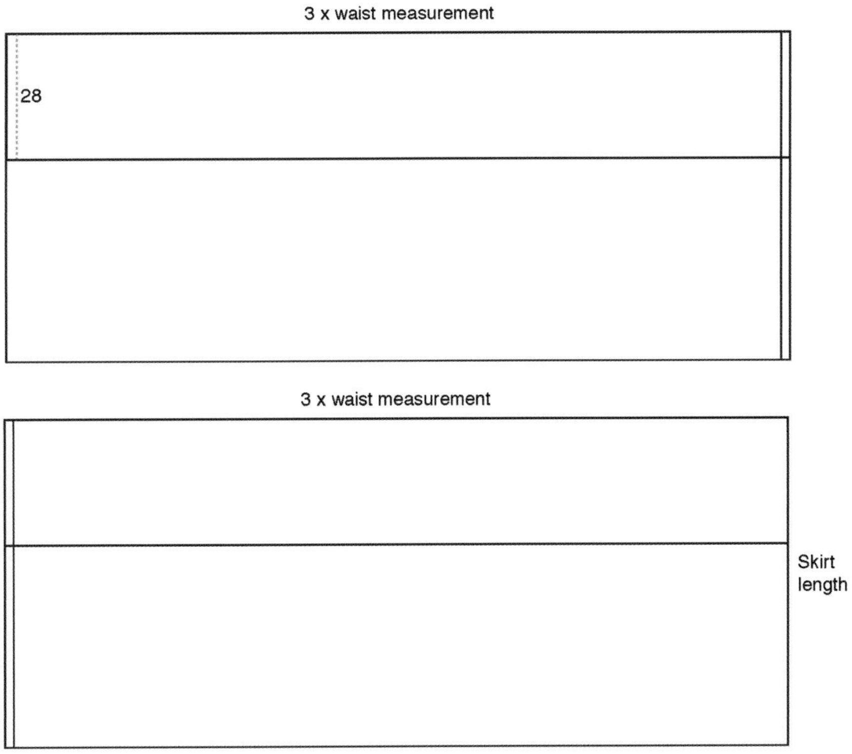

Fig. 7.37 Block dimensions for dirndl skirt.

SS.

7. Remove and true up. The spaces between the notches will give an indication of how much cloth is required to create the gathers. As a rule of thumb, whatever the waist measurement is you will need 2.5 to 3 times the amount for gathering.
8. Repeat for the skirt back.
9. Trim off the excess calico, leaving a 2cm allowance around the side and waist on the front and back.
10. Check the drape by re-aligning the front and back pieces on the mannequin, then folding the calico back under along the sewing line at the SS before pinning to the SS for the front panel. Make any alterations necessary and re-mark in a different colour before taking the calico off the stand and transferring it to a master.

Fig. 7.38 Arranging waist gathers under the elastic.

Flared Skirt with Gathered Waistband

The technique for this is almost the same as for the dirndl but this time, by levelling the gathers at the waist, it gives the drape more of an A-line silhouette to the skirt (Fig. 7.39). The SS flares out as the excess volume is transferred into the hemline and not absorbed into the volume of gathering at the waist. As a result the pattern piece ends up being curved at the waist and hem rather than straight as per the dirndl. If your fabric was wide enough you could drape the dirndl with only one seam at the CB but for the flared skirt you are likely to need SSs, unless you begin with a huge amount of calico above the waist. Repeat all the steps for the dirndl but for steps 4 and 5 start to ease the calico downwards from the CF to the SS, pushing the volume of fabric into the hem so that it swings outwards, creating a more fluted look. Also worth noting is how the hipline, normally on the cross grain, changes direction onto the SG as it travels beyond the PS.

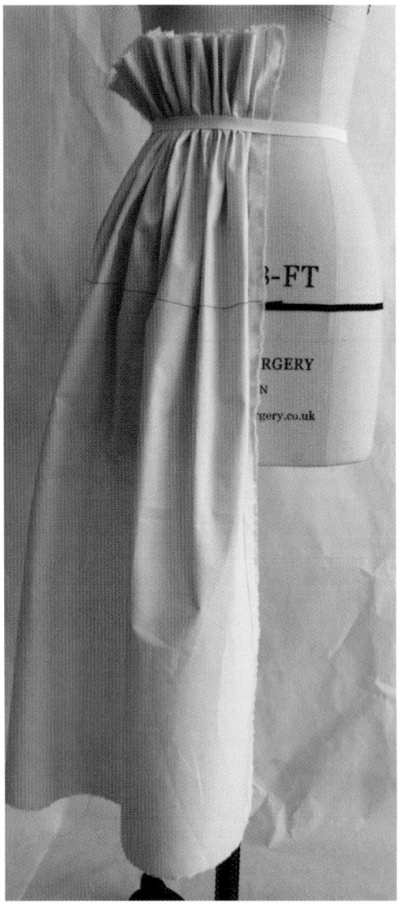

Fig. 7.39 Levelled gathers at waistline create flared silhouette to skirt.

Fig. 7.40 Jupe bombée. (Photo: Yousef Al Nasser)

Jupe Bombée (Gathered Skirt on a Yoke) (Fig. 7.40)

This is a more sophisticated variant on the gathered skirt but with a yoke, so that the gathers begin at the hip and not the waist. The yoke here is a smooth fitted area of fabric around the waist and hip and it reduces the amount of fabric which could add bulk at the waistband seam. It is something I have seen used to varying degrees in Victorian petticoats where all sorts of visual tricks were employed in addition to corsetry to make the waist seem smaller. Staggering the petticoat layers onto a yoke meant more volume could go into the dress hem without making the waist thicker and the yoke could fit over the corset exactly. My yoke is fitted through the waist to the hipline and cut straight, but stylistically the bottom of your yoke can be any shape you want.

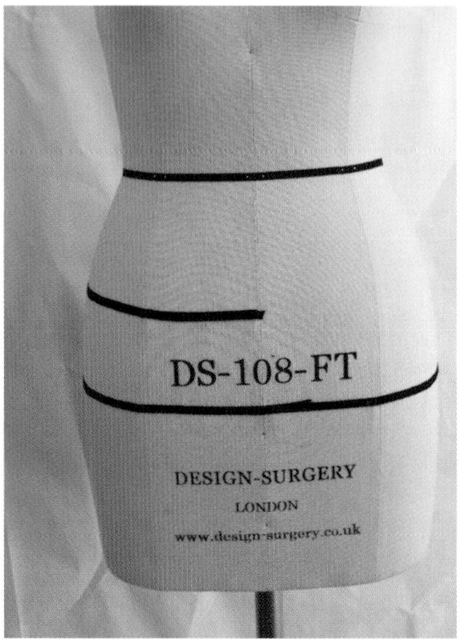

Fig. 7.41 Mannequin taped with yoke.

You will need to drape the yoke first then drape the skirt to the yoke.

1. Tape up the mannequin with waist- and hiplines and a tape to indicate the end of the yoke (Fig. 7.41).
2. Prepare and block the calico as per the measurements in Fig. 7.42.
3. For the yoke you will need to drape from the hip upwards, so align the calico at the CF where it intersects the hipline and pin. Smooth the calico upwards and pin it to anchor.
4. Ideally you want to eliminate the waist dart on the yoke as per the A-line skirt so that it is one flat panel (Fig. 7.43). As the calico is smoothed up to fit the waistline it will start to move downwards off

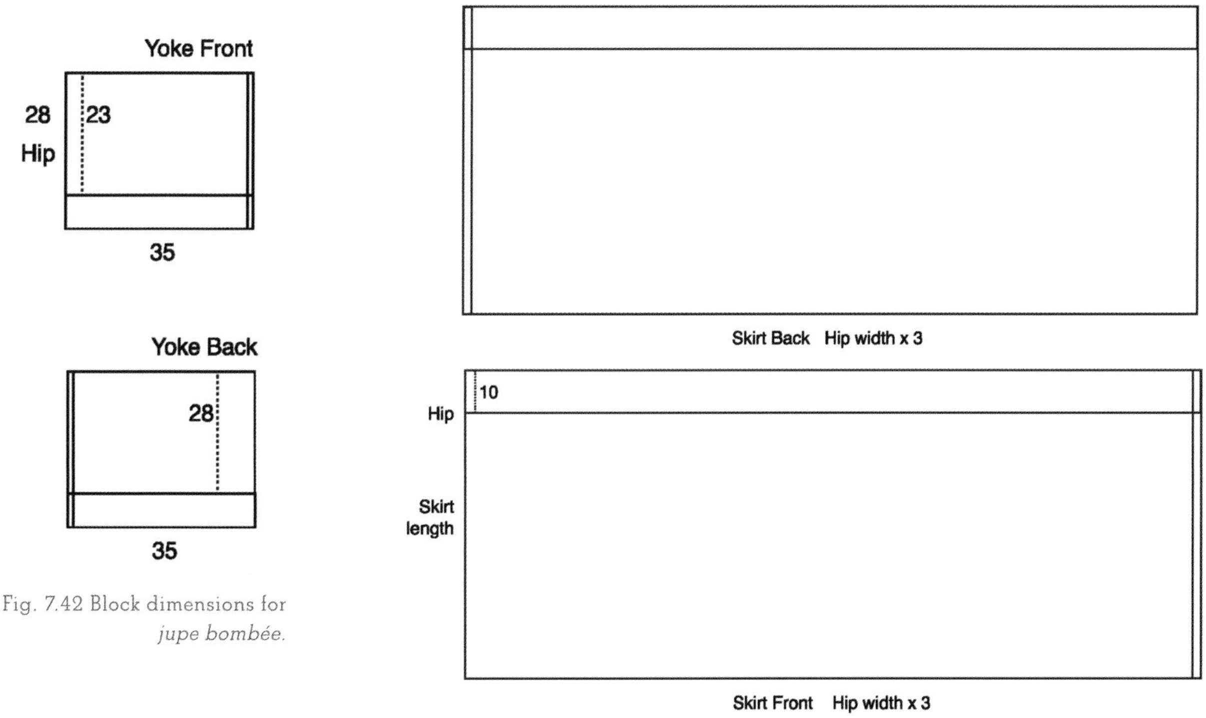

Fig. 7.42 Block dimensions for *jupe bombée*.

the hipline, going off grain, but the dart will be eliminated automatically and a better fit will be achieved. Don't drape the yoke too tightly; it will have to accommodate the additional bulk of the gathering later on.

5. You may need to snip down towards the waistline and around the SS to ease the tension in the calico and smooth it evenly over the mannequin.
6. Using a mechanical pencil, mark off the waistline and the SS, and add notches at the PS.
7. Remove and true up (Fig. 7.44).
8. Repeat for the skirt back.

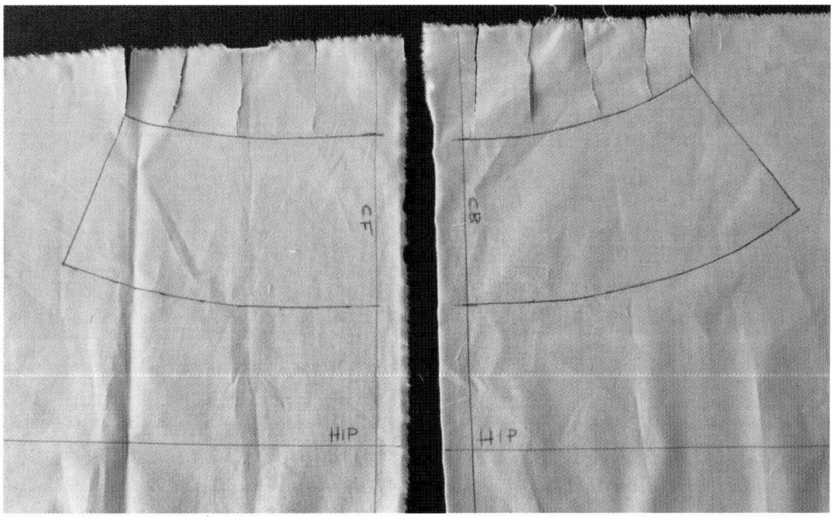

Fig. 7.44 Trued-up yoke drape on the flat.

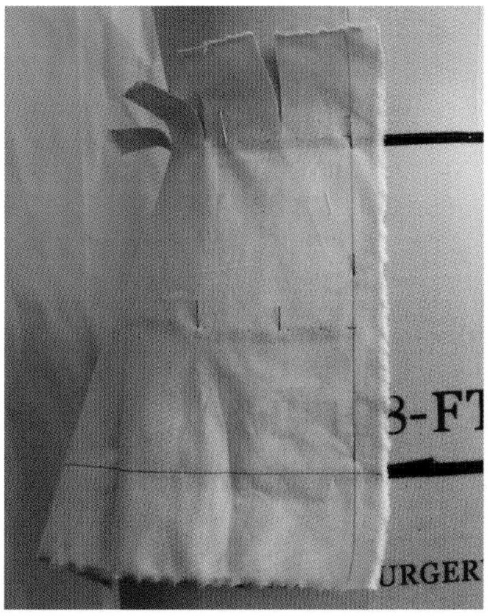

Fig. 7.43 Draped yoke piece.

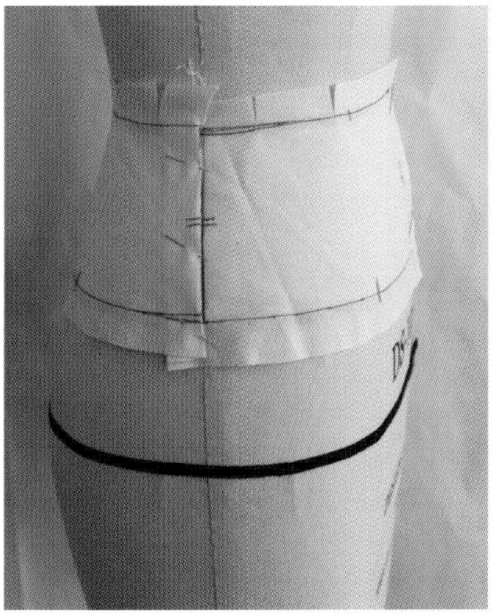

Fig. 7.45 Finished yoke drape with adjustments.

Fig. 7.46 Arranging the gathers under the elastic at style line.

9. Trim off the excess calico leaving a 2cm allowance around the side and waist on the front and back (Fig. 7.45).
10. For the skirt, tie a piece of elastic around the style line or position of the bottom of the yoke to begin.
11. Push the blocked calico under the elastic, aligning the hipline and CF.
12. Pin down the CF to hold and arrange the gathers (Figs 7.46, 7.47 and 7.48).
13. Repeat stages 5–9 as listed for the dirndl skirt. If a more flared silhouette is required then angle the calico downwards as per the flared gathered skirt. You will need extra notches along the style line/hipline and you will also need to mark them off on the corresponding drape for the skirt piece.
14. To check the drape keep the skirt on the stand, align the front and back pieces, then turn the calico back under along the sewing line of the back and pin to the SS of the front. Then re-align the pieces of the yoke on the mannequin in the same way. Turn the yoke hemline up, laying it over the gathers of the skirt. Match up the notches and pin it in place. Make any alterations necessary and re-mark in a different colour before taking the calico off the stand and transferring it to a master. It is worth noting that the gathering can create a lot of additional bulk so an alternative method for checking the drape is to put the yoke on first and pin the skirt panel on top. If you don't want to see the raw edges of the gather, turn the skirt piece upside down to pin the gathers onto the yoke from the underside. Once anchored in place drop the volume of the skirt back down over the gathers. The disadvantage with this is obviously that it is more awkward to make adjustments accurately (Fig. 7.49).

Fig. 7.47 Trimming down excess to 2cm allowance and pinning gathers in position on stand.

Fig. 7.48 Trimmed skirt panel.

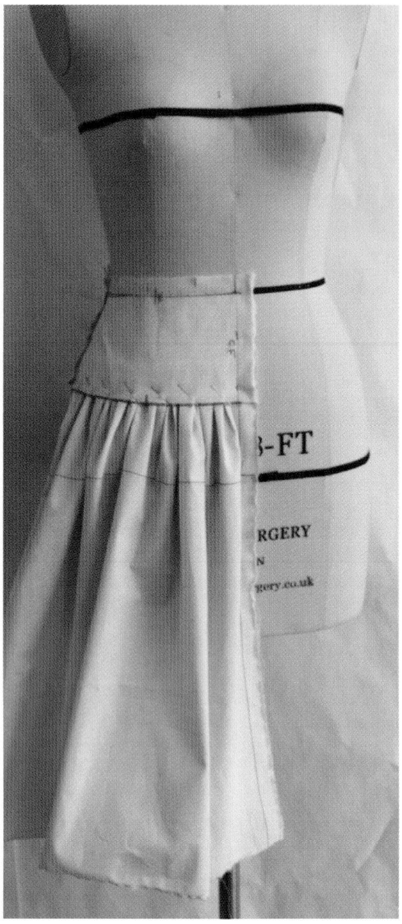

Fig. 7.49 Final drape with yoke overlaid on skirt; note series of notches added to yoke and skirt to align gathers for production pattern.

Levelling Skirt Hems

Once you have toiled up your production pattern you will need to level off the hem so that it is parallel to the floor. If your mannequin is light enough, lift it up onto the table so that the skirt is at eye level. Use a metre rule and measure from the floor up to the desired length. Move the mannequin round, slowly marking off the required hem length as you go. Be careful not to tilt the metre rule at an angle or the measurement will be wrong. Also note that although the hem looks parallel to the floor by eye, if you transfer onto your paper pattern it will actually be curved (Fig. 7.50).

Waistbands

Your skirt can be finished with a facing on the inside of the waist seam but a more common finish is to add a folded-over band at the waist edge to give a clean finish. The waistband usually includes additional allowance for your fastenings so it is useful to know what these are before draping and creating the pattern.

Straight Waistband

This is probably the commonest treatment and it can be any depth you want. Note that the deeper it becomes,

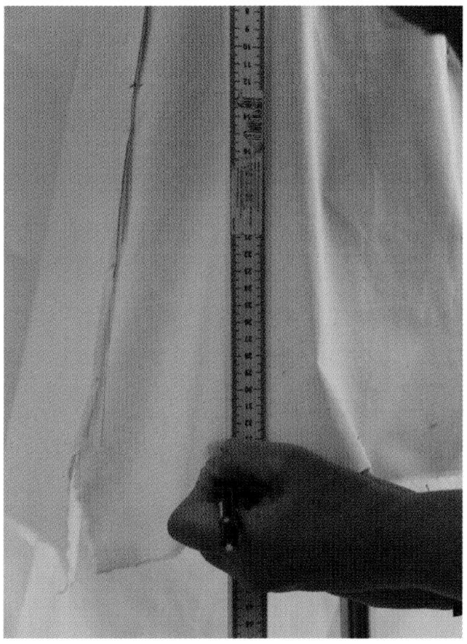

Fig. 7.50 Levelling skirt hem with a metre rule and working from the ground up.

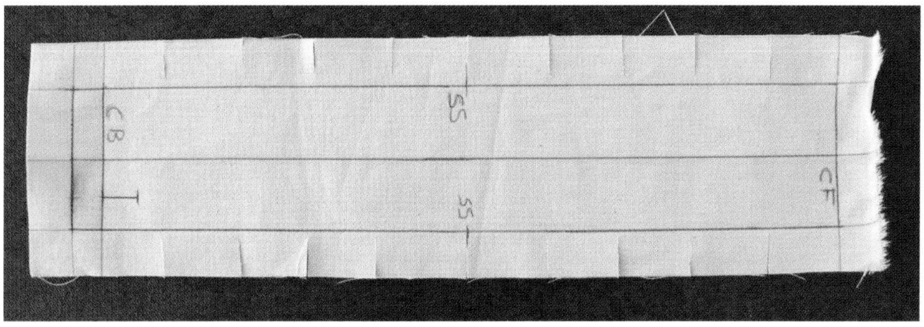

Fig. 7.51 Straight waistband.

the more shaping it will require to fit the widening of the body between the waist and bust. From a fitting point of view, a straight waistband suits a straighter figure with a wider waist (Fig. 7.51).

1. To create a straight waistband measure the waist. Halve that measurement as you are only working on the right side of the stand. Add a button wrap – the width of your button plus 0.5–1cm depending on what looks best proportionally.
2. Decide on the depth of your waistband and double it.
3. Block a piece of calico and mark off the CF. Draw in a rectangle to the dimensions you have just measured, leaving an extra 2cm all the way around the outside edges for alterations.
4. Fold and position on the mannequin where the CF and waist intersect.
5. Pin the waistband into position along the waist from CF to CB. A narrower band depth will give a closer fit.
6. Add notches at the PS and SS.
7. Remove from the stand and true up before transferring to a master on paper.

Curved Waistband

I have also included a curved waistband where the top edge is reduced to get a more tailored fit which will suit a curvier figure.

1. Begin as for the straight waistband (Fig. 7.52).
2. Position the calico on the mannequin where the CF intersects the waist and snip into the SA for a smoother fit.
3. Pin out the suppression and mark off.
4. Repeat for the back from the CB and transfer everything to the master.
5. For the production pattern, trace off the front pattern, then trace off the back, joining them through the SS to create one long curved pattern piece.
6. If you are using buttons add a button wrap, either at the side or the CB depending where the fastenings will be on your design. The button wrap should be the width of your button plus 0.5–1cm.

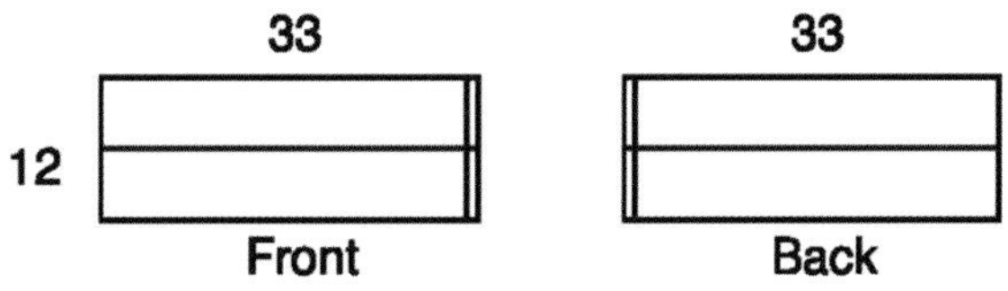

Fig. 7.52 Block dimensions for curved waistband.

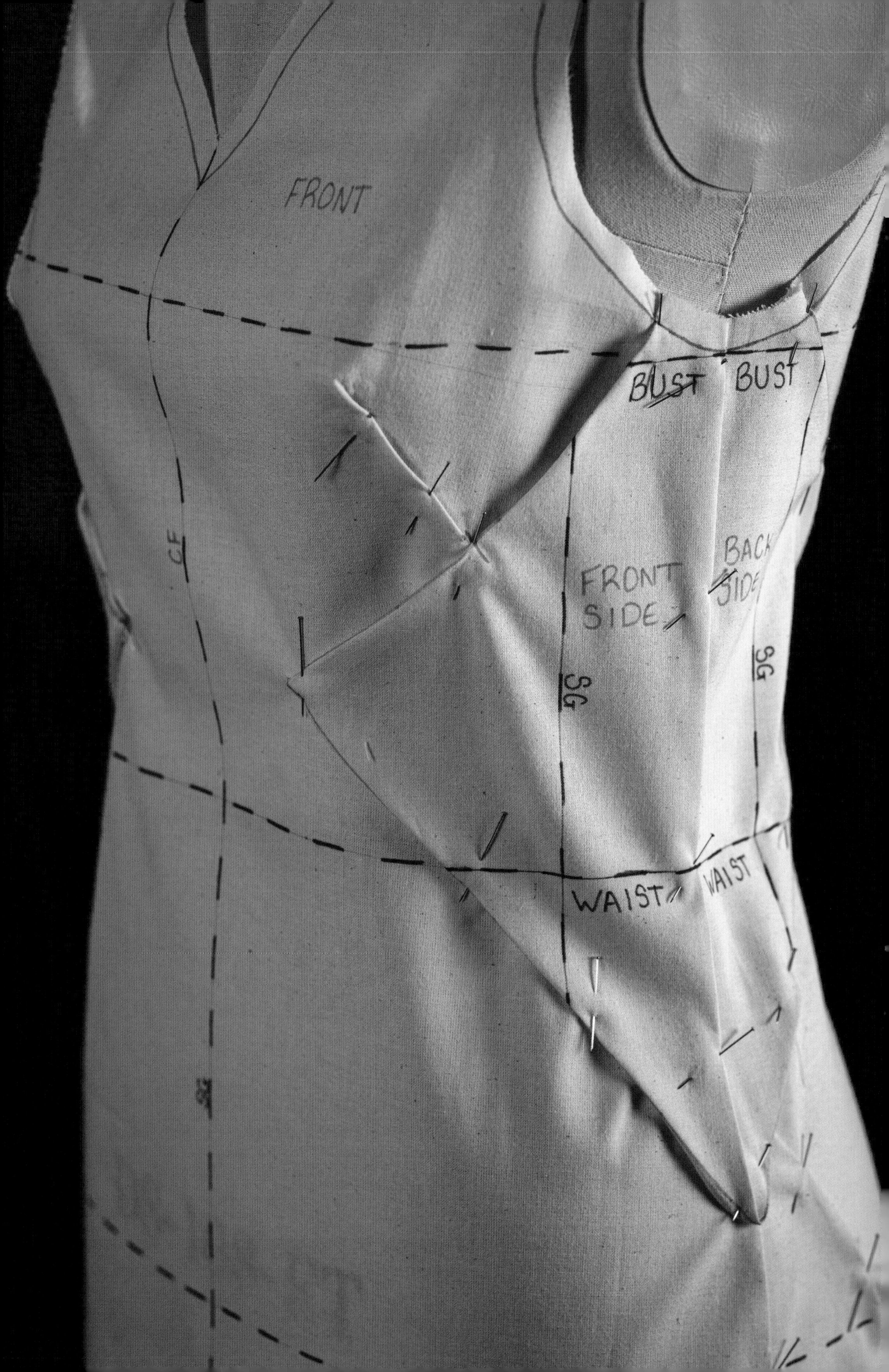
FRONT
BUST
BUST
CF
FRONT SIDE
BACK SIDE
SG
SG
WAIST
WAIST

The Dress

8

The dresses in this chapter are all either derivative of a traditional sleeveless shift dress or a flared dress. The shoulder line is equally important in the draping of both styles even though they are radically different with regard to volume and fit. I have included a little bit of dress history to set the context for their evolution before describing how to drape variants on the respective styles.

Sleeveless Shift Dress

The shift hangs straight from the shoulder and is fitted through the body with darts or panels. Its simple classic style makes it both flattering and practical. The flapper dresses of the 1920s were the first popular shift dresses and were a stark contrast to the corseted nipped-in waists so pervasive in previous decades. This period coincided with the advent of sportswear for women that provided clothing that was much easier to wear and move around in, giving a much more fluid silhouette. The shift became a symbol of women's independence during an era where women began to have more active lifestyles and spending power. The shift had something of a renaissance in the 1960s where it evolved to have bust darts with a straight or A-line hem with no shaping at the waist, as seen in Mary Quant's minis. Couturier Hubert de Givenchy in particular made a significant contribution to the dress's legacy: he designed Audrey Hepburn's iconic black dress for the movie *Breakfast at Tiffany's* and was responsible for many of the shift-and-jacket two-pieces worn by former First Lady Jackie Kennedy.

The basic fitted sleeveless dress block has long darts running from the BP through the waist to the hip. On the flat, the elongated dart looks like an elongated diamond shape. It also has a shoulder dart running down to the BP which allows for an easy manipulation into a PS style. If the block has been drafted rather than draped the darts tend to have sharp straight lines running to the suppression points but if you drape it, the sewing lines of the darts take on a more curved appearance that more closely reflects the curvature of the female body. I used the drape for a longer-line bodice in Chapter 5 to introduce the draping process: we will be revisiting it here for the shift. It was draped to the bottom of the hip or widest part of the body. By extending from this downwards on the flat to the desired hem length, the simplest shift dress can be created.

SHIFT DRESS BASICS

The essence of draping a shift dress is that you start by pinning a boxy shape then begin to put the shaping in at the waistline, running out to bust and hip. You want the intake to be the same at the front and back waist.

1. Tape up your mannequin with bust, waist- and hiplines. Make sure the hipline is parallel to the floor by stepping away from the mannequin to check.
2. Prepare and block your calico as

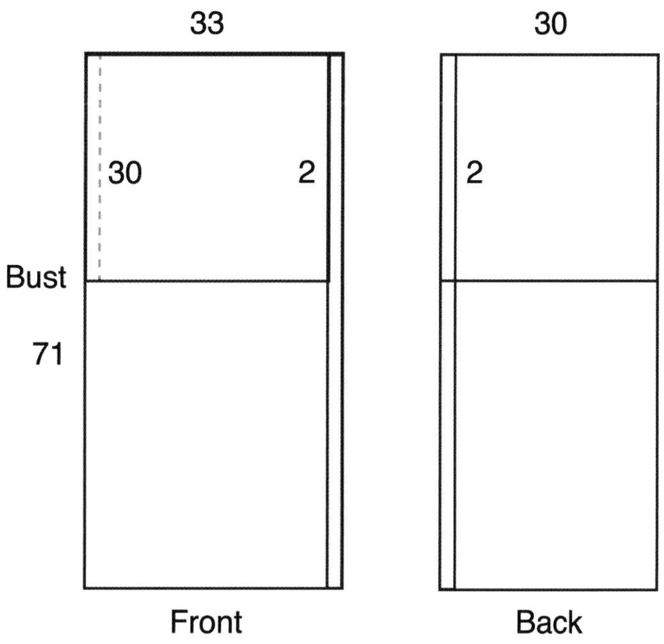

Fig. 8.2 Block dimensions for longline bodice/basic shift.

Left: Fig. 8.1 Fitted, panelled shift dress. (Photo: Yousef Al Nasser)

per the dimensions in Fig. 8.2. Note that you are draping to the hipline only and will be extending the length on the flat once you have the master.

3. Position the calico onto the mannequin aligned at the CF and bustline and pin it to hold.
4. Smooth up to the neckline and pin at the neck point. Snip round the neckline to release the tension and smooth across the shoulder.
5. Roughly pin in the shoulder dart to the bust and pin across the rest of the shoulder line to hold.
6. Smooth the fabric around to the SS and create a rough waist dart (Fig. 8.3).
7. Pin in the SS and snip in towards

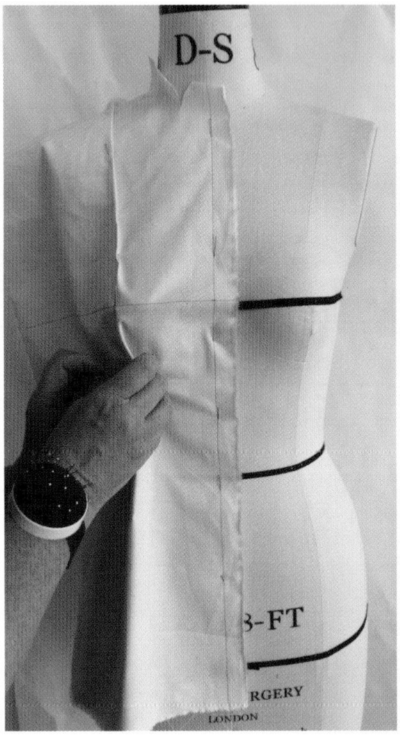

Fig. 8.3 Pinning in waist dart; shoulder dart is already in place.

the waist to release the tension and get a smoother fit (Figs 8.4 and 8.5).

8. Adjust the fit and mark off the darts, neck, shoulder, SS, armhole, arm plate and hipline with dots. I have also used the adhesive style tape to include the waistline on the CF and SS but have not drawn it in

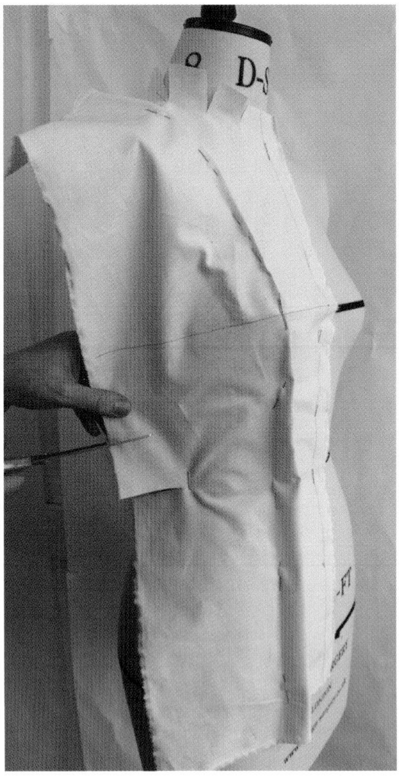

Fig. 8.4 Snipping into waistline and along SS to release tension.

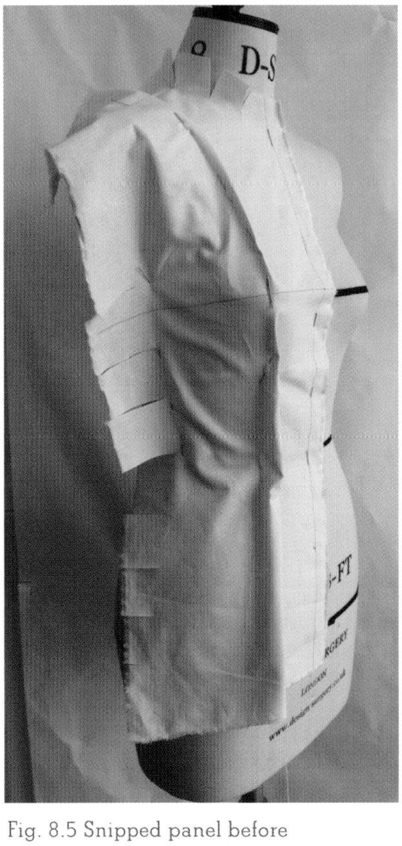

Fig. 8.5 Snipped panel before adjustments to smooth fit.

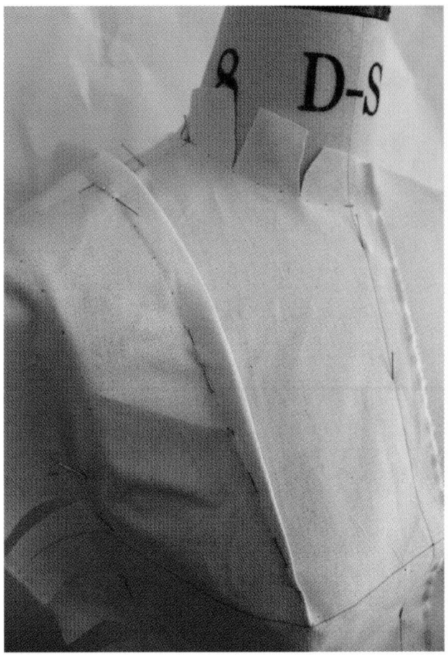

Fig. 8.6 Marking off darts with dotted line.

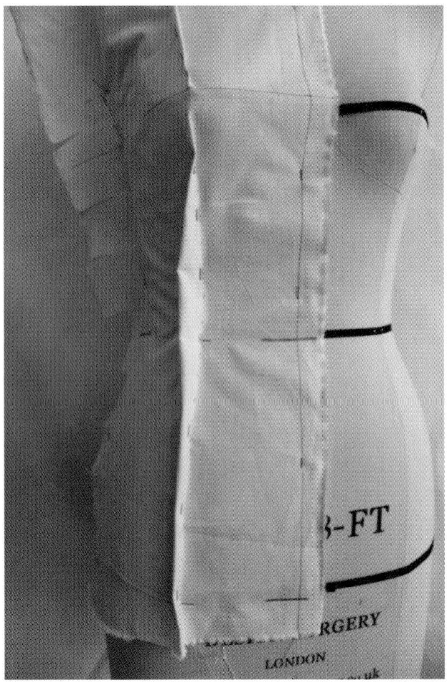

Fig. 8.7 Marking off waist- and hiplines.

(Figs 8.6 and 8.7).

9. True up on the flat. Drop the neckline at the CF by 1cm and the armhole down by 2cm and out by 1cm. Add notches (Fig.8.8).
10. Align the calico to the CB and bustline.
11. Ease the calico into the neck point and pin. There will be some pulling, so release the tension by

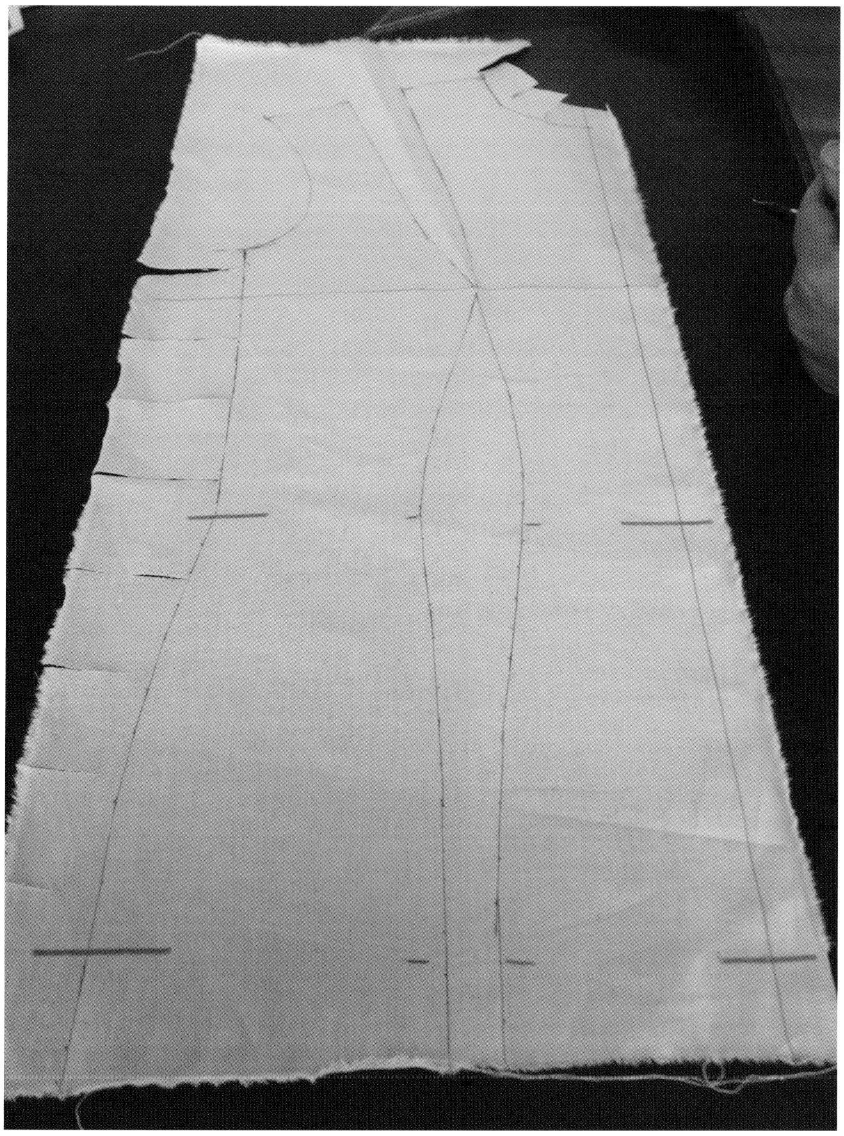

Fig. 8.8 Drape front trued up on the flat; note long dart.

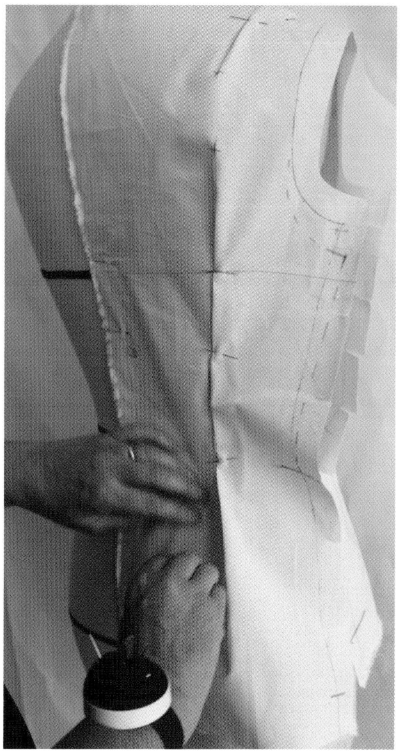

Fig. 8.9 Positioning back drape to check fit.

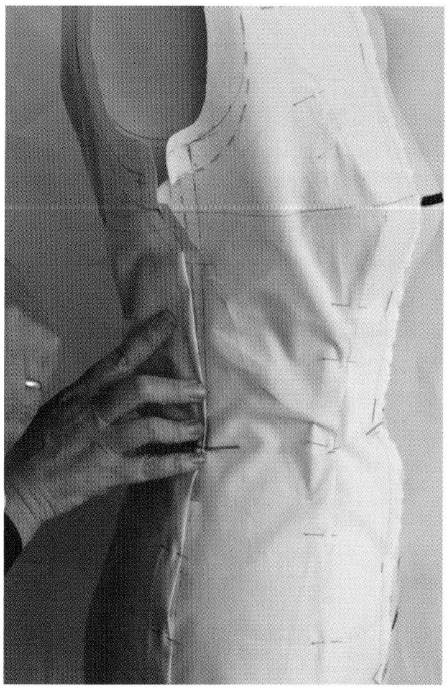

Fig. 8.10 Pinning back over front to join at SS.

snipping round the front neck and trim away the excess fabric as you did on the front neck.

12. Smooth the calico along the shoulder seam of the mannequin, fold a small dart approximately 1cm in depth on top of the PS and pin it. This shoulder dart allows for ease of movement at the shoulder bone and should taper out just above the middle of the shoulder blade.
13. Pin at the SS just under the arm plate, allowing the volume to swing into the back of the calico, and shape the dart by folding the fabric. Ideally the dart should taper out towards the bustline and must not join up to the shoulder dart.
14. Using a mechanical pencil, apply a series of dots to mark off the neckline, darts, SS and waist. Also mark off the position of the armhole and the position of the bottom of the arm plate where it joins the SS. Use dashes to indicate corners or junctions where seams intersect one another and crosses to denote the fine ends of your darts.
15. Remove the calico from the stand and true up as per the front. Repeat the process for dropping and drafting the armhole only. As the back neck is already a good fit this time you do not need to adjust it. Trim down leaving a 2cm allowance around the adjusted drape.

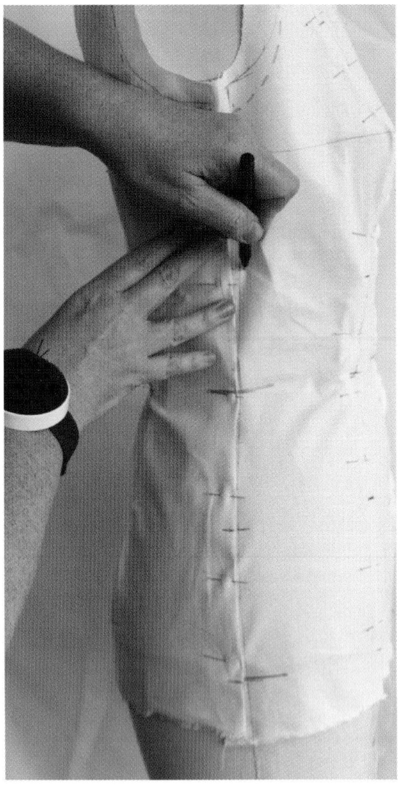

Fig. 8.11 Marking off adjustments.

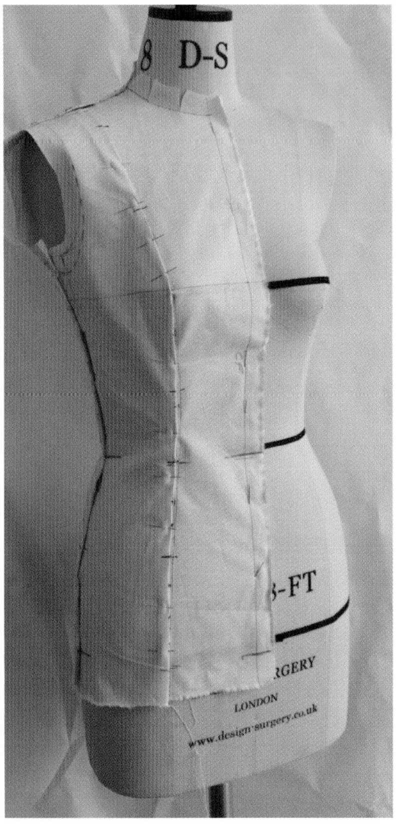

Fig. 8.12 Basic shift final fit, front view.

16. Put the pieces back on the stand starting from the CF. Pin the darts (placing them diagonally), then position the back at the CB and put the back darts in. Turn the SA under; lay it over the front SA at the sides and shoulders and pin together to check the fit (Figs 8.9, 8.10 and 8.11).
17. Make any final alterations to the fit before removing from the stand and converting to a master pattern. Extend the length of the bodice on the flat to create the dress pattern (Figs 8.12 and 8.13).

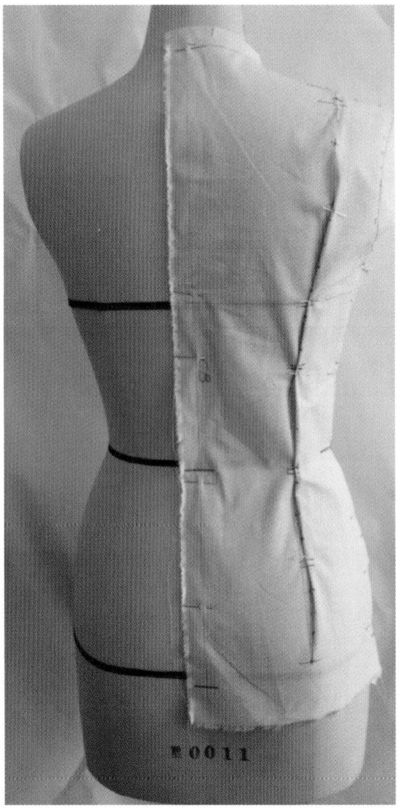

Fig. 8.13 Basic shift final fit, back view.

WAIST DARTS

Recapping on what has already been learned, waist dart lengths depend on the fullness of the bust and hip. The fuller these are, the shorter the dart. The dart should not end any closer than 1.3cm from the BP and 2.5cm from the hipline.

Panelled Shift Dress (Figs 8.14 and 8.15)

This particular style continues to use the techniques explored with the draping of the bodice in Chapter 6. The main suppression points of bust, waist and hip have been repositioned into a side panel with a demi-French dart at the bust. As there isn't a dart running through the bust, waist and hip, the suppression is now all in the SS running through the side panel. The panel needs to remain as two pieces for the front and back to create the fitted silhouette. A close-up of the dress bodice can be seen in Fig. 8.1. The SS has been eliminated in the skirt below the hipline so the calico for draping the skirt panel is quite a big piece to allow it to wrap all round the body from the CF to the CB. The dress is symmetrical, with a V neck and a CB seam which can include a zip fastener at the back neck and a split or vent at the hem on the production pattern.

1. Tape up your mannequin with bust-, waist- and hiplines. Make sure the hipline is parallel to the floor by stepping away from the mannequin to check.
2. Prepare and block your calico as per the dimensions in Fig. 8.16. Note that you are draping to the bottom of the stand only and will be extending the length on the flat once you have the master.
3. Add the style lines for the V neck and side panel. This dress has a much lower armhole than the one on the fitted bodice in Chapter 6 so you can either tape it on to the mannequin or drape to the arm plate and alter the armhole on the flat. As the dress is symmetrical you only need to tape on the right-hand side (Figs 8.17, 8.18 and 8.19).
4. Starting with the CF panel, align to the bustline and CF and pin to hold it in position. Smooth across the BP and pin, then pin the rest of the CF in place. Smooth excess towards the SS (Fig. 8.20).
5. As this design is draped from the CF to the CB, now bring the fabric

Fig. 8.14 Panelled shift dress, front view. (Photo: Yousef Al Nasser)

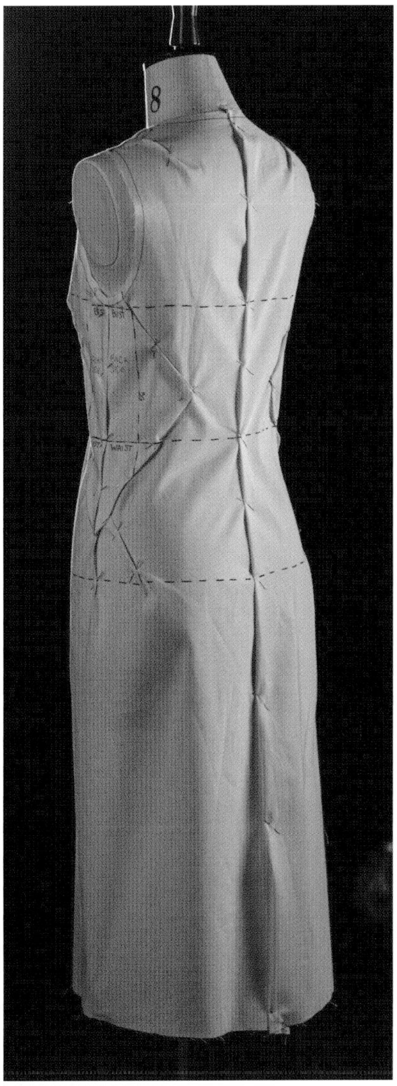

Fig. 8.15 Panelled shift dress, back view. (Photo: Yousef Al Nasser)

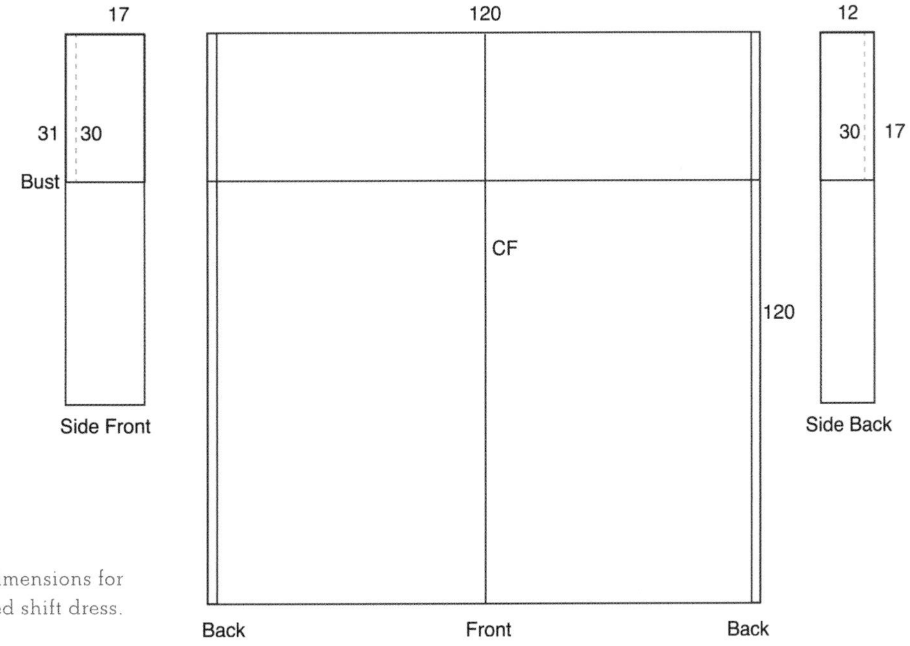

Fig. 8.16 Block dimensions for panelled shift dress.

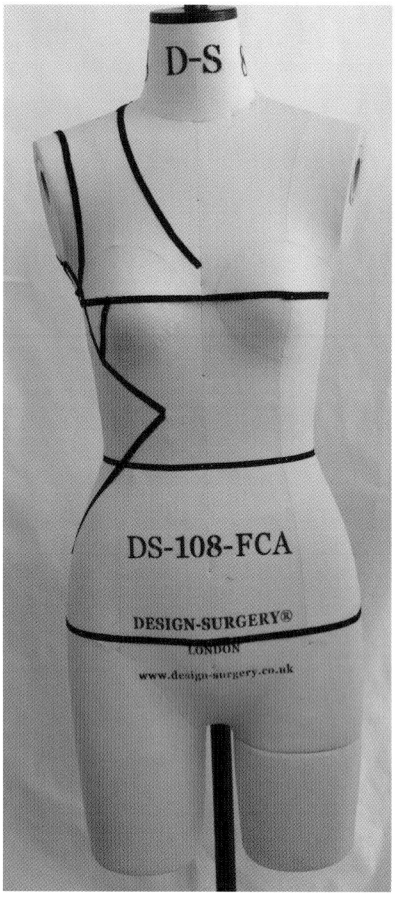

Fig. 8.17 Style lines, front view.

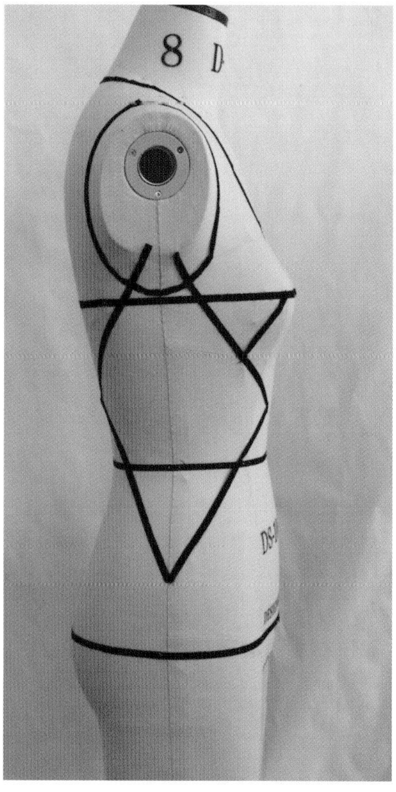

Fig. 8.18 Style lines, side view.

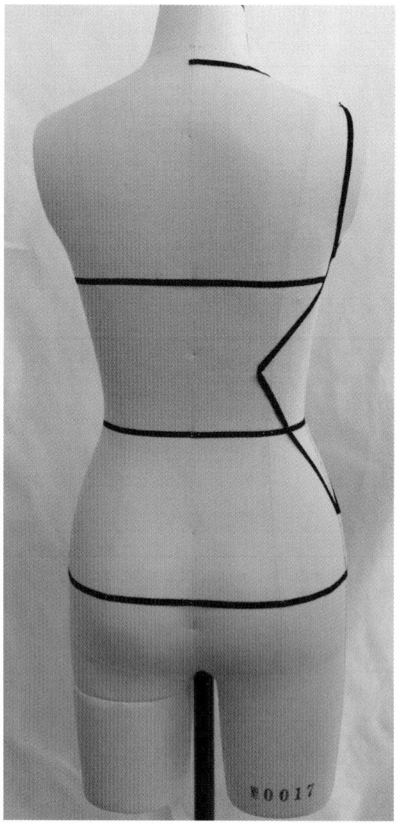

Fig. 8.19 Style lines, back view.

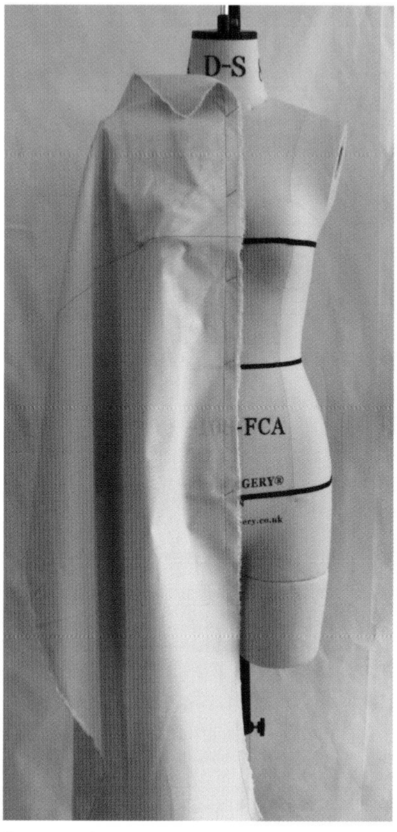

Fig. 8.20 Positioning calico at CF with excess at SS to be folded around to CB.

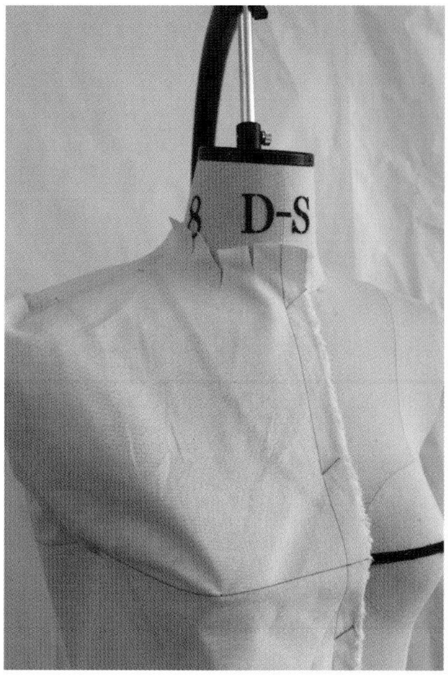

Fig. 8.21 Trimmed and fitted drape along shoulder and neckline.

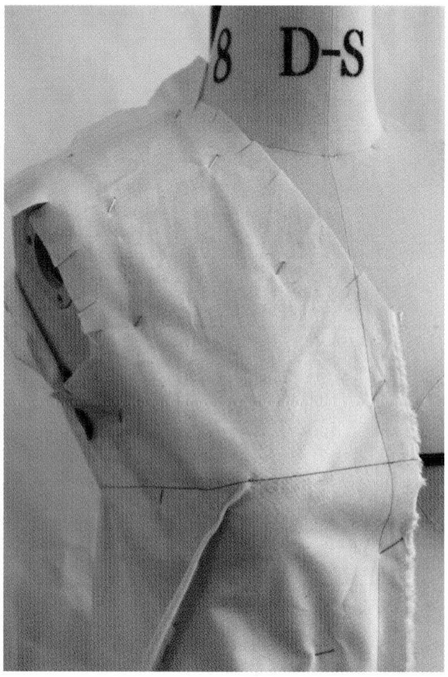

Fig. 8.22 Trimmed arm plate and neckline that now follow style lines beneath.

around the body and repeat to position the CB to the bustline again, easing the excess calico towards the SS. Make sure that the calico is not too tight across the hip and thigh and that it has not gone off grain.

6. At the front, smooth the calico upwards to the shoulder and into the neck point. Pin and snip into the neck point to release the tension.
7. Smooth the calico along the style line for the neckline and pin to the tape. Roughly cut away some of the excess at the CF to reflect the neckline (Figs 8.21 and 8.22).
8. Smooth the calico along the shoulder line and pin it, then work your way round the front armhole. There will be some tension as the fabric is going all the way around the body from CF to CB, so slash down to the bottom of the arm plate to release the tension in the fabric. Then snip into the front towards the taped style line to release it and you will be able to see the fabric relax onto the mannequin. Focus on getting this sitting snugly and adjust the fit through the back if you need to. Just drape to the arm plate for now and not the armhole but mark the latter's position onto the calico.
9. Now repeat the process on the back but include a small shoulder dart as you would for a back bodice, as in Chapter 6.
10. There will be quite a lot of surplus fabric at the waist through the side, front and back. This is where the position of the suppression needs to be resolved with a series of darts that feature in the end design. The final garment has three darts over the bottom and back hip and one French dart at the BP. These have been created by pinching the calico in and pinning to get the most aesthetically pleasing silhouette (Figs 8.23, 8.24 and 8.25). Aim for something skimming rather than skintight, but this stage is very much trial and error to get the balance of suppression right and achieve a pleasing fit. I have spread the excess evenly through the SS and used two diagonal darts running from the bust through the waist to the top hip at front and back so experiment with the best position – if you are working from a sketch you can always adjust it afterwards. The bottom of the front dart is going to effectively be lost in the side panel once the excess has been cut away outside of the style line for the centre panel. I have also extended a dart down over the hip below the bottom tip of the side panel at the side. This excess has later been eliminated on the front as it can be eased away with pressing at the toile stage but the excess at the back has been redistributed into the small darts at the back hip. The darts are at a right angle to the side panel seams to give it a geometry which works well visually.

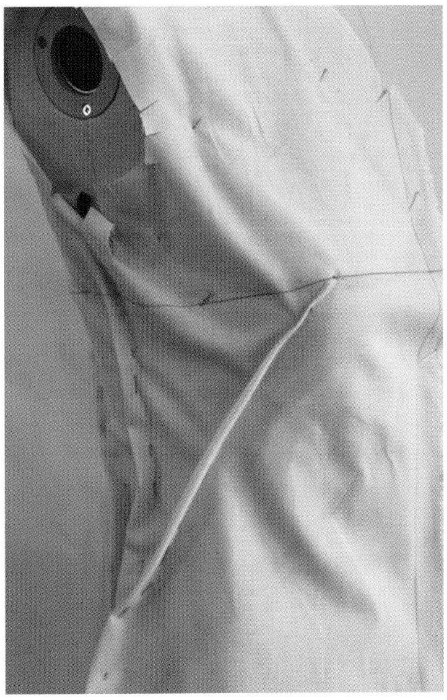

Fig. 8.24 Suppression split between SB and SF through waist to create both defining fit and design of the dress.

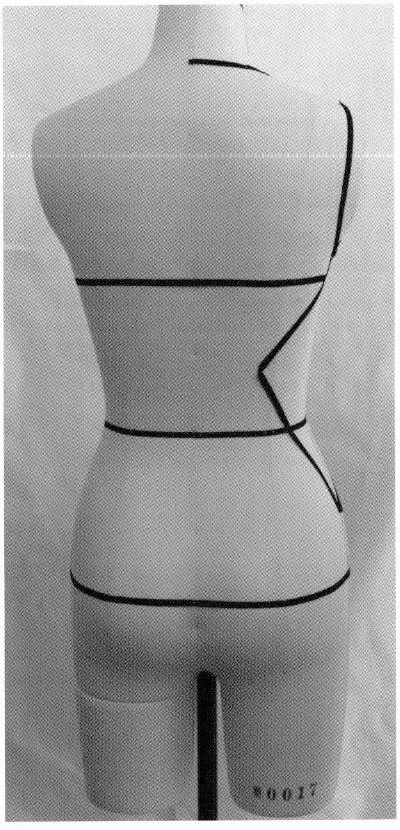

Fig. 8.23 Rough shaping of dart leading into French bust dart.

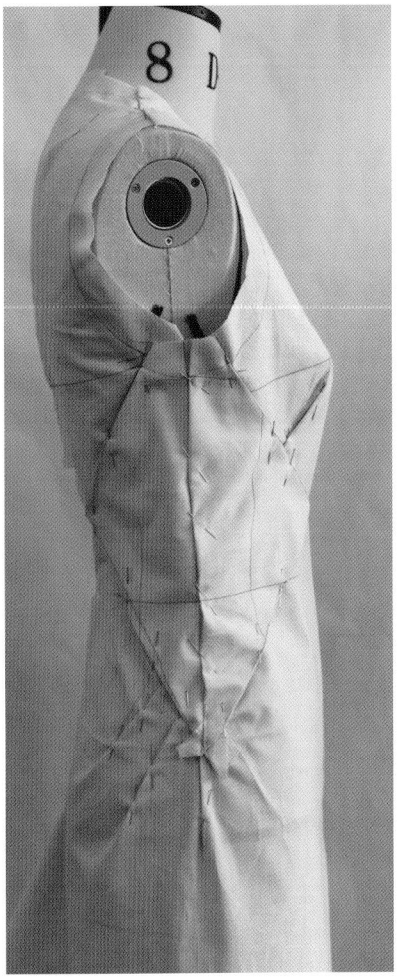

Fig. 8.25 Dart positions over hip and bottom.

11. Pin along the style line for the side panel at front and back and cut away the excess calico at the SS, leaving the main front and back panel with a generous SA. Cutting will release some of the tension created by the bulk in the darts so you should be able to make adjustments to the fullness and position of the darts in the main panel of the dress. The darts are functional but they are also a design feature so it is fine to reposition these until you are happy.
12. Using dots, mark off the neckline, all the darts and panels. Also mark off the armhole style line and the position of the arm plate. Check all notches are in place. Remove the calico from the stand.
13. Look at Figs 8.26 and 8.27. To drape the side panel align the blocked calico to the SS on the front and where it intersects the waistline. Usually I would align the bustline but it is rather small in the panel that is wanted so I have gone for the biggest, more stable option of the waistline. Pin in position and smooth up and across to the PS, then down and out to the SS. In effect the fabric is being fitted using a clockwise motion. Pin along the style line for the panel seam and anchor along the SS. Mark off with dots and cut away the excess calico leaving about 4cm round the seams. Remove from the stand.

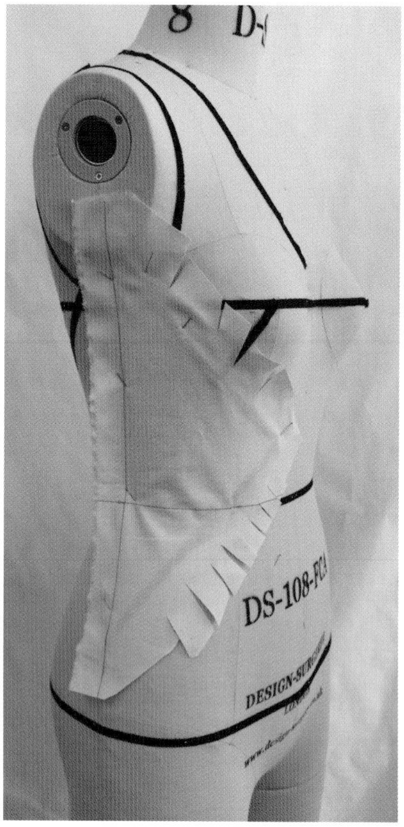

Fig. 8.26 Draping SF panel.

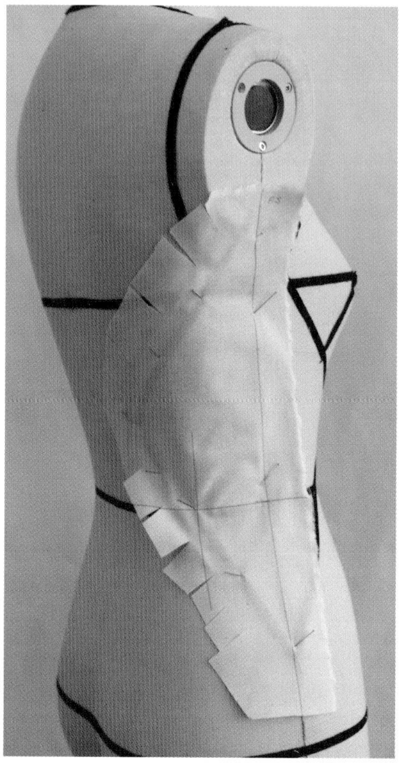

Fig. 8.27 Draping SB panel.

14. Repeat for the back panel.
15. True up and cut the excess SA down to 2cm round all of the seam lines (Figs 8.28 and 8.29).
16. Reposition the drape on the stand, starting with the realignment at the bustline and the CF.
17. Turn the edges under to the sewing line on the side front panel and position it on top of the main panel. Pin from the top. Repeat for the SB panel and mark any adjustments (Fig. 8.30).
18. Remove from the stand and transfer to the master on paper.

Some Notes for Toiling

As the design is symmetrical this has been recut for the photos with the calico on the fold. Measure the drape pieces to see how wide the dress needs to be – remember the drape is only half of a dress that goes all the way around the body from CB to CB so you are going to need quite a wide piece of cloth. Fold the calico in half, selvedge to selvedge, and pin the CF of your pattern to the fold line. If your fabric is narrower than the drape, consider where the additional seams will need to go on the production pattern. The dart position can be transferred to the cloth by tracing with carbon paper (Fig. 8.31).

Fig. 8.28 CF and CB pattern piece trued up on the flat.

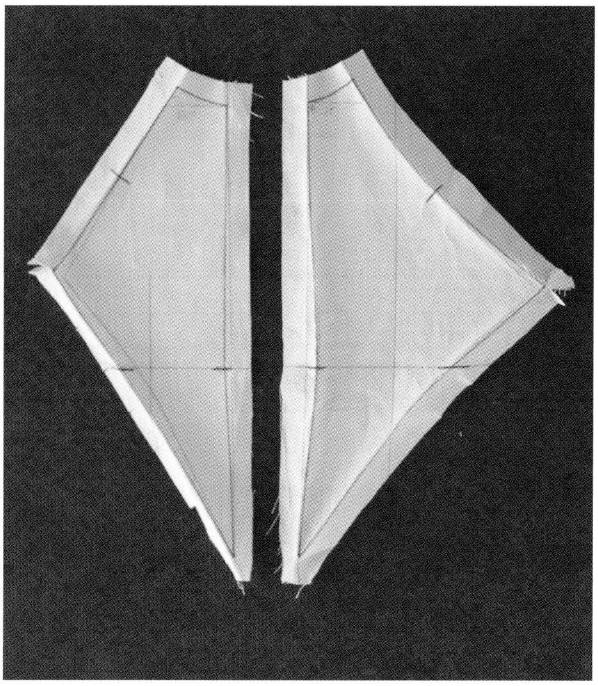

Fig. 8.29 Trued-up side panels on the flat.

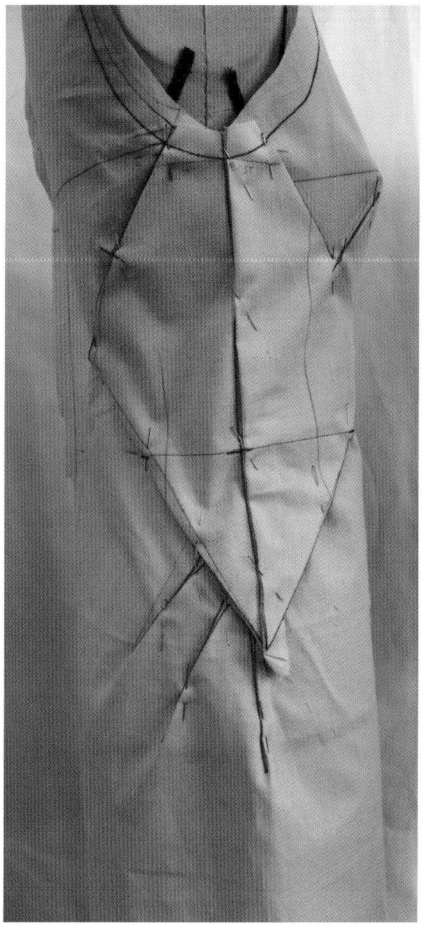

Fig. 8.30 Checking drape by pinning panels together from top.

Fig. 8.31 Using carbon paper.

Sleeveless Flared Dress (Fig. 8.32)

The flared dress or trapeze line is a relatively modern silhouette that emerged in the late 1950s as a derivative of the A line. This term was first used to describe a silhouette created by Dior. The new A line offered something new, clean and unfussy, with the A-line shape beginning either from the shoulder with a bust dart or just under the bust and gradually widening towards the hem, creating the silhouette of the capital letter A. For his collections from 1954 and 1955 Dior named his collections after the shapes reminiscent of the letters H, Y and A and cut his cloth accordingly. The shapes were considered very modern (or 'mod') and a deliberate departure from his previous New Look collections dominated by the nipped-in waists of his Bar Suit and the Corolla Line. Another Parisian couturier working with the A-line silhouette was Jacques Fath who introduced the swing coat in the late 1940s. The coat's popularity is thought to be for practical as well as stylistic reasons. It hung directly from the shoulder or yoke, often with pleats or tucks to get more volume in, making it a suitably discreet style for women during a post-war pregnancy surge. Showing your pregnancy bump was still considered slightly indecent – a throw-back to society's Victorian sensibilities – so this was an excellent design solution. Dior died in 1957, making way for a new designer and successor, Yves St Laurent, who introduced his own version of the A line called the 'Trapeze Line'. The style was often fuller at the hem than Dior's and the dresses flared directly from the shoulder with no shaping at all at the bust or hip. YSL hemlines fell just below the knee and the style was worn with low-heeled shoes. This style captured the spirit of the moment, as Balenciaga and Hubert de Givenchy also introduced their own versions at the same time. Eventually this style would adapt to become the 'baby doll' tent dress of the 1960s alongside the more practical A-line mini dress.

Fig. 8.32 Asymmetric sleeveless flared dress with asymmetric hem. (Photo: Yousef Al Nasser)

By contrast to the panelled fitted shift dress and in keeping with its history, this style has no suppression at all and therefore no darts. It is all about volume at the hemline. To create the flare, volume must be added into the front of the dress from the shoulder line. The objective is to create volume without putting pleats or tucks in at the shoulder or adding additional panels and seams. For this style I also decided on the finished length in advance to see the handkerchief hem before levelling. However, there is no reason why you couldn't keep that as a feature if you wanted to (Fig. 8.33).

1. Tape up your mannequin with bust-, waist- and hiplines. Make sure the hipline is parallel to the floor by stepping away from the mannequin to check.
2. Prepare and block your calico as per the dimensions in Fig. 8.34.
3. Align the calico at the CF and bustline and pin to hold.
4. Smooth the calico upwards to the shoulder line and pin the neck point.
5. Snip into the neck point and adjust for a smooth fit before snipping into the front neckline and trimming off the excess.

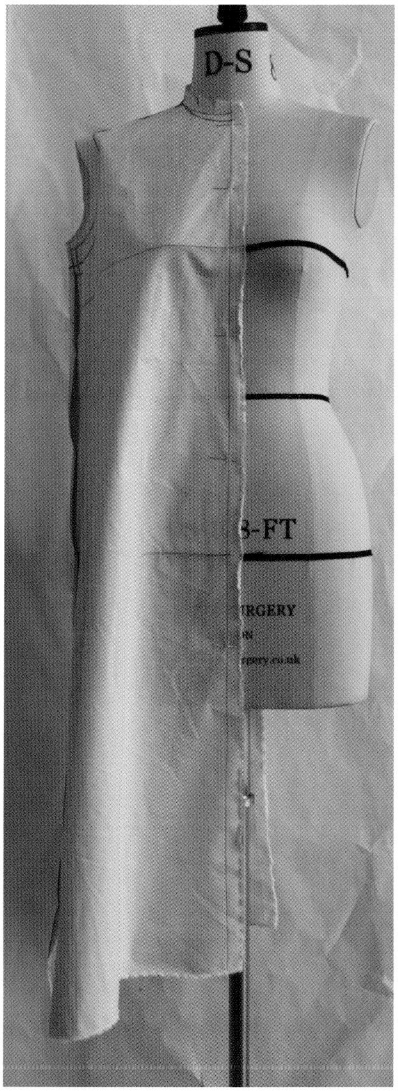

Fig. 8.33 Aligning CF for sleeveless flared dress.

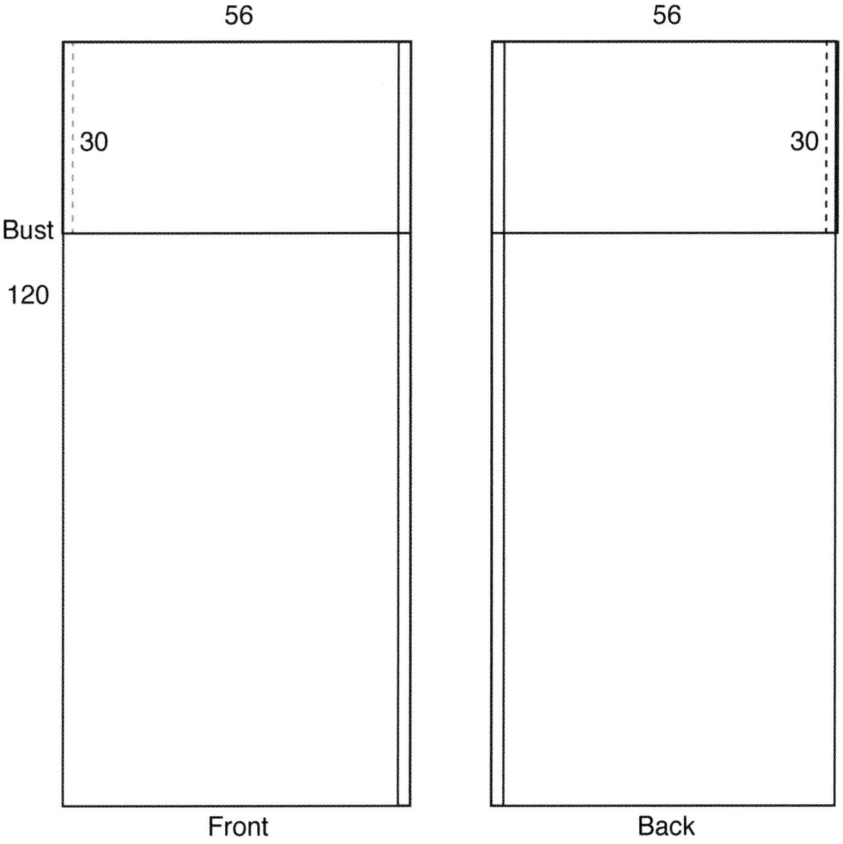

Fig. 8.34 Block dimensions for sleeveless flared dress.

6. Start to gently angle the calico down from the neck point and pin it about 2cm from the neck point along the shoulder line. Snip in towards the pin, letting the fabric drop a bit.
7. Repeat this process, angling, pinning and snipping the calico all the way along the shoulder line until you get to the top of the arm plate. You should be able to see the amount of flare you have created forming along your hemline (Fig. 8.35).
8. If you are happy with it, put a couple of holding pins into the calico at the SS.
9. Transfer all the information you need to the drape by marking your neckline, shoulder line, armhole and SSs with a dotted line and all the corners with a bar and junctions with a cross. Also include your new bust-, waist- and hiplines. I find these easier to do in a broken line in a different colour simply because of the volume of cloth now standing away from the bottom of the stand. If you have done this correctly these lines will now be curved when you take the drape off the stand.

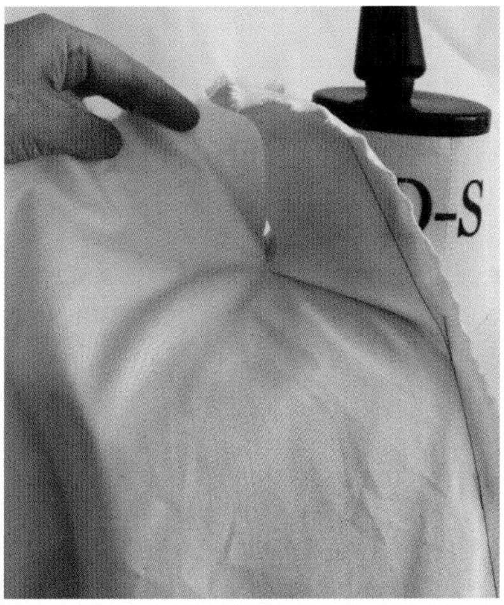

Fig. 8.35 Angling volume of cloth into front from neck point to shoulder.

10. Remove the calico and true up (Fig. 8.36).
11. Drop the neckline by 1cm at the CF and the armhole down by 2cm and out by 1cm at the underarm, then re-mark.
12. Trim the excess SA down to 2cm.
13. Repeat the whole process, steps 3–12, for the back. Note that no shoulder dart is needed (Fig. 8.37).
14. Put the front and back pieces back on the stand and pin the back to the front through the shoulders and SSs. Remember to leave the SA flat for the front and turn under to join up at the position of the sewing line for the back. Pin together from the

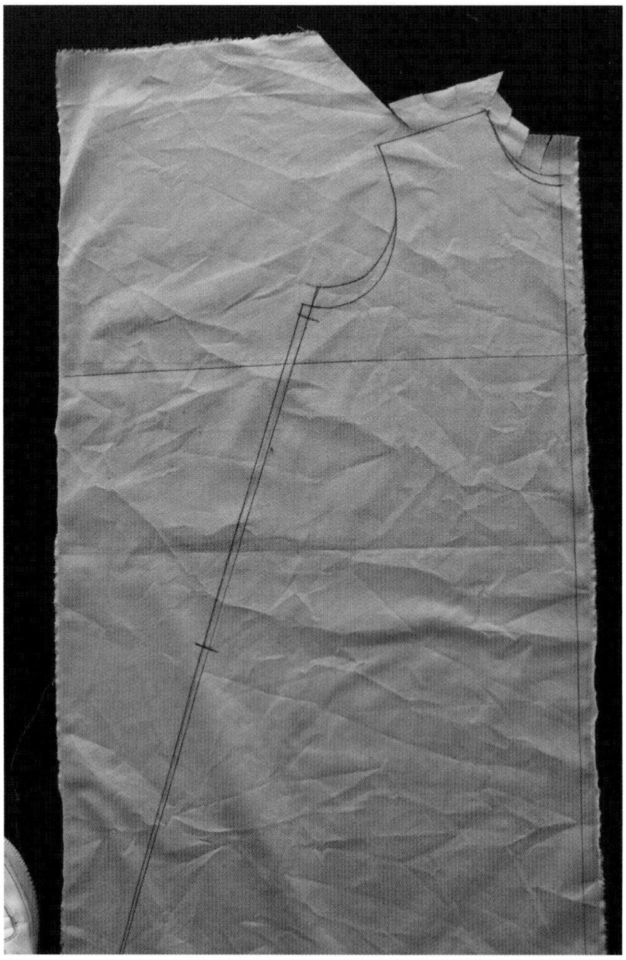

Fig. 8.36 Flared dress front on the flat; hemline is A-line shape and armhole and neck hole have been dropped.

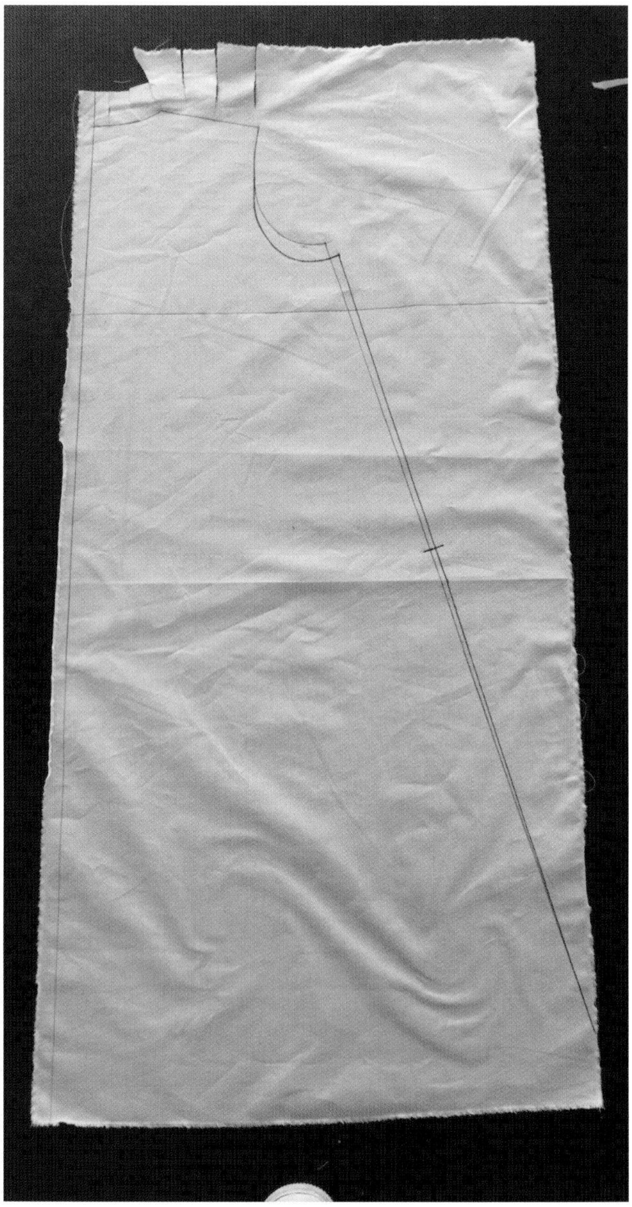

Fig. 8.37 Flared dress back on the flat.

top – remember you are still draping, not preparing a toile to sew, and may still need to unpin, make adjustments and re-pin (Fig. 8.38).

15. Unpin, make your adjustments and re-pin.
16. Level the hem.
17. Transfer to your paper master.

Changing the Neckline and Armholes

This can be done to the dresses and the bodices in this book. You have three points of intervention for this and the method you use is up to you. Keep these in mind when looking at the variations for the flared dress.

1. One is at the outset so that you are draping, for example, a V neck by taping it onto the mannequin and draping to it.
2. The alternative is a more revisionist approach where you have already draped a basic neckline or armhole and want to modify or change it altogether. Pin on a stay tape or use the adhesive styling tape to 'draw' the neckline or armhole into the shape you want directly on top of your drape. Adjust until you are happy, then mark it off with your series of dots, dashes and crosses and transfer to your paper master with a tracing wheel (Figs 8.39 and 8.40).

BIAS SEAM STRETCH

With the flared dress and its variations, the SS is on the bias so it is likely to stretch. It is therefore advisable to leave the finished version on the stand to drop for at least 24 hours before marking off the final length and the hem.

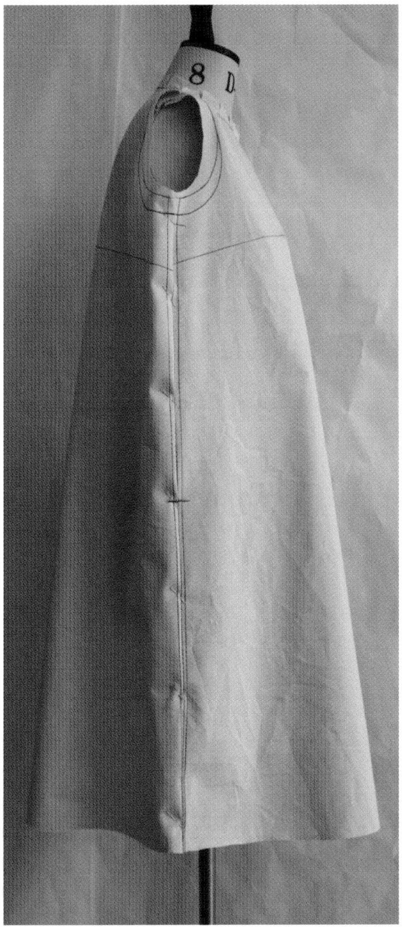

Fig. 8.38 Flared dress with hem levelled.

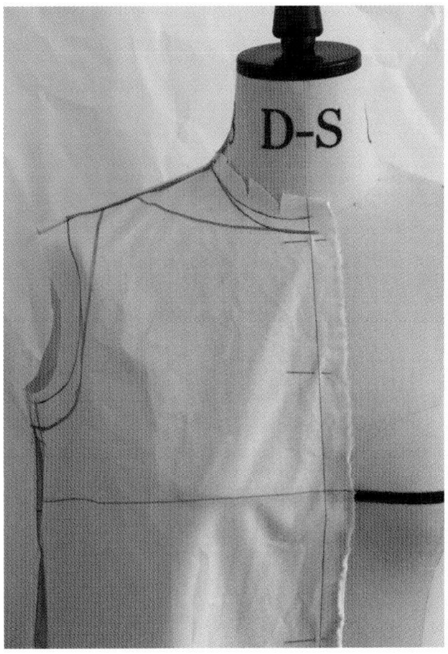

Fig. 8.39 Using adhesive tape to draw in new neckline on existing drape, front.

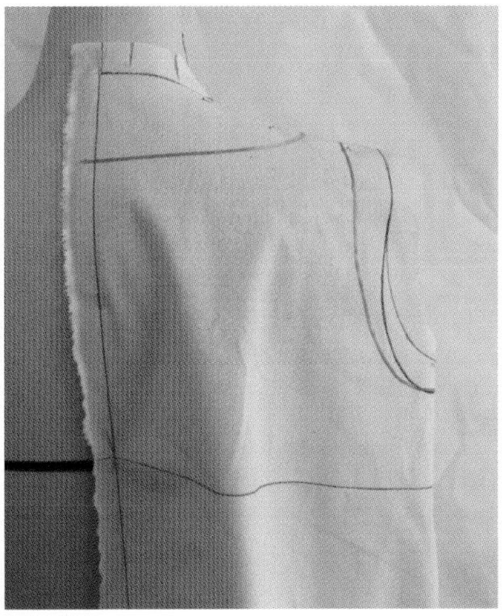

Fig. 8.40 Using adhesive tape to draw in new neckline on existing drape, back.

3. Draw the new neckline onto the paper master itself and transfer to the calico using carbon paper and a tracing wheel. Be warned – it can get a bit messy but it is really quick. You can also transfer calico to calico with carbon paper.

Flared Dress with Overlay (Figs 8.41 and 8.42)

My starting point for this was my existing flared dress drape and master. This time I also decided on the finished length of the overlay and marked it off on the original drape, transferring it to the master pattern. There is no need to block and drape from scratch for this overlay as it is the same dimension as the dress beneath it. If I had intended to toile this dress the overlay would have been joined to the underdress

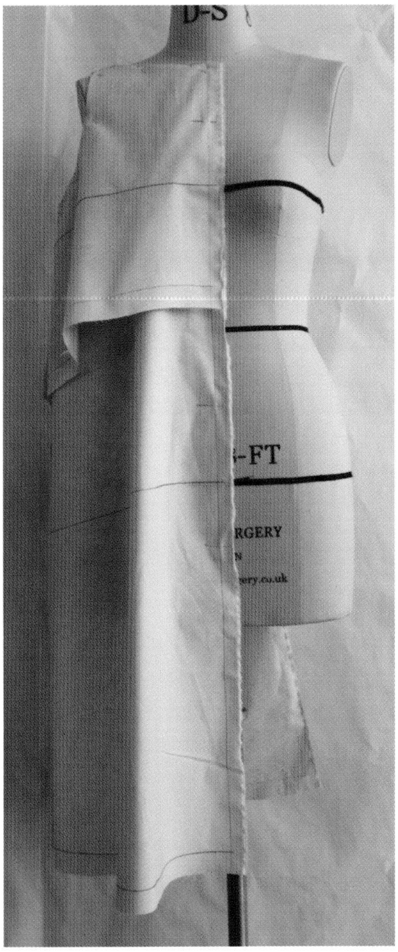

Fig. 8.41 Half drape for flared dress, with overlay and boat neck.

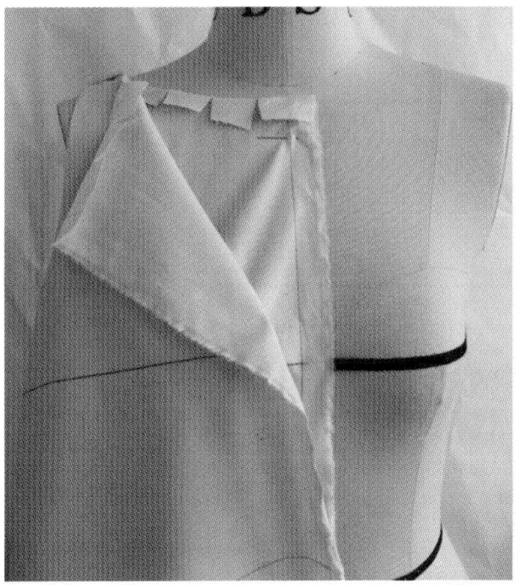

Fig. 8.43 Snipping into SAs of underdress.

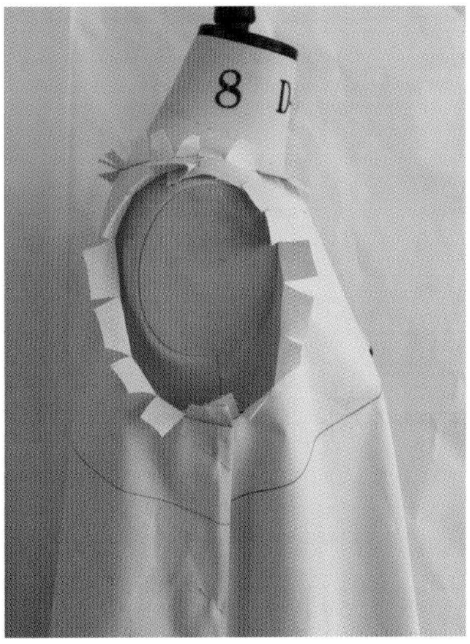

Fig. 8.44 Turning allowance inwards on dress and overlay neckline to pin together.

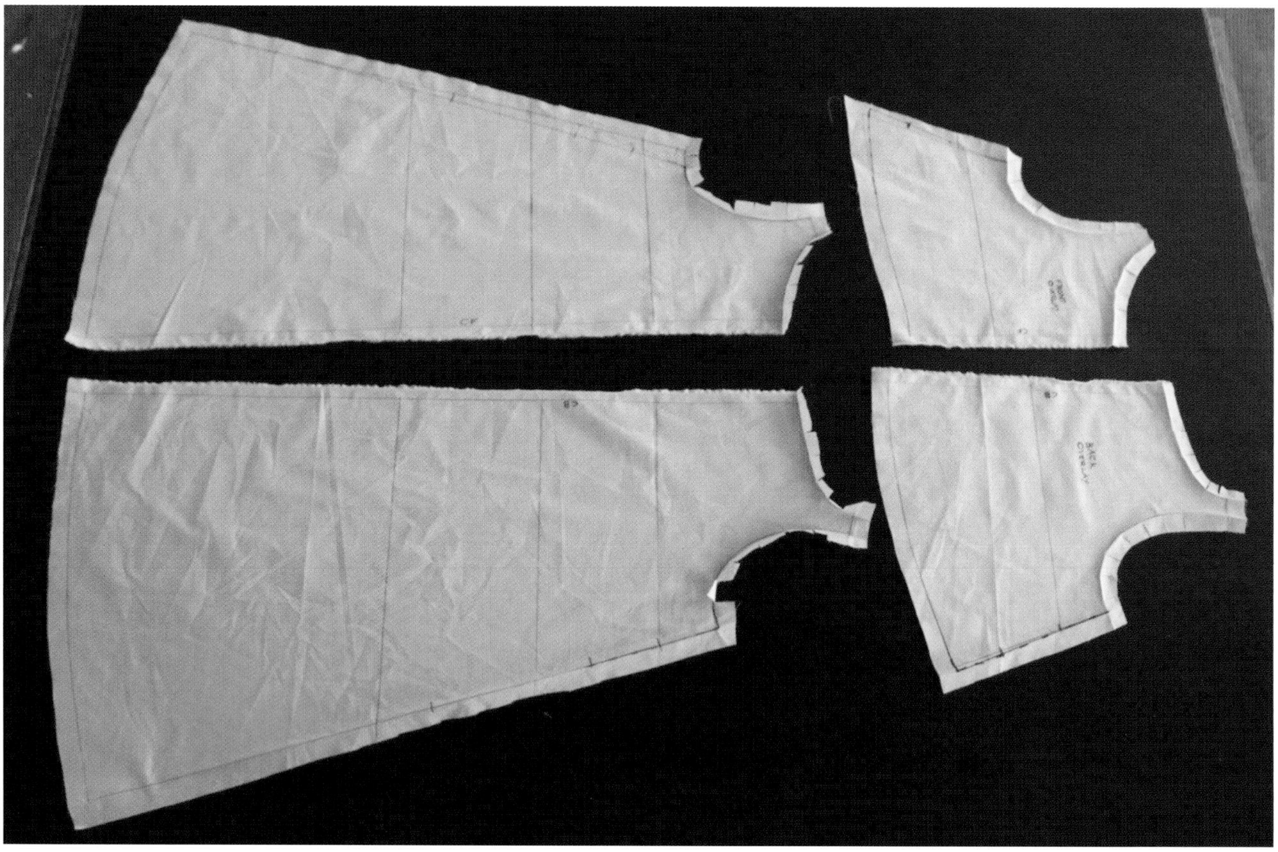

Fig. 8.42 Flared dress with overlay drape on the flat.

through the neck and armholes with a shaped hem over the waistline. So that is reflected in the way I pinned it to check the drape.

1. Using carbon paper, trace the overlay onto calico from the master. True up and, leaving a good 4cm SA, trim away the excess calico. Snip into the neckline and armholes towards the sewing line and finger-press the SA on the dress outwards on the top and the SA on the overlay inwards underneath (Fig. 8.43).
2. Put the existing flared dress drape on the mannequin and align the CF and bustline of the front overlay to the CF and bustline of the dress. Ease the overlay up to the neck point and along the shoulder. Adjust the edges around the neck and armholes so that the two layers of calico are aligned, and pin together (Fig. 8.44).
3. Fold the back SS and overlay onto the front, aligning them at the sewing line. Pin and make any adjustments in a different coloured pen before taking off, truing up and transferring to the master pattern.

Asymmetric Flared Dress (Fig. 8.45)

This style is something you often see in summer dresses for fashion-forward high-street brands like COS or in collections from ready-to-wear designers like Roland Mouret and Commes Des Garcons. This particular style marries up many of the draping skills we have already explored for the bodice and skirt we are simply applying them to a different area of the body to create a different garment type. There is significantly more volume in this half of the design, with the hemline going onto the bias. I have also left the corners on for this to highlight the design's asymmetry. I have used the drape from the original flared dress for the left half of the

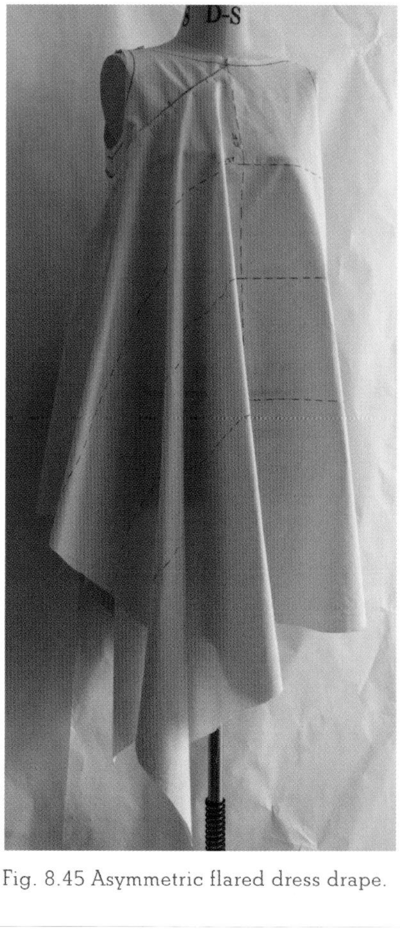

Fig. 8.45 Asymmetric flared dress drape.

design and then draped a new right half with different style lines and yoke to contrast.

I actually joined the two halves together at the CF and CB to form new single pattern pieces and a new design. If I hadn't already had a pattern to adapt I could have draped the whole of the front with one large piece of calico instead, then repeated for the back. This dress has SSs but from a design point of view these could also be eliminated, leaving just the seam at the CB. This would have to be draped from one large single piece of calico, which is a more sophisticated approach to the draping process. However, the downside of draping with such a large amount of calico is that it is really unwieldy to manage when you are first learning to drape, so using this approach of draping in two halves gives you much more control.

Volume-to-Length Ratios

This is not always easy to gauge but, as a rough rule of thumb, the more volume you want the longer and wider your calico needs to be, so add on an extra 20cm more than you think you need to drape. I slightly misjudged the amount of volume-to-length ratio when I draped the bias section of this style and started with a piece of calico that ended up being too narrow for the finished length I wanted. The solution is obviously to add an extra piece on where it is needed but keeping the insert on the same grain as the body of the dress it is being attached to, so that the calico continues to behave as though it were one continuous piece. As my hemline is on the bias I was able to join it selvedge to selvedge. I pinned mine but you can also overlay the pieces and machine stitch or baste together by hand; if you are feeling bold you can use a bit of PVA glue and wait for it to dry (Fig. 8.46).

1. Tape up your mannequin with waist- and hiplines. Make sure the hipline is parallel to the floor by stepping away from the mannequin to check. Also tape your neckline and armhole, keeping them the same as the original so that you don't have to re-drape them later. Also tape in the style line for the yoke but only on the side you are now draping. Include notches so you can align the panels later (Figs. 8.47, 8.48 and 8.49).
2. Prepare and block your calico for the new half of the dress as per the dimensions in Fig. 8.50. Begin with the yoke panel as it is the smallest (Fig. 8.51). Align the calico at the CF and bustline and

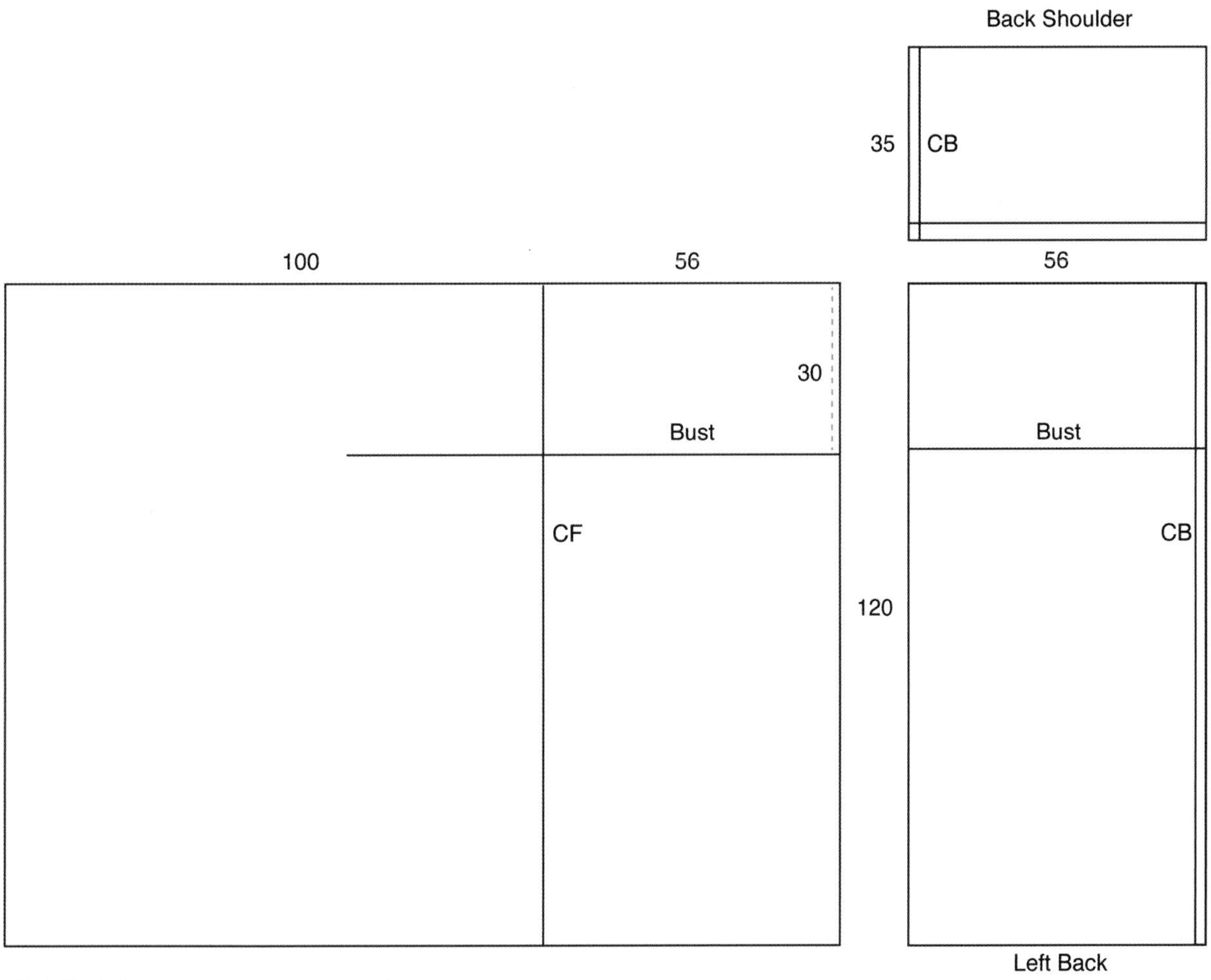

Fig. 8.50 Block dimensions for asymmetric dress.

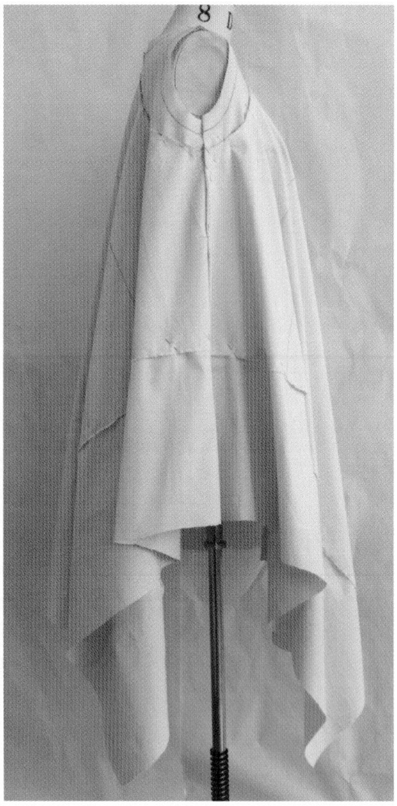

Fig. 8.46 Pinned insert of calico on bias side of asymmetric dress can be seen in this side view.

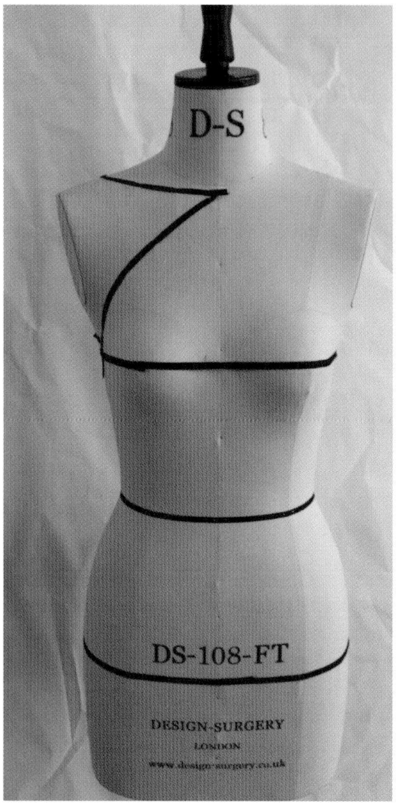

Fig. 8.47 Taping style lines for asymmetric dress, front.

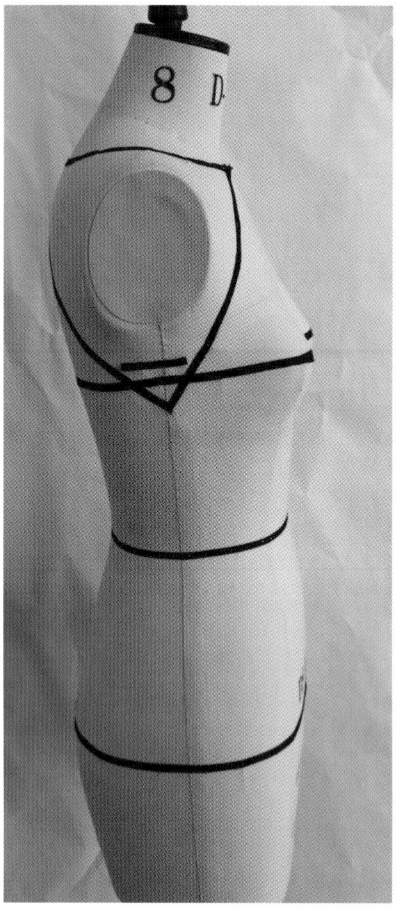

Fig. 8.48 Taping style lines for asymmetric dress, side.

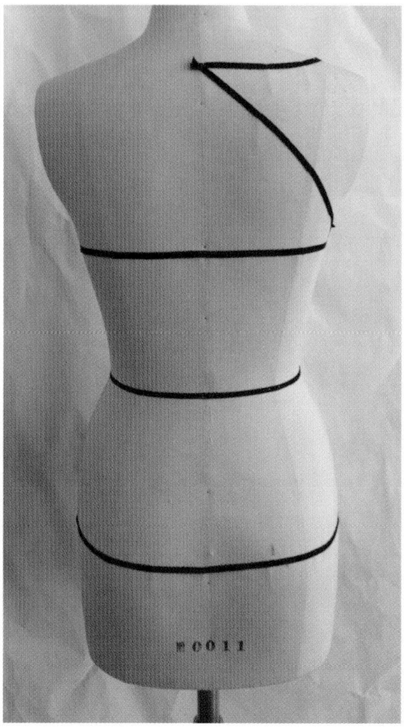

Fig. 8.49 Taping style lines for asymmetric dress, back.

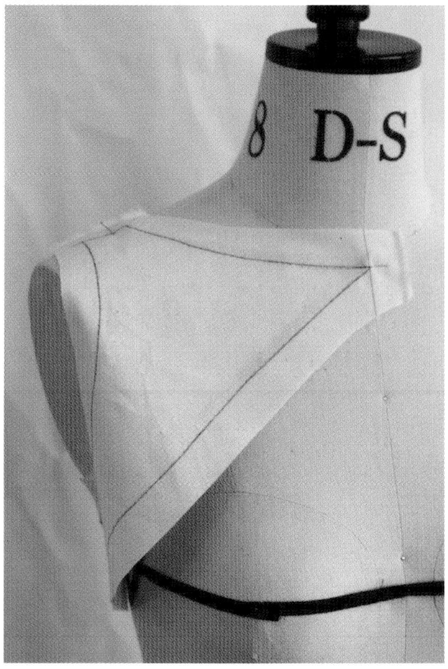

Fig. 8.51 Asymmetric dress yoke drape.

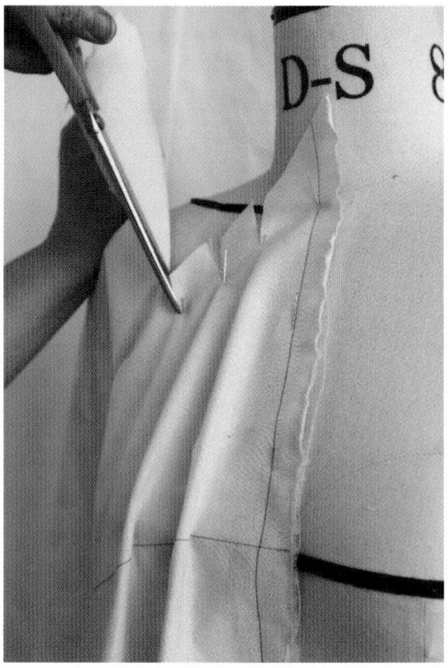

Fig. 8.52 Snipping into fabric and angling calico forwards to create volume.

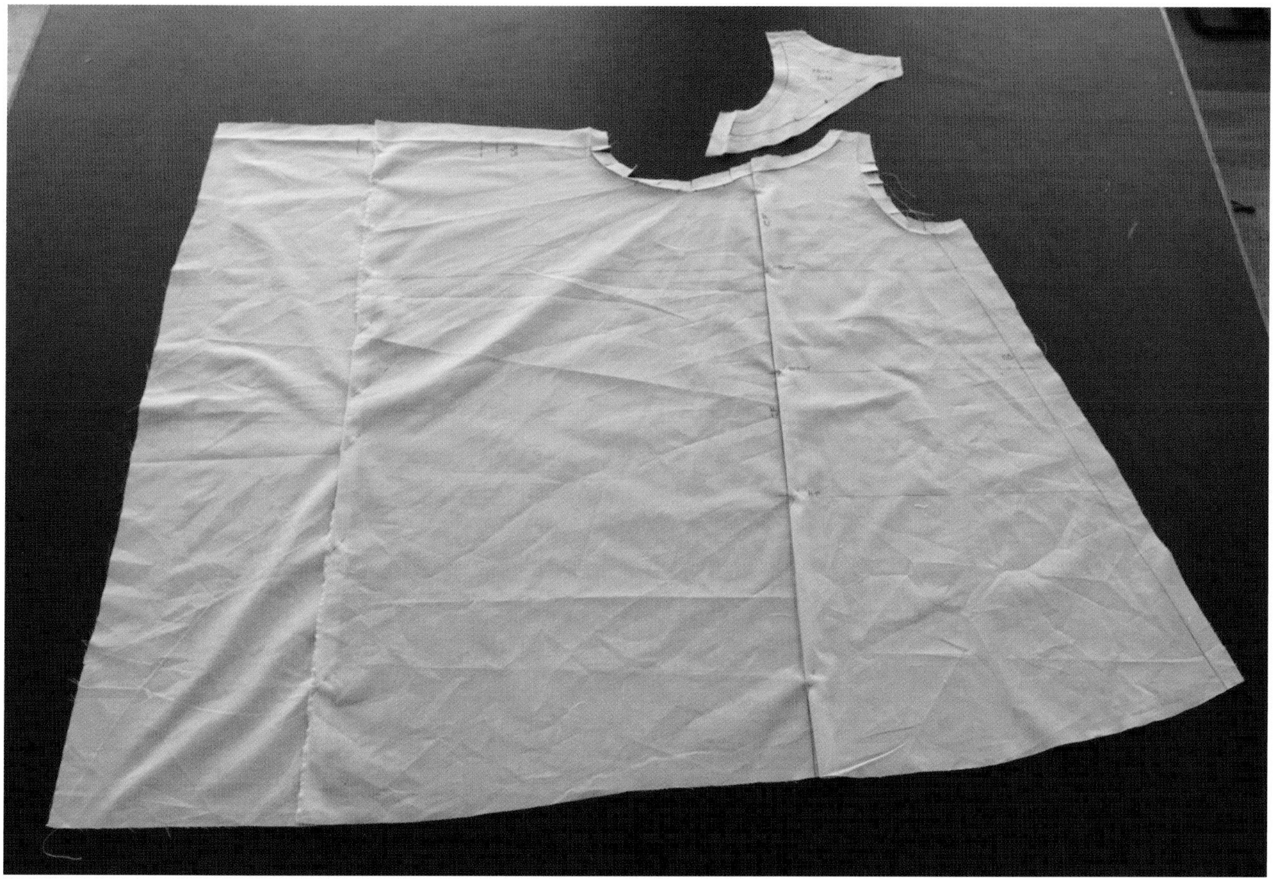

Fig. 8.53 Trued-up drape on the flat.

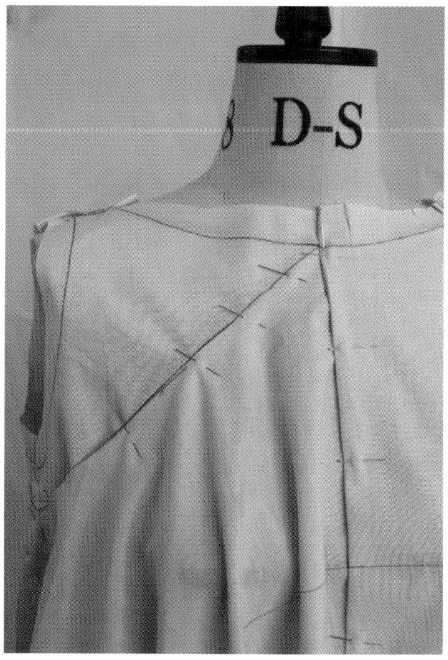

Fig. 8.54 Drape front pinned together from the top of the calico.

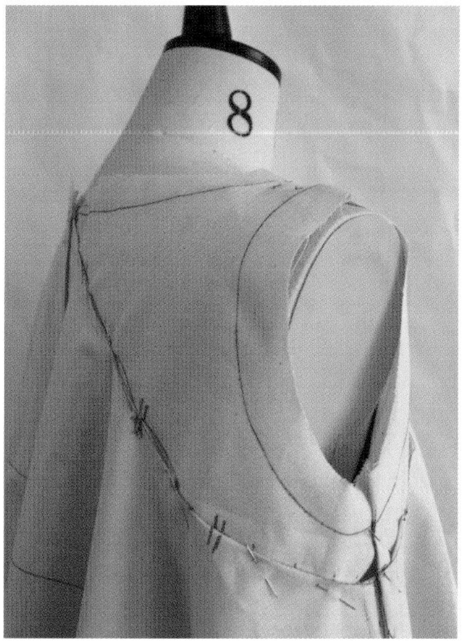

Fig. 8.55 Drape back pinned together and adjusted with notches.

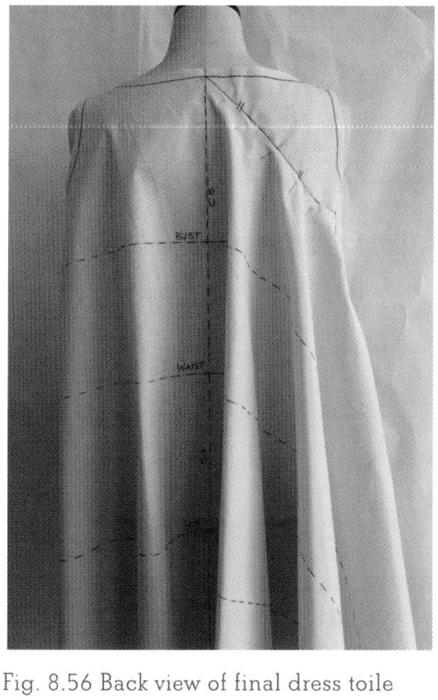

Fig. 8.56 Back view of final dress toile with additional CF and SS eliminated.

pin to hold, smoothing your fabric up to the neck point. Pin and smooth out along the shoulder. Pin along the style lines and mark off with dots and bars for corners and notches.

3. The skirt section of this drape is based on the technique used to drape the circular skirt in Chapter 7, where the volume is formed by turning and manipulating your calico along the style line of the bodice yoke. As the volume falls from the yoke you will need to align your calico where the bustline and CF intersect and pin to hold.
4. Smooth the calico along the bustline and pin 2cm along the style line. Snip downwards to the pin and start to angle your calico downwards from the bottom of your snip and the point where you have inserted the pin.
5. Repeat this process of pinning and snipping along the yoke style line until you get to the SS. As you turn the fabric downwards from the snips you are pushing volume into the front and creating the characteristic flared shape at the bottom of the hemline. It is a question of aesthetics how much volume you put into the front and also where you place it but by using this method you can see exactly where it is going to sit and how it is going to look (Fig. 8.52).
6. Repeat the process for the dress back.
7. True up all the pieces on the flat and adjust the armhole if you need to. Make sure the left and right armholes are the same. The best way to do this is to trace off the armhole from the side you are most happy with and transfer it over to the other side before truing up the SSs as you did for the bodice in Chapter 6. Trim down, leaving a 2cm SA on all pieces (Fig 8.53).
8. Reposition all the draped pieces back on the stand, starting with the skirt panel at the CF and overlaying the bodice piece onto it along the sewing line, turning the SA under. Pin together from the top, ensuring the notches match up. Join the front to the back at the SS. Again, turn the edge of the back under along the sewing line and pin onto the SF from the top. Be aware that if you are not pinning straight down the SS it will affect the hang of the dress (Figs 8.54, 8.55 and 8.56).
9. Adjust and re-mark as necessary.
10. Remove from the stand and trace off onto paper to create your master pattern.
11. To create the production pattern for this dress re-trace half the front and half the back of each, joining them through the CF and CB, then cut out in calico to toile (Figs 8.57 and 8.58).

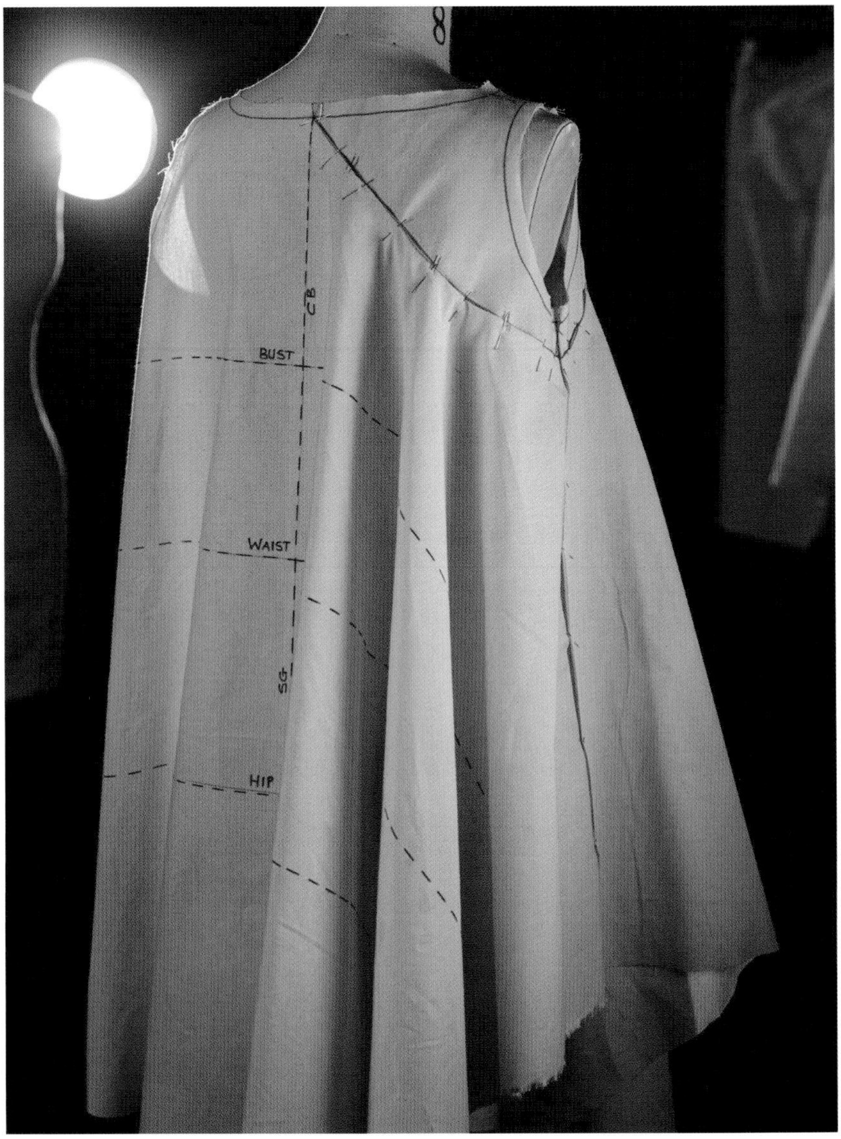

Fig. 8.58 Asymmetric dress finished drape, back view.

Fig. 8.57 Asymmetric dress finished drape, front view.

0-S 8
CF

The Sleeves

9

The purpose of the sleeve is obvious from a functional point of view: we can all see the necessity for arm coverage and protection in some garments. In addition, sleeves must also offer freedom of movement and comfort. Beyond their practical function, different styles of sleeve can add to a garment's aesthetic silhouette and style and create movement and structure. The set-in sleeve – described below and the style we are most familiar with today – requires a higher standard of tailoring than a grown-on sleeve which is cut in one with the body of the garment. Historically speaking, this level of skill was very much in evidence for centuries in Chinese and Eastern cultures and regularly seen in variants of the kimono. However, in many ancient cultures that have helped shape Western society, the sleeve played virtually no role at all. In the West, where it existed, the sleeve was usually roughly cut in one with the garment and had very little shaping or regard for fit or aesthetic.

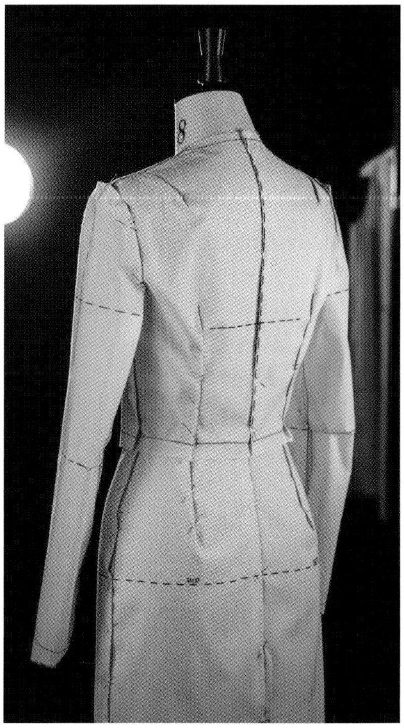

Fig. 9.2 Finished drape for set-in one-piece sleeve back. (Photo: Yousef Al Nasser)

In this country the sleeve didn't really come into its own until the Tudor period where, according to portraits of the time, shaped detachable sleeves started to appear in the dress of wealthy men and women. Occasionally sleeves were stitched directly to a bodice or the doublet but in the main part they were tied or buckled onto the rest of the garment at strategic points like the shoulder. The advantage of the detachable sleeve was that it provided movement without too much shaping but, more importantly, it was interchangeable and could be worn with a variety of bodices and dresses to create a wider range of looks. Traditionally, Tudor ladies' bodices were quite plain, with the focus being on elaborate sleeves and their embellishments: this provided more opportunities to showcase the wealth of the wearer. Design features of the time demonstrate the importance of expressing your wealth and status through the vehicle of clothing in Tudor society. For example, the 'slashed sleeve' was named after the intricate cuts that ran down the length of the sleeve, allowing the wearer to show off not one luxurious cloth but two or more, often with a velvet outer sleeve and layered silk and organza inner sleeves or underlinings. The head of the sleeve was often puffed, with extra volume created by gathering and pleating or with long and voluminous cuffs. This design sensibility influenced the style of the sleeve in Europe up until the 1800s.

The advent of the Industrial Revolution saw radical changes to the cut and construction of Western fashions, with the introduction of mass production and synthetic dyes. Women's sleeves were now attached at the armhole and whilst the forearm from the elbow downwards was narrow and fitted, the shoulder was a puffed or a voluminous bell shape. The notion of detachable elements survived into the Victorian era with the use of *engageantes* or false sleeves made of lace or linen which sat under the sleeves of day dresses and were easy to remove and launder.

Revivals of past styles make up a considerable part of a fashion designer's armoury today. At the time of writing, the statement sleeve has been an overwhelming trend in the past few seasons on the catwalk and has been the focal point of many womenswear garments. Such sleeves can be described as an over-sized balloon sleeve or bishop's sleeve. Regardless of their practicality for modern-day lifestyles they allow for freedom of movement and comfort far more than their historical counterparts as a result of modern-day pattern cutting, construction methods, fabrication and laundering.

Types of Sleeves

There are three basic types of sleeve: set-in, kimono and raglan. All other sleeve styles are a derivative of one of these, regardless of how loose, flowy, puffy, structured, long or short they are or how many panels and pieces they have to them. When cutting patterns on the flat the kimono and raglan are created by manipulating the set-in

Left: Fig. 9.1 Finished drape for set-in one-piece sleeve front. (Photo: Yousef Al Nasser)

sleeve pattern. If this is incorrectly drafted or draped then everything else will be wrong thereafter in your pattern so it is important to get it right.

Similarly, note that the back waist darts of a fitted garment with sleeves should not finish above the underarm of the armhole. This would hinder the smooth fit that you are looking for.

Set-in sleeves: These are made in one piece and sewn into the bodice armholes. All set-in sleeve styles have to be eased, gathered, darted, tucked and sewn into the bodice arm scye seam. They can be fitted, flared, long or short, with hemlines finished in a variety of ways. The closer the armhole to the armpit, the greater the range of movement to the arm.
Raglan sleeve: This has part of the sleeve attached to the bodice. In its basic form a diagonal seam is formed from the neckline to the underarm.
Kimono sleeves: These are cut all in one with the front and back bodice and have a deeper arm scye than the set-in sleeve. There is less of a range of movement to the arm with these styles and they are also characterized by extra volume of cloth under the arm.

The Anatomy of a Sleeve

There is some terminology for the anatomy of the basic set-in sleeve that is useful to know. It is shown in Fig. 9.3 and this correlates to the position of the tapes on the arm of the mannequin in Fig. 9.4. You will need an arm for your mannequin. You will also need a bodice with a decent armhole that suits the type of sleeve to be draped; for example, a fitted sleeve requires a smaller armhole than a wider sleeve. If shoulder pads are being used they need to be positioned on the stand before draping the bodice and sleeve so the extra height is accommodated in the shoulder line and the armhole deepened from the outset.

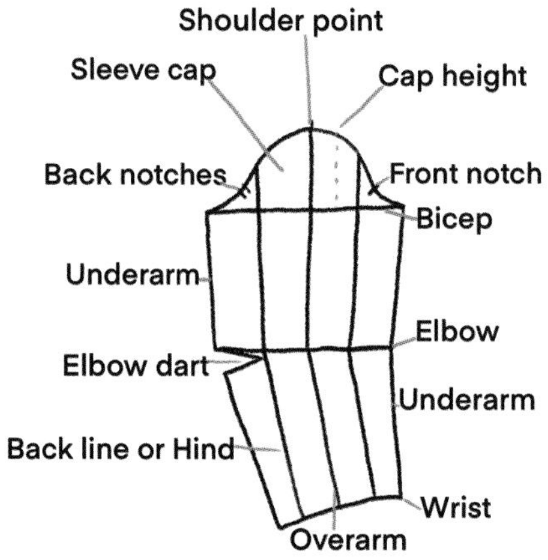

Fig. 9.3 Anatomy of a sleeve.

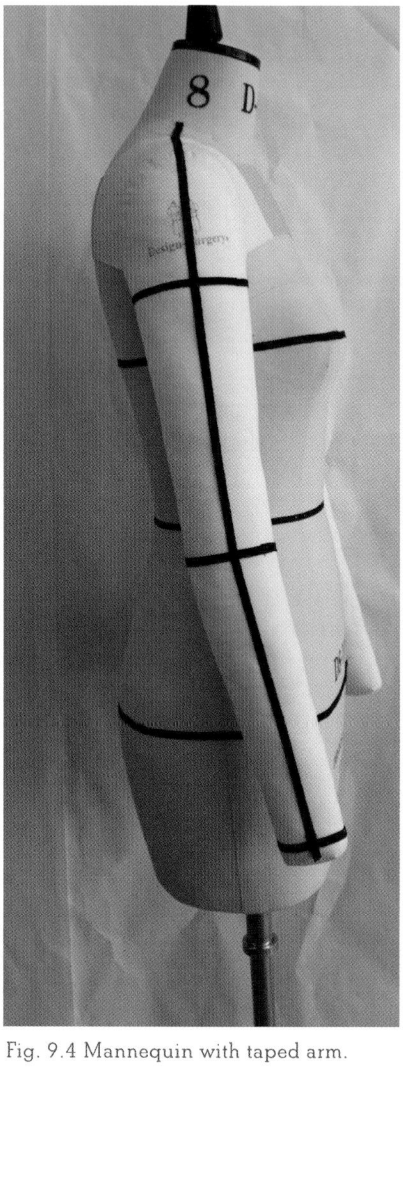

Fig. 9.4 Mannequin with taped arm.

Set-In Sleeve

There are many methods of drafting sleeves on the flat using precise measurements. The pattern book in Figs 9.5, 9.6 and 9.7 shows some pages from an old tailoring manual in the UCA archive. This seventh edition of the manual, entitled *The Climax System for Cutting Gentlemen's Garments*, was reprinted in 1917 and signed by the authors, W.E. Leggatt and T.W. Hodgkinson, both of whom were members of the Master Tailors Association of Great Britain and Ireland. It contains a series of instructions and diagrams for drafting on the flat for a variety of frock coats, ecclesiastical garb and gentlemen's sporting wear, all of which use derivatives of their one-piece set-in sleeve. This particular one-piece sleeve was deemed suitable by the authors to be used most notably for 'angling, golf and rock climbing'! Accompanying the book is a drafted one-piece sleeve in buff, along with collars, pockets and other pieces of ephemera that indicate the level of engagement the original owner would have had with the book's contents. The shape of the sleeve head in particular appears to be the most variable aspect of the drafts and dependent on the nature of the activity the garment is intended for, and much attention is given over to the process of the first fitting on a client. Written in a similar period to the wonderful Women's Institute of Domestic Arts and Sciences series, this manual had its own set of instructions for drafting and adapting a basic set-in sleeve. It is interesting to see in both publications how similar and how in-depth the level of instruction is for those pursuing the art of tailoring their own bespoke garments.

Draping is obviously a far more organic process than the Climax System but it does need some core measurements to get started. Sleeves can either be draped from scratch directly on the mannequin or can be created using a hybrid approach with a relatively unrefined but simple one-piece sleeve draft drawn onto paper or direct onto the calico as a starting

Useful Dimensions for Draping Sleeves						
Size UK/US	**8/4**	**10/6**	**12/8**	**14/10**	**16/12**	**18/14**
Sleeve length	57.2	57.8	58.4	59	59.5	60
Underarm length	40.6	41.3	41.9	41.6	43.2	43.8
Bicep	27.9	29.2	30.5	31.7	33	34.3
Elbow	23.5	24.8	26	27.3	28.6	29.9
Wrist	18.4	19	19.7	20.3	21	21.6

All measurements are in centimetres.

This table is based on industry guidelines for sizing but obviously not carved in stone so it is always best to take your own measurements, as in Chapter 2. The sleeve length does not include a cuff, so if you want to work with the cuff taken into account in the sleeve length then add on another 5cm.

Fig. 9.5 Frontispiece and title page of *The Climax System For Cutting Gentlemen's Garments*.

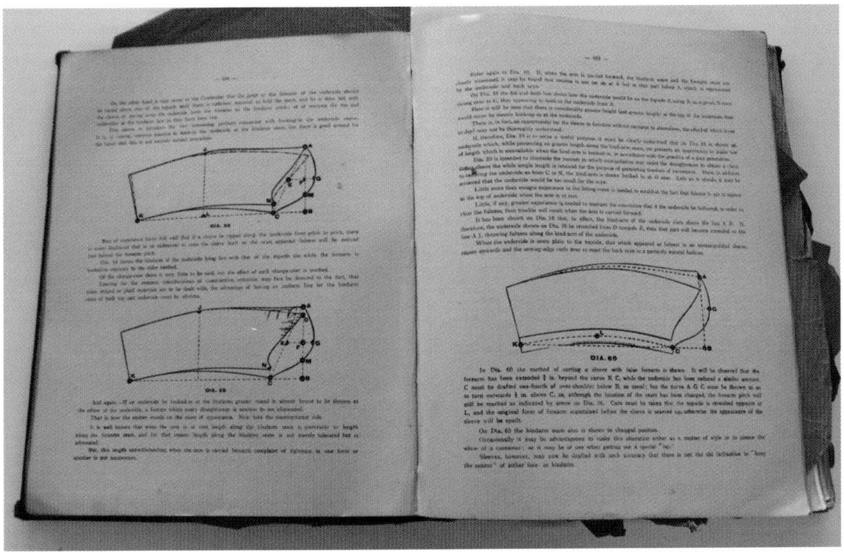

Fig. 9.6 Instructions for drafting an ecclesiastical sleeve.

point. The benefit of drafting a rough sleeve shape first is to save time and set the general parameters of the sleeve before fine-tuning the drape once it is on the mannequin. In *Draping: The Complete Course*, Karolyn Kiisel has an excellent method for this that also includes a rough draft for the sleeve cap. My preferred method begins in the same way with a few basic measurements marked onto the calico but I prefer to drape the cap of the sleeve direct to the armhole. I am working on a full-length sleeve for this drape and have used a series of measurements in accordance with that. Note that the blocking dimensions used are the same for the set-in sleeve, the fitted sleeve and the raglan sleeve.

1. Prepare and block your calico 45cm wide and the desired sleeve length plus 10cm. It should look something like mine in Fig. 9.8.
2. Place a vertical grain line in the centre of the fabric.
3. Draw a horizontal line 2cm up from the bottom of the calico for the wrist.
4. Measure the distance from the wrist to the elbow on the arm and mark off on the calico.
5. Measure the distance from the elbow to the bicep on the mannequin and mark off on the calico.
6. In the middle of the calico pin in a pleat all the way down measuring 4–5cm in total. The raised part of

Fig. 9.7 Part of a two-piece sleeve block inside the book.

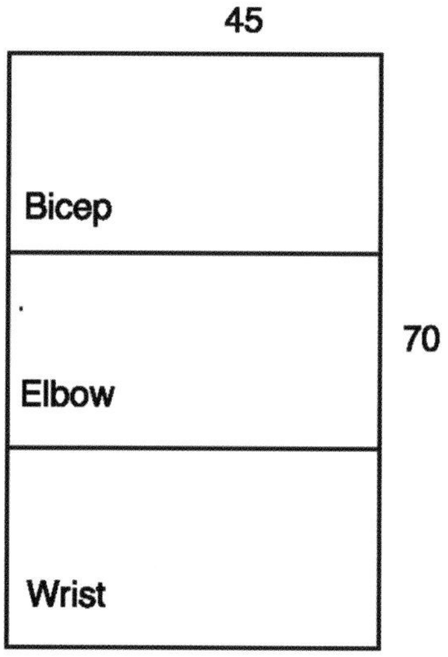

Fig. 9.8 Block dimensions for set-in sleeve.

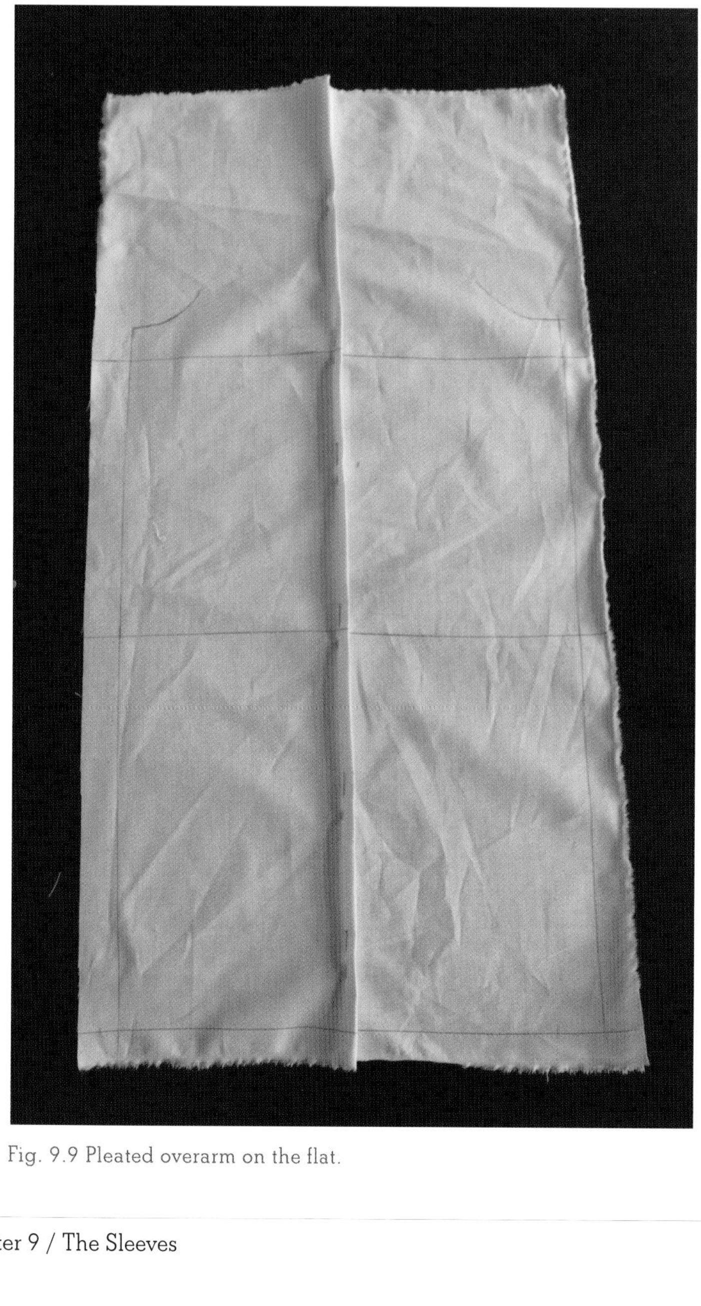

Fig. 9.9 Pleated overarm on the flat.

the pleat should be 2–2.5cm in height. This is going to create extra width for the drape so that it is not skintight on the arm on the master pattern and also provides ease at the sleeve head (Fig. 9.9).

7. This step can be done with the arm either attached to the mannequin or flat on the table if it is easier. Align the elbow and bicep lines on the calico with the corresponding elbow and bicep tapes on the arm. Pin the fold and grain line of the calico to the overarm tape on the mannequin's arm (Fig. 9.10).
8. Pin one side of the calico along the underarm seam. Then cut the excess calico away leaving a generous 2cm allowance. Fold the other side towards the inner arm seam, folding the excess calico underneath. Pin the two sides of the calico together with this side on top of the other. Obviously, this process is easier if you turn the arm over on the table top with the inner arm upwards. If your arm is attached to the mannequin then manoeuvre the arm position backwards a little so you can see what you are doing before taking it off to check and marking off the underarm seam on the calico. Cut away the excess fabric, leaving about 4cm allowance, and also roughly shape around the base of

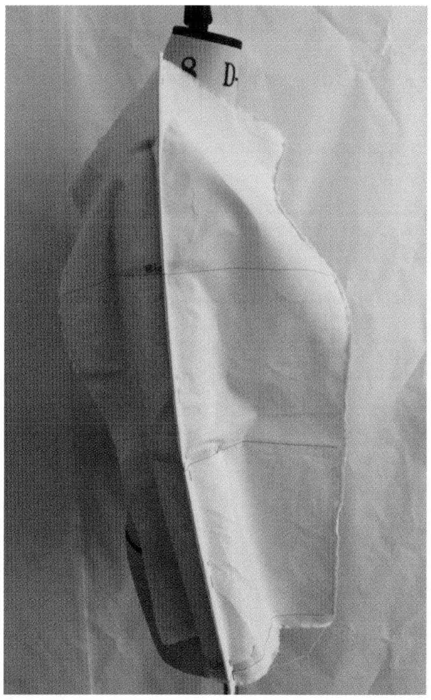

Fig. 9.10 Pleated overarm positioned, with elbow and bicep aligned.

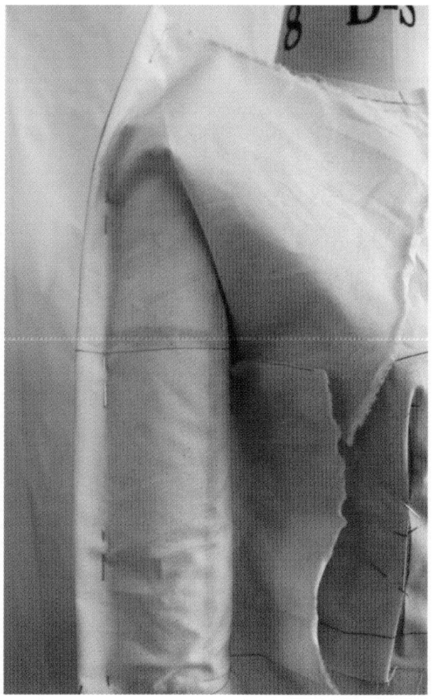

Fig. 9.11 Edges pinned to underarm seam position.

the arm so that it is easier to shape the armhole (Fig. 9.11).

9. The bottom of the armhole should sit on the bicep line. Align with the bottom of the armhole on the bodice and trace off with a dotted line. Remove the sleeve from the arm and true up.
10. There are balance points at the front and back of the sleeve head so just true up to the balance points. On the front this will be 9.5cm from the end of the underarm seam, 7.5cm on the back. Mark with a single notch at the front and a double one at the back.
11. Cut down the excess calico to 2cm allowance, following the curve of the underarm and leaving enough to drape the crown of the sleeve head (Fig. 9.12).
12. Pin the sleeve back together along the underarm seam – put a ruler under it to use as a backing if you need to. Unpin the pleat at the overarm.
13. Put the arm back on the mannequin. Align the underarm of the sleeve drape with the bottom of the armhole on the bodice and

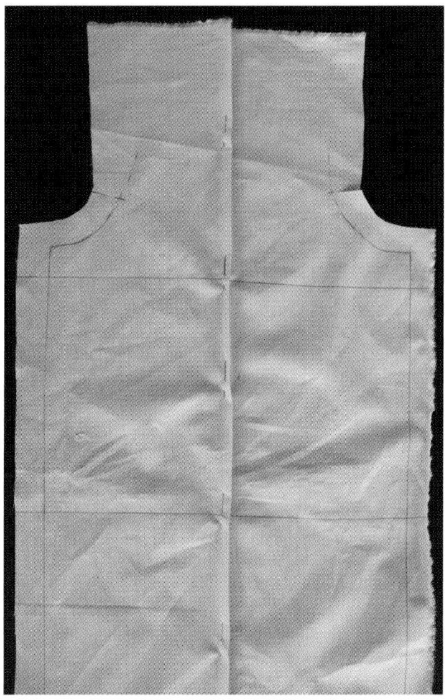

Fig. 9.12 Trimmed bottom of armhole marked on calico on the flat.

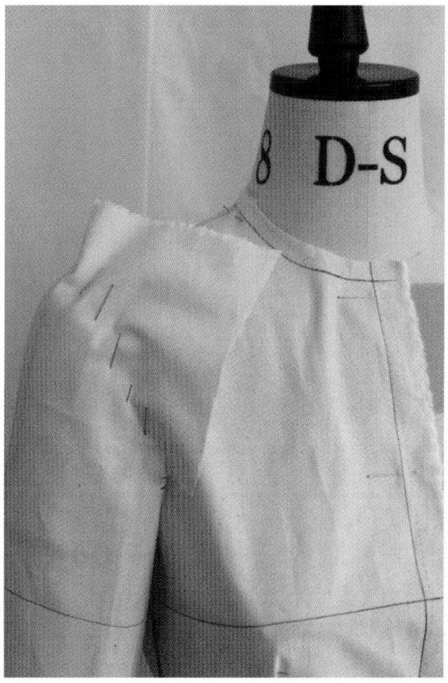

Fig. 9.14 Front view of allowance for draping sleeve crown.

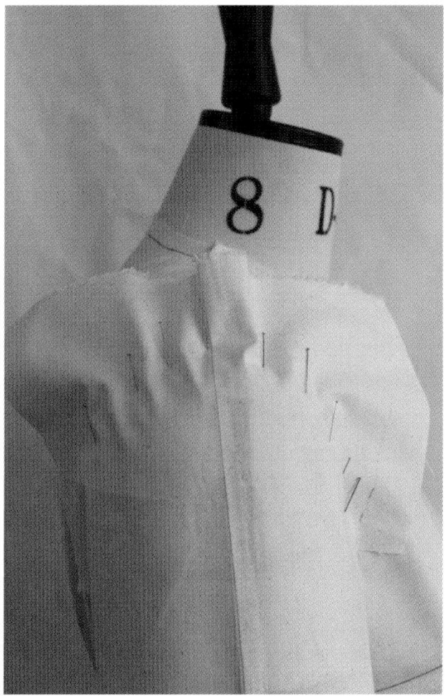

Fig. 9.13 Positioning sleeve back on stand to pin sleeve head.

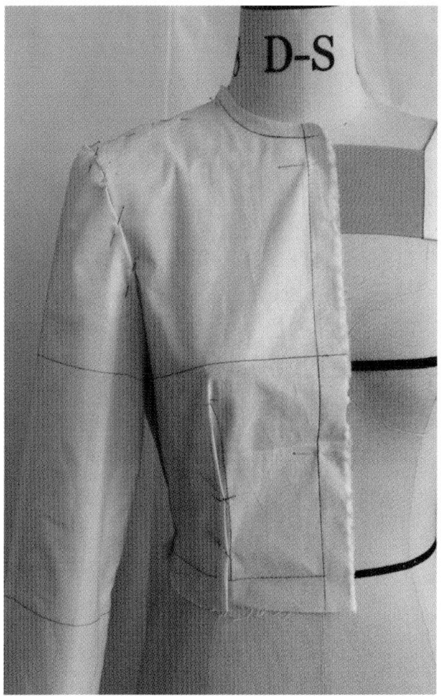

Fig. 9.15 Sleeve inserted into bodice armhole and pinned in position, front view.

mark the front and back notches onto the armhole to correspond with the notches on the sleeve. Snip horizontally into the allowance at the notches, leaving the underarm pinned inwards and the rest of the allowance for draping the crown outwards (Figs 9.13 and 9.14).
14. Fold the upper piece of the sleeve across the armhole and pin the head to the shoulder seam of the bodice with a holding pin. Divide the rest of the sleeve drape equally around the armhole to the notches, pinning with a holding pin and adjusting to get it as even as possible.
15. Cut away surplus fabric leaving a 2cm allowance. Note that the grain line of the sleeve does not necessarily have to connect to the shoulder seam; it is more of a visual guide to check that the sleeve is hanging properly, so adjust accordingly making sure that the sleeve is not swinging backwards.
16. Pin the SA inwards and make sure that you divide the calico equally. Snip into the calico allowance if you need to get a smoother curve over the sleeve head. Mark off the sleeve head with dots and include an additional notch for the top of the sleeve head where it joins the shoulder seam (Figs 9.15 and 9.16).
17. Remeasure for the desired sleeve length and mark off the wrist line.
18. Remove from the arm and true up (Fig. 9.17).

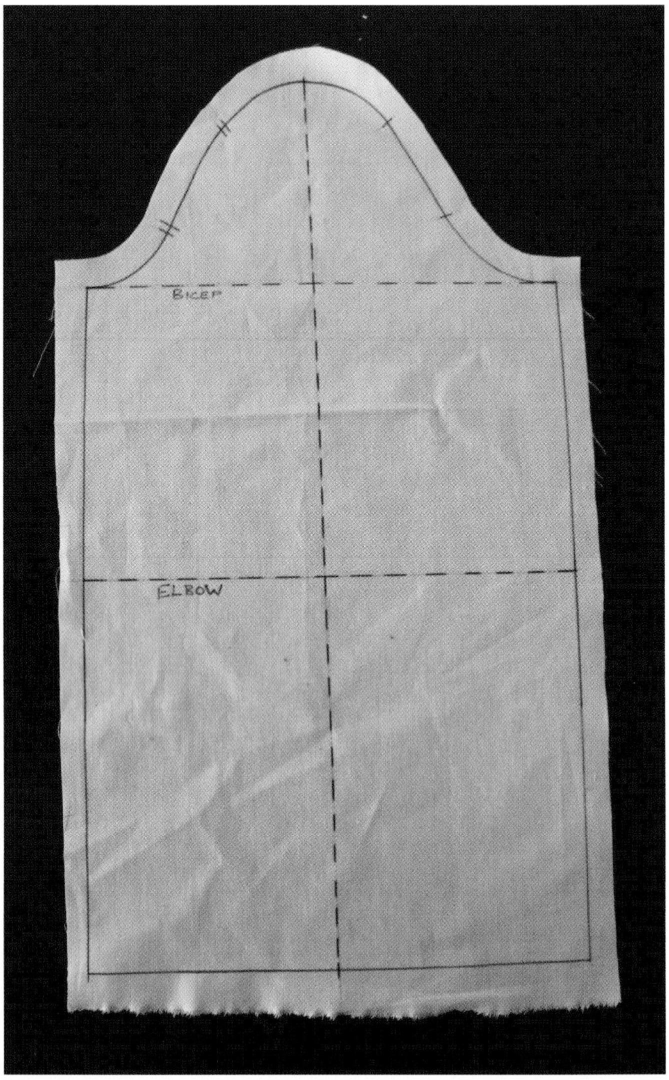

Fig. 9.17 Basic sleeve trued up on the flat.

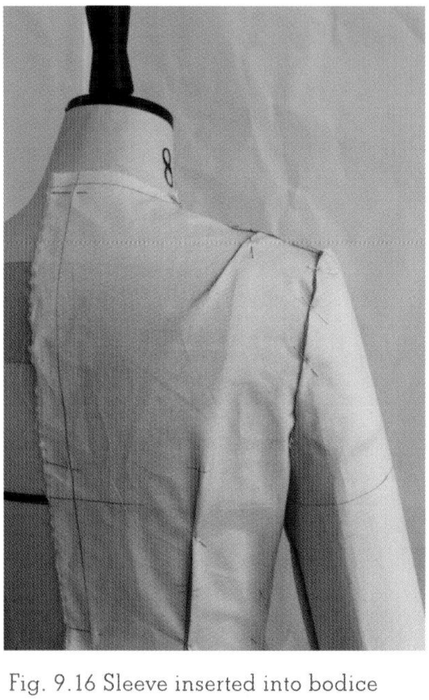
Fig. 9.16 Sleeve inserted into bodice armhole and pinned in position, back view.

SLEEVE INSERTION

Avoid creating angles at the top of your armhole at the shoulder line and at your underarm. Each section of the pattern piece or drape should end with a right angle, encouraging the transition from one pattern piece to the next to be a smooth flat line with no pointy bits.

Fitted Sleeve

This is a variant of the one-piece sleeve. It has the same sleeve head but has more shape between the elbow and the wrist, with a small elbow dart giving a slightly more curved look. This sleeve has also has the width reduced at the wrist slightly to create a more tailored look.

1. Repeat the entire process for the set-in sleeve.
2. When pinning the underarm seam on the back or left-hand side only put a dart in at the elbow and re-pin the underarm to close.
3. Using a dotted line, mark off the underarm and the dart and cut

away the surplus fabric.

4. Remove the sleeve from the arm and true up the lines. It should now look like Fig. 9.18, with the wrist of the sleeve curving downwards from the hind quarter at the elbow.

Raglan Sleeve (Fig. 9.19)

The raglan sleeve comes in a variety of guises depending on how closely to the neck point you take the seam. It can be a one- or two-piece sleeve and its most distinctive characteristic is the two-pronged sleeve head areas known as the raglan horns (Fig. 9.20). These are effectively where the shoulder is removed from the bodice and attached to the sleeve head instead (Fig. 9.21). The raglan sleeve is named after the 1st

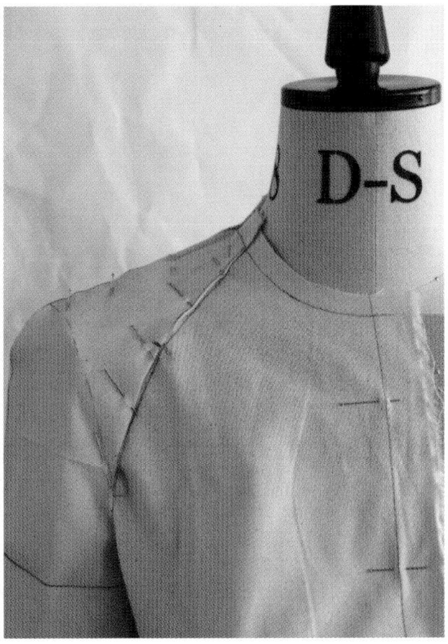

Fig. 9.19 Raglan sleeve drape.

Baron of Raglan who is said to have worn a coat with this particular style of sleeve after the loss of his right arm at the battle of Waterloo. He continued to work in the army in spite of his disability and didn't want his lack of movement or inability to dress himself hinder his progress. In consultation with his tailor he discarded the set-in sleeve and devised this alternative design that now extended in one piece to the collar, with a diagonal seam allowing Lord Raglan greater movement to swing his sword! Many decades later the ease of movement was transferred and popularized in the iconic three-quarter baseball T- shirt and continues to be a popular sportswear cut. Not surprisingly then, the seam line can be run into the shoulder rather than the neck or indeed across the chest and back to the CF and

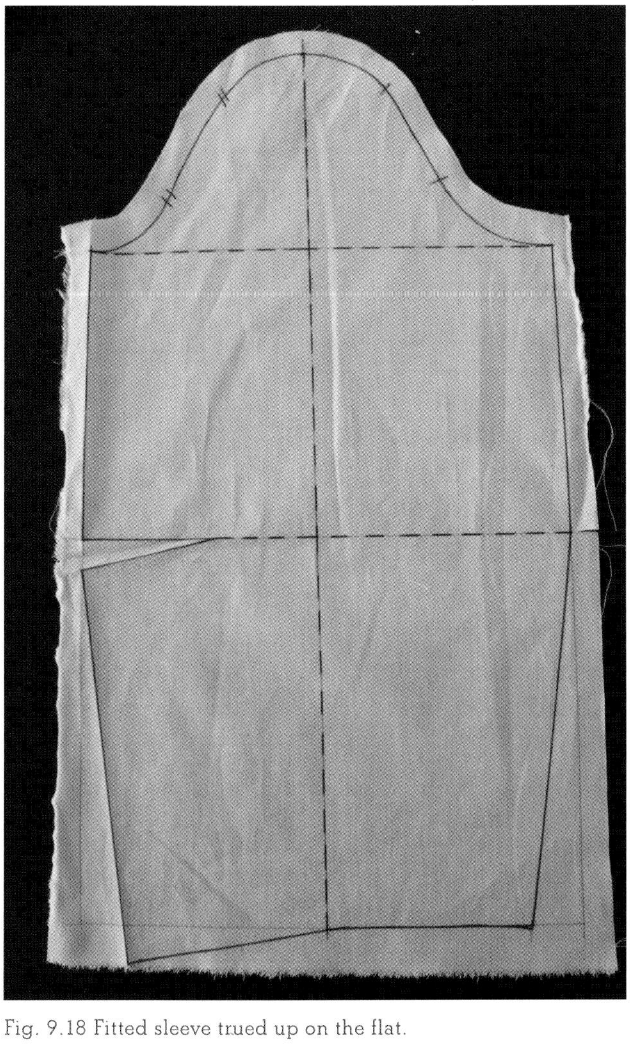

Fig. 9.18 Fitted sleeve trued up on the flat.

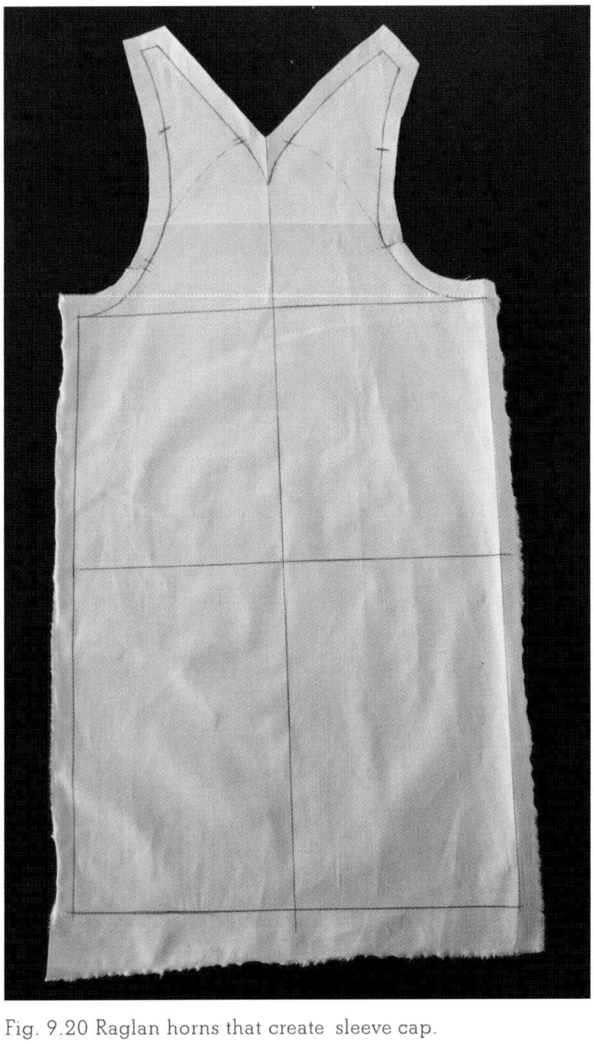

Fig. 9.20 Raglan horns that create sleeve cap.

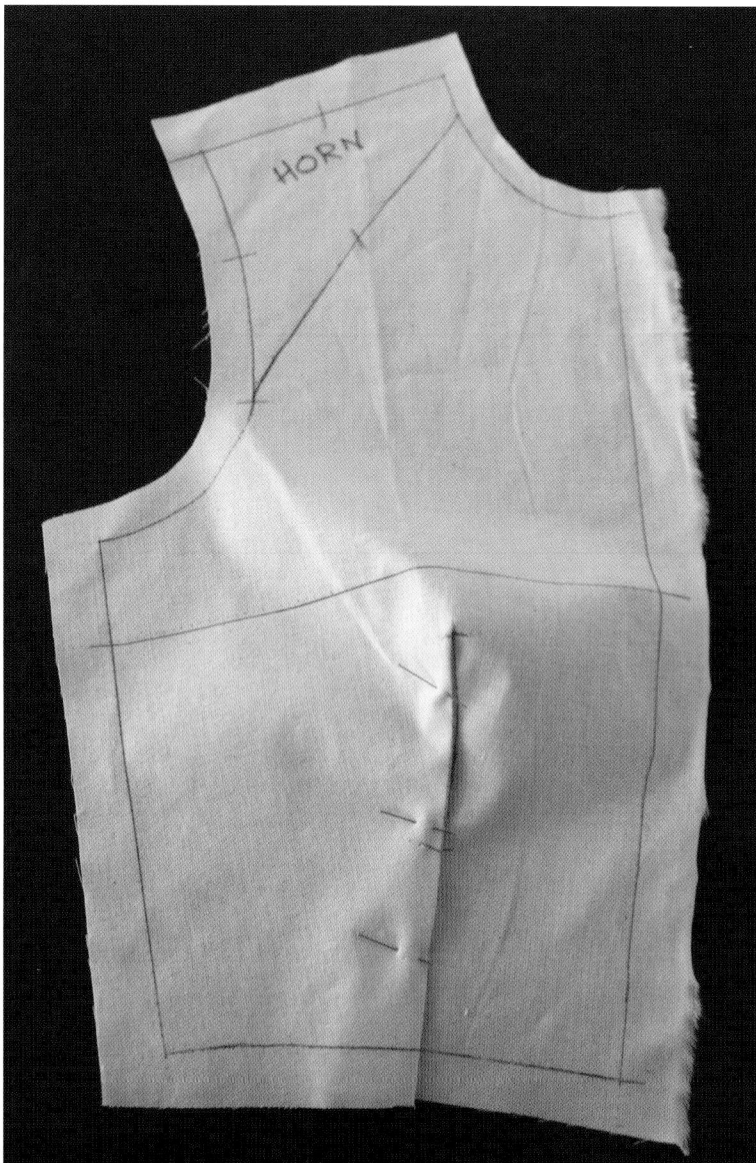

Fig. 9.21 Top of the bodice shoulder becomes raglan horns.

CB. Figs 9.22, 9.23 and 9.24 show the stand taped up in preparation to drape some of these variants. Note that if you are draping one of these styles the width of the calico needs to be wider to drape with so that the raglan horn will reach beyond the CF and CB.

1. Prepare and block your calico 45cm wide and the desired sleeve length plus 20 cm. It should look something like mine in Fig. 9.25, with the extra length at the crown of the sleeve above the bicep line.
2. On the mannequin use tape to mark off the position of the raglan seam and include a notch on the front and the back so you can align the sleeve head back up with the bodice. Refer to Figs 9.26, 9.27 and 9.28. This seam will need a

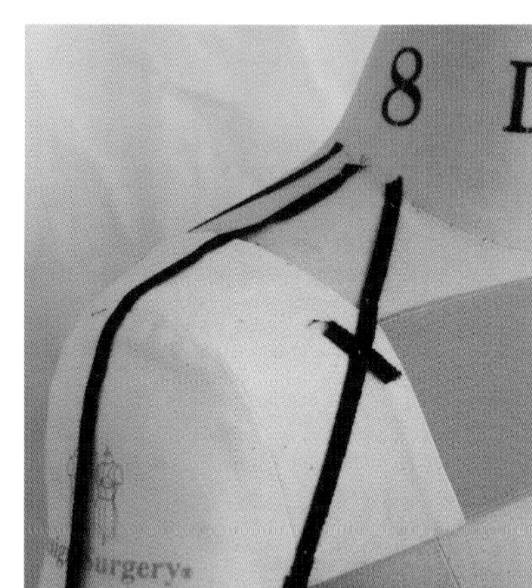

Fig. 9.24 Traditional raglan with seams running into neck either side of neck point.

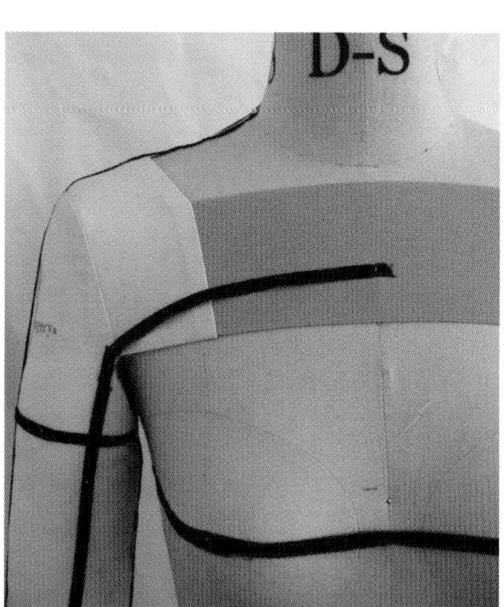

Fig. 9.22 Variation on raglan style that finishes across CF.

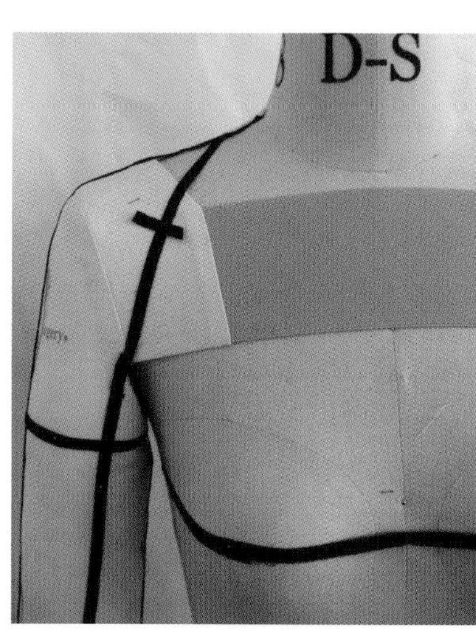

Fig. 9.23 Demi-raglan that finishes mid-shoulder.

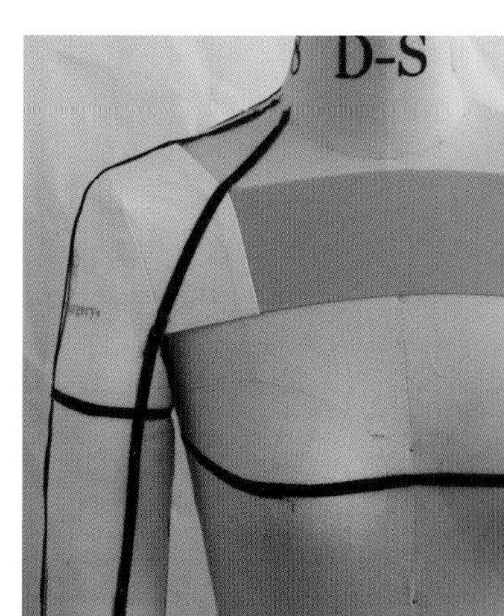

Fig. 9.26 Mannequin taped for raglan sleeve, front view.

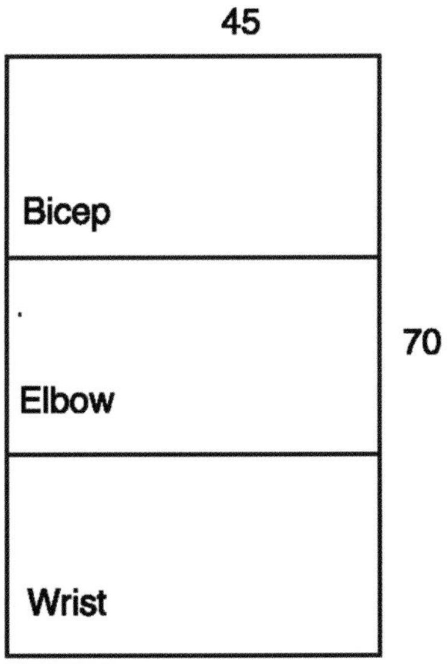

Fig. 9.25 Block dimensions for raglan sleeve.

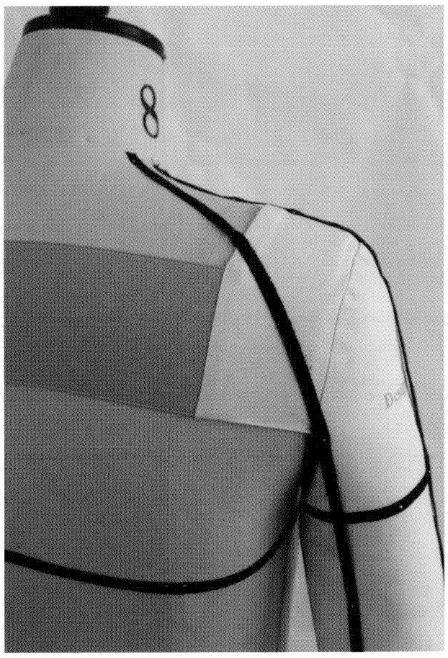

Fig. 9.28 Mannequin taped for raglan sleeve, back view.

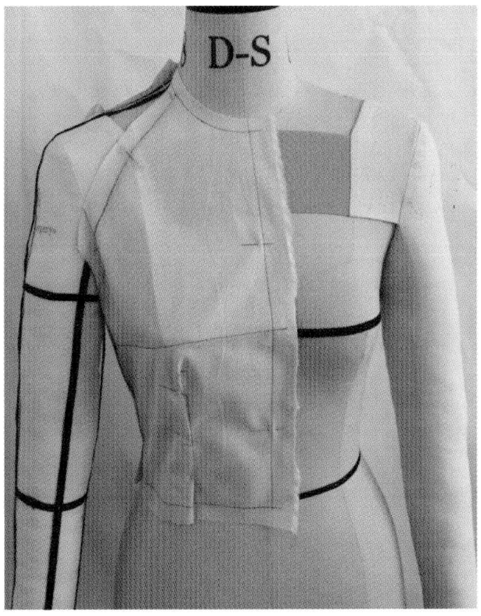

Fig. 9.29 Raglan bodice trimmed to sleeve line, front view.

small amount of curve to sit properly over the shoulder and collarbones but try to keep it as straight as possible. I have gone for a higher raglan that fits closer to the armpit and started my seam from the armhole notch, blending it into the bottom of the armhole on the flat. The lower the seam, the deeper the armhole and the more

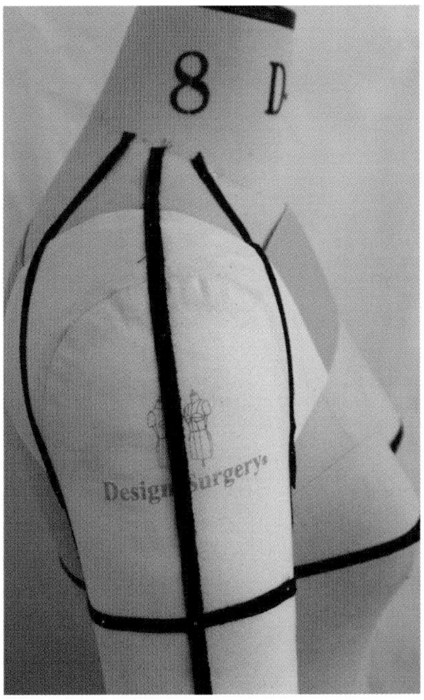

Fig. 9.27 Mannequin taped for raglan sleeve, side view.

fabric there will be under the arm.

3. Drape the bodice to the new seam lines (Figs 9.29 and 9.30). Note that the bodice will include the bottom tip of the back shoulder dart. Leave this in and it can be eased onto the raglan sleeve later, allowing more ease of movement over the shoulder blade.
4. Remove the bodice pieces from the stand and true up (Fig. 9.31).
5. Undo the tip of the back shoulder

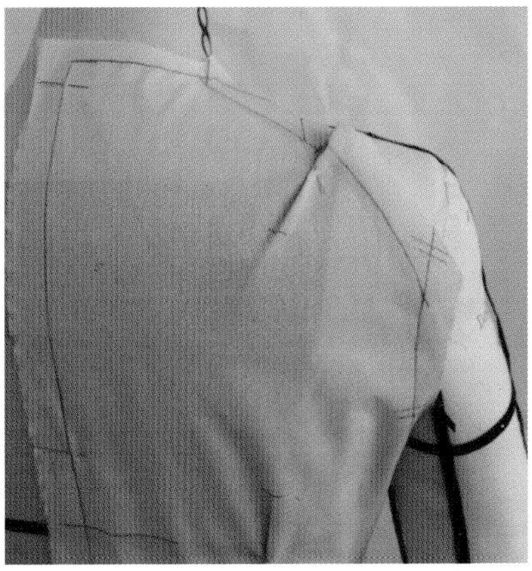

Fig. 9.30 Raglan bodice trimmed to sleeve line, back view.

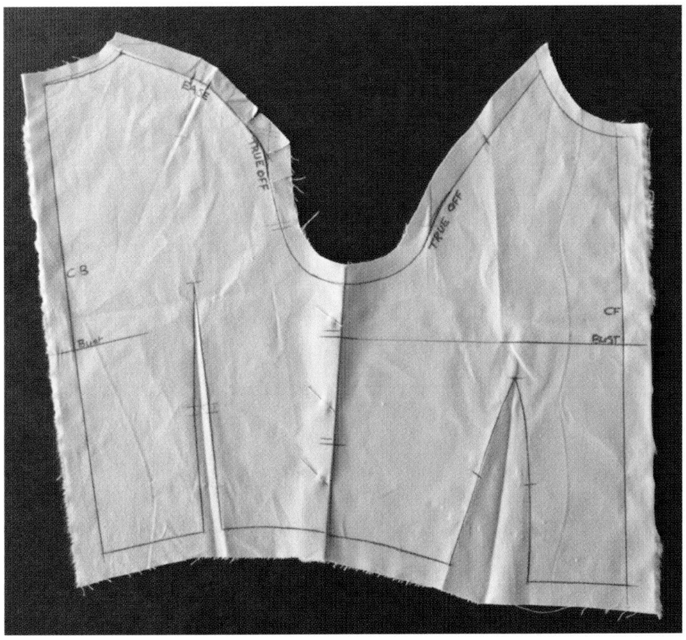

Fig. 9.31 Raglan bodice trued up on the flat.

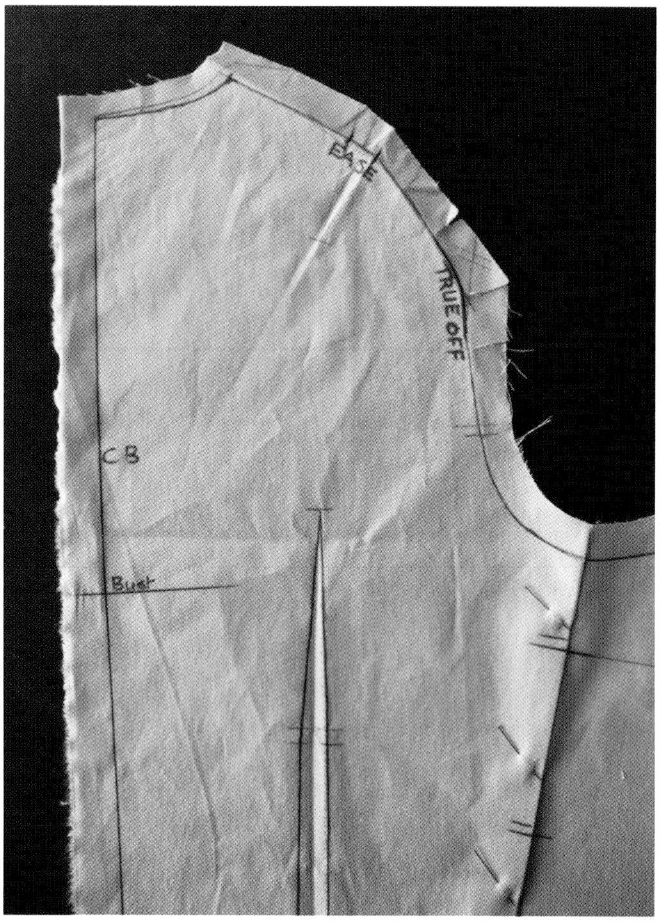

Fig. 9.32 Raglan bodice back, including intersected shoulder dart marked as ease.

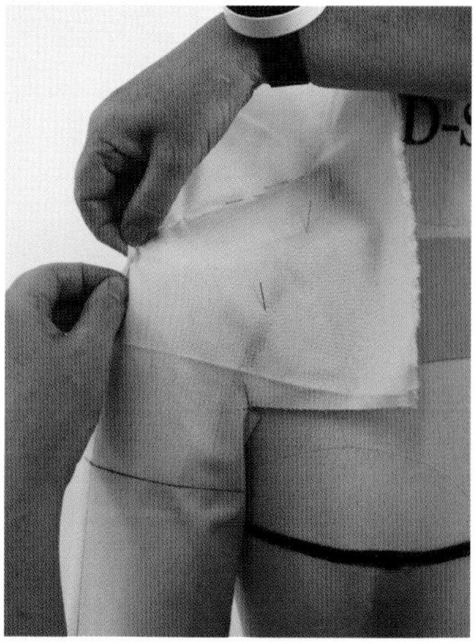

Fig. 9.34 Creating sleeve head, front view.

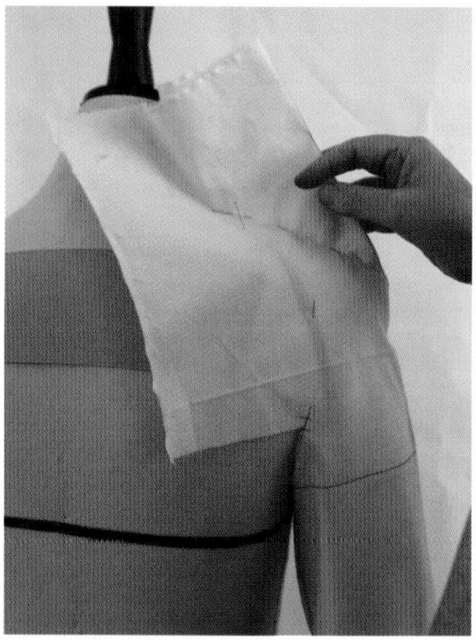

Fig. 9.35 Creating sleeve head, back view.

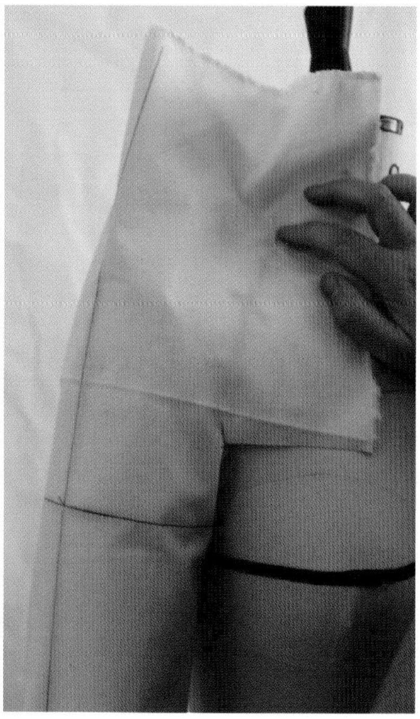

Fig. 9.33 Repositioning sleeve with extra sleeve head allowance.

dart and mark it as ease with some notches. When pressed it will disappear, whilst providing a little more movement at the shoulder blade (Fig. 9.32).

6. Repeat steps 1–13 listed for the set-in sleeve and reposition back on the arm.
7. Lay the shoulder part of the sleeve from the front notch smoothly across the shoulder of the mannequin front, pinning along the style line (Fig. 9.33).
8. Repeat on the back.
9. Smooth the calico front and back over the shoulder and pin along the shoulder line, tapering to a point and ending in a dart at the shoulder point (Figs 9.34 and 9.35). Keep looking on both sides of the pins to make sure that both the front and back remain flat.
10. Mark off the sleeve line with a

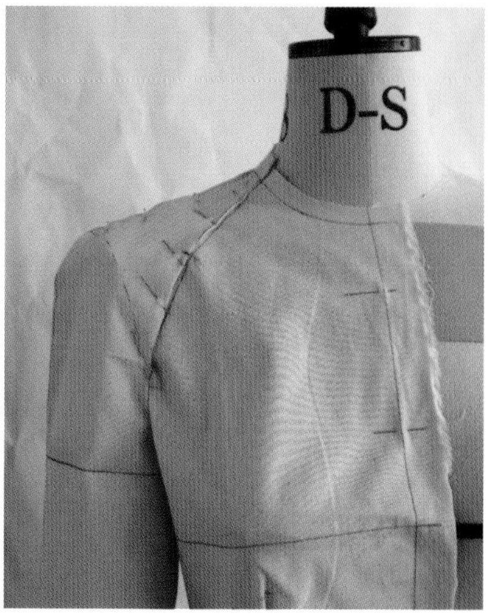

Fig. 9.36 Checking fit on front.

dotted line and trim away the excess calico to a 2cm allowance. Decide on the sleeve length and mark off the neckline, shoulder seam and hem.

11. Remove the sleeve and true up on the flat; it should look like the raglan sleeve in Fig. 9.17.
12. Put the raglan bodice back on the stand and pin into position.
13. Put the sleeve back on and fold the SA under on the front.
14. Align the front horn edge to the raglan bodice using the notch and pin together on top of it (Fig. 9.36).
15. Close the raglan dart on the shoulder line and pin.
16. Align the back horn edge to the raglan bodice, including the ease from the base of the shoulder dart. Pin together from the top of the calico.
17. Check fit and make alterations before removing from the mannequin and transferring to the master (Fig. 9.37). Check that the shape of the seam is smooth at both front and back and neaten up if you need to (Fig. 9.38).

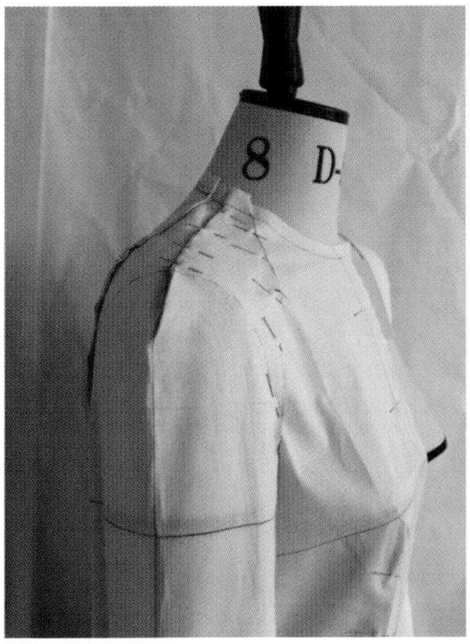

Fig. 9.37 Checking overall fit.

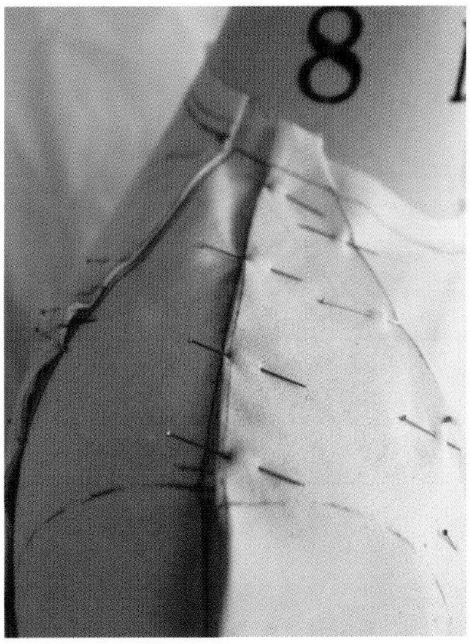

Fig. 9.38 Checking fit on shoulder dart with adjustment.

Kimono Sleeve (Fig. 9.39)

In Japanese culture kimonos vary considerably for different occasions and their sleeves have special meanings; for example, they indicate the age and marital status of women: a young single Japanese woman would traditionally wear a *furisode,* a kimono with long flowing sleeves almost touching her feet. A married woman might wear a *tomesode*, a kimono with short sleeves. In a modern Western fashion context, the term 'kimono sleeve' is understood as describing an extended sleeve with a wide hem cut as one with the bodice. The kimono was widely adopted in Western fashions in the 1950s as the fashionable shoulder line softened and the focus moved to the waistline. A trend emerged for a smooth sloping shoulder which was

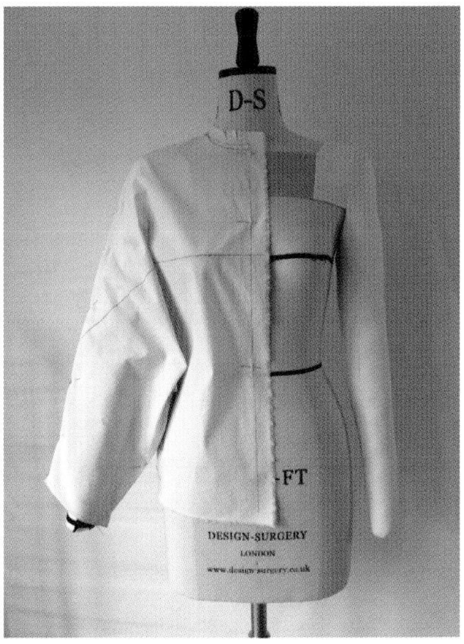

Fig. 9.39 Draped kimono.

softer and often without padding. By now many women had their own sewing machines at home and the one-seamed kimono sleeve was far easier to construct for most home dressmakers than fitting a set-in sleeve into the armhole.

The kimono is also known as a 'grown-on' sleeve as it is formed by creating the body of the garment and the sleeve from the same continuous piece of fabric rather than separate sleeve and bodice pieces, with a seam running along the top of the sleeve on the overarm as well as underneath to join the back and the front. A close-fitting or 'high' kimono may also include a gusset panel under the armpit: this is a diamond-shaped piece of fabric which allows for ease of movement. The version I have draped

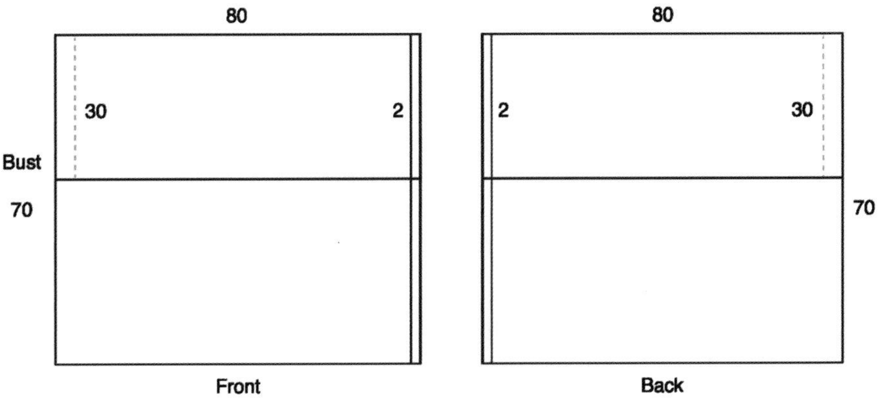

Fig. 9.40 Block dimensions for kimono sleeve.

is a low kimono. Be aware that this style does have excess fabric under the arm and will also restrict the range of movement so decide how high you want to lift your arms before you start and angle the arm of your mannequin accordingly. The tighter the fit through the body, the higher the position of the underarm seam and potentially slimmer the sleeve, so decide on the silhouette you want before you start.

1. Prepare and block the calico as per the dimensions in Fig. 9.40.
2. Adjust the arm on your mannequin to the desired position (I used black tape to raise the arm and kept it in position by tying the tape onto a dress rail) and on the stand in line with the shoulder seam (Fig. 9.41).
3. Tape up the mannequin with the bust- and waistlines and the arm with elbow, bicep and overarm.
4. Position the CF and bustline intersection on the calico with the corresponding position on the mannequin.
5. Smooth the calico up and down the CF and pin to hold.
6. Smooth the calico into the neck point, pin and snip in to release the tension and create a smooth neckline cutting the excess away.
7. Smooth the calico over the shoulder and pin. Adjust the calico down the arm, pinning to the overarm to create the top seam of your design (Fig. 9.42).
8. Mark off with dots and cut away the excess calico leaving a 2cm allowance (Fig. 9.43).
9. Fold the calico down out of the way whilst you repeat on the back. Remember to include a small shoulder dart.
10. With the CF and CB pinned into position, smooth both the front and back pieces of calico up to meet each other at the overarm. This seam is on the bias, as you will be able to see from Fig. 9.43 where the bustlines meet each other and form a 45-degree V shape. It will also be slightly curved if the position of the arm is lower than shoulder height. This area in particular may stretch a little so be careful to pin the overarm seams together evenly without gathers on one side or the other. Don't try to pin one seam on top of the other at this stage.
11. Decide on the fit through the body and try not to pull or distort either side as you smooth the front and back pieces together under the arm and down the SS. Pin from the bottom edge upwards towards the arm, shaping the underarm hole as you go. This part is trial and error and takes a while to get the underarm flat with a pleasing shape so be prepared to experiment. Stylistically, you might want to pin over the hip and then use the adhesive style tape to experiment with the shape first before committing to it, although I did mine by eye with pins and kept stepping back to take a look at my handiwork,
12. When you have the shape and fit you want, pin and mark off with a dotted line (Fig. 9.43).
13. Remove from the stand and true up the overarm and underarm and drop the neckline at the CF by 1cm. Cut away the excess to a 2cm allowance. Don't cut away on the stand: again it is really awkward to get underneath the arm properly.
14. Put the back on first and then lay the front on with the overarm SA turned under so you can pin through the layers of calico from the top.
15. Repeat for the side and underarm seams with the front SA folded and pinned on top. Be warned that this is quite awkward to get to and pin properly because of its shape and you may get some buckling in the fabric. Depending on the curve of the underarm you may also need to snip into the allowance to release some of the tension in the fabric to fold more accurately and get a better fit (Fig. 9.44).

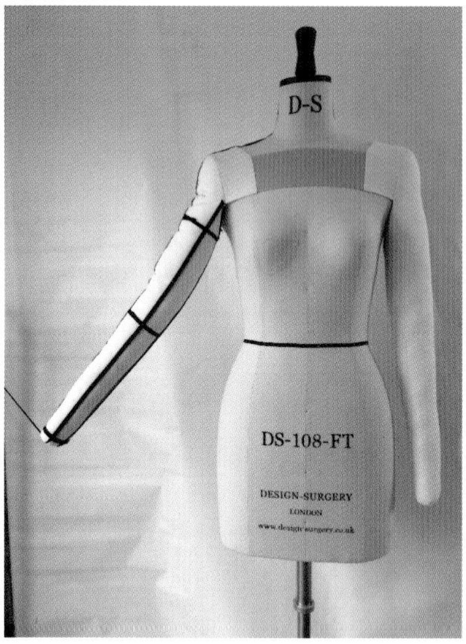

Fig. 9.41 Mannequin arm adjusted to desired height before draping.

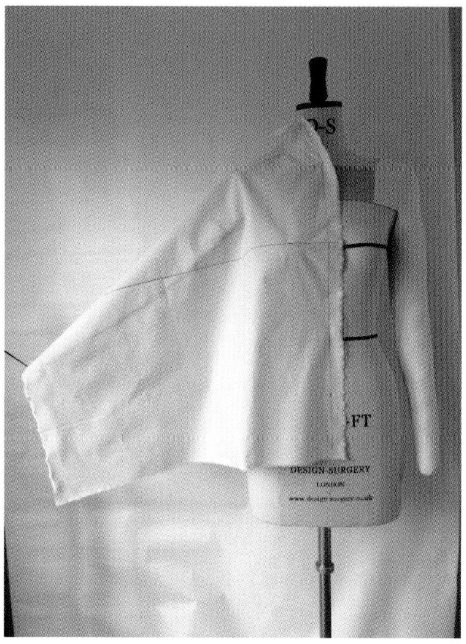
Fig. 9.42 Smoothing calico for front over body and down overarm.

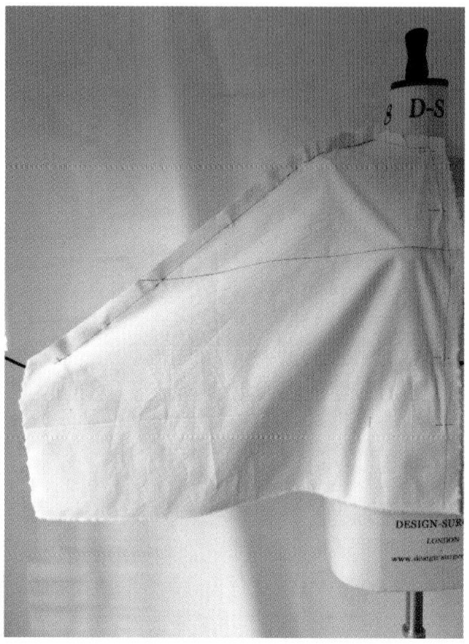

Fig. 9.43 Pinned overarm seam with 2cm allowance for adjustments.

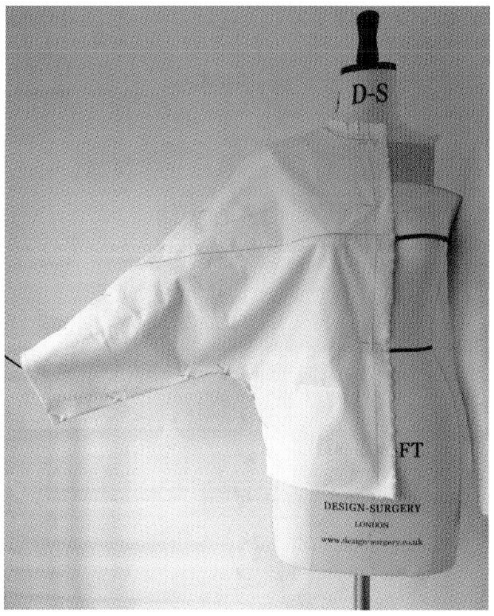

Fig. 9.44 Pinned underarm.

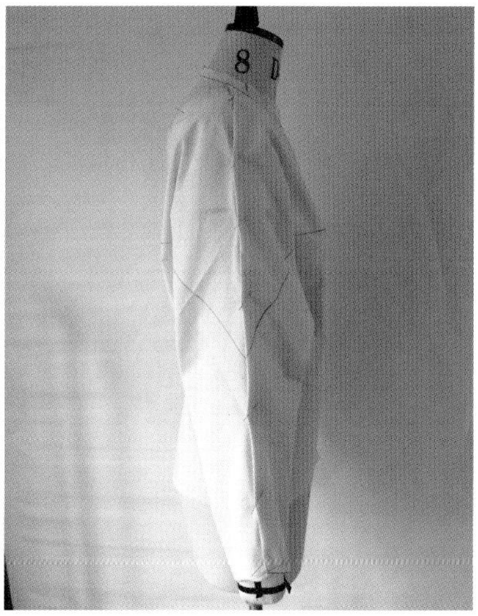
Fig. 9.45 Adjusted final drape, side view.

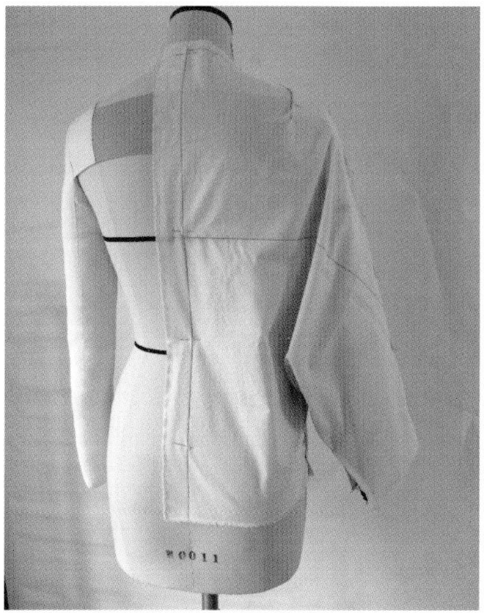
Fig. 9.46 Adjusted final drape, back view.

16. Refer to Figs 9.45 and 9.46. Make any other adjustments before removing from the stand and transferring to the paper master pattern. Include notches on both the over- and underarms and indicate if there is any ease on the overarm seam.

One-Piece Gigot Sleeve (Fig. 9.47)

This sleeve style has consistently been a micro trend for several seasons, with its distinctive upper body silhouette, and is having a bit of a fashion moment right now (as I write in 2021), with designers like J.W. Anderson using the historical pattern as reference for a more contemporary interpretation. The sleeve was named for its unusual shape which resembles the hind leg of an animal. 'Gigot' is a French term meaning 'leg of lamb' and has been anglicized to the more familiar 'leg o' mutton' expression we now associate with Victorian-era clothes. Its distinctive silhouette is created by a voluminous gathering of fabric at the sleeve head tapering to a normal sleeve at the wrist or elbow. In the late 1500s both men and women wore huge versions of this style of sleeve, with additional padding and horsehair to hold its shape. The combination of this widened shoulder line and a fuller skirt

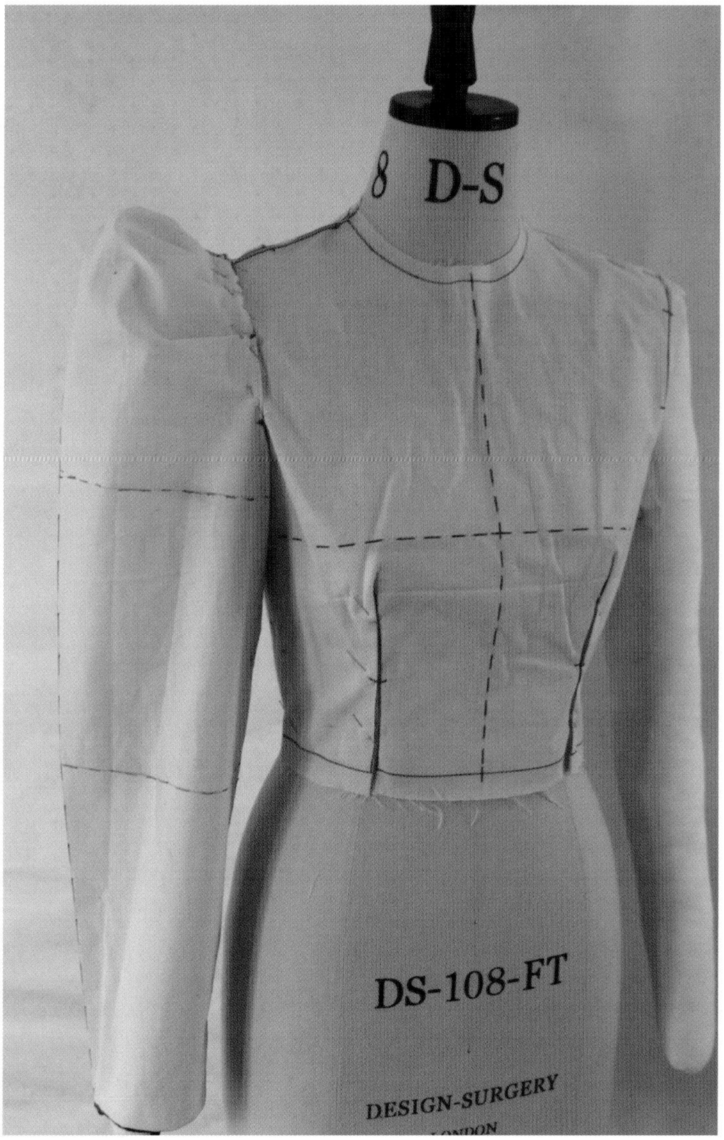

Fig. 9.47 Gigot sleeve compared to normal set-in sleeve.

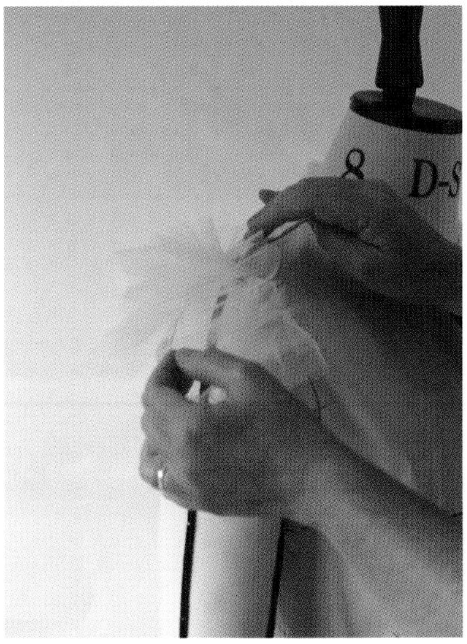

Fig. 9.48 Arranging the net support.

or hose to balance the ensemble was to make the waist look smaller whilst showcasing wealth through the wearer's choice of fabric and embellishment. Obviously, the more fabric the more surface area for adornment and ostentatiousness. The social politics of this were also not lost on the Victorians who adopted it for much the same reasons, although for women only as it re-emerged in the 1820s and 1830s before disappearing and returning again in the 1890s. As the voluminous balloon sleeves became bigger, they were often supported by sleeve supporters – think whale boning for your arms – in much the same way that a large skirt would be supported with a crinoline cage. The average girth of a dressed bicep in 1829 was twice that of the waist so they would not have maintained their shape without help. Garment patterns became very complex, with a substantial requirement of nearly two yards (1.8m) of fabric for the proper amount of fullness in a lady's blouse in 1895 according to *The Fairchild Books Dictionary of Fashion*. The fad was much ridiculed in the media for its impracticalities and social elitism and was very short-lived as women found the girth of their sleeves made them unable to do mundane things like walking through doorways facing forwards, and the restrictions of a heavy sleeve and a small armhole indeed prevented them from moving their arms at all. Incredibly, each time the trend lasted, the gigot was applied to nearly every item women wore, including seaside costumes and riding and walking ensembles, even though the style's limitations prevented them from engaging as fully in such activities as modern women would expect.

In the 1900s the sleeves transitioned to puffs and a variety of sleeker smaller forms that acknowledged the more physical lifestyles of the gentlewomen of the day. Traditionally this sleeve would have had a tight, high armhole to allow for more movement when attached to a very fitted bodice and corsets and thus created the contrast of volumes. The true gigot is cut in one piece and uses quite a lot of cloth. To counterbalance the often huge sleeve heads of the gigot and therefore the fabric wastage, prudent Victorian dressmakers introduced the demi-gigot, which is cut with a puffed top sleeve which ends at the elbow and is joined onto a separate tight-fitting sleeve from elbow to wrist, thus making better use of the cloth by using smaller pattern pieces.

The silhouette of the sleeve can be dictated by the angle of the pleats and their volume so it is worth playing around with this to see what you get before committing to your design content. This version is cut in one piece, with the extra volume starting from the front armhole notch, running over the shoulder seam and round to the back armhole notch. There is no additional fullness under the arm. The extra volume is created by a higher and wider sleeve cap. To help support the shape I have gathered some net onto the shoulder of the bodice and pinned it through to the mannequin's shoulder before draping. It is folded in half and staggered to create a bit more lift in the right places (Figs 9.48 and 9.49). Whether or not you need this inside your garment would depend on the final choice of fabric being used but I would keep it in for toiling. You can also decide how you want to control

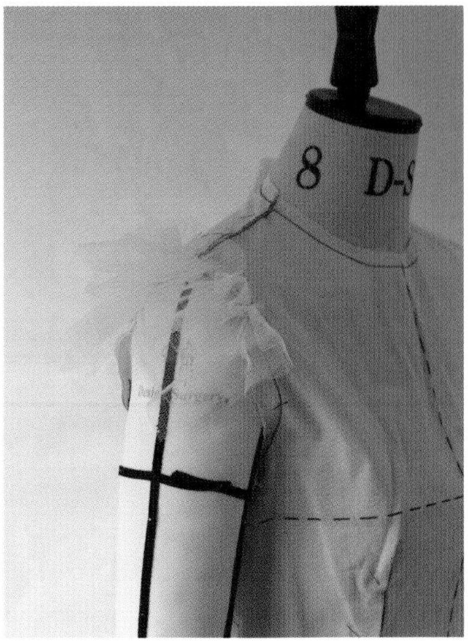

Fig. 9.49 Finished net support.

the fullness in the crown. A pleated sleeve head will look very controlled in comparison to a gathered one and where you chose to taper the crown into the overarm will also impact on your silhouette. For example, if you taper into the bicep line you will have a more controlled, higher puff of a sleeve head with a leaner arm, or you may chose to run it out at the wrist as I have done for a more evenly balanced sleeve overall.

1. Prepare and block your calico 70cm wide by the desired sleeve length plus 30cm. It should look something like mine in Fig. 9.50.
2. Place a vertical grain line in the centre of the fabric.
3. Draw a horizontal line 2cm up from the bottom of the calico for the wrist.

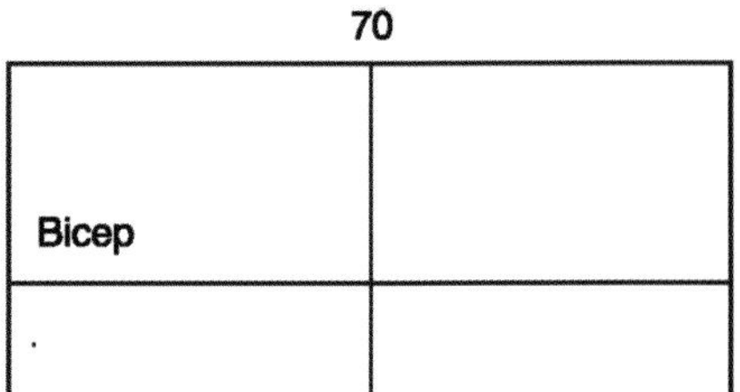

Fig. 9.50 Block dimensions for gigot sleeve.

4. Measure the distance from the wrist to the elbow on the arm and mark it off on the calico.
5. Measure the distance from the elbow to the bicep on the mannequin and mark it off on the calico.
6. Fold the calico along the overarm and pin a triangle measuring 20–30cm in total at the top and running out to 4cm at the wrist. This is going to create extra width for the sleeve head and create the characteristic ballooning shape of the gigot. Fig. 9.51 shows this additional girth once the underarm sleeve is in position on the mannequin.
7. Follow steps 7–13 given for the set-in sleeve.
8. Put the sleeve back onto the stand and pin the underarm into position. Pin the sleeve at the crown and begin putting in pleats either side of the shoulder point for the front and back until you have utilized all the excess fabric and fitted it into the armhole above the balance points on the armhole. If you are happy with the height and volume of the crown and position of the pleats and gathers, then pin frequently and firmly to hold them in place (Figs 9.52 and 9.53). Cut the excess fabric away.
9. Mark the sleeve head with a dotted line and the pleats with dashes. Mark off the top of the fold as well as the bottom and include arrows for the direction of the pleat.
10. Remove from the stand and true up on the flat. Trim the remaining allowance down to 2cm and finger-fold under. The sleeve head should be abnormally large to accommodate the additional volume created by the gathers (Fig. 9.54).
11. Put the sleeve back on the mannequin and line up the notches. Pin the sleeve to the bodice at the armhole to check the fit (Fig. 9.55).
12. Adjust and remove to transfer to the master pattern.

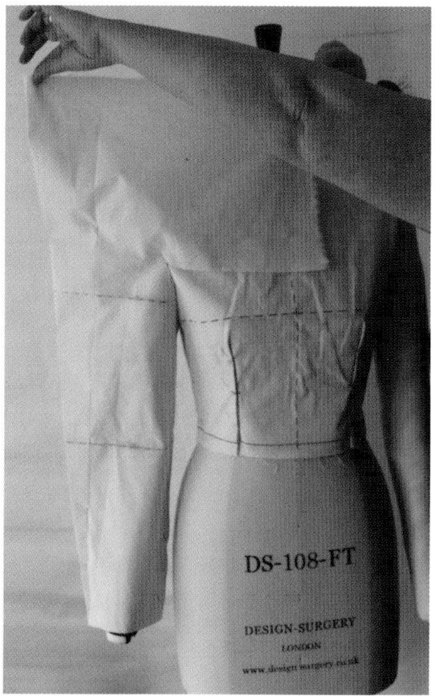

Fig. 9.51 Extra 30cm pinned out on overarm to create fullness in sleeve head.

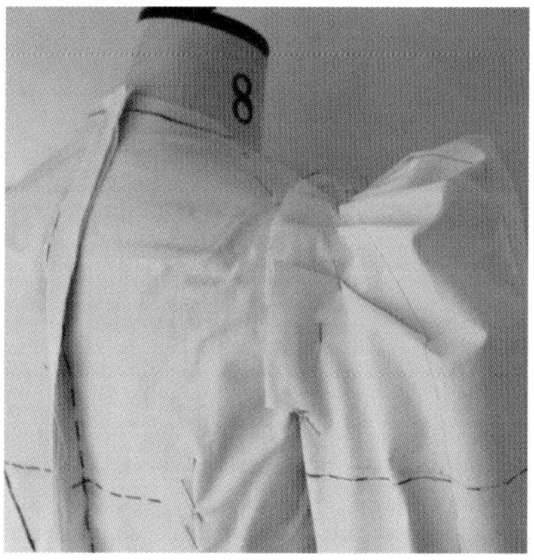

Fig. 9.52 Pinning sleeve head, back.

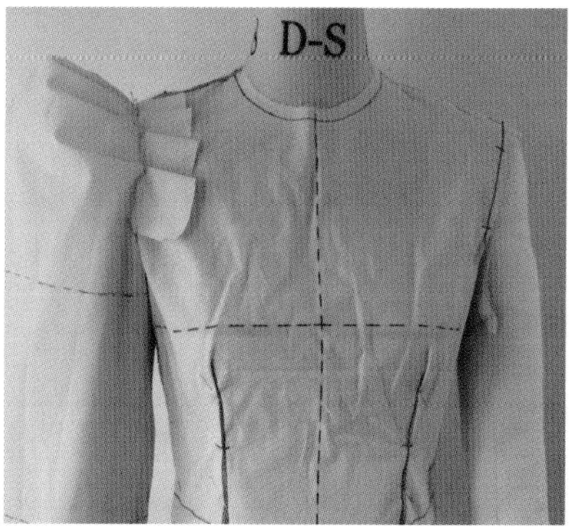

Fig. 9.53 Pinning sleeve head, front.

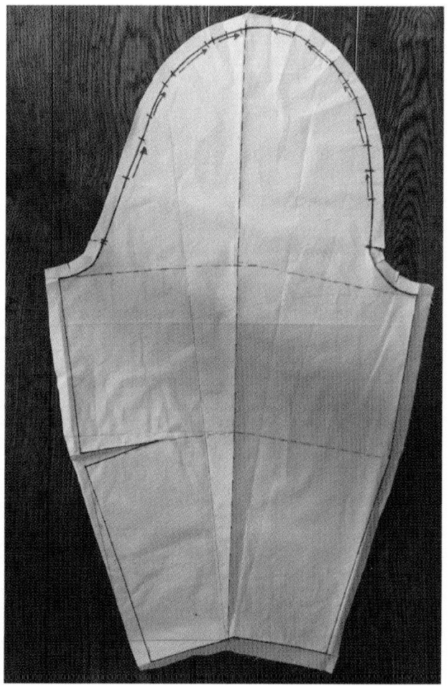
Fig. 9.54 Gigot drape trued up on the flat.

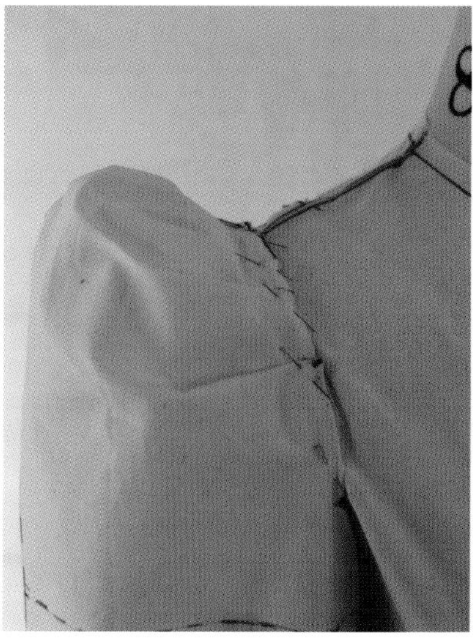
Fig. 9.55 Finished gigot.

TRUING A CURVE

You may not hit all of your dots when producing in a curved line. Don't worry; the goal is to achieve a smooth continuous curved line rather than one with odd indentations. With practice this can be achieved freehand as you build up 'muscle memory'. To begin with, just keep repositioning your set square or curve tool until you achieve the best line.

D-S
BUST

The Collar

10

Whilst Paul Poiret and some of his Parisian counterparts were busy waging war over the length and silhouette of women's dresses, another battle was being fought over the softness of men's shirts – specifically their collars! Since the 1830s men's collars had been stiff and starched and sold separately, which probably contributed to our stereotype of a rigid, stuffy, Victorian gentleman. Detachable collars saved on laundering as they were the part that needed the most frequent cleaning and replacement. Soldiers fighting in WW1 were issued with soft shirts with attached collars, prioritizing ease and comfort over laundering, and after that there was no going back. The war over collars raged in Britain in particular where more conservative gentlemen resisted the change and fought back in their clubs, the media, universities and courtrooms for their right to remain stiff and starched. Collars at this time were often also very tall – some of the stands were as much as 7.5cm (3in) in depth.

Collars were usually white with rounded edges; the attached collar was deemed very casual and working-class, particularly if it was worn without a tie or not buttoned up. This was exacerbated when men's shirts also received an explosion of colour and pattern from the late 1920s onwards.

With so many other fashion rules being tossed aside during this period, it was the perfect time for women to plunder the male wardrobe and see what could be adapted in terms of comfort and fit. Until the 1920s women had worn blouses – usually white with a lace insert – which had flat collars that were soft and pointed, but this was the next piece of clothing to go (after the corset) in favour of the man's buttoned-down shirt with a pointed collar and stand. Chanel was at the forefront of this particular revolution that blurred the boundaries between masculine and feminine dressing. Characteristically her shirts were cut with a slightly deeper V-shaped neckline and a leaner fit for her female clients. Interestingly, the woman's collar was also often white, detachable and required starching even up until the 1960s, and it is puzzling that whilst men were abandoning this in favour of something softer and easier to wear, women were adopting it regardless of its lack of comfort for socio-political reasons and to make a fashion statement.

The collars in this chapter are draped for the high neckline of the fitted bodice we draped in Chapter 6 and are therefore the basic forms (Fig. 10.2). The collars run from CF to CB and are best worked on over a half-draped bodice so that you have a neckline already marked off to drape to. Alternatively, you can come down 1cm from the CF neck seam as you would with the bodice on the flat and mark it out with black tape as a draping guide line. There is nothing to stop you from experimenting with the methodology. Here, for example, you can see a slightly lower V shape like Chanel's, produced by lowering the neckline at the CF by 2cm or more and reshaping it from the neck point to the CF or finishing the collar before it meets the CF and giving the collar a wider 'spread' (which is the name given to the gap between the two front collars at the neckline).

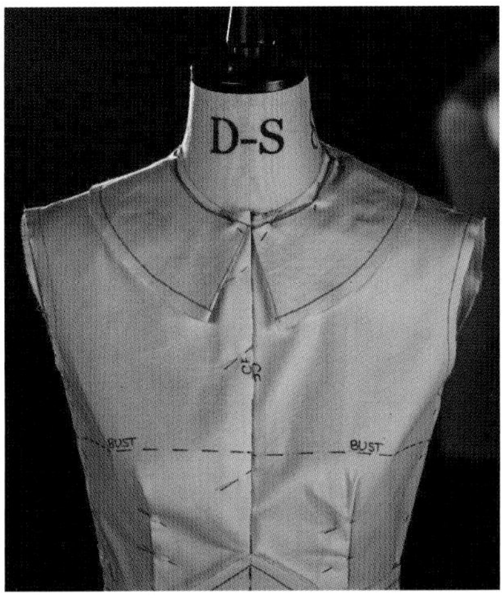

Fig. 10.2 Draped flat or 'Peter Pan' collar. (Photo: Yousef Al Nasser)

Frequently Used Collar Terms

Neckline edge: The bottom edge of the collar where it attaches to the neckline of the garment.
Collar edge: The outside edge of the collar, where design variations are most evident.
Collar tip: The shaped end of the neckline edge – again, where design detail is very visible.
Collar stand: The amount by which the collar 'stands up'. It is the distance between the neckline edge and the line where the collar rolls over. It can either be embedded (for example, for a convertible collar) or separate (as in a

SEAM ALLOWANCES ON COLLARS

When draping any part of a garment, extra SA is added in case adjustments are needed later. For collars the pieces seem particularly oversized. In industry the standard SA is 6mm (¼in) at the neck and armhole and 1cm at the SS and shoulder so this need adding onto the production pattern to toile.

Left: Fig. 10.1 Draped collar, with stand. (Photo: Yousef Al Nasser)

two-piece collar).

Roll line: The visible or invisible join line between collar and stand where the collar changes direction.

Collar spread: The distance between the collar tips at CF – again, one of a collar's most 'designable' features.

Flat Collar

This collar lies flat on the torso and has soft curved corners. It is also known as a Peter Pan collar, named after the collar worn by the leading actress Maude Adams for her performance as the character in the 1905 stage version of J.M. Barrie's novel.

1. Prepare and block your calico as per the dimensions in Fig. 10.3.
2. The collar will drape from CF to CB so it is important to position the blocked calico correctly where the CF and neckline intersect. Put a holding pin in whilst you adjust (Fig. 10.4).
3. Lay the fabric smoothly across the front panel over the shoulder towards the back (Fig. 10.5).
4. Remove the tension this creates by snipping downwards towards the neck point and shoulder seam and make additional vertical cuts towards the neckline so that the fabric begins to lie flatter to the body all the way round from the CF to CB. Note that your fabric will have gone off grain at the CB. The finished piece will look like Fig. 10.6.
5. Cut horizontally through the excess calico to create a neckline and SA, then snip down further towards the neck seam to refine the shape.
6. Use tape to indicate the shape of the collar. I have used an adhesive one here from Design-Surgery® but could just have easily used the black stay tape. Your style line can be plotted to your own design and I have included some variations in Figs 10.7, 10.8 and 10.9.
7. When you are happy with the style line, mark it off with a series of dots. Also mark off the CB and use bars to indicate the corners. Mark

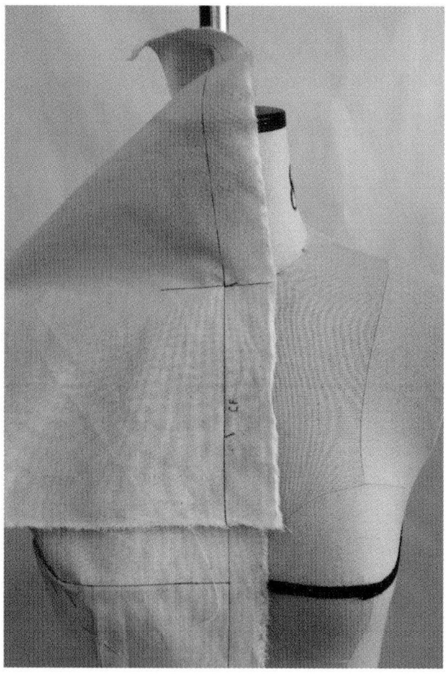

Fig. 10.4 Positioning calico at CF.

Fig. 10.5 Calico smoothed round to CB is on the bias and needs to be drawn in.

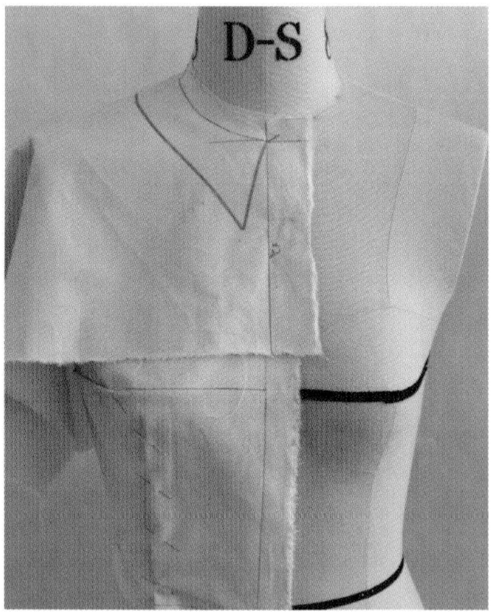

Fig. 10.7 Pointed collar tips on flat collar variation.

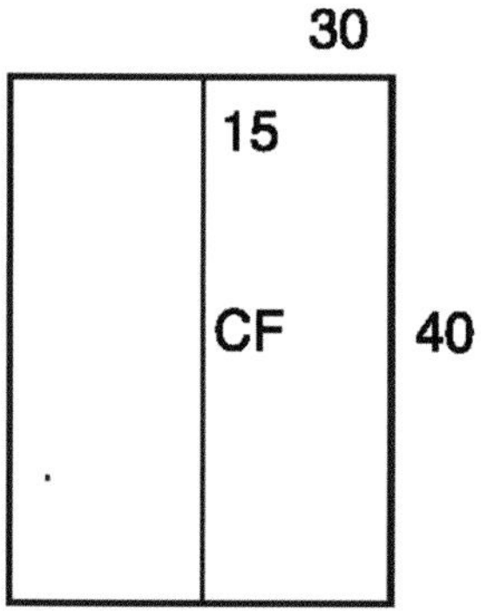

Fig. 10.3 Block dimensions for Peter Pan collar.

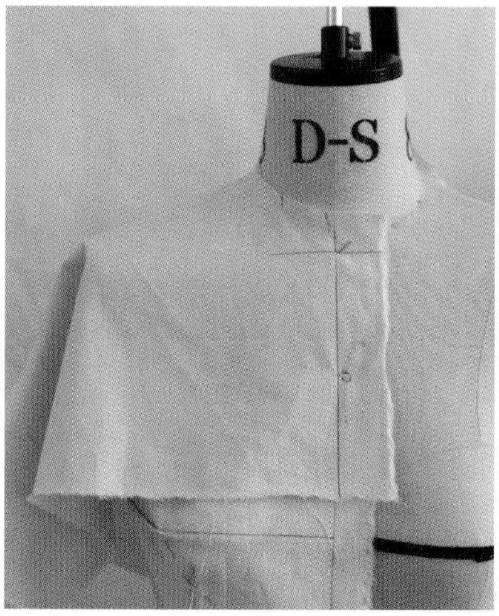

Fig. 10.6 Positioned calico lying flat to body after neck has been snipped into.

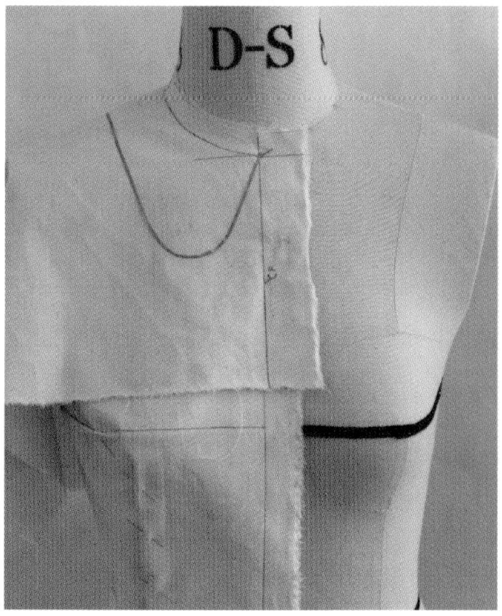

Fig. 10.8 1970s long, round, tipped collar variation.

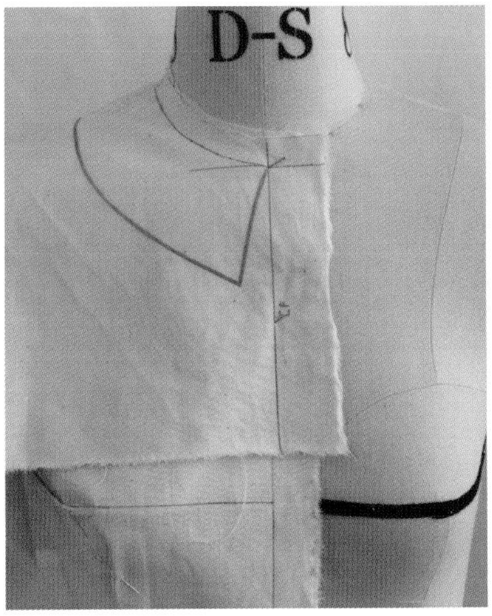

Fig. 10.9 Traditional Peter Pan collar variation.

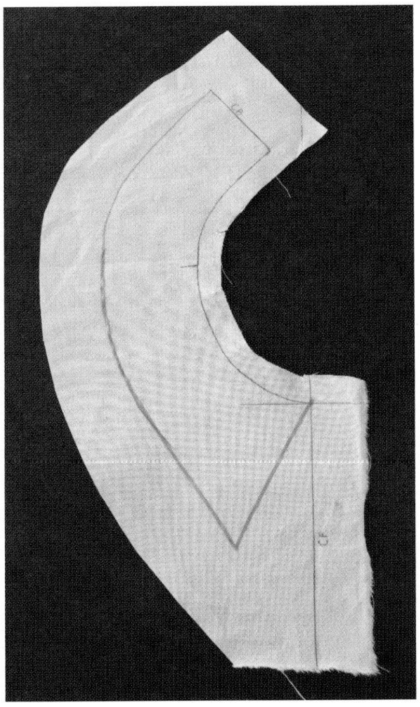

Fig. 10.10 Peter Pan collar on the flat.

off the neck point where the shoulder seam intercepts the neckline: this will become a notch on your production pattern later.

8. Remove from the mannequin and true up (Fig. 10.10).
9. Trim down to a 2cm allowance all the way round. Snip into the allowance towards the style line and turn the edges under so that it can be pinned to the neckline and the fit can be checked.
10. When you are happy, transfer to a paper master and make sure to include the neck point and the SG.

COLLAR EDGE

Put the undercollar on the bias so that it rolls satisfactorily. On your production pattern trim 2mm (bare ⅛in) off the top edge of the undercollar and from the curved edges of the inner collar stand. When the topcollar is sewn to the undercollar, it will roll over the stitch line and conceal it, giving you an edge without a stitch line on it.

Stand Collar (Figs 10.11 and 10.12)

This is a narrow stand-up collar that normally opens at the front. Sometimes it is called a mandarin collar as the style originated in China where it was originally worn by Qing-era bureaucrats and later became synonymous with images of Chairman Mao. In India it is the distinctive feature of the Nehru jacket, named for the late Indian Prime Minister Jawaharlal Nehru. Russia also has its own version called a cossack collar although this opens at the side of the neck and not the CF. The stand collar's original function was military: it protected soldiers' necks from chafing when carrying heavy gear during deployment.

1. Prepare and block your calico as per the dimensions in Fig. 10.13.
2. Using tape, mark off the desired top edge of your collar on the neck of the mannequin, starting from the CB. The SG will be on the CB; the CF will be off grain.
3. The collar will drape from CB to CF so it is important to position the blocked calico correctly where the CB and neckline intersect. Put a holding pin in whilst you adjust.
4. Smooth the calico around the neck

Fig. 10.11 Stand collar drape, front view.

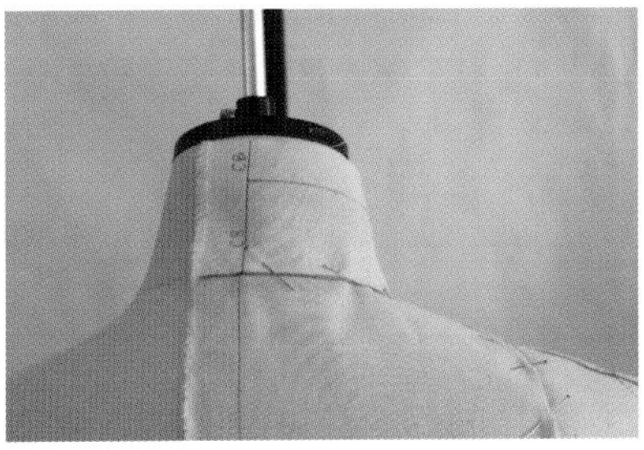

Fig. 10.12 Stand collar drape, back view.

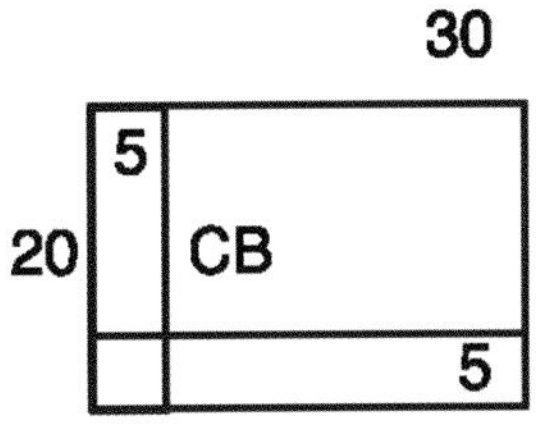

Fig. 10.13 Block dimensions for stand collar.

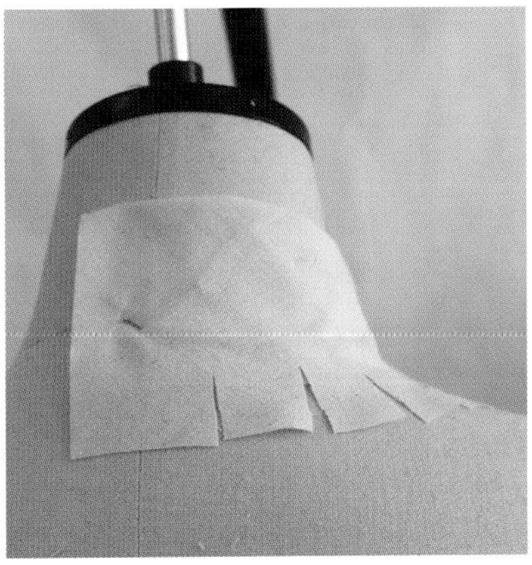

Fig. 10.14 Snipping into neckline to release tension and achieve fit for stand collar.

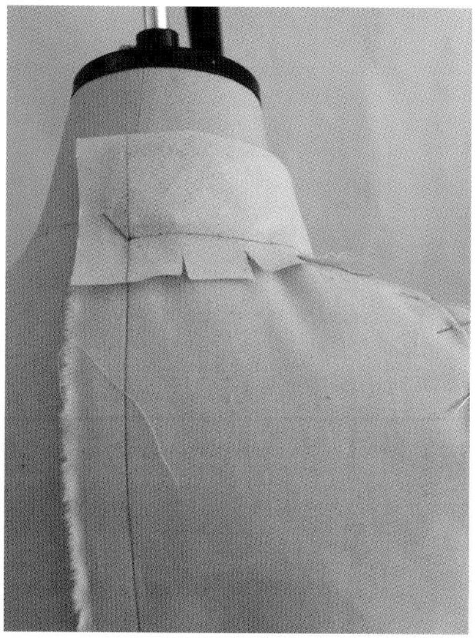

Fig. 10.15 Marking off collar line in pencil.

from CB to CF, snipping as you go to release the tension and allow the calico to sit flat around the neck (Fig. 10.14).

5. When you are happy, mark off the style line with a dotted line, using bars for the corners and where the seams intersect. Also mark the neck point (Fig. 10.15).
6. Remove from the mannequin and true up. The collar should swing up at the CF as in Fig. 10.16.
7. Trim down, leaving a 2cm allowance, and turn the bottom edge under.
8. Align the collar to the neckline and pin. Make any adjustments; your final drape should look like Figs 10.9 and 10.10. For the master pattern your collar will finish straight at the CF; this will give you a collar with an edge-to-edge finish. Variations for this collar are discreet and can be done on the production pattern before you toile, so you could extend at the CF to include a button wrap, or shape the collar tips to produce notched tips or rounded corners. You could also experiment with its height. (Note that the mandarin collars in the images featured have all had the tips trimmed away slightly from the CF. This is a small refinement that creates a better fit at the throat. This is done once the collar has been drafted with the edges to meet but not overlap at the CF.)

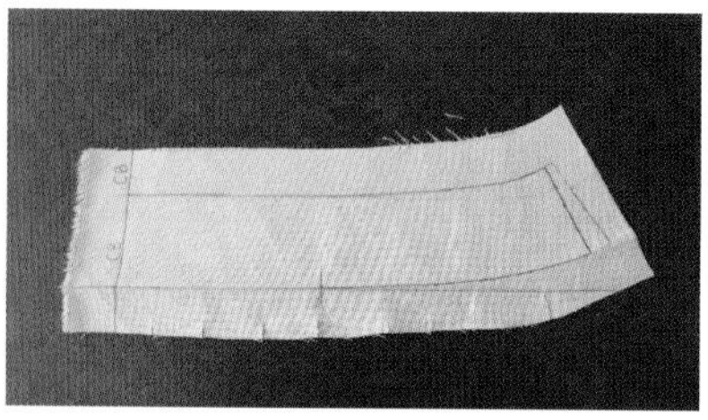

Fig. 10.16 Stand collar trued up on the flat.

Convertible Collar

This is a one-piece collar that can be worn either open or closed at the neck. Worn open it creates a lapel for a tailored, almost jacket-like opening.

1. Note that this collar is draped on the bias to allow it to stand and roll over smoothly. Prepare and block your calico as per the dimensions in Fig. 10.17.
2. The collar will drape from CB to CF so it is important to position the blocked calico correctly where the CB and neckline intersect. The CB is on the bias. Put a holding pin in whilst you adjust (Fig. 10.18).
3. Smooth the calico up the CB. Decide on the depth of the collar at the CB and put a pin in so that you have an anchor point from which to start creating the roll line (Fig. 10.19).
4. With the calico still standing upwards, smooth it around the neckline of the bodice towards the

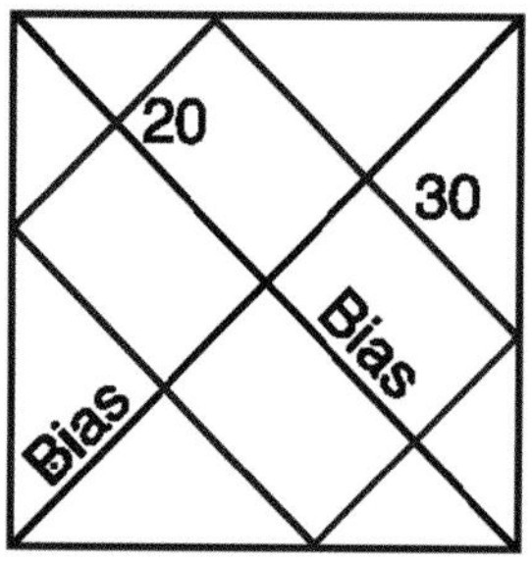

Fig. 10.17 Block dimensions for convertible collar.

Fig. 10.18 Positioning convertible collar at CB; note grain line on the bias.

Fig. 10.19 Pinning roll line position and smoothing calico around back neck to neck point.

Fig. 10.20 Snipping to release tension and allow drape to lie flat at back.

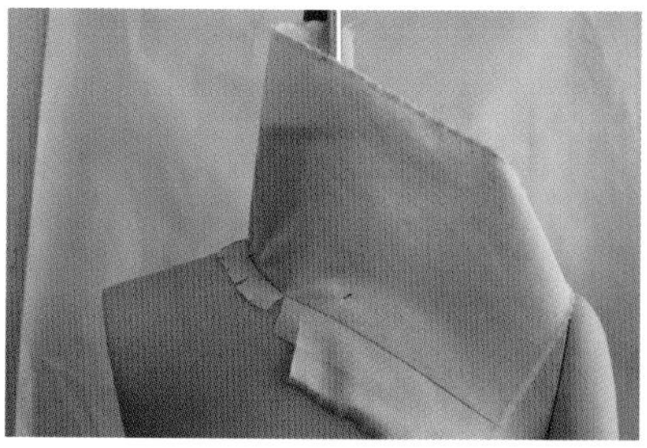

Fig. 10.21 Snipping in to ensure collar travels round neck from CB to CF.

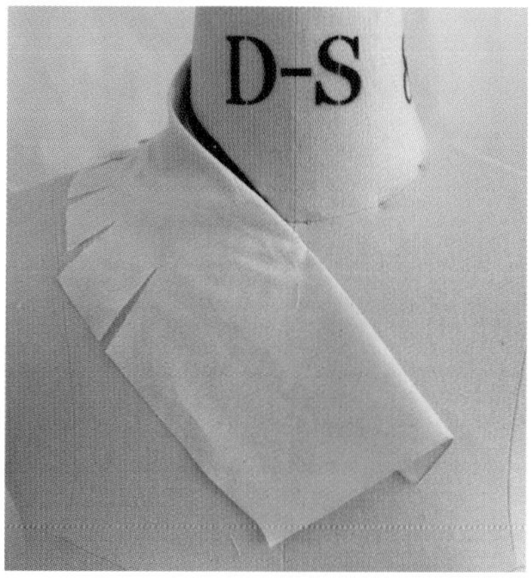

Fig. 10.22 Creating roll line and getting convertible collar to sit flat along outer edge.

CF, snipping in as you go to shape the collar bottom (Figs 10.20 and 10.21).

5. From the pin on the neck of the CB, fold the calico downwards to create a roll. The fold should run out at the CF. You may need to snip into the outer edge of the calico to allow it to sit flatter as it goes over the torso from front to back (Fig. 10.22).
6. Using tape, mark out the collar shape. I have used black stay tape but you could just as easily use an adhesive one from Design-Surgery®. Your style line can be plotted to your own design so consider the width and shape of the collar tips (Fig. 10.23).
7. When you are happy, mark off the neckline edge, collar edge and roll line with a dotted line and a bar for corners and where the roll line intersects at CB and CF. Mark off

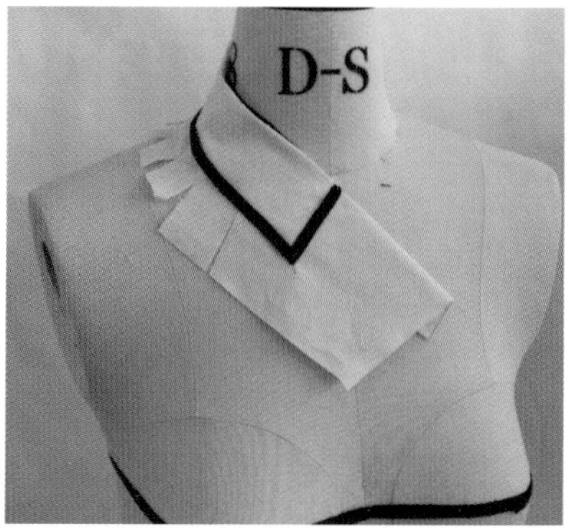

Fig. 10.23 Taping collar style line.

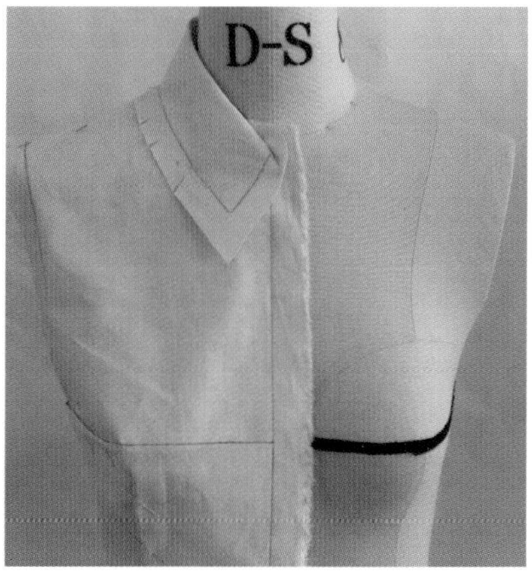

Fig. 10.24 Drawn style line for convertible collar.

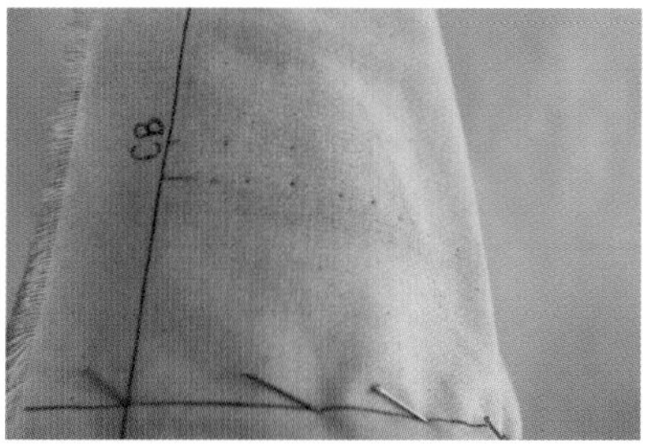

Fig. 10.25 Lifting collar up to mark off roll line.

the neck point where the shoulder seam intercepts the neckline; this will become a notch on your production pattern later (Figs 10.24 and 10.25). The markings should be on both sides of the calico so you need to transfer them all to the same side when truing up.

8. Remove from the stand and true up as per Fig. 10.26. Trim down to a 2cm allowance all the way round.
9. Fold the neckline edge under and reposition it back on the mannequin, pinning onto the neckline of the bodice. Reposition

Fig. 10.26 Convertible collar trued up on the flat.

the roll line at the CB with a pin and fold the top edge over to check the design and roll line. Mark off any adjustments.

10. Remove from the stand and transfer to a paper master pattern.

Two Piece Collar (Fig. 10.27)

This is the collar with a separate stand; it is most traditionally seen on men's shirts. The stand is draped on the SG and the collar segment is on the bias. You have two choices with regards to the stand. You can repeat the process for the stand collar so that you see the stand at the CF and it will have a button wrap and button fasten. Alternatively, the top edge of the stand can be curved downwards and run out at the CF in which case the extra height will be transferred onto the collar segment itself.

1. Prepare and block your calico as per the dimensions in Fig. 10.28. You will need two pieces, one for the stand and one for the collar itself.
2. Begin with the stand and follow the method for the stand collar. Once draped, the top edge of the stand may need to be brought a little closer to the neck so put a small fold in the calico at the neck point and true the neck edge off.

Fig. 10.27 Two-piece collar. (Photo: Yousef Al Nasser)

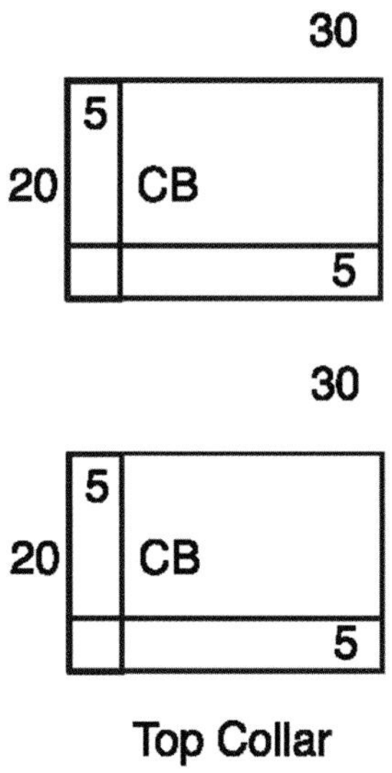

Fig. 10.28 Block dimensions for two-piece collar with stand.

On the pattern this will have the effect of giving the stand more of a curved shape. You will also need to add 1.5cm onto the CF as a button wrap.

3. Pin the neckline edge of the collar onto the neckline of the bodice. Align the CB of the collar segment to the CB of the mannequin.
4. In their *Fairchild Books Dictionary of Fashion* Duborg and van der Tol place their topcollar piece behind the collar stand at this point to create the adjoining seam. I find it hard to tell if the calico is sitting flat this way and prefer to put mine on top of the collar stand instead, as in Fig. 10.29. As per the convertible collar, put snips into the bottom of the calico piece so that it will mould around the neck nicely and fit the stand well. Pin to hold (Fig. 10.30).
5. Fold the collar calico down and check that it rolls well over the top edge of the stand from CB to CF (Figs 10.31 and 10.32).
6. Create your style line and determine the form of your collar with tape (Fig. 10.33). Mark off with a dotted line. Include the CB, collar edge and roll line but also mark in a notch that is directly above the neck point on both the stand and the collar: this notch will be used to align the pattern pieces on your production pattern later.
7. Remove from the mannequin and true up on the flat. Trim away the excess leaving a 2cm allowance around the collar.
8. Reposition the collar stand.
9. Turn the bottom edge of the collar under and align at CB and neck notch on the top edge of the stand and pin together (Figs 10.34 and 10.35).
10. Mark off any adjustments and transfer to the paper master pattern.

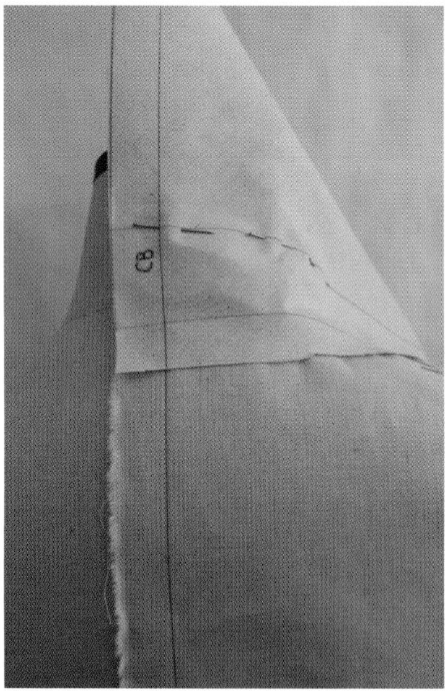

Fig. 10.29 Topcollar being positioned on collar stand for two-piece collar.

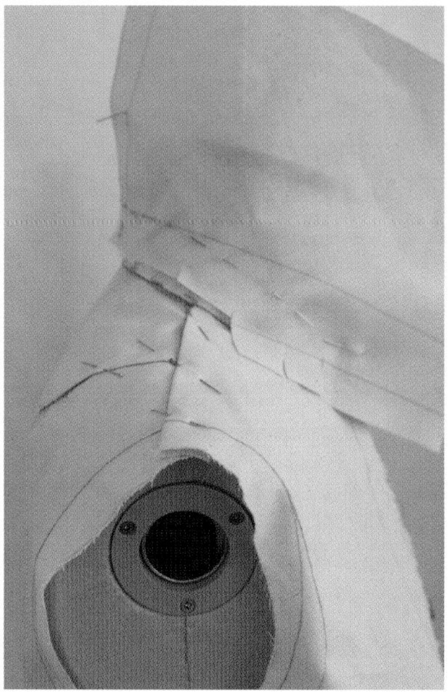

Fig. 10.30 Snipping into topcollar where it joins collar stand.

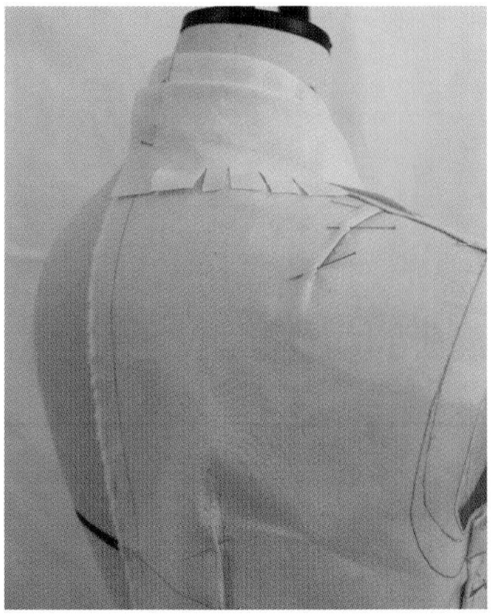

Fig. 10.31 Snipping into outer edge of topcollar, back view.

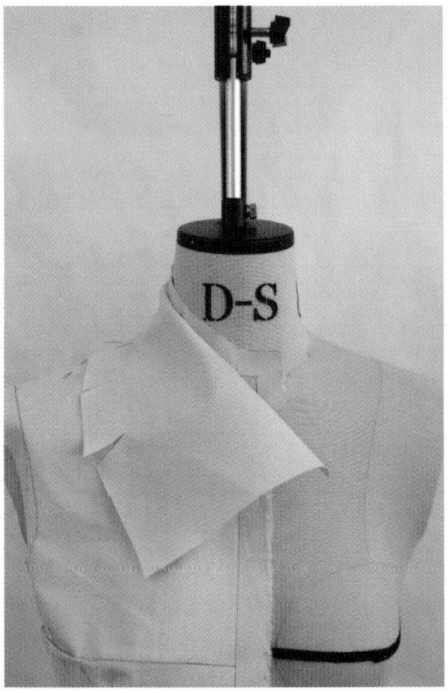

Fig. 10.32 Snipping into outer edge of topcollar, front view.

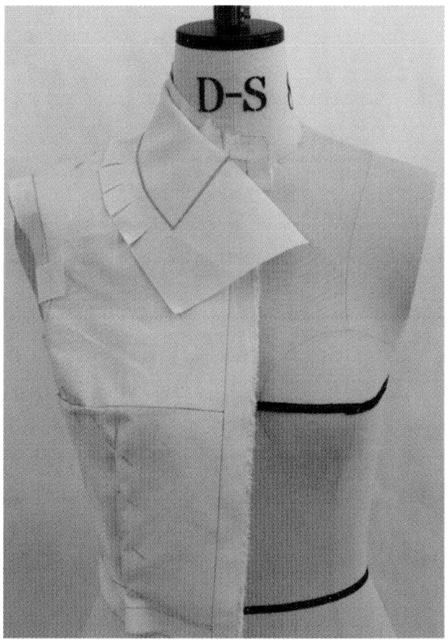

Fig. 10.33 Marking off style line for collar.

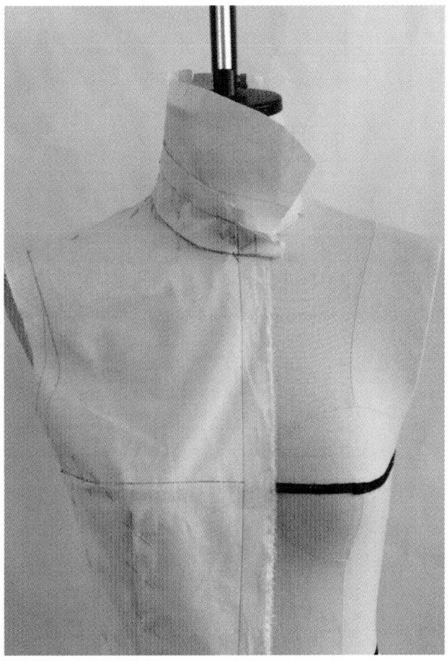

Fig. 10.34 Collar pieces pinned back together for adjustment; note extra at CF of stand for button wrap.

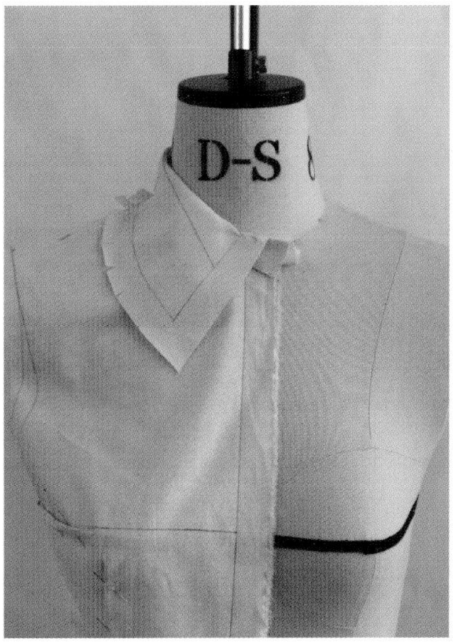

Fig. 10.35 Topcollar pinned and folded over collar stand; note topcollar finishes at CF and not at end of button wrap as per stand.

Probably Vionnet. 1933 T.203-1973.

Evening Dress about 1933.

Satin with paste buckle

"... the fashionable low back is taken to the extreme - it nearly reaches the waist whereas at the front the neckline is high and almost demure. The bias cut garment appears simple but the cut and the construction are complex and immaculately executed. The box shaped sleeves are supported by an interlining of cream grosgrain.

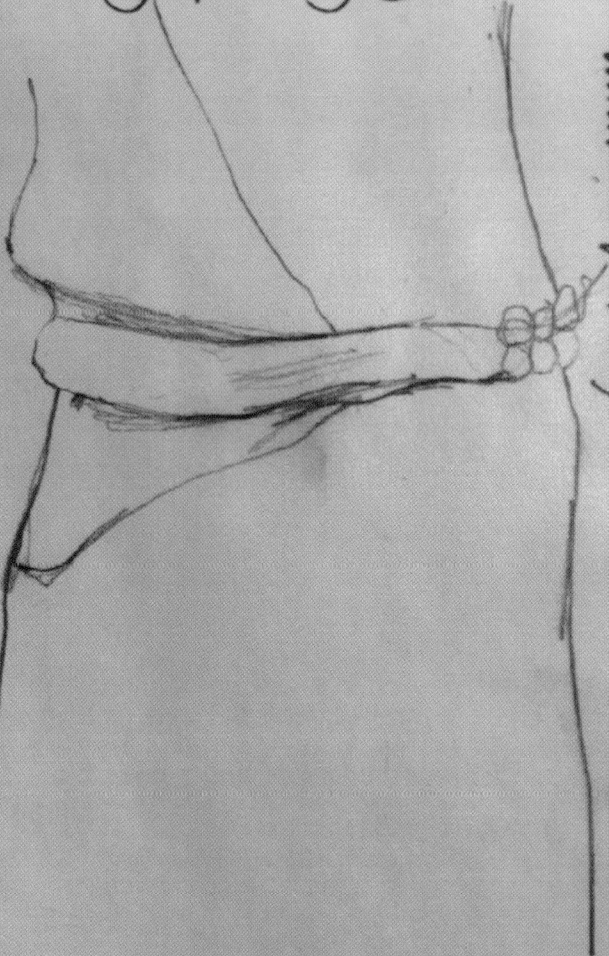

V and A museum. 5 April 2000

1.94

11

The Bias

For this chapter I have made extensive use of the Stuart Aitken Research Files archive at the UCA. The archive comprises collated notes, interview transcripts and illustrated sketches covering all aspects of fashion and clothing from 300 CE to the present day. The illustrations in this chapter are taken from Aitken's Architecture of Fashion: The Modern Period, Book 1 which focuses on the work of Worth, Poiret, Chanel and Vionnet.

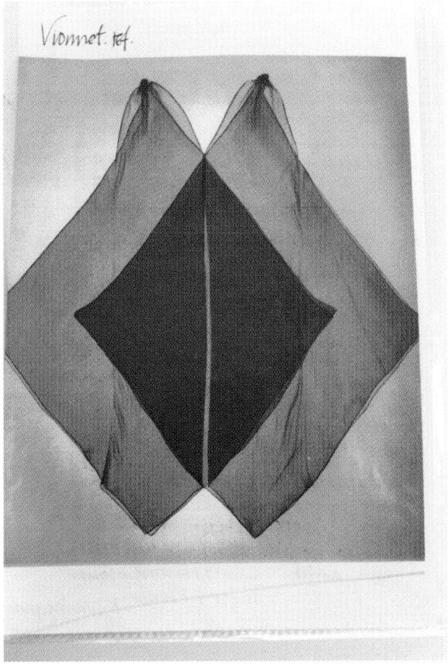

Fig. 11.3 Vionnet dress on the flat. (Stuart Aitken Research Files, UCA)

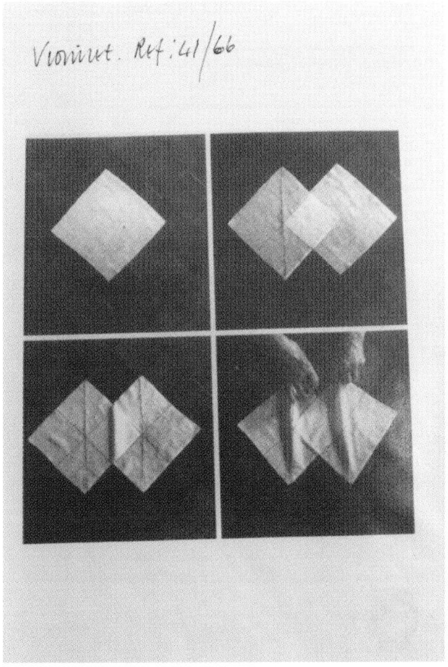

Fig. 11.4 Three-dimensional sketches with geometric squares. (Stuart Aitken Research Files, UCA)

I have already given a brief history of these influential figures in this book's introduction but cannot have a chapter on bias cutting without again mentioning Vionnet and Grès as they have been so integral to the development of the fashion industry's understanding of these practices. For example, the sketches of Vionnet's designs clearly show where she has taken advantage of the bias grain to construct dresses around the female form in a way that skims the body and highlights the wearer's curves while eliminating the need for excess seams and structure. Her work is uncluttered, often using a purist and geometric approach, such as working with an uncut square held at the shoulders and fixed at the waist. Really a precursor to the zero waste movement of the last couple of decades, Vionnet sought to use the fewest cuts and seams possible and created her designs through twisting bias-cut rectangles and half-circles to cinch in fullness and create a good fit whilst adding a decorative element. Figs 11.3 and 11.4, also taken from the Stuart Aitken Research Files, show a photograph of a Vionnet dress on the flat along with Stuart Aitken's own experimentation with the overlaying of two bias squares in response.

Fig. 11.2 Detail of bias panels wrapping over one another for a Vionnet dress. (Stuart Aitken Research Files, UCA)

Bias cutting is notoriously unstable and as a more advanced technique it therefore seems appropriate to leave it until the last chapter in the book. So far, the drapes in this book have all been on the SG to give them structure and stability; fit has been achieved by using suppression to create darts, panels, seams or gathers. Where we have worked on the bias it has been as a by-product of working on the SG rather than as an intention. The only time we have used the bias so far is to create the convertible collar where we needed the calico to roll over the break line more smoothly without creating kinks. For bias cutting, traditionally softer fabrics like crêpes and georgettes are used to drape, although any fabric can be cut on the bias and calico still works. The bias requires larger pieces of fabric to drape with because of the

Left: Fig. 11.1 Vionnet bias-cut dress sketch. (Stuart Aitken Research Files, UCA)

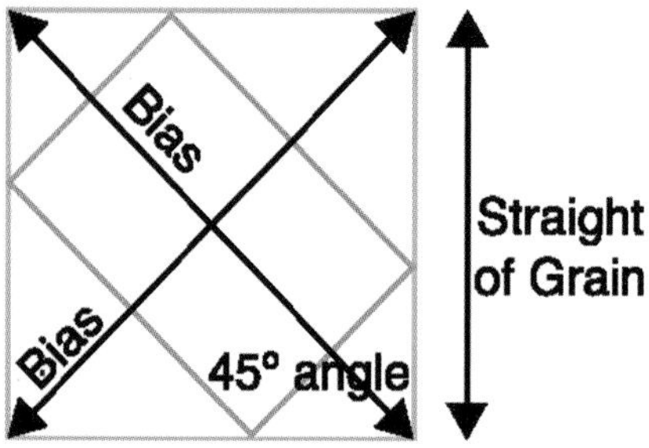

Fig. 11.5 Diagram of the bias grain.

characteristic tilting of the pattern pieces: this means that there can be a lot of waste fabric. Cutting on the SG can generate on average around 15–20 per cent waste whilst working on the bias can generate up to 45 per cent waste if the pattern pieces are all big and shaped. This puts the cost of bias gowns and wedding dresses into perspective where a client is paying for the cloth that is effectively not being used as well as the cloth that is. If the pieces of a bias design are more considered and strategically seamed they can wrap around the body like a spiral and the pattern will fit almost as economically as an SG garment (Fig. 11.5).

A bias-cut garment is cut with the warp and the weft at a 45-degree angle allowing the weave to open and spread a little. This creates the soft drape that is characteristic of bias cutting whilst allowing the fabric to stretch a little and mould around the body. This allows for some really creative draping and cutting without the need for darts or even seams. Figs 1.16–1.22 in Chapter 1 demonstrate the fluidity of fabric when it is placed at 45 degrees on the mannequin in comparison to when it is placed on the SG, so the secret to working with the bias is to let the behaviour of the fabric dictate the final aesthetic of the garment more than you would normally allow it to do as part of the design process.

FORETHOUGHT

Do a stretch test with the fabric to see how stretchy it is before working with it. Pull it across the bias first, then cut a 20cm square. Pin it to the wall overnight hanging from one corner. Measure it again in the morning and see if gravity has caused it to 'grow'. This method also has the added advantage of enabling you to see how the fabric drapes and decide on its suitability for the garment.

Working at Half Scale (Fig. 11.6)

The miniature mannequin can be seen in Fig. 1.12 in Chapter 1; this can be an invaluable tool for designing in three dimensions. It is synonymous with Vionnet's design approach and there are many photos of the designer working out her design ideas on a doll-sized mannequin atop a spinning piano stool so she could check the evolution of her idea all the way round. As she pieced the fabric squares together she would make diagrams of the pieces and shapes she needed, along with the dimensions of cloth. This was effectively her sketch – something more akin to geometry which addressed her concerns over shape, size, relative position of panels or folds and the properties of space than a traditional fashion sketch or *croquis* that we are more used to seeing. Having resolved her design rationale at half scale Vionnet was then better equipped to scale up and cut out the relevant-sized fabric pieces to achieve the design, either on a full-scale mannequin or directly onto a client's body.

Fig. 11.6 Working at half scale.

When I teach my students how to work on the bias we begin with a bias slip then move onto a fabric manipulation using a knot to create supple folds and volume. I find 2.5m of heavyweight chiffon or georgette is enough to do both full size with a little bit left over for them to 'free style' at half scale and develop three-dimensional 'sketches' for their own designs. Partly as an homage to Vionnet and partly out of necessity because I wrote this chapter during lockdown with limited access to resources like calico and voile, I draped all of the bias techniques in this chapter at half scale. The benefits to this have been obvious: I can see how the pieces of fabric will look all the way around the body in half the time using half the cloth. It has been a great method for working out key features and fit. However, it is also true that it is a bit more fiddly and has forced me to be a lot more precise, meaning a half-scale stand is not necessarily easier to learn to drape on than a full-scale stand. There are pros and cons to working at half scale. Other drawbacks are that it is hard to gauge the length of a finished garment because you can't adjust the height of a mini mannequin. It is also worth noting that there are often some discrepancies when changing the cloth or the scale of a design to full size, so it is not fail-safe. However, the important thing is that the process for achieving the idea has already been more or less resolved in a fraction of the time and there are only minor adjustments left to make when scaling up.

Something beginners find perplexing about half scale is how to transfer their design idea to full scale so I would suggest one of the following:

- Take your drape and double all the measurements to create the full-scale master.
- Double the fabric you used and then faithfully replicate the half-scale processes you used on a full-scale mannequin and adjust as you go.
- If the drape pieces fit, enlarge on a photocopier to create a series of 'tiles' you can piece together with an adhesive stick or tape at full scale.

Establishing Your Own Working Process for a Bias

Like Vionnet, my students do not start the draping process for working with bias with a specific design in mind; rather they enter a state of creative 'freefall' to see where the fabric takes them. This can be a really exciting part of the design process provided you learn to embrace the bad ideas along with the good. In Vionnet's day this aspect of the design process would have required lots of sketching and note-taking to visually record every step. To cement my students' understanding, they experiment broadly with a variety of fabrics and ideas, documenting the process with diagrams, measurements and lots of photos on their mobile phones! As you've got this helpful device then, every time you position and pin the fabric you can take a photo. If you swipe left in your photo gallery you can see the garment being deconstructed back to the original placement of calico on the stand at the start and if you swipe right you can see the garment being constructed in sequence. This is extremely useful when transferring what will no doubt look like very abstract pattern pieces to a master or onto the real fabric and you need to know what the folds look like. It is also invaluable when you try to repeat the design idea in the real fabric full-scale and can't remember exactly what you did the first time. Armed with this knowledge you can then develop your fashion illustrations on a *croquis* more meaningfully if you need them afterwards.

Accommodating the Stretch in a Bias Drape

As noted under 'Forethought' above, bias-cut garments have a tendency to stretch over time; how much and how quickly depends entirely on the fabric you are using and how it responds to gravity when it is hanging. In the past I have worked on jersey dresses that appear to have grown by nearly a foot overnight and the waist, hip and bust had to be re-marked and the hem levelled before I could transfer the drape to a production pattern. I would suggest doing your drape and leaving it on the stand, if you can, for 24 hours then checking against your original dimensions to see what has shifted. Some common issues to look out for are as follows:

- Bias fabric commonly veers off at the side of the hip or the whole hipline drops in skirts and dresses. Correct this by re-marking the hipline to correspond with the hipline you taped to your mannequin before beginning the drape.
- Sometimes a pouch of fabric is created, either through the stomach or the back waist of a dress or close-fitting garment. This is caused by the garment torso stretching. As the hips are the widest part of the body, the fabric stops growing when it hits them, causing a pillowing effect around the waistline. The only thing you can do is undo the pins at the SS and adjust the fabric, then leave the drape alone again to see what happens.
- Draping too tightly will cause the grain line to distort and result in a drape and consequently a production pattern that is too small. Be particularly wary of pulling the fabric tightly over the bust and between the BPs. Your drape should be skimming the body, not contouring it – you are not working with lycra!
- The dropping of the hem and the progress toward unevenness may be caused by the SSs stretching or a partial stretch over one particular area of the body. Leave the garment on the stand as long as you can before levelling it. If you have to remove it from the stand then hang it up well above the floor and let it drop on a hanger. Check it again on the mannequin to level the hem.

Blocking for Bias Garments

The malleability of bias fabric is both an advantage and a disadvantage. Its ability to stretch and be moulded to create body-skimming and fluid garments has already been mentioned as a plus; however, its instability can make it really unpredictable and difficult to work with. Regardless of the cloth you have chosen to drape with, take your time to cut it out accurately.

- Work with a single layer and smooth it out as flat as possible: if you cut doubled or on the fold it will never be symmetrical.
- Remove the selvedge edge as the weave is very tight at the edge – snip and rip as in Chapter 4.
- Use a piece of pattern or tissue paper under the fabric to stabilize it and then you have a straight edge along which to pin the SG. Start in one corner and smooth the fabric across the weft and up the warp, pinning as you go to ensure that the cloth lies flat without any distortions. Any distortions to the grain will pull unattractively and as you cut the fabric out they will snap back, reducing the size of your cut piece of cloth at that point and leaving you with a very wobbly edge.
- Use fine pins and plenty of them – not weights because the cloth will move around. Don't pin so tightly that the fabric stretches or it will shrink back from the pins as you cut.
- Keep a separate pair of really sharp

scissors for cutting through fine fabrics and paper combined and this will give your drape a clean edge. If you can use a rotary cutter then do so.

- Tape up your mannequin for bust, waist and hips and measure the distance between them. Mark off the CF and CB on the fabric, then, using these dimensions, mark off the bust-, waist- and hiplines. You can do this with thread marking in a coloured thread or with a coloured pencil or pen. Be aware of the amount of extra fabric you will need above the bustline to create a variety of necklines.
- Lightly dry-press if you need to but don't use steam. It is best to know your fabric content before you start: silks and pure wools are great to work with but anything synthetic will react to heat and may disintegrate if the iron is too hot. Always test your fabrics with the iron first to see how they behave.

Fig. 11.7 Sketch of Vionnet bias-cut slip. (Stuart Aitken Research Files, UCA)

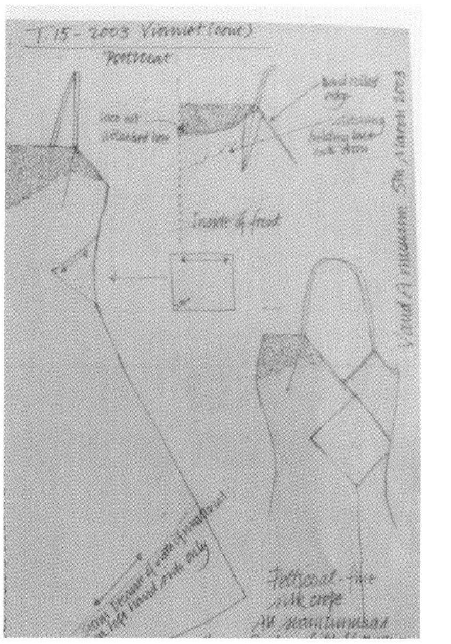

Fig. 11.8 Pattern analysis sketch of Vionnet bias-cut slip. (Stuart Aitken Research Files, UCA)

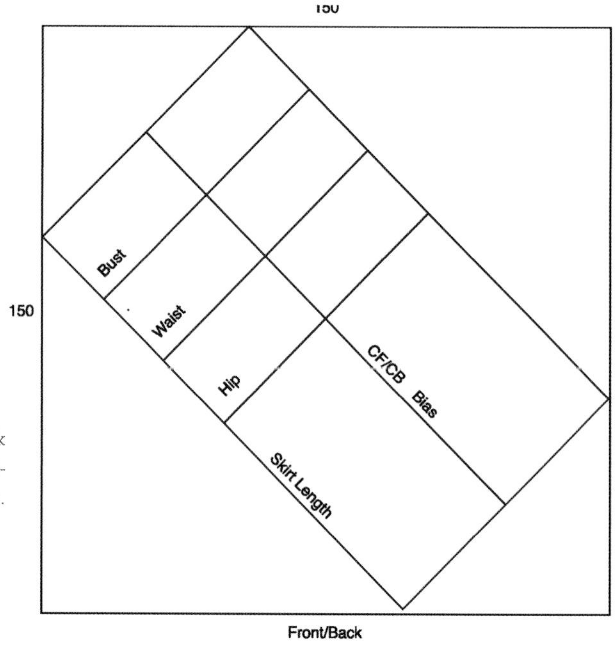

Fig. 11.9 Block dimensions for full-scale bias slip.

PRESSING

When working on the bias, it is especially important not to iron heavily: you will drag your fabric out of shape, rendering it useless. Instead, place the hot iron on top of the fabric and gently press, then lift the iron, move it along and place it down again gently.

Spaghetti-Strap Bias Slip (Figs 11.7 and 11.8)

Although not quite as complex as the Vionnet slip in Stuart Aitken's sketches, this one follows the same principles and is a good starting point for getting used to working with the bias. The shift is effectively draped of two tilted squares, one for the front and one for the back, which are joined through the SS. Like the sketch, the volume is supported from the shoulder and the fit should offer enough ease to allow you to get the slip on and off over the head easily without fastenings. Rather than draping on the right-hand side you are going to drape the whole front and the whole back to see how the fabric performs. The bias grain runs down the CF and CB and the garment fits by stretching gently over the bust, waist and hips.

1. Tape up the mannequin with bust-, waist- and hiplines and the style line for the neck and armhole.
2. Prepare and block your calico as per the dimensions in Fig. 11.9.
3. Pin the CF bias line onto the CF of the mannequin where it intersects with the bustline and pin at the BP (Fig. 11.10).
4. Starting on the right side, smooth the fabric across the mannequin and pin down the SS from the bustline to the hipline only. Leave the fabric below the hipline for now.
5. Repeat on the left-hand side.
6. Snip into the waist and along the SS allowance to release some of the

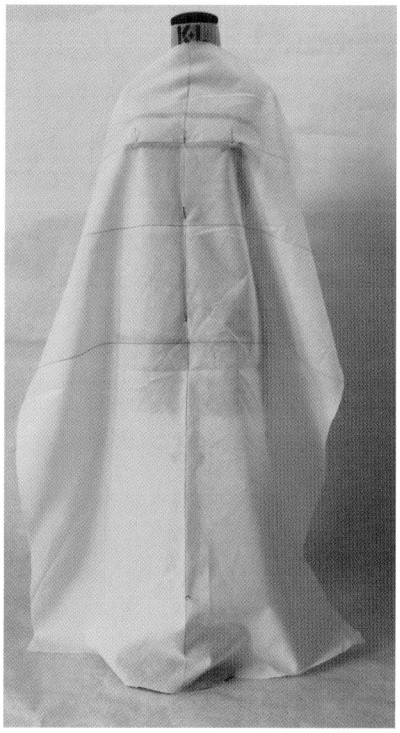

Fig. 11.10 Positioning CF and BPs.

tension through the suppression points and keep adjusting the fit of the front of the slip without allowing it to become too tight. This will take time to get exactly right and remove ripples in the fabric (Fig. 11.11).

7. Smooth the fabric up and over the BP, pinning as you go to hold the fabric in position, and smooth across the style line. Take a separate piece of non-adhesive stay tape and wrap it around the over bust along the style line and pin into place. The tape is going to become a template for the binding used to finish the neckline. Where ease is concerned, it may be possible to press a slight fullness away but if you can't then it needs to be stabilized as it is eased onto the bound neckline or facing. If your fabric doesn't sit flat then you may need to create some ease along the neckline. Even it across the neck tape until you are happy and indicate its position with pins to hold. Either thread mark or mark off the position of the ease with notches on both the fabric and the tape (Fig. 11.12).
8. If you are happy with the fit, trim the excess allowance away and mark off the SS and neckline with a series of dots, or thread mark if you prefer.
9. At the hipline, the object of the exercise will be to ease the volume of fabric forwards a little to create the characteristic fluting associated with the hemlines of bias garments. Snip into the hemline and ese the fabric round from the SS towards the CF and the volume will move from the side of the body to the front. Move as much in as the allowance will let you. Pin the front drape from the

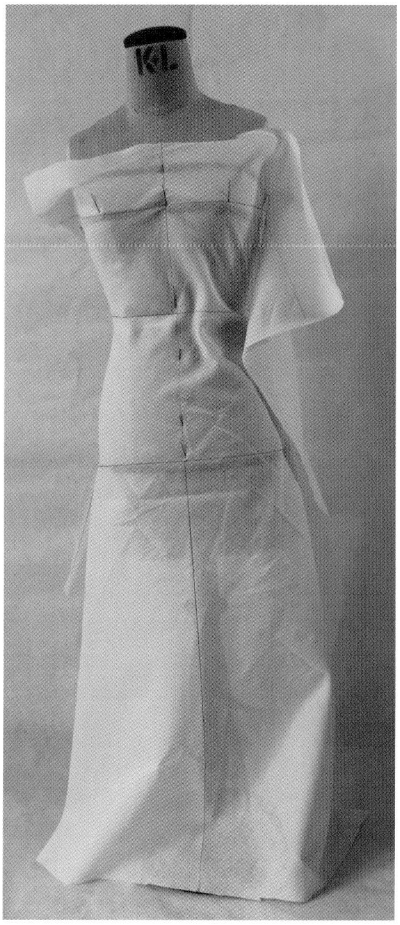

Fig. 11.11 Smoothing fabric over mannequin to create fit.

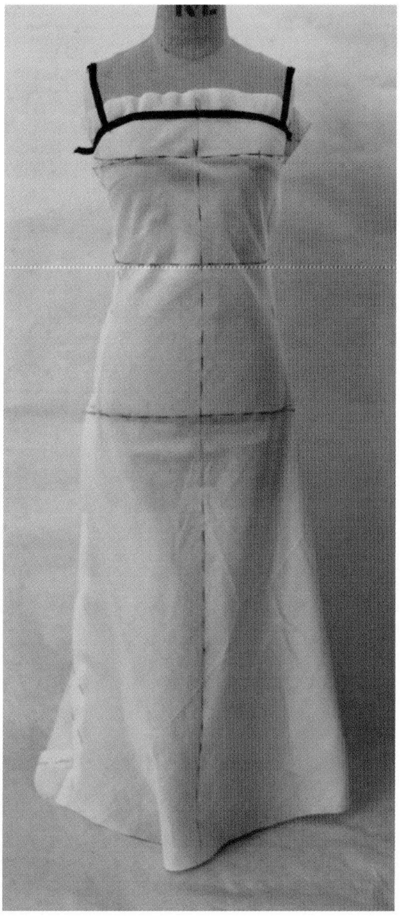

Fig. 11.12 Using twill tape to create neckline and strap position; note puckering of ease across chest.

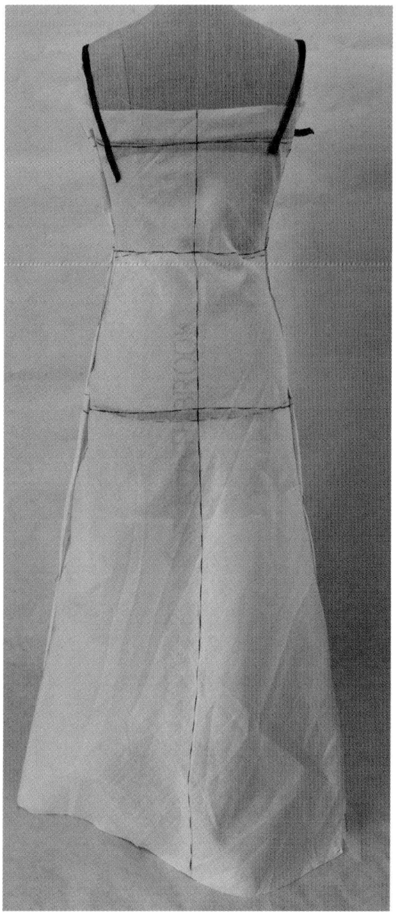

Fig. 11.13 Process repeated on the back.

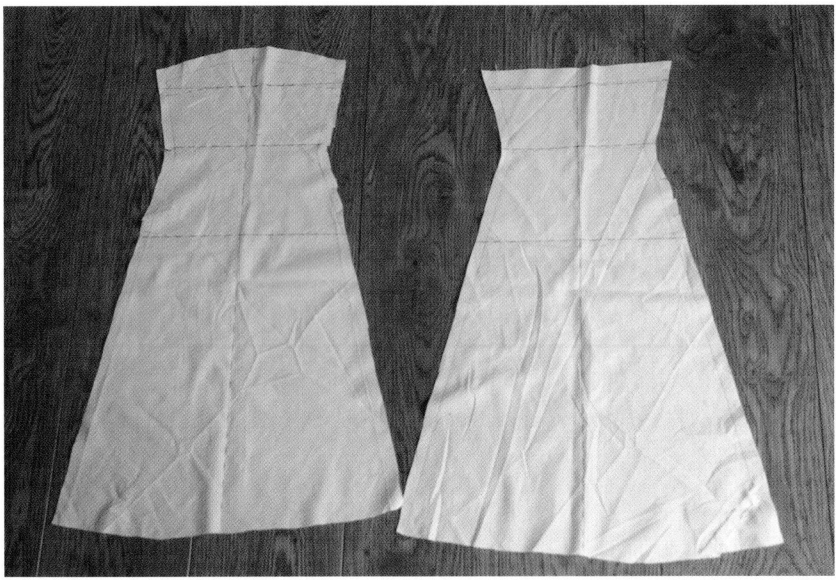

Fig. 11.14 Trued-up bias slip on the flat at half scale.

hip down to the bottom of the mannequin and mark off the extended SS.

10. Remove from the mannequin and true up if you need to. Trim the allowance away, then repeat the process for the back of the shift (Fig. 11.13).
11. To check the fit, return the front to its position on the stand and pin it, checking to see if the bust, waist and hip are still in alignment with those taped on the mannequin.
12. Re-align the back, folding the SS allowance under and aligning the edge to the SS of the front piece. Pin diagonally from the top through both layers of the fabric but not along the SS. Don't pin to the stand.
13. Re-mark the position of the bust, waist and hip if the fabric has dropped already.
14. Reposition the tape across the CF and CB and mark off the position of the spaghetti straps with more black twill stay tape. Mark off additional corresponding notches on the bodice and the straps.
15. Adjust if necessary and mark the alterations in a different colour before transferring the adjusted drape to a paper master pattern ready to toile (Fig. 11.14)

Bias Camisole with Panel Neckline and Draped Overlay (Fig. 11.15)

The neckline here is a stylistic variant on that of the bias slip. The neckline has been raised, with an additional panel rather like a facing inserted above the style line of the drape; the drape itself is a third piece inserted into the style line seam that rolls over on itself before being trimmed away to the desired finished length and volume. The drape could have been in one continuous piece but would be a lot less stable and this technique builds the drape's support piece into the design from the outset. Stylistically the garment is also obviously just a shorter version of the long slip dress but do consider the length-to-volume ratio you are after here. The longer the garment the more of the characteristic fluting at the hem you will have.

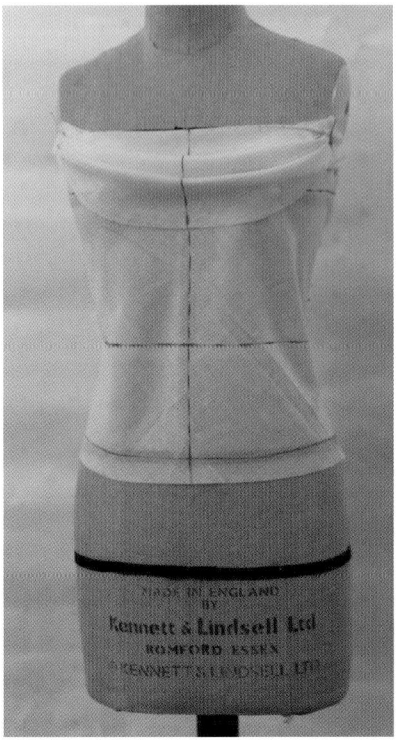

Fig. 11.15 Finished drape for bias camisole with neck panel and overlay.

1. Tape the new neckline onto the stand (Fig. 11.16).
2. Prepare the calico for draping (Fig. 11.17).
3. Repeat all the steps given for the

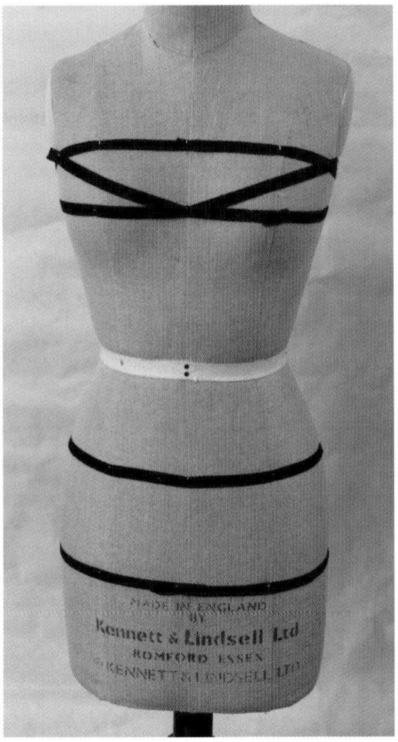

Fig. 11.16 Taped panel position.

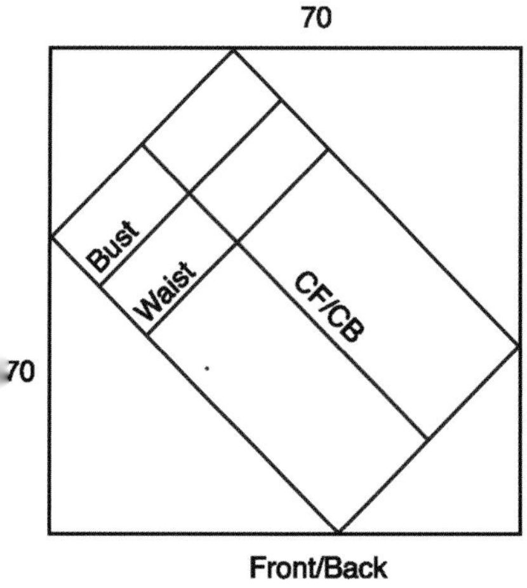

Fig. 11.17 Block dimensions for draping camisole.

spaghetti-strap slip but finish just beyond the desired hem length for the camisole (Figs 11.18 and 11.19).

4. Drape the top facing or support panel on the SG by aligning to the CF. Mark the style line off on the bottom edge with a series of dots and true up on the flat, cutting the allowance down to 2cm (Figs 11.20 and 11.21).
5. To create the draped overlay fold the fabric in half along the bias and position the centre of the piece with the CF. The drape will be suspended from the armhole and held in place with the bias spaghetti strap so experiment with the position of your pinning and adjusting until you like the look of the drape created. Make sure it is deep enough at the CF (Fig. 11.22).
6. Shape the bottom edge of the draped overlay, making sure it covers the bustline but reveals the insert at the CF.
7. Set the straps but remember to keep the underarm area high to prevent the side of the bust being exposed.
8. Adjust if necessary and mark the alterations in a different colour before transferring the adjusted drape to a paper master pattern ready to create the production pattern and toile (Fig. 11.23).

Fig. 11.18 Positioning calico on the bias to drape camisole body to hip.

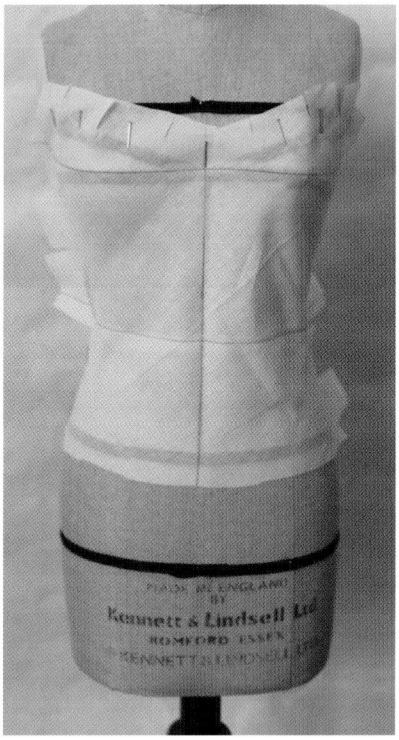

Fig. 11.19 Fitting calico to stand on the bias for camisole body.

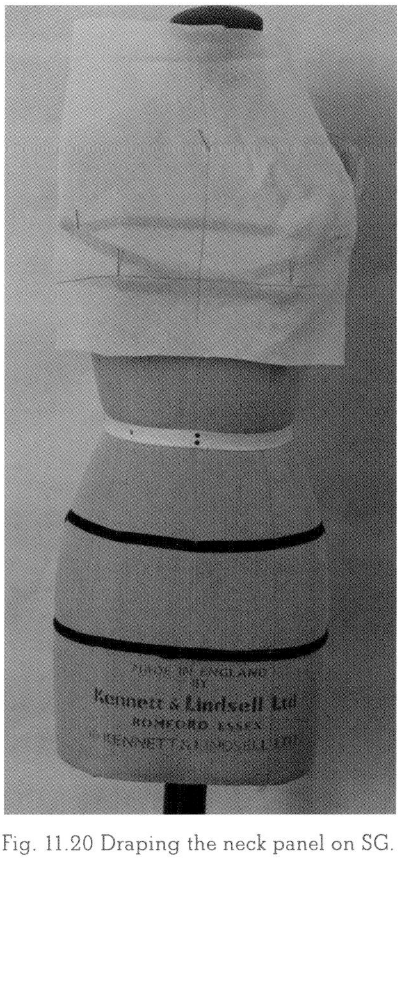

Fig. 11.20 Draping the neck panel on SG.

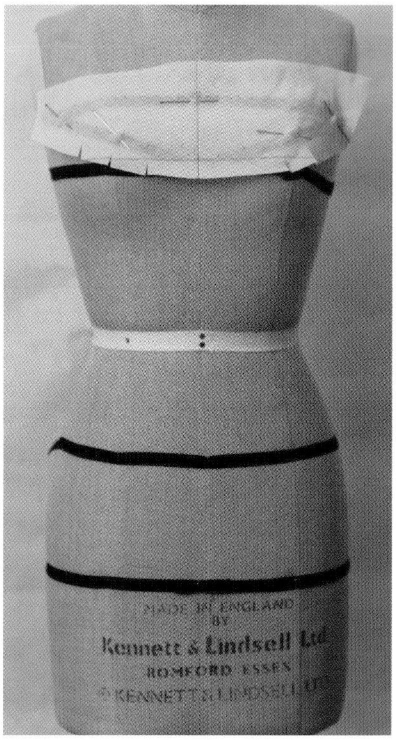

Fig. 11.21 Trimmed-down neck panel.

Draping is really about the arrangement of the fabric in folds, flares and flounces from a fixed point. For the following bodices the fixed

Fig. 11.22 Creating the draped overlay.

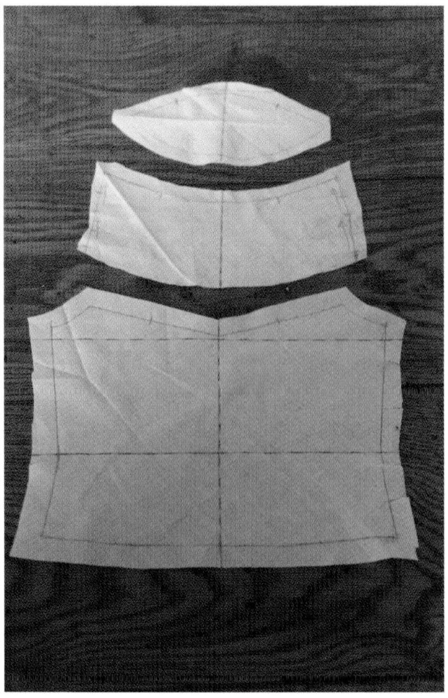

Fig. 11.23 Finished trued-up drape for camisole.

point is the front neck and the drape is on the right-hand side. Where the volume is asymmetric I have draped a left-fitted bodice and the back on the SG to make each piece look more complete.

Bodice with Waterfall (Fig. 11.24)

This technique is actually much simpler than it looks and can be done with skirts, with the volume falling from the waist as well. For this design I have draped the waterfall on the right-hand side with the waterfall and the fitted bodice embedded into one piece. You could easily drape the left side of the bodice across the front to the right-hand PS. The waterfall panel could be basted over the SA of the left-hand piece and machine stitched on the top of the design to toile as a complete garment with the waterfall as its key feature. Alternatively, you could drape the whole of the front bodice first and use this as an overlay instead.

1. Tape the mannequin with bust- and waistlines.
2. Block the calico according to the diagram (Fig. 11.25).
3. Pin the bias at the CF where it intersects the bustline and pin above and below the bustline to hold.
4. On the right-hand side smooth the calico into the neck point and pin. Smooth the calico along the shoulder line and pin to hold.
5. Ease the calico across the right-hand side of the mannequin to the SS and pin to hold. Snip into the SS allowance to release the tension if necessary and fit to the stand snugly.
6. Snip into the waist and cut away a section from just below the waist to the PS. The object of the exercise here is to fit the calico through one

Fig. 11.24 Waterfall drape.

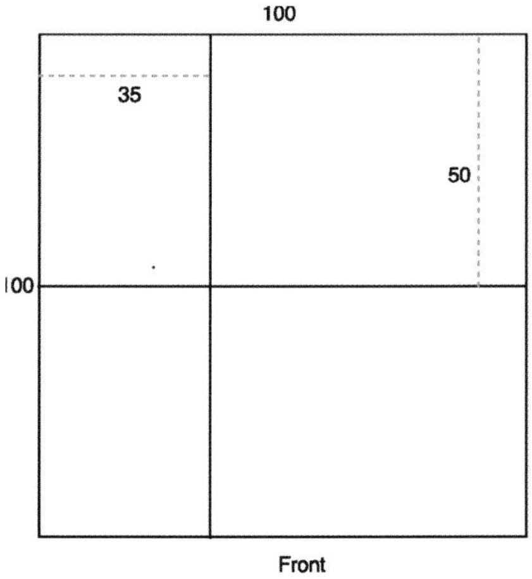

Fig. 11.25 Block dimensions for draping waterfall.

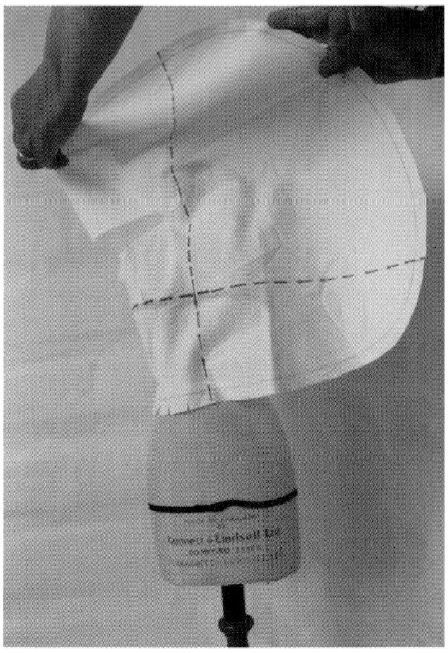

Fig. 11.26 Positioned calico fitted to right side of body with shoulder snipped.

side of the body whilst keeping the length at the CF as it will form part of the waterfall.

7. Leaving 2cm allowance at the shoulder, cut along the shoulder seam towards the neck point (Fig. 11.26).
8. Pivot the fabric above the shoulder seam forwards and let it drop down the bodice front from the neck point to create the waterfall. Initially it will be quite bulky but the volume can be cut to your desired aesthetic. If you are not sure where to cut, use the black tape to mark it off first (Fig. 11.27).
9. Remove from the stand and true up on the flat. The waterfall element should look like a mis-shaped circle, depending on how you have trimmed away the extra volume and length, but with the distinctive shape of a shoulder, armhole and SS embedded into it on one side (Fig. 11.28).
10. Put the pieces back together on the stand and adjust if necessary. Mark the alterations in a different colour before transferring the adjusted drape to a paper master pattern ready to create the production pattern and toile.

Fig. 11.27 Calico being pivoted around from neck point to create folding drapes.

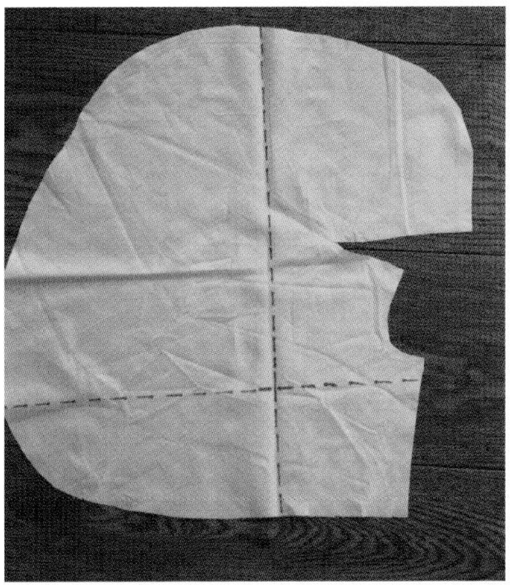

Fig. 11.28 Trued-up waterfall drape.

Fitted Bodice with a Draped Front (Fig. 11.29)

This style is similar to a cowl but with controlled drapes at the shoulder that form the drapery at the CF. As the back of the body is flatter than the front, this feature sits equally well the other way round. Avoid trying to do it on both the front and the back simultaneously because you need the high neck of one to anchor the drapes of the other in place without building bulk at the shoulder line.

1. Tape the mannequin with bust- and waistlines.
2. Block the calico according to the diagram (Fig. 11.30).
3. Fold the fabric double along the bias and pin a big triangle out of the CF, running it out at the back waist point. This will create the volume of your fold so think about its depth before you start. It is a similar principle to creating the volume for the sleeve head of the gigot in Chapter 9.
4. Slash up the CF just below where it intersects the waist. The triangle is

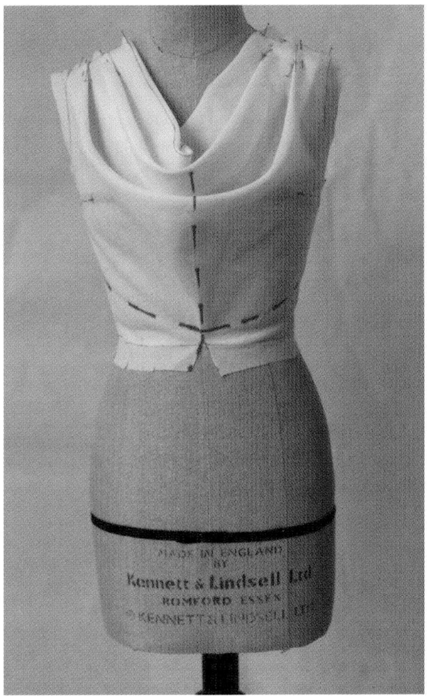

Fig. 11.29 Fitted bodice with draped front.

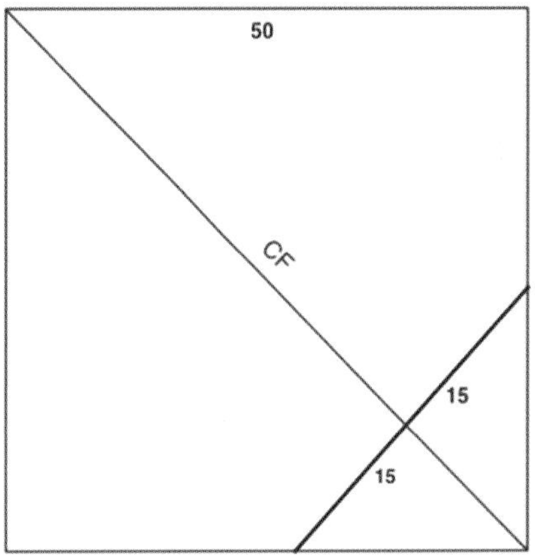

Fig. 11.30 Block dimensions for bodice with draped front.

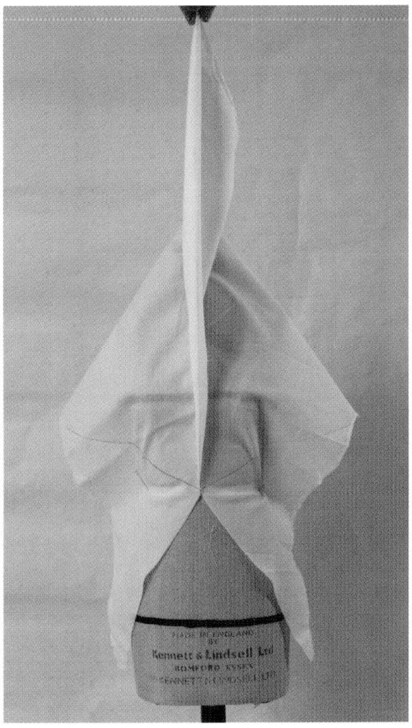

Fig. 11.31 Fitting bodice with extra volume at CF and slash up to waistline; note that waistline has swung up towards SS.

going to create the drape so the size of this depends on the amount you pin out at the CF to start. The pin line is now the CF (Fig. 11.31).

5. Align the pinned CF to the CF of the mannequin and pin from the neck to the waist to hold.
6. Smooth the panel out towards the SSs and shoulder and pin to hold.
7. The original waistline will swing upwards. Cut off the excess fabric under the mannequin's waist and snip up into it to ease the tension and get a smoother fit.
8. Partially pin the shoulder and mark off the SS and armhole, cutting away the excess allowance to approximately 2cm.
9. Undo the pins on the centre segment and start to create symmetrical pleats either side of the CF to form the drapes. The original CF/bias drawn onto the fabric is now the CF of the drape (Fig. 11.32).
10. Mark off the shoulder and pleats. Use notches to indicate the pleat position and the top and the bottom folds.
11. Remove from the mannequin and true up on the flat. Mark the alterations in a different colour before transferring the adjusted drape to a paper master pattern ready to create the production pattern and toile (Fig. 11.33).

Fig. 11.32 Armhole and shoulder are fitted and drapes temporarily pinned into place.

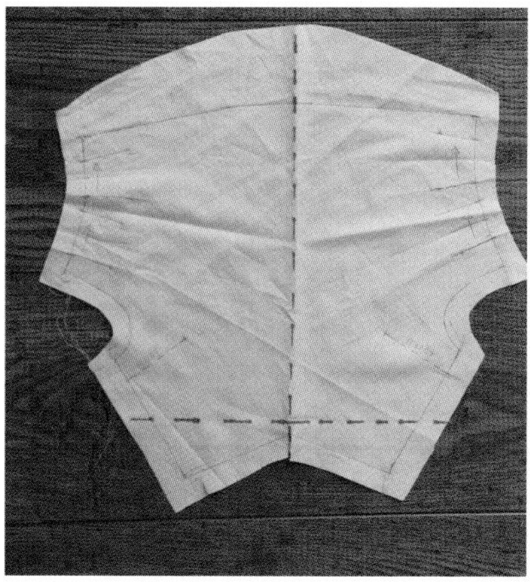
Fig. 11.33 Trued-up final drape.

The Knot (Figs 11.34 and 11.35)

The knot technique is slightly different in that you have to prepare it first on the flat rather than draping it straight onto the body. In this design, the knot is at the waist on the CF but it doesn't have to be: for example, the Stuart Aitken sketches in Figs 11.34 and 11.35 show the front and back view of a design with the knot at the neck. Once the drape is stable enough to lift up vertically, it is worth thinking about the position where you want the knot to sit on the body, then position accordingly before fitting the rest of the cloth to the mannequin and completing the drape. You might, for example, consider having the knot at the neck or collarbone or you might move it to the lower back or the hip. Experiment with this first – this really highlights the benefit of working in three dimensions to design and generate more unexpected ideas as a result of having instant visual feedback, as in Fig. 11.36. The construction seams that create the knot and hold its shape will disappear into the drapery and effectively create the illusion of this design being cut in one piece and not two. I used the CF to create a simple V neckline rather than cutting into it so it would be useful to re-mark your CF at the end. Although it is not essential for you to do so, I put in a bustline to demonstrate what happens to the SG with this technique. As you can see from the final drape, this has been manipulated round by 90 degrees in a quarter-circle (Fig. 11.37).

Fig. 11.34 Vionnet knot dress, front, drawn by Stuart Aitken. (Stuart Aitken Research Files)

Fig. 11.35 Vionnet knot dress, back, drawn by Stuart Aitken. (Stuart Aitken Research Files)

1. Tape the mannequin with bust- and waistlines.

2. Block the calico according to the diagram (Fig. 11.38).
3. Cut along the bias line so that you have two right-angled triangles with the CF on the long cut edge/bias.
4. Finger-press the bias-cut edge under to keep the CF looking clean and finished (Fig. 11.39).
5. On the flat, lay one triangle over the other, aligning at the CF, and smooth flat.

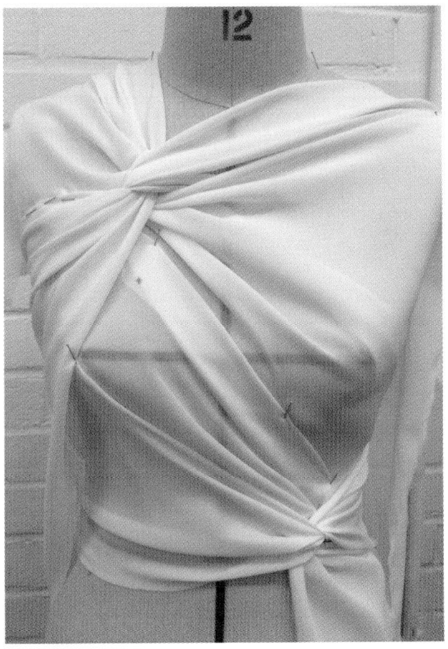

Fig. 11.36 Multiple knot bodice in georgette.

Fig. 11.37 Different version of multiple knot bodice.

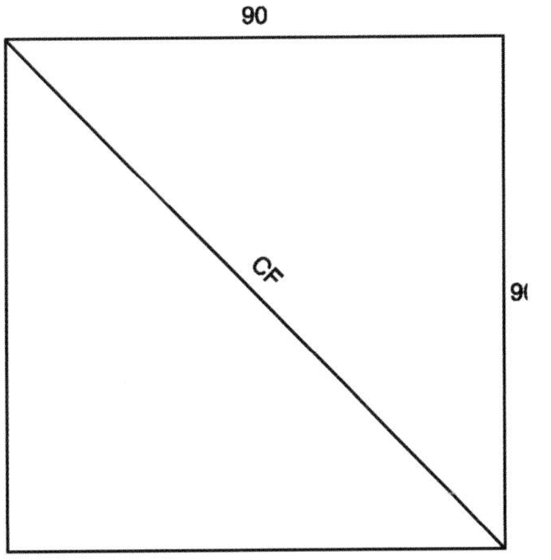

Fig. 11.38 Block dimensions for the knot.

Fig. 11.39 Two right-angled triangles of calico with finger-pressed edges at the CF.

6. Measure across from the CF to the widest point and mark off a third of the way in from the triangle point.
7. Measure and mark off the same distance along the outer edges of the triangle's point.
8. Join the points together with pencil in an arc and cut away the triangle's corner along this line.
9. Separate the two triangles again, laying them flat on the table next to each other, CF to CF (Fig. 11.40).
10. Gather up the volume across the middle of the triangles from the cut-away to the CF – one in each hand (Fig. 11.41).
11. Cross the bottom half of the left triangle over the bottom half of the right to create a loose 'butterfly' shape. Arrange the drapes a little as you go (Fig. 11.42).

Fig. 11.40 Triangles with outer corners cut away in an arc.

12. Complete the butterfly stage by taking the bottom half on the left side (formerly the right-hand bottom half) and cross it over the right-hand side, creating a more solid knot or twist at the centre (Fig. 11.43).
13. Adjust the volume of the pleats so that the CF is not too bulky and smooth out the butterfly again so that you can see the outside edges of the arcs you cut away on each side.
14. On the left side start at the outer edge of the arc and pin the edges together to create a horizontal seam. Pin as far as you can towards the CF, stopping when you hit the bulk of the knot. Mark off the position of this opening with a notch on both the top and the bottom of the seam (Fig. 11.44).
15. Repeat for the right-hand side.
16. Pinning the arcs closed should help to stabilize the knot and hold it in place. You should now be able to lift the whole piece up off the table and position it on the mannequin.
17. Position the knot where the CF and

Fig. 11.41 Gathering up each triangle through its centre.

Fig. 11.43 Butterfly stage 2: crossing new left over right to create a more solid knot.

waistline intersect and pin to hold.

18. Smooth the fabric up the CF to the neck and shoulder line and pin to hold.
19. Smooth towards the SSs and pin to hold. You will most likely need to adjust the drapes and folds of the knot: ideally you need them to run out before they hit any seam positions or you will be creating bulk with a pleat in the seam. The seams created by the arcs will most likely sit along the waistline and be concealed under folds so you shouldn't be able to see them. If you need to adjust the fit at the front then unpin them to reshape before re-pinning for the desired fit.
20. When you are happy with the drape and position of the knot, trim the excess allowance away.
21. Mark off the neck point, shoulder, SS and armhole with a dotted line.
22. Inasmuch as you can, mark off the CF across the top and bottom of the folds in the knot. At this stage you might also find it helpful to mark off the position of each pleat or fold in the drape along with its direction. Also mark off the tip of the pleat where it runs out. On the Fashion Atelier course, because we are using couture techniques and I am teaching techniques, I get my students to thread mark each fold at this stage – it is very time-consuming but the design is consistent each time it is put it back on the mannequin and we also get to see how the fabric performs and whether or not it stretches and alters the fit.
23. Remove from the stand and true up on the flat. Alter your armhole shape if you need to and trim down the SA (Fig. 11.45).
24. Re-pin the pieces back together from the top and put back on the stand. Check the fit and mark off any adjustments before removing from the stand and transferring to the master.

Fig. 11.42 Butterfly stage 1: crossing left half over right.

Fig. 11.44 Creating horizontal seam in knot to stabilize drapes.

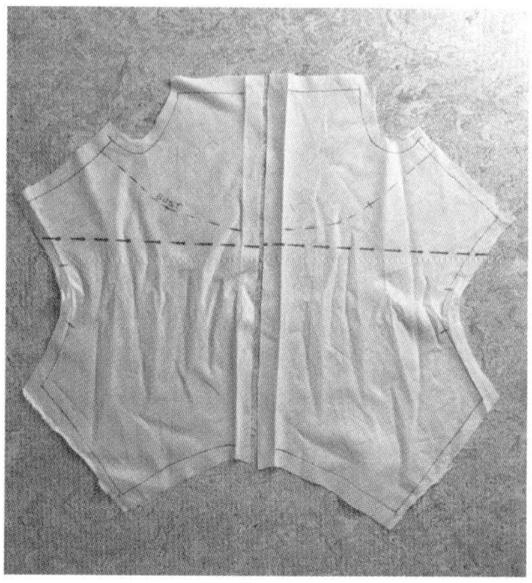

Fig. 11.45 Knot drape trued up on the flat.

Stockists for Workroom Supplies

Croft Mill, Lancashire (UK),
www.croftmill.co.uk
Fabrics

Design-Surgery®, Barnet (UK),
www.design-surgery.com
Mannequins

Eastman Staples Ltd (UK),
www.eastman.co.uk
Pattern-cutting and workroom supplies

Empress Mills, Lancashire (UK),
www.empressmills.co.uk
Sewng supplies and fabrics

Ernest Wright, Sheffield (UK),
www.ernestwright.co.uk
Scissors and shears

Fabric Land Ltd (UK),
www.fabricland.co.uk
Fabrics and haberdashery in shops nationwide

Hunter & Hyland, London (UK),
www.hunterandhyland.co.uk
Workroom supplies, including scissors, pins, rules, etc.

Jaycotts, Chester (UK),
www.jaycotts.co.uk
Sewing machines and patterns, etc.

John Lewis & Partners (UK),
www.johnlewis.com/haberdashery
Haberdashery and fabrics in shops nationwide

Kennett & Lindsell Ltd, Essex (UK),
www.kennettlindsell.com
Dressforms and pattern-cutting supplies

London Trimmings Ltd (UK),
www.londontrimmings.co.uk
Trimmings and other sewing supplies

MacCulloch & Wallis, London (UK),
www.macculloch-wallis.co.uk
Fabrics and haberdashery

Merchant & Mills, Sheffield (UK),
www.merchantandmills.com
Scissors and shears

Morplan, London (UK),
www.morplan.com
Mannequins and pattern-cutting supplies

Pattern Making Supplies (UK),
www.pgmdressform.com
Dressforms

Sew Essential (UK),
www.sewessential.co.uk
Sewing supplies

Whaleys (Bradford) Ltd (UK),
www.whaleys.bradford.ltd.uk
Fabrics, especially calico in different weights

William Gee, London (UK),
www.williamgee.co.uk
Haberdashery and sewing supplies

Suggested Reading and Information Sources

Books

Aldrich, W., *Metric Pattern Cutting for Womenswear,* 6th edn (Wiley, London, 2015)

Amanden-Crawford, C., *The Art of Fashion Draping,* 5th edn (Fairchild Books, London, 2018)

Boucher, F., *20,000 Years of Fashion: The History of Costume and Personal Adornment,* expanded edn (H.N. Abrams, New York, 1987)

Chunman Lo, D., *Pattern Cutting (Portfolio Skills)*, illus. edn (Laurence King, London, 2011)

Duborg, A., van der Tol, R., and Schacknat, K., *Draping: Art and Craftsmanship in Fashion Design,* 4th edn (ArtEZ Press, Arnhem, The Netherlands, 2014)

Fashion: *The Definitive History of Costume and Style* (Dorling Kindersley, in assoc. with the Smithsonian Institution, London, 2012)

Fernault, H., *Haute Couture Ateliers: The Artisans of Fashion* (Thames & Hudson, London, 2014)

Kiisel, K., *Draping: The Complete Course,* 1st edn (Laurence King, London, 2014)

Kiisel, K., *Draping: The Complete Course,* 2nd edn (Laurence King, London, 2020)

Leggatt, W.E., and Hodgkinson, T.W., *The Climax System for Cutting Gentlemen's Garments,* 7th edn (Minister & Co., London, 1925)

Long, T.A., *Charles James: Designer in Detail* (V&A, London, 2015)

Mears, P., *Madame Grès: Sphinx of Fashion* (Yale University Press, New Haven CT, 2008)

Mida, I., and Kim, A., *The Dress Detective: A Practical Guide to Object-Based Research in Fashion,* 2nd edn (Bloomsbury, London, 2018)

Miyake, I., and Kirke, B., *Madeleine Vionnet,* 3rd edn (100th Anniversary edn) (Chronicle Books, San Francisco, 2012)

Saillard, O., *Madame Grès: Sculptural Fashion*, bilingual repr. edn (Cannibal/Hannibal Publishers, Veurne, Belgium, 2014)

Sterlacchi, F., *Draping: Techniques for Beginners* (Laurence King, London, 2019)

Tortora, P.G., and Keiser, S. (illus. Bina Abling), *The Fairchild Books Dictionary of Fashion,* 4th edn (Fairchild Books, New York and London, 2014)

Websites

brightonmuseums.org.uk

clothingindustry.blogspot.com/2018/01/pattern-making-garment.html

collections.vam.ac.uk/item/O17899/evening-dress-gres-madame/

collections.vam.ac.uk/search/?listing_type=&offset=0&limit=15&narrow=&extrasearch=&q=John+Galliano+wedding+dress&commit=Search&quality=0&objectnamesearch=&placesearch=&after=&before=&namesearch=&materialsearch=&mnsearch=&locationsearch=

spectorbooks.com/the-couture-secrets-of-shape

thedynamicarchive.net/component/the-architectural-perfection

thedynamicarchive.net/component/the-sculptural-approach

visforvintage.net/2012/03/15/a-line/

www.fashionera.com

www.fitnyc.edu/museum

www.metmuseum.org/art/collection/search/159347

www.refinery29.com/en-us/2018/02/189721/skirts-political-history

www.seamwork.com/issues/2015/01/a guide-to-working-on-the-bias

www.telegraph.co.uk/fashion/

www.thecuttingclass.com/grainlines/

www.thegoodtrade.com/features/what-is-slow-fashion

www.vam.ac.uk/articles

www.wdl.org/en/item/7333/

Glossary - An A-Z of Fashion Terms for Draping

Apex: Location of bust point.
Arm plate: Mannequin terminology for the flat plate attached to the arm socket where an arm would sit. Depending on the mannequin this is either a plate to attractively finish and cover the raw edges of the canvas cover or it is an attachment that allows a full arm to be added to the stand. The arm plate is not the same depth as an armhole although it is used as a guide when draping them.
Arm scye: Technical term for the diameter measurement of an armhole or the fabric edge to which the sleeve is sewn. The scye depth is the total length of this edge and the width is the total distance across the hole at its widest point.
Asymmetric: Where the two sides of the garment have different silhouettes and/or fit.
Atelier: The French term for a workshop or studio used by a professional artist or designer. Nowadays, in fashion terms it means a design studio where a number of assistants, apprentices and interns can work together to create finely crafted clothing released under the design house's name.
Balance: When the front and back of a garment hangs perfectly at the side seam.
Basic block/sloper: A basic fitted bodice template. It will include the front and the back with or without darts and gets manipulated during pattern cutting to create a range of different designs and features for production patterns. They do not usually have seam allowances on and are therefore termed 'nett'. They are accurate and precise, based on individual body measurements or a standardized size chart. The basic block is usually used for pattern drafting and is the equivalent of the master pattern if you are draping.
Basting: Temporary stitches made either by hand or machine to hold parts of the garment together until you are ready to sew them permanently.
Bias cut: Rather than following the straight line of the weave, the bias cut places the pattern at a 45-degree angle on the fabric. At this angle the fabric's threads are a bit more elastic and the natural stretch this creates makes the bias excellent for accentuating body lines and creating more fluid curves and soft drapes.
Bicep: Fullest part of the upper arm circumference; located between the elbow and the armhole.
Blocking: Process of manipulating calico or muslin so that the warp and weft are at right angles to each other.
BP: *See* Bust point.
Bust circle: 2–3cm radius around the apex or bust point where your darts should finish once they have been foreshortened at the pattern drafting stage.
Bustline: Horizontal line at the apex or widest part of the bust; runs parallel to the floor.
Bust point: The very tip of the bust, usually where the princess seam and bustline intersect on a mannequin and a guide for where darts should stop if they are going to control the fit. The bust circle can be drawn with a radius 2cm from the bust point all the way round the bust point. It is best to foreshorten darts by 2cm from the bust point on production patterns to reduce the risk of creating an unsightly bulge on top of it when sewing, particularly where there is more than one dart converging on it.
Calico: A plain woven textile made from unbleached and often semi-processed cotton. Its unfinished appearance makes it cheap and easy to work in for toiling.
Cap height: Vertical measurement from the top of the shoulder to the bottom of the armhole or underarm line.
Carbon paper: A transfer paper used to copy stitching lines from cloth to cloth or paper to cloth. The paper is impregnated with coloured ink which creates a track mark or dotted line when the tracing pencil or wheel is passed over it.
CB: Vertical centre back of the body or mannequin.
CF: Vertical centre front of the body or mannequin.
Chiton: A long woollen tunic worn by men and women in ancient Greece and Rome.
Contour dart: Dart with shape; may be convex, concave, French, etc.
Crêpe de chine: French for 'crêpe of China'. Refers to a light woven dress fabric produced either with all-silk warp and weft or a silk warp and hard-spun worsted weft. It is light and floaty in appearance with a rippled surface and is idea for bias cutting.
Cross grain: Fabric grain that goes from selvedge to selvedge. If you are unsure if your cloth is straight of grain or cross-grain try folding it and will be much bouncier on the cross grain.
Dart manipulation: Moving darts to different areas of the body.
Darts: The Business of Fashion (BoF) describes darts as a dressmaker's 'punctuation marks'. They are the technique used for shaping garments by curving the fabric straight to the body or mannequin. They are created by pinning out and sewing a long thin wedge of fabric to a pinch point, usually at the bust, hip or shoulder, which is then pressed to one side. They vary in width, length and position depending on the type of fit the garment requires and can be inserted at the neck, shoulder, bust and waistline by being tapered at one or both ends.
Detachable arm: Mannequin attachment for draping sleeves.
Ease: This is also known as tolerance in the industry. Patterns must be created larger than the actual dimensions of the body for the garments to allow for

ease of movement and comfort. It is not a given but for woven fabrics like wool you could expect the bust to be up to 7.5cm bigger all round on the pattern than on the stand and the waist to be 1.25cm bigger. An armhole could be a minimum of 2cm bigger depending on the style of the garment.

Elbow dart: One or two darts made at the elbow to create a fitted sleeve.

Elbow line: Line denoting the elbow circumference; runs parallel to the floor.

Fast fashion: Inexpensive clothing produced rapidly by mass-market retailers in response to the latest catwalk trends. Up until the mid-twentieth century, the fashion industry ran on four seasons a year, with designers working several months ahead to plan for each season and predict what they believed customers would want. Instead, today we now have brands producing as many as 52 micro seasons in a year, with high-street stores like Zara having entirely new collections hitting stores weekly to remain on trend and bring inexpensive styles that are cheaply produced in cheap fabrics to the public.

Finger-press: Using the fingers to press a temporary crease or fold on the fabric as you drape, usually for seams and darts.

Fitted: A garment that sits close to the body.

Flared: Extending outwards from a natural or straight line or side seam.

Fold line: Indicates where to turn fabric up or under on a pattern, such as for a hem.

Gather: A technique that manages the volume or areas of fullness (such as a sleeve into an armhole or a skirt onto a waistband), allowing you to attach a longer piece of fabric onto a shorter one.

Georgette: Lightweight semi-sheer cloth with a grainy feel. The cloth is woven in highly twisted yarns on the warp and weft making it slightly rough or dry to the touch. It is named after the French dressmaker Georgette de la Plante, who popularized its use at the beginning of the twentieth century.

Grain line: Direction of the threads in a fabric weave. It is customary to follow the vertical thread or warp for the grain line and this is indicated with a long arrow on the paper pattern or master.

Handle: Industry term used to describe the way cloth feels – heavy, dry, light, stiff, creased, stretchy, and so on.

Haute couture: The literal translation from the French would be 'high dressmaking' but the term is applied to garments created as one-off pieces for a specific client. To qualify as an official haute couture house the brand has to be selected by the Chambre Syndicale de La Haute Couture. Members must design made-to-order clothes for private clients, with more than one fitting and using an atelier that employs at least fifteen full-time staff. They must also have twenty full-time technical workers in one of their workshops. Finally, they must also present a collection of no less than fifty original garment designs for both day and evening wear to the public every season in January and July at the Paris Fashion Week.

High hip: Horizontal style line 10cm down from the waist and running parallel to the floor.

Hip: The widest part of the lower torso, usually about 18cm below the natural waist and parallel to the floor.

Holding stitch: A temporary machine or hand stitch used through the development and adjustment stages until a permanent stitch is made.

House model: Also known as a fit model. This is a person who is employed by a fashion designer to check the fit, drape and visual appearance of a design on a real human being: effectively they act as a living mannequin. They are used a lot for toile reviews as well as for modelling the final garments to clients. Live models first appeared in the dressmaking salons of Charles Fredrick Worth in the nineteenth century and were referred to, confusingly, as 'the mannequin' whilst the garments created on their bodies that they exhibited to customers in the salon were known as 'the model'. The model gown was a one-off garment that did not go into production and the prototype design could be sold either to a client or a buyer to replicate. Worth's wife was an in-house model and modelled exclusively for the House of Worth from 1858–78, after which she continued to train the in-house mannequins. She is credited with institutionalizing the profession of modelling and establishing a precedence that each couture house should have its own set of carefully selected and trained house mannequins rather than using the occasional petits mains or seamstress. The earliest fashion models inspired admiration for their beauty and disapproval because they wore fashionable and often risqué dresses in public for money.

Jabot: A frilled ruffle that hangs at the front of a shirt. In the seventeenth century they were the equivalent of a gentleman's tie and were often made of lace and cambric sewn directly to both sides of the opening of a man's shirt. Later they became an add-on secured at the neck with a band or pin. They still form part of the robes of judges and barristers in court today.

Kimono: A loose-fitting T-shaped robe worn as part of the traditional national dress of Japan. It has wide sleeves, typically cut in one piece with the rest of the garment, and is full length, wrapping over to close at the front of the body.

Mannequin: A stylized version of the human form. Also called a dress stand, dress form or tailor's dummy.

Master pattern: When the drape is complete in calico it is transferred to a paper master pattern. This has a specific lay-out with all the pattern pieces in the design being transferred onto it in the same sequence as they would appear around the body. If you are short on paper all of the pattern pieces can be drawn one over another provided the balance lines of the bust, waist and hip are consistent across all the pieces. The master will have notches and notes but will not have facings and seam allowance. The production pattern will be traced from the master and the toile made from that. The master is never cut up, only

traced from, and any alterations on the pattern are made to the production pattern so if anything goes wrong the cutter can go back to the original drape on the master and start again.
Moulage: The science or practice of making casts or moulds, in this instance in fabric to create three-dimensional fashions on a mannequin.
Muslin: A loosely woven bleached or unbleached plain cotton fabric used in fashion for toiling.
Neck point: The point on a mannequin where the neck seam and shoulder seam intersect.
Notches: Small marks made on the pattern and drape to ensure that one pattern piece will match up to the pattern piece next to it. They are also used to indicate the size of the seam allowance on a production pattern and as markers on two pieces of fabric to ensure that they come together correctly when sewn.
Object analysis: A research technique where knowledge is inferred by the examination of existing objects and garments. The knowledge is then cross-referenced with other archives or through practice to expand the research content.
Off grain: Describes when a garment is not draped or cut on the fabric grain as defined by the warp. It may result in an unbalanced, ill-fitting garment.
Off the peg: Ready-made garments in standardized sizes.
On the flat: Pattern drafting in two-dimensions on a flat surface, ideally a purpose-built pattern cutting table.
Pattern cutter: A professional practitioner who is employed in the fashion industry specifically to cut or drape patterns. They may also be responsible for making first toiles and doing fittings, depending on the size of the company they work for.
Pattern making: Also called pattern cutting, this is the process of creating a two-dimensional diagram or template of a garment, either through draping or on a flat surface.
Petersham ribbon: A thick, stiff, corded ribbon used by milliners and tailors as a facing. It is woven so that, once steamed, it will take on and support a particular curve or seam of fabric.
***Petits mains* (les):** The literal translation from the French is 'small hands' and refers collectively to the 2,500 or so seamstresses who work in ateliers to painstakingly bring haute couture pieces to life. They are highly skilled, fiercely loyal to their fashion house and usually spend their entire career working for one brand.
Pre-shrink: Fabric or trim that has been shrunk before use – usually by using steam when it is pressed – to avoid additional shrinkage once the garment or toile is sewn, pressed or washed.
Press: Industry term for an iron and also for the action of ironing or pressing a fabric before use to smooth it.
Prêt-à-porter: Designer clothes sold ready to wear rather than made to measure. The garments are still of a high quality but factory-produced using a standard sizing system and not bespoke to an individual client. These pieces are not intended to fit perfectly or require a tailor and that is the key difference between *prêt-à-porter* and couture.
Princess line: Associated with Charles Frederick Worth who introduced the silhouette in the 1870s. The princess line is cut in long vertical panels without horizontal seaming at the waist and uses long seams to absorb suppression and shape the garment to the body. The princess seam starts at the mid-shoulder point and on the front; it runs through the bust point down through the mid-waist and hip to the hem of the garment. The style line can also be displaced from the apex of the bust point but only by up to 2.5cm or a good fit will not be achieved.
Production pattern: A schematic plan of a garment design; it is generated by manipulating the basic block or tracing off from the master. Seam allowance, notches, labelling for the design and facings are added to complete the pattern ready for cutting out in fabric and sewing up.
PS(s): Princess seam(s).
SA: Seam allowance.
Sartorial: An adjective that refers to a tailor or tailoring and is derived from the Latin sartorius, the long leg muscle that gets used when our legs are crossed. Traditionally, tailors sat cross-legged to work, hence the link. However, it is now also used as a general term to describe clothing and styles of dress.
SB: Side back.
Seam allowance: Extra material extending beyond the stitching line. For draping as a general guide start with at least 5cm and trim down to 2cm when checking the final drape.
Seam line: The stitching line of a garment, usually denoted by a pencil line on a drape.
Selvedge: The self-finished edge of fabric where the weave is denser, which keeps it from unravelling and fraying. It always runs parallel to the warp.
SF: Side front.
SG: *See* Straight of grain.
Shoulder dart: A dart positioned in the middle of the shoulder seam and running over the shoulder blade on the garment back. Usually about 7.5cm long, it aligns or is parallel to the princess seam. On the front it usually finishes at least 2cm from the bust point. The front shoulder dart is more for function and fit than aesthetics and is usually manipulated into a more desirable position as part of the design process.
Slash: A cut or snip into the fabric to release tension built up in it as it is smoothed over the contours of the body, such as around the neckline or at the neck point; it allows the creation of a smoother style line and fit.
Slow fashion: A term coined by Kate Fletcher, Professor of Sustainability, Design and Fashion at the University of the Arts, London (UAL). It is the movement for designing, creating and buying garments for quality and longevity with slower production schedules, better-quality makes and cloth and less regard for trends. It combines a brand's practices with a customer's shopping habits, rather like the model for haute couture!
SS(s): Side seam(s).
Stay stitch: Machine or hand stitch used to control an area of cloth and stop it from stretching, particularly on

curved seamlines, such as around the neck and armholes.
Straight of grain: For woven textiles, the grain refers to the orientation of the warp and weft threads. The straight of grain runs parallel to the selvedge edge and the centre front and centre back of a garment are most frequently placed on it. If you are off grain it can cause the garment to twist and buckle so it is important to get this right.
Style line: Lines on a drape or pattern that denote the desired garment design.
Style tape: By-the-metre tape positioned on a mannequin to create design lines. It can be a pinned twill tape or a plastic tape with adhesive backing.
Suppression and suppression points: Suppression points are the apex of a dart from which it radiates, such as the bust, waist or hip. Suppression is the amount of volume in the dart needed to contour the garment to create the desired fit.
Symmetric: A mirror image from one side of the garment to the other. It is assumed for most of the drapes in this book that the left and right side of the garments are the same so only a half drape is required.
Thread marking: A hand basting stitch used to mark garment hems, centre lines, notches, stitching lines and fastening positions temporarily, rather than other types of temporary marking like a tracing wheel and carbon paper.
Toile: A prototype version of a finished garment made up in a cheap material like calico or muslin so that the design can be tested for fit, proportion and aesthetic.
Toiliste: The highly skilled technician who makes the toiles.
True up: Its generic meaning is an accounting term which means to match or reconcile two or more balances with the help of an adjustment. For fashion it means the neatening or adjusting of draped and hand-drawn seam lines – usually denoted by a series of dots, with dashes for the corners and intersections – so they match up properly with corresponding seams next to them.
UCA: University for the Creative Arts.
V&A: Victoria and Albert Museum, London.
Vanishing point: Where a dart ends.
Waist tape: Tape used to denote the waistline on a mannequin. The natural waist has a slight dip at the centre back.
Warp: The lengthwise threads of a cloth that are attached to a loom before weaving begins.
Weft: The horizontal threads woven back and forth through the warp to make fabric. It is a derivative of an old English term 'wearp' meaning 'to throw across'.
Yoke: A frame or bar fitted to a person or animal that helps to spread and carry weight evenly. In fashion terms it is a frame or pattern that is fitted at the shoulders or the waist to emphasize the structure of a garment. Bodice yokes were first seen in fashion in the 1880s and in skirts in 1898. They can be stitched in or overlaid as a decorative element. They can also be outside of the garment and tied around the waist with a sash: such a yoke is called a plastron.
Zero waste fashion: A fashion garment, accessory or process that eliminates waste materials from their production. Viewed as being part of a wider sustainable fashion movement it has two approaches: pre-consumer intervention, which eliminates waste during manufacture; and post-consumer intervention, which encourages the consumer to buy less, mend and repair, buy second-hand clothing or rework existing products to give them a longer or entirely new lifecycle.

Acknowledgements

It normally takes me two years to write a book part-time, with all the research, designing and making the projects and the photography being done in the first year and the writing-up and organization being done in the second. This time I am even more aware of the passage of time between starting and finishing, with the division of labour being defined as work completed 'pre-Covid' and work completed 'during lockdown' during the ongoing Covid 19 pandemic. I would very much like to thank The Crowood Press for their patience, advice and understanding when my timescale went out of the window! I would also like to thank eagle-eyed copy editor Jane Read for help with the clarity of my instructions and images and whose patience I probably tested. Also, in this context perhaps my biggest thank you of all goes to my husband Gary for his pragmatism in such unprecedented times as he acted as a sounding board for what was realistically possible in the midst of a hectic family home where every flat surface became a work station for someone! This book is dedicated to you, the kids and our extended lockdown family bubble.

Of course, he is not the only one to have been so supportive and this project would not have been possible without the help of lots of other people generously giving their time and sharing their knowledge and skills. I need to give a huge thank you to Jan Bigg-Wither, a great pattern cutter in her own right, and her business partner and partner in life David Bigg-Wither from the Design-Surgery® for their continued support and the generous two-year loan of mannequins for me to drape on.

In terms of research, I would very much like to thank Suzanne Smith from The Clothworkers' Centre for the Study and Conservation of Textiles and Fashion at the V&A for kindly allowing me access to the Madame Grès dresses and the John Galliano wedding dress for my object analysis, as well as her insightful conversation about couture processes. I would also like to thank Gerry Connelly, Senior Curator at the Worthing Museum and Art Gallery, for access to the brilliant Women's Institute box set and other 'making' ephemera in the museum archive. Thank you also to Tanya Perkins and Lisa Moore at the University for the Creative Arts library for granting me access to the Architecture of Fashion files in the Stuart Aitkin Research Files archive and other pattern-cutting and tailoring manuals from the collection. I have actually used all of these resources not just for this book but also in my teaching practice on the Fashion Atelier BA Honours course, where sharing new knowledge with my students has been a wonderful and precious thing. Likewise, I am grateful to Chip Harris from the Fashion Atelier BA Honours course and Donna Ives, Programme Director for Fashion Design at UCA, for access to the studios and workshops I needed more or less on demand over the summer of 2019 when the majority of the practical work was completed.

Many thanks also to Tony Hassan and John Sullivan from the UCA Photography Department for giving me access to the photography studios. My sincerest gratitude has to go to the talented Yousef Al Nasser for his fantastic studio photography and particularly sympathetic lighting – you did a wonderful job of making calico toiles look so much more than they are normally perceived to be. A special thanks also to Ruby Parker who did all of the supplementary photography during lockdown and who effortlessly converted a bedroom into a photography studio for the mini mannequin shots. Finally, I would really like to acknowledge the significant contribution made by my friend and colleague Poppy Miles for her technical skill and indefatigable patience: I have been blessed with such an outstanding assistant for this project and it has been great to share this technical journey with her.

Index